Administrative Management of Physical Education and Athletic Programs

Clayne R. Jensen
Brigham Young University

WAVELAND PRESS, INC.

Prospect Heights, Illinois

#4522991

For information about this book, write or call:

Waveland Press, Inc.
P.O. Box 400
Prospect Heights, Illinois 60070
(847) 634-0081
www.waveland.com

PREFACE

Every one of the 50 states in the United States includes physical education as one of the subjects taught at the various grade levels in the public schools, and competitive athletics and intramural activities are important aspects of the educational system of every state and territory. In addition to the programs in public schools, the great majority of colleges and universities sponsor athletics, physical education, and related programs. This means that every year the great majority of the youth of this country participate in physical education and many of them are involved in school athletics.

Because of the extensive participation in these activities and the large amount of time and funds spent in their support, these programs must be administered effectively so as to fulfill important purposes with respect to the individuals involved and to society as a whole.

This book is aimed toward improving physical education and athletic programs at all school levels by helping those who manage them to implement better content, methods, and procedures. The book takes cognizance in a related fashion only of curricular content, teaching methods, and counseling. The main focus is on effective *planning, organization,* and *management.*

The Book Is Divided into Five Sections

Part I deals with the basis of administrative leadership. This section is designed to help the reader better understand the need for and the means of developing a sound basis for effective administration.

Part II emphasizes methods and procedures that will help guarantee success in any kind of management position. The content is "success oriented."

Part III deals with management techniques and processes that enhance efficiency and positive results.

Part IV provides pertinent information about administration as it relates to the specific content of physical education and athletics. It is designed to help the reader gain insight into what really needs to be done and how to approach it.

Part V consists of related information that every administrator in this field needs in order to function effectively as a well-informed, insightful, and integrated member of the profession.

iv • *Preface*

The book was written specifically for upper division or graduate students who have particular interest in administrative work. But the content will also serve well those preparing for or serving in teaching and coaching positions, because their jobs include some elements of management, and they must know how to work effectively with the school administrators.

This third edition includes updating of the total content of the book, and certain sections have been expanded in order to better provide the reader with current and useful information. Special attention has been given to computerization in the administrative process. Further, Chapters 22 and 23 have been added to help the reader gain insight into some important changes that will occur in the near future.

In sum, the material in this book has been carefully selected to help current and potential administrators gain the knowledge, skills, and insights that are needed to effectively administer high quality physical education and athletic programs. The information is purposely presented in a manner that can be easily understood.

Special appreciation is expressed to the following individuals for contributing to the book and for their critical reviews of certain sections: Linda Carpenter, Joyce Harrison, Bruce Holley, Boyd Jarman, Mary Bee Jensen, Jay Naylor, Betty Vickers and Pete Witbeck.

Provo, Utah   Clayne R. Jensen

CONTENTS

Part I
BASIS OF ADMINISTRATIVE LEADERSHIP

Chapter *1*

RATIONALE FOR THE STUDY OF ADMINISTRATION

In a book about administration, it seems important at the outset to discuss the rationale for studying the topic, and to establish certain meanings relative to it. Furthermore, we need to examine the nature of administration and how it functions in the educational system, and to describe some of its basic tools.

Administration has been described in a general way as the art of getting things done. But, it is more adequately described as getting the right things done the right way for the right reasons. The practical activities of administration involve both deciding and doing, and those two tasks—deciding and doing—are closely integrated processes that pervade the entire organization.

One might ask, "Why study administration?" Especially, why should college students study the topic when administrative assignments for them are not imminent, and many of them have no intention of pursuing administration as a career. Certainly, the study of administration has more direct and immediate value for one who is preparing to become an administrator or is already an administrator and wants to improve. However, all teachers and coaches should have a basic understanding of administrative theory and practice. This is especially true because every teacher and coach has some administrative responsibilities, such as student records, selection and ordering of books and class materials, and helping with selection and ordering of equipment and supplies. Furthermore, all else being equal, a teacher who has knowledge and insight about administrative processes will be able to work more effectively with those in administrative positions.

Physical educators are more likely to have administrative assignments than most other teachers because of the related out-of-class programs that must be administered, such as interschool athletics and intramural activities. Athletic coaching has administrative aspects because the coach must be able to deal effectively with other members of the coaching staff, members of the team, those who care for equipment and facilities, the school administrators, parents of athletes, other members of the public and media personnel. Athletics includes responsibilities pertaining to finances and public relations that do not exist to the same degree in the assignments of most other teachers.

Good administrative procedures in connection with physical education and athletics have been made even more important by the increased emphasis on participation by women. This has escalated the need for women and men to share facilities and use those facilities more efficiently. It has also enlarged the programs and thereby contributed to the financial squeeze that is being felt in many schools. Therefore, a need has developed for more adequate budgeting and better financial management. Furthermore, with the national trend toward school consolidation, physical education and athletic departments have become larger and more complex, therefore requiring better administrators. It is also interesting that in their later professional years a high proportion of physical educators and coaches pursue administrative work outside their own discipline. Many have become deans of students, guidance counselors, school principals, and superintendents.

NATURE OF EDUCATION

It has been rightfully stated that next in importance to freedom and justice is education, without which neither freedom nor justice can be permanently maintained. *Education,* in the broad sense, can be defined as any act or experience that has a formative effect on the mind, character, or physical ability of an individual. In other words, it is the process of positive change. In this sense, education never ends, because we learn from experience throughout our lives. *Formal education* is the process by which society, through schools, colleges, universities, and other institutions, deliberately transmits its cultural heritage—its accumulated knowledge, values, and skills—from one generation to another. Its purpose should be to help people succeed, not cause them to fail. Formal education involves planned programs and distinct methods for accomplishing the educational objectives.

Physical education is an element of the total field of education, and it can be viewed in two different ways: education *through* the physical and education *of* the physical. Education *through* the physical can cause changes in the total individual—knowledge, values, skills—as a result of participation in muscular activities. Much can be learned about our environment, about others, and about ourselves through this form of participation. Furthermore, it can significantly influence the development of one's personality and ability to function effectively in society. Education *of* the physical causes development of the physiological systems. It emphasizes the body's ability to perform efficiently. The total thrust of the physical education program ought to emphasize both of these aspects in proper balance.

MEANING OF ADMINISTRATION

The need for effective administration of educational programs is obvious, especially when one considers the important role that education serves in society and the tremendous amount of public and private resources devoted to it. However, exactly what is meant by the term *administration* is not so obvious. Let us analyze what the term includes and what methods and techniques are involved.

A meaningful way to describe certain aspects of administration is by use of the term *management.* Every organization or business must be managed, and if it is managed well, it stands a better chance of success. In the general sense, management is the process of working with and through people to achieve the organizational goals. This definition includes two very important assumptions: (1) involvement of other people in a participative manner and (2) clearly defined organizational goals.

The complexity of management varies in accordance with the size and nature of the organization. Let us relate this idea to the educational system. A teacher in a one-room school would have teaching as the primary responsibility. But even in this basic educational setting, there would be certain administrative duties. The facility would have to be provided and cared for, supplies and equipment kept on hand, student records maintained, and certain student information submitted to a higher authority. A budget would have to be worked out to cover the teacher's salary and the expenses of the facility and equipment. There would be public relations considerations involving parents and local citizens. The school would operate under some form of local authority, such as a committee, council, or board, and this would involve an administrative relationship between the teacher and the higher authority. Therefore, it is apparent that even in the basic setting of the one-room school, the teacher, being the sole employee, would need to devote a portion of time to the managerial functions inherent in the situation.

As one-room schools became less prevalent and more than one teacher was employed, it was apparently decided that most of the administrative tasks should be handled by one of the teachers, and a portion of that teacher's time should be given for this purpose. Such a person has become prevalently known as the school principal. As the educational system became even more complex, each state created a state department of education with a state superintendent in charge. Each state became subdivided into school districts with a district superintendent appointed to administer the educational programs of the district.

In a similar fashion, colleges and universities became large and complex. They were organized into colleges, schools, and departments, with an administrative head over each unit. Each of these steps of development resulted in administrative positions that had previously not existed.

In a general sense, the areas of administrative duties are the same under today's large and complex system as they were in the one-teacher school. But, the complexity and involvement of each aspect of administration has increased immensely.

Even in our present educational arrangement, no school employee is totally free of administrative tasks and procedures. Those in full-time teaching positions must still provide some managerial leadership. For example, they must make sure that the facilities are properly scheduled and ready for use and that the necessary supplies and equipment are readily available. Student data must be recorded and processed. Adequate attention to public relations is expected, including relationships with parents, other teachers, administrators, and the public. Physical educators and athletic coaches normally have more public relations involvement than do other teachers.

Even though a teacher cannot be totally separated from management responsibilities, such involvement should be carefully controlled in order to maximize effective teaching. Administrative tasks should be handled mostly by those in administrative positions. Supposedly, those given administrative assignments are prepared to handle these tasks, whereas those given full-time teaching assignments are supposedly well prepared to teach.

Even though many of the responsibilities of an administrator are managerial in nature, an educational administrator is certainly more than a manager. In addition to direct management of the organization, he or she must (1) be an educational leader who will provide both enthusiasm and direction; (2) be an insightful leader on both curricular and noncurricular matters; (3) provide broad and far reaching leadership toward overall planning, including budget, personnel, and facilities; (4) help define and interpret goals and provide continuing leadership toward achieving them; (5) provide opportunities for improvement and enrichment of employees; and (6) give positive leadership concerning public sentiment.

In actual fact, some administrative positions are largely managerial with the focus on the efficiency of the daily operation, whereas other administrative positions are much broader in scope. To give examples, the head of a physical education division in a high school has primarily managerial responsibilities. The principal of the same school is also involved in management, but on a broader basis. The principal, additionally, has to give adequate attention to the overall objectives of the educational system of which that school is a part and to how the school fits into the system and contributes toward the objectives. The principal must be analytical about the organizational divisions within the school and how well they function in relationship to each other. The principal is concerned about the balance of educational experiences the students receive, as well as the quality of those experiences. The well-being of the employees, their productivity, and their continuous professional improvement are of concern. These are administrative responsibilities which extend beyond direct managerial functions. In a like manner, the school superintendent's responsibilities are broader and more far-reaching than those of the principal. The superintendent's job involves less attention to the direct and specific aspects of management and more emphasis on the broader aspects of educational administration. A good administrator must be an effective human being who is proficient in three general areas: (1) desirable personal characteristics, (2) technical knowledge, and (3) management skills.

SOME ELEMENTS OF ADMINISTRATION

In education, the philosophies of those in leadership positions have significant influence on the nature of programs, their underlying purposes, established goals, and methods employed. The decisions the leaders make are, in a sense, expressions of their philosophic concepts toward education and life. Therefore, it is of crucial importance of educational leaders to have personal philosophies that emphasize the objectives and desired results of the educational system. More will be said about this important topic in subsequent chapters.

Ideas about education in general, and physical education and athletics in particular, have developed from analysis of social and individual needs and from experiences with the total environment, including educational, social, economic, religious, and political aspects. Ideas originated as untested, unrefined, and unvalidated notions. These notions, along with opinions and intuitions, form general concepts, which help formulate theories, principles, and laws, which in turn help to form the basis of our programs and our procedures.

Unproved and untested ideas become verified through reasoning, constructive and critical thinking, analysis, evaluation, interpretation, and the testing of hypotheses. All of these are valuable methods of the administrative process. These methods help us determine and apply useful goals, standards, criteria, policies, principles, and procedures. These elements of administration are discussed in more detail.

Goals

The term *goals* is often used as all-inclusive of aims, objectives, and expected outcomes. For example, it would be logical to state a broad and remote goal labeled the *aim,* and then state several more specific goals labeled *objectives,* following by numerous immediate goals called *expected outcomes* (or expected results). Such a structure of goals gives definite purpose and direction to the program and to those involved with it (Figure 1-1).

Having clearly stated goals that are both challenging and realistic is of utmost importance. Administration without them is similar to going on a trip with no plan in mind and, therefore, no determined route to follow. Socrates expressed it well when he said, "for a ship without a destination, no wind is favorable." Organizational success clearly depends upon having correct goals and mapping out an exact plan to reach them.

Goals may be expressed from different points of view. For example, goals are set by administrators, teachers, students, and those who sponsor the educa-

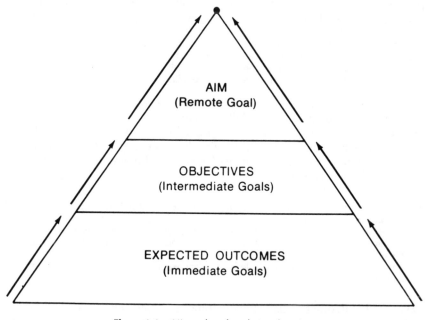

Figure 1-1. Hierarchy of goals in education.

tional program. There can be goals for the educational program as a whole and goals for specific areas such as physical education and athletics. In addition, each individual has some personal goals that relate to the situation and should be considered in the total plan.

Goals that are carefully thought through and properly stated have a strong element of stability. They should not be thought of, however, as static and never-changing. As circumstances change, it naturally becomes necessary to update goals. One of the challenges of educational leaders is to maintain the right balance between keeping goals current with changing circumstances and maintaining sufficient stability and continuity.

Goals should be stated in terminology that is understood by those involved. They should be clear, concise, and meaningful. Goals should express concepts to which people relate, which motivate, and cause them to aspire to achieve. They should be measurable, and a time frame for their accomplishment should be stated. Each goal should include the implied *action*, expected *results*, and *time frame*. It is interesting that sometimes the process and the goal are one and the same. This is largely true of teachers who carry on the process of effective teaching. Effective teaching is a worthy goal as well as a process.

It is apparent that a comprehensive treatment of goals is complex; but when the goals are dealt with properly at each level and in connection with each aspect of the program, the process becomes simplified. Swanson[5] added considerably to the understanding of the importance of goals in physical education.

Aims. An aim may be defined as a broad statement of purpose or a desired result to point toward. It is a remote level of achievement toward which efforts are directed. In education, an aim is usually thought of as a broad, inclusive, and remote goal stated in a manner that gives general direction to the broad spectrum of the educational program. The following is an example of how an aim might be stated for a department of physical education and athletics.

The overall aim of the department is to provide the highest quality programs and leadership possible in the areas of physical education and competitive athletics for the benefit of the total student body. Further, the aim is to contribute maximally to the self-fulfillment of each student and to help develop each student's potential to the fullest.

Objectives. Educational objectives are desired goals for which one strives in the attainment of knowledge, skills, and appreciations. The achievement of specific objectives leads toward the aim, which is more general and more remote. Objectives are related to the aim, but they are not synonymous with it. They are steps toward achievement of the aim. Following are some examples of intermediate objectives.

1. To sponsor a strong and well-balanced program of interschool athletics for both boys and girls with proper emphasis on the development of each individual participant.
2. To sponsor a high quality and varied program of physical education instruction consisting of interesting and beneficial activities arranged in logical sequence and proper gradation of difficulty.
3. To make optimum use of the available facilities and equipment for the benefit of the program and the students.

Expected Outcomes. Expected outcomes are statements of anticipated immediate results. They serve as short-range goals on which to focus. They are steps toward the attainment of objectives, which are broader and more long-range. An expected outcome in a beginning swimming class might be for each student to *swim 100 yards nonstop by a specified date*. For a basketball team, an expected outcome might be the achievement of *shooting 50% or better from the field during early season*. A track athlete might have an expected outcome of *running the mile in 4 minutes 30 seconds by a particular date in mid-season*. For an administrator, some expected outcomes might be (1) to have the head secretary in each department become proficient in word processing, (2) to cause every professor in a department or college to adhere strictly to the prescribed schedule and guidelines for conducting final examinations, and (3) to cause teachers to post their schedules indicating the hours available to meet with students and adhere to the posted schedule.

Standards

As used in education, the term *standard* refers to a defined level of performance against which other performances or achievements are compared. The standard may be quantitative or qualitative. For example, it might be determined that ninth grade boys should be able to run the 100-meter dash in *14.2 seconds* in order to receive a rating of *good*. This means 14.2 seconds is the standard for a *good* rating. Some universities hold to the rule that a student must meet a standard of a *3.0 GPA* (grade point average) in order to *qualify for graduate school*. In his 12-minute run test, Kenneth Cooper established the standard of *1.6 miles* for men between ages 30 and 40 years to receive a rating of *excellent* in cardiovascular fitness. Each teacher determines certain standards or levels of performance a student must meet in order to earn a particular grade. In a well-developed educational program, many standards of achievement and behavior are applied. Standards evolve from criteria, and they serve as guides toward assessment and achievement. They help to evaluate the success of students, teachers, and curriculum content. In educational programs, only reasonable and useful standards should be applied, while artificial and nonconstructive standards should be avoided. Standards should be applied only for the true benefit of the students and the programs.

Criteria

Criteria are measures or data that form the basis for establishing standards. As with standards, criteria may be either quantitative or qualitative. The reason some universities have the standard of 3.0 GPA for entrance into graduate school is that a substantial amount of *data* has been gathered and evaluated that supports the idea that students with less than a 3.0 GPA have marginal chances for success. These data are the criteria on which the standard is based. Likewise, in order for Kenneth Cooper to establish 1.6 miles as the standard of *excellence* in the 12-minute run for men between ages 30 and 40, a large amount of data was gathered and became the criteria for the standard.

A defined set of criteria can form the basis for making judgments or evaluations. For example, leadership can be evaluated with increased objectivity if the evaluation is based on specifically stated and valid leadership criteria. The same would be true in the case of judging or evaluating social adjustment, basketball playing effectiveness, or other characteristics where objective and precise measuring methods are not applicable. Validity and reliability are essential characteristics of criteria. Without these characteristics, criteria can be misleading and useless. (For information about validity and reliability, refer to Chapter 18.)

Administrative Procedures

Proper administrative procedures are of crucial importance for effectiveness. Procedures that are clearly defined and applied consistently become *standardized*. Once standardized, a procedure is automatic and generally accepted by those concerned. Procedures that have been carefully thought out, properly refined, and tried and tested, provide a distinct advantage toward overall efficiency. However, not all procedures can be standardized, because some procedures must remain flexible in order to accommodate various and changing circumstances.

To aid the administrative effort, many organizations have a *procedure manual,* and this contributes significantly toward standardizing the procedures and communicating them to others in the organization. It is highly desirable for the procedures to be understood and supported by those affected by them. Here are some procedural statements[4] of the kind found frequently in procedural manuals pertaining to physical education.

1. Teachers of physical education classes for which students change into activity uniforms are expected to start the class five minutes after the regular beginning time and end ten minutes prior to the scheduled ending time. This is to allow for dressing and showering.
2. In the case of an accident that results in injury to a student, the instructor or supervisor in charge is fully responsible for the administration of emergency care in accordance with the procedures described in the American Red Cross First Aid Manual. Further, he/she is expected to exercise prudence and sound judgment in caring for the injured person.

Policies

A policy is considered a governing statement: a statement that defines the procedure to be followed under given circumstances. Policies are often closely related to the underlying philosophies of those who establish them. They are also related to the nature of the particular organization and the circumstances. The primary purpose of policies is to serve as guides in the administrative procedure. Some policies are strict in nature and not subject to exception, whereas others are considered guidelines and are subject to exception for good reason. A school district might have the policy of *keeping parents informed about student absenteeism,* but the exact procedures for implementing the policy might vary from one school to another. Furthermore, the exactness with which each school implements the policy might vary. Perhaps it is a policy of a particular university that *faculty members who are not going to be reemployed will be notified by March 12;* otherwise reemployment can be assumed. The exact procedure in notifying each person affected by this policy might vary within the different administrative units, but the basic policy would be consistent throughout.

It is important to have clearly stated policies that are understood by all concerned. Further, there should be a strong element of consistency in their application. Lack of consistency can result in confusion and have a demoralizing effect. Teachers are frequently involved in helping to determine policies because such participation is inherent in the nature of a teacher's preparation and service.

Following are sample policies taken from a college policy manual.[4]

1. Even though available facilities and teachers must be taken into account in determining the class schedule, these factors should not dictate the content of the program. Instead, the program needs should dictate the availability of facilities and teachers insofar as this is feasible. This is an important element in the long-range planning of the organization.
2. Classes that need not be taught every semester should be placed on a rotation schedule, which results in an optimum combination of economy for the university and convenience for the students.
3. When a teacher will be absent from class, both the reason for absence and the substitute arrangements must be approved by the department chairperson.
4. No one is permitted to enter the swimming pool unless a certified life guard or a qualified swimming instructor is present and in charge.

In addition to policies that are normally formalized and written, an organization usually has a number of "practices" that have not been established as rules or regulations and are not formally enforced but are nevertheless observed in the organization by reason of custom and practicality. Often the line between policy and practice is fuzzy, unless the organization follows the "practice" of providing written definitions of each.

Principles and Laws

A principle may be defined as a fundamental truth, a uniform result, or a universal guide. Often principles serve as cornerstones for a particular body of knowledge. They can form the basis for defining methods and procedures or for conduct and behavior.

Principles are used in a variety of ways in education. For example, some principles give direction to the overall educational effort, such as the *seven cardinal principles* stated by the U.S. Commission of Education in 1917. For many years, these principles served as a guiding light for the public education programs of America. They are still referred to often, and they are still basically sound. Certain physiologic and mechanical principles (or laws) are applied in athletic conditioning and performance. Examples are the *law of use* as it applies to the human organism (with proper use, the organism improves, while in the absence of use, it deteriorates), and the *principles of leverage* as they apply to movement of body parts and the application of external objects. Also, there are principles of administration such as those sated below.

1. The assignment of responsibility should be accompanied by the delegation of authority to correspond with the responsibility.
2. The best public relations instrument is an excellent program.
3. It is not possible to accomplish today's work with yesterday's tools and methods.

Furthermore, the field of education has *principles of conduct* (often stated in the form of ethics). Some examples of principles pertaining to athletics appear in Chapter 15.

Theories

A theory is one step beyond an assumption or hypothesis. It is a guide, which has some evidence in its support, but is still not validated. Theories are useful in education in the formulation of administrative practices. Sometimes, a theory gradually evolves into a standard procedure, a policy, or a principle after sufficient evidence has been accumulated to support it. In other cases, theories become discarded because attempts to prove their validity and usefulness are unsuccessful. Theory can be viewed as a starting point for the development of facts, policies, principles, and laws. Administrative theory precedes administrative practice and nurtures it.

REFERENCES AND RECOMMENDED READINGS

1. Bucher, C.A.: Administration of Physical Education and Athletic Programs, 9th Ed. St. Louis, C.V. Mosby, 1987, pp. 2-20.
2. Frost, R.B., Lockhart, B.D., and Marshall, S.J.: Administration of Physical Education and Athletics, 3rd Ed. Dubuque, IA, William C. Brown, 1988, pp. 1–12.
3. Horine, L.: Administration of Physical Education and Sport Programs, 2nd Ed. Dubuque, IA, William C. Brown Publishers, 1991, Chapter 1.
4. Jensen, C.R.: Policy and Procedure Manual, Revised Ed. Brigham Young University, Provo, UT, College of Physical Education, 1992.
5. Swanson, J.: Developing and implementing objectives in physical education. JOPER, 50(3):68, 1979.

Chapter 2

A SOUND PHILOSOPHY

It has been said that in a democracy, "those who hold steadfastly to correct ideals eventually determine the law." It is also true that such individuals form the foundations of society's institutions and the lasting programs that benefit the people. Thus, it is apparent that in order to be really useful, an educational administrator must be professionally ethical and moral and must believe, represent, and foster desirable attitudes, concepts, and practices. This means that perhaps the most important characteristic an administrator has is a personal philosophy, because this influences all else. Thus, it follows that in striving to be an effective administrator, the phrase "know thyself" is certainly applicable.

The term *philosophy* is derived from both Latin and Greek, and it means "love of truth" or "love of wisdom." It implies the need to find the real truths and values in life and apply them correctly.

Philosophy has two important themes: (1) to gain a greater understanding of life and of the universe in which we live; and (2) to sharpen one's ability to think clearly and logically. Both of these aspects are of vital importance to an educational administrator.

Those who are credited as being philosophers are usually viewed as deep thinkers who have unusual insights and express superior wisdom. Philosophers think more analytically than the ordinary person, concentrating on life's fundamental values and vital issues. The serious philosopher approaches a hypothetic question much like a scientist approaches a scientific problem.

Most people have personal beliefs or ideas about life, just as they have favorite remedies for aches and pains. However, the philosophic beliefs of some people are fuzzy and poorly defined, because they are unknowledgeable or have not really analyzed matters thoroughly. Others express definite beliefs based on superficial thought, emotional reaction, or incorrect information. Still others have deep and well-defined beliefs based on thorough knowledge and careful analysis.

Some people try to make a distinct separation between *philosophy* and *science,* and thus, individuals are often labeled "philosophers" or "scientists," but usually not both. Such clear separation is not totally appropriate. Scientists should be philosophers in the sense that they should carefully consider the reasons for pursuing scientific discovery and the application of the results.

Further, philosophers should be scientists in the sense that they should take an organized and systematic approach to philosophic inquiry, and the inquiry should be inclusive of important scientific facts and concepts. Through the scientific approach, discoveries are made about such things as matter, composition, and energy. Through the philosophic process, decisions are made about where, when, and for what purposes those discoveries should be used. Scientists who have no concern for the purposes of their discoveries could be considered irresponsible; philosophers who fail to test their beliefs through critical investigation are equally lacking.

In order to comprehend more clearly the nature and meaning of philosophy, it is helpful to know the processes involved. These include the following[3]:

1. *Metaphysics,* which attempts to answer the question, "what is reality?" It includes a study of the science of being, the science of fundamental causes and processes, the nature of the mind and the body, and the nature of self. As Aristotle said, "it is associated with principles of being."
2. *Epistemology,* which is concerned with knowledge—its sources, authority, validity, principles, and limits.
3. *Logic,* which deals with reason: what constitutes sound reasoning and logical thought, what are the characteristics of it and the criteria by which it is measured?
4. *Ethics,* which is associated with morals: what is right and wrong, the criteria for determining good and bad, and an understanding of the foundation on which moral character rests. Ethics attempts to answer the question, "what is the highest good?"
5. *Aesthetics,* which is pertinent to personal taste and preference and discriminates between beauty and ugliness. Its basis is appeal and quality of form or technique.
6. *Politics,* which is a study of the various forms of government and social structure, such as anarchism, aristocracy, communism, democracy, and socialism. Much of the behavior of humans is politically related in terms of cause and results.

Within the framework of the processes listed above, philosophers utilize the following methods for arriving at philosophic beliefs: *reason, observation, experience, intuition,* and *revelation.*[7]

Reason is probably the predominant method in philosophic analysis. The principal tools of reason are the inductive and deductive processes. The deductive process begins with a general idea or principle and uses reason to arrive at (deduce) specific conclusions based on the general principle. Inductive reasoning builds on specific ideas or facts to arrive at a general concept or principle.

Discovering truth through observation is a highly accurate approach. Observation of physical results, events, and discoveries through the five senses might seem inconsistent with the theoretic analysis of the philosophic process. Observable truth, however, is essential to philosophy as well as to science.

Experience, like observation, involves the senses. Experience, however, results in learning through active participation, as one might learn through the senses that the rays of the sun are hot. Observation, on the other hand, separates the person from direct experience, in the way that a spectator in a sport is separated from the participants on the playing field.

Intuitive learning is a nebulous concept in the minds of many scholars. One's intuition is that form of native intelligence that enables a person to become the initiator of ideas. It involves awareness, perception, interpretation, judgment, and a sense of truth.

Some philosophers believe that truth may be gained through *revelation* from a higher power—an extraterrestrial source. Many believe that revelation is the purest form of truth since it comes from a source more perfect than the earthly environment, a supernatural being.

BUILDING A PERSONAL PHILOSOPHY

The question here is not whether each of us has a philosophy, but rather what the philosophy includes. With a weak or poorly developed philosophy, a person lacks clear understanding and direction. Certainly life cannot be highly successful or satisfying without a philosophy that leads to a purposeful existence.

It is often helpful for a person to put in written form what he or she truly believes about the various aspects of life, because putting thoughts into writing contributes clarity to one's ideas and concepts. It follows the claim that writing makes an *exact* person. This process forces decisions about one's philosophy that might otherwise never be made. It is recommended that prospective administrators follow this procedure, and in doing so, apply the following guidelines.

Some Suggested "DOs"

Ask these questions as you write your beliefs.

1. Why do I believe this, if there are worthy contrary beliefs?
2. Is this a "best guess," an expedient opinion, or do I really believe it?
3. Is this a prejudiced belief? A narrow one? A closed-minded one?
4. Is this a belief that is attuned to the past, the present, or the future?
5. Is this a belief that is too restricted in some way (time, place, condition, or circumstance)?
6. Beneath and beyond all rationalization, why do I believe this?
7. Is this a necessary or important belief for me to hold?
8. What facts or near-facts support this belief?
9. Is this belief probably permanent or will it likely change with increased experience, additional facts, and new ideas?

Some Suggested "DON'Ts"

1. Don't start wondering in general, "What *do* I believe?" Be exact and proceed with an orderly design.
2. Don't think that a written account of your philosophy has to be fancy or filled with "big words." It is possible to be complex and still express yourself in simple terms.
3. Don't believe that you have to agree with the "great minds," or the half-great, or your friends, or even the instructor. Just be yourself.
4. Don't write anything that is not sincere or truthful. In philosophy, loss of integrity is loss of everything.
5. Don't be ashamed of beliefs that may be linked to the idealistic, the beautiful, the artistic, or any other area that symbolizes a keen sensitivity and awareness of life, thought, and experience above the common and the ordinary.

6. Don't just skim the surface. Dig deep into your basic beliefs and concepts, and don't stop digging just because you hit hard-pan.
7. And finally, don't make hard work of the process. Let the words come easily. After all, you are only writing about the things you believe.

Building (or perfecting) a personal philosophy involves putting one's thoughts into a logical order, beginning with the most basic items. For example, how did I come to exist, for what reasons am I here? In light of this, what are my responsibilities and what contributions should I strive toward? Some helpful suggestions follow:

1. Am I here (a) simply to exist; (b) to achieve enjoyment; (c) to contribute to the betterment of mankind; (d) to improve myself through constant progress and self-realization.
2. Where am I going? (a) toward maximum accomplishment of self; (b) toward achievement for the benefit of society; (c) toward a joyful and happy life?

Once a person's basic premise is fairly well established, it is helpful to continue with such questions as these:

3. What are my goals and how can I accomplish them?
4. Do I have responsibilities to others and to society? If so what are they?
5. How should I incorporate elements of my philosophy into my profession and my associations with other people?
6. Are my daily actions consistent with my beliefs?

Answers to questions such as these will go a long way toward perfecting the fundamental aspects of your philosophy. The nature and strength of these aspects will have a firm influence on your daily actions and your responses to life's various situations.

THE IMPORTANCE OF VALUES

Significant progress has been made toward structuring useful philosophical thought, but still there is much truth to Aldo Leopold's statement that ". . .history consists of successive excursions from a single starting point, to which man returns again and again to organize yet another search for a durable scale of values." The task of ferreting out what you believe with reference to your own specialized discipline, say physical education, is not easy. This relates to even larger questions, such as the purposes of education in general, and those of life itself. But, for any particular individual, the purposes of life, of education, and of physical education depend upon the person's *system of values*. For that matter, the methods of instruction one chooses are dependent upon values, as are the activities selected for the program.

Let us investigate further the significance of *values*. Do you think some phase of administration, or some activity in the program, or some method of instruction, or some technique of discipline is desirable because:

1. It satisfies you as an individual?
2. It is developmental to those involved?
3. It calls for interaction between individuals and the environment?

4. It is based on the greatest good for the greatest number?
5. It is in and of itself desirable?
6. It is good for society?
7. It contributes to some divine plan?

Obviously, no major purpose, no program of activities, and no method of instruction, can serve all of these results. Thus you must choose, and your choices will be influenced by your system of values.

If you wish to refine and perfect your system of values you must ask the question, "Why?" "Why have you selected a particular idea or held to a certain premise?" If you have the fiber to persist in this line of questioning, you begin not only to think crisply but to really understand. Moreover, because there are often good reasons for selecting any one of several alternatives, you begin to understand yourself better and become more tolerant, more understanding, and more respectful of others and their views.

A person's values shape life by influencing one's thoughts and actions in both personal and professional relationships. Indeed, the kind of person that an individual is as an employee, neighbor, friend, teacher, or administrator is strongly influenced by the sum total of one's values or lack of values.

Some of our values change as we develop and expand our understanding. More experience, further education, and broader exposure may alter our values. In turn, our values affect our experiences, and in fact, determine which experiences we have by the choices we make.

It is said that values cannot be taught. But certainly teaching values is possible in the sense that values may be influenced by one's experiences. And one of the processes of education is to provide carefully selected experiences. However, it is also true that people do not consistently adopt values simply by being instructed to do so. The development of values results from a complex interaction between a person and experiences.

It is, therefore, important for teachers, administrators, and others who influence educational programs to make value-based decisions in educational settings. Values influence such things as (1) one's objectives in education, (2) the selection of learning experiences and how they are arranged, (3) the relative emphasis on different subject matter, (4) the provision of facilities and other resources in support of the various areas of education, (5) teaching methods, (6) the administrative organization and procedures, and (7) the standards by which employees are to conduct themselves.

The fact that no two people have exactly the same value system indicates the complexity of the topic, and because of their complexity, values defy comprehensive classification. Certain groups of values are identifiable, however, and some meaningful distinctions can be made. Values may be expressed as *intrinsic* or *extrinsic; subjective* or *objective; individual* or *social; absolute* or *relative.*[3]

Intrinsic versus *extrinsic* values provide an interesting contrast. Intrinsic values are those that have worth in and of themselves and do not depend on extraneous factors. These are the more permanent and less changing values in life, and they relate mostly to nonphysical qualities. They form the moral and spiritual fiber upon which society depends, superseding prestige, fame, wealth, or influence. Intrinsic values play a significant role in education, community, and family life.

Extrinsic values are those that lead to something of greater worth and are instruments of attaining another end. For the most part, these values lie in the practical affairs of everyday life: physical items such as clothes, automobiles, and sporting equipment; and also such things as the accumulation of money, power, and facts of practical use. Youngsters, for example, earn money in order to finance their education. The work they do represents a value which is extrinsic toward the end of gaining an education. Some aspects of education are instrumental (extrinsic) toward achieving a desired lifestyle or fulfilling lifelong aspirations. Conversely, some aspects of education involve intrinsic values, because they result in the gaining of knowledge for its own sake, and the development of the person, for no reason other than a more complete person.

Some philosophers feel that all values are basically intrinsic because even in using something as a means to something else, the individual gains in basic worth. Others feel that all values are extrinsic because it is impossible to achieve or apply a value that does not lead to something else. Obviously, there is no clear-cut division between intrinsic and extrinsic values. It is a matter of relative emphasis.

Values also may be labeled as *subjective* or *objective*. A person emphasizing subjective values would be relatively nonmaterialistic and would hold that truly valuable things exist in the mind in the form of knowledge, attitudes, appreciations, and ideals, in the state of well being, and in human relationships. Furthermore, significance, worth, and beauty exist within the person rather than in objects.

Conversely, objective values are those exist in the material world, whether or not they are observed. Such values do not depend on the imagination, hopes, or aspirations of the individual. They exist independently and need only to be discovered. Objective values emphasize that beauty and worth are inherent in the object or the thing itself and not in one's mental perception or interpretation.

Values are also classified as *individual* or *social*. Since only individuals can have values, this terminology is somewhat inaccurate. In a given society, however, there becomes a unity of values among individuals; these values become prominent characteristics of the society and are sometimes labeled "social values." They are concerned with such factors as respect for the rights and property of others, respect for the law, volunteer service to others, and accepted standards of social conduct.

One of the most clear-cut classifications is *absolute* versus *relative*. Values that are absolute are universal and unchanging. The advocates of absolute values believe that such values have always existed and will continue to exist indefinitely. Absolute values are not related to time nor circumstance. These values are often related to a supreme being or deity, and they include such things as truth, virtue, love, and goodness. Other people relate absolute values to the natural order, emphasizing that the laws of nature are consistent, predictable, and everlasting; therefore, they are universal and absolute.

Relative values fluctuate with circumstances and time. One who takes the position that all values are relative would emphasize that the world is in a constant state of physical and social change, and therefore, values must remain adjustable.

Within the framework of the philosophic dichotomies that have been explained, some people live by *positive* thoughts as opposed to those who emphasize the *negative*. Positive thinkers look for the inevitable good. They are optimistic in the face of adversity and are easily encouraged and often encourage others. Conversely, the negative thinkers look for the worst. Such persons tend to destroy optimism, enthusiasm, and creative ideas by always finding reasons to feel reserved, reluctant, and discouraged.

As adults who are especially concerned with the development of young people, it is imperative that educators understand the importance of providing positive models. Furthermore, as parents, teachers, and administrators, we have a responsibility to provide an abundance of developmental experiences for children and youth (as well as adults) that contribute toward sound values. The development of values is a major function of education.

Each of us has established a value system, however perfect or imperfect, which guides and directs us in all of our activities and influences our behavior. It forms the basis for our aspirations, dedications, and actions. To a large extent, our system of values dictates the meaning of life, forming the foundation of what we are and what we hope to become. It determines our most marvelous intentions and structures our actions.

But we must recognize that our system of values is never complete or final. It is always more or less in a state of development and flux, due to new experiences and changing circumstances. In view of this, each of us must consistently try to keep our values on track, developing in a manner that will be for our good and the good of others whose lives we influence. For this reason it is especially important for each of us to remain thoughtful and open-minded about new ideas and changing circumstances.

All that has been said in this chapter about personal philosophy and values should be applied toward increasing one's authenticity. The authentic person is one who has a high degree of internal consistency in terms of an integrated philosophy that possesses unity and coherence. In the words of psychologist Abraham Maslow "authenticity is the reduction of phoniness and fuzziness to the zero point."

REFERENCES AND RECOMMENDED READINGS

1. Harper, W.A.: The philosopher in us. JOPERD, 53(1):32, 1982.
2. Harper, W.A.: The Philosophical Process in Physical Education, 3rd Ed. Philadelphia, Lea & Febiger, 1977, p. 336.
3. Hartvigsen, M.F.: Unpublished papers on establishing a personal philosophy. College of Physical Education, Brigham Young University (updated, 1992).
4. Pierce, J.L., and Newstrom, J.W.: The Manager's Bookshelf, 2nd Ed. New York, Harper Collins Publisher, 1990, pp. 135–150.
5. Romance, T.J.: Promoting character development in physical education. Strategies, 1(5):16, 1988.
6. Vickers, B.: Lecture notes on Philosophy of Physical Education and Athletics. Brigham Young University, 1992.
7. Ziegler, E.F.: Philosophical perspective. JOPER, 51(11):40, 1980.

Chapter 3

LEADERSHIP STYLES AND METHODS

Leadership is an intriguing quality that is found in people of various ages, female and male, members of different races, and from various cultural and economic backgrounds. No segment of society has a hold on leadership. But, what is a leader? What qualities differentiate such a person from others? Why do certain leadership approaches function well in some situations and not in others? These are interesting questions and they relate to the concepts dealt with in this chapter.

A typical dictionary definition of leadership includes such descriptions as the following: one who directs others; one who goes before to guide or to show the way; one who conducts; one who has authority to preside.

The emphasis in these descriptions is on guiding, directing, and presiding. Some specialists on leadership, however, stress that the leader is a *persuader* or an *enabler*. In this context, a leader could be one who persuades others to seek particular objectives; one who has the human qualities that bind a group together and motivate it toward goals; or one who demonstrates the art of coordinating and stimulating individuals and groups to achieve desired ends. Leadership may also be described as the capacity to help others achieve their own desires. British Field Marshall Montgomery described leadership as "the capacity and will to rally people to a common purpose."

Unfortunately, some effective leaders produce negative results because of divisive intent or a confused sense of values. Adolf Hitler is a dramatic example of this. Of course, in education, our efforts should always be towards *positive* influence.

Leadership is more than just authority. It is more than enthusiasm or inspiration. In the most serious sense, leadership is a tool for achieving objectives, and its success must be judged in terms of what is accomplished. Leadership is *influencing* the actions of individuals and organizations. The key word is "influence." A person who is well liked and admired but does not influence results is ineffective as a leader.

Some of the definitions of leadership found in the literature that emphasize *influence* including the following:

1. Leadership is influencing people so that they will strive willingly toward the achievement of group goals.
2. Leadership is the process of influencing the activities of an organized group in efforts toward goal setting and goal achievement.
3. Leadership is getting people to do what the leader wants them to do because he has influenced or inspired them.
4. Leadership is influence, the dynamics of which are a function of the personal characteristics of the leader and followers and the nature of the specific situation.

Exerting significant influence in an organization is a complex process. Influence is exercised through an intricate system of authority, responsibility, persuasion, and communication. Given the exertion of influence, each level of leadership still leaves an area of discretion to the level below. Even the lowest ranking employee exercises some judgment in determining particular actions.

In addition to the influence of direct leadership, employees are also governed by standardized policies and procedures, organizational loyalty, and other factors built into the environment. This emphasizes the importance of a leader who can create an environment that will help produce the desired results. One of the most successful forms of leadership is the creation of conditions conducive to motivation and effective performance by the employees.

Further, the truly effective leader, instead of being "the boss," is a resource to the organization, an expert in communication, and a catalyst to fellow workers. The leader's functions include facilitating, as well as directing, and maintaining a healthy flow of communication up, down, and across the organization, instead of merely issuing orders.

Leadership can be either *direct* or *indirect*. Direct leadership involves immediate contact between the leader and those being led. Indirect leadership is purposeful influence upon people without contact between the leader and them.

An example of direct leadership is a department chairperson's supervisory influence on how well other employees perform their responsibilities. From such a position, the leader is expected to direct the program and account for its accomplishments. Another example of direct leadership is a person who gives public speeches, thereby changing people's knowledge, concepts, and feelings about certain matters. A teacher is a direct leader who regularly influences people's lives along a set pattern toward educational goals.

Examples of *indirect* leadership are an educator who writes materials that influence those who read them, or one who communicates indirectly to a large number of people through a small number who function as "disciples." Another form of indirect leadership is the role model. Both colleagues and students are influenced by models with whom they relate. One who has achieved unusual professional success is often identified as a model by others who aspire to the same kind of success. Outstanding teachers and coaches serve as worthy models for students and also for others in the profession. The effective administrator serves as a model for those who aspire to administrative positions.

ELEMENTS OF LEADERSHIP SITUATIONS

Every leadership situation has four basic elements.

1. The leader—with abilities, personality traits, responsibilities, and authority.
2. The followers—with their abilities, personalities, and responsibilities.
3. The situation—with its special features.
4. The purpose or task—with which the individuals, program, or organization is concerned.

Analysis of these elements shows that people who emerge as leaders in one setting might not emerge, or at least not to the same degree, in other circumstances. Leadership is, after all, a functional relationship between the *leader,* the *followers,* the *situation,* and the *purpose* or *task.* Thus, different circumstances call for different leadership qualities.

In terms of the significance of the administrator, it is important to highlight the following logic.

1. The personal characteristics of the administrator will influence the choice of a particular leadership style.
2. The leadership style will determine how the person carries out the administrative functions.
3. How the administrator carries out the functions will have a profound influence on the overall effectiveness of the organization.

In describing the importance of administrative appointments, management specialist Peter Drucker stated the following.[3]

> For the spirit of an organization is created from the top. If an organization is great in spirit, it is because the spirit of its top people is great. If it decays, it does so because the top rots; as the proverb has it, "trees die from the top." No one should ever be appointed to a senior position unless top management is willing to have his or her personal and professional character serve as a model for the organization.

FORMS OF LEADERSHIP

The basic forms of leadership can be labeled *autocratic, participative,* and *laissez faire* (the latter two are democratic in nature). The main distinctions between autocratic and democratic leadership are seen in the contrasts between totalitarian and democratic governments. But, less pure forms of these contrasting styles can be found in various organizations, and among individual leaders in the same organization. In a general sense, autocratic leaders think of others as working *for* them and subject to their commands, whereas democratic leaders think of others as working *with* them *not for them.* They view others as partners in the work and members of the team.

Autocratic

The characteristics of *strict autocratic* (authoritarian) leaders have been documented as having protective and paranoid tendencies, combined with a lack of security, frequently bolstered by arbitrary displays of authority. Also, they tend to be remote from other members of the group and demand to have activities and attention centered on them. The apparent stability of the group is somewhat artificial, and is maintained largely under threat. Typically, there is a tight authoritative structure in which any deviation or disloyalty is met with chastisement. Negative expression against the organization or leader is discouraged, although some "constructive criticism" of organizational practices is usually allowed.

The autocratic leader insists on exercising the decision-making power. Often seen as "heavy-handed" and "hard-boiled," the leader issues the orders and expects subordinates to be unfaltering in their subservience. Typically, such a leader is a hard worker and a hard driver.

Many autocratic leaders threaten and use negative sanctions to enforce their authority. They may show little concern for the needs and problems of others. Subordinates often respond to such leadership by being tense, subtly resentful of the "system," and quarrelsome among themselves.

A modification of strict autocratic leadership is known as *benevolent authoritarianism*. Its practitioners employ positive techniques toward gaining support by providing incentive awards to followers, hoping that this will produce the desired obedience. Although subordinates may respond more positively to this style, they still do not share in important decision making.

Authoritarian leaders of either the strict or modified pattern usually insist on exact compliance with rules and regulations, and they place heavy emphasis on mechanical considerations of operational efficiency. In fact, adherence to rules frequently becomes so important to the authoritarian that the achievement of organizational goals is subordinated to procedural perfection.

Participative

Participative leadership emphasizes the concept of planning with people, not for them. It represents an intermediate position between the extremes. Under this style, members of the group are participants or contributors to decision making, but the one in the leadership position makes or strongly influences the final decision, after taking into consideration input from the others. The leader shares authority and decision making with subordinates but ultimately retains the authority and the associated responsibility. Participative leaders thinks of others as working with them, not for them. They see followers as partners in the work and glorify the team spirit.

Directions are issued and adherence is expected under this system, but the expectations are likely to be accompanied by positive rewards as well as negative sanctions, with emphasis on the positive. Goal achievement is stressed at least as fully as adherence to rules and procedures.

With participative leadership, decision making sometimes follows a time-consuming and cumbersome process. The advantage, however, is that it adds stability since it does not depend too much on the power of only one person. There are checks and balances that do not exist in autocratic leadership.

Certain dangers should be avoided with leadership that is highly participative. It can become almost leaderless, unstructured, and chaotic. While subordinate tension may be reduced by minimizing heavy-handed rule enforcement, it is also true that productivity may be adversely affected by too much emphasis on the participative technique.

The preferred degree of participative leadership is one in which the leader exercises enough command to move things along at the desired pace and keep the organization responsive and alive, while showing adequate sensitivity toward other members of the organization and permitting sufficient involvement and influence by them.

William Hitt, an advocate of participative management, listed the following ten characteristics of this style of leadership.[7]

1. Confidence and trust prevail throughout the organization.
2. Staff feel free to discuss job problems with their supervisor.
3. There is group participation in goal setting.
4. Personnel at all levels feel responsibility for the achievement of organizational goals.
5. Information flows down, up, and across.
6. There is substantial cooperative team work throughout the organization.
7. Staff members are actively involved in decisions that influence their work.
8. Responsibilities for review and control are widespread throughout the organization.
9. Control data are used for self-guidance and coordinated problem solving, rather than criticism and chastisement.
10. Formal and informal processes mesh together and tend to become one and the same.

Laissez Faire

This pattern of leadership allows extensive freedom to act without interference from the leader. The leader is available to serve as a resource person and to assist in accomplishing individual or group goals. Such leaders will generally provide materials, information, guidance, and support when needed, but little uninvited direction. They encourage co-workers to set their own objectives, make their own decisions, and proceed on their own and often appear to be bystanders, observers, or subtle mediators without getting deeply involved in the activities of the group.

Management experts and behavioral scientists generally agree that the probability for disorganization, instability, low output, and chaos is just too great to advocate the laissez faire technique. However, in unique circumstances such an approach can work effectively. Possible examples would be a group of competent and dedicated researchers, a mature departmental faculty at a university, a law firm staff, or a medical staff in a clinic.

Leadership Continuum

A continuum graph is a helpful method of viewing the complete range of leadership styles from one extreme to the other. This concept has been presented in a variety of forms by different writers and lecturers. Figure 3-1 is the author's version of a leadership continuum illustrating the range from the extreme autocratic to the extreme democratic approach. At one end is the autocratic administrator who makes all the decisions, which the other employees

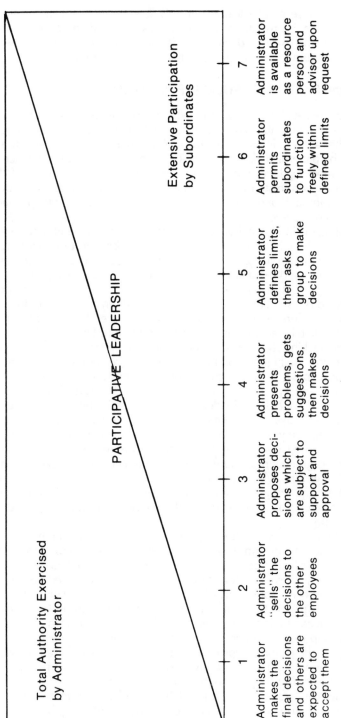

Figure 3-1. A continuum graph, illustrating the range from extreme autocratic to extreme democratic leadership in decision making. Modeled after How to choose a leadership pattern, Tannenbaum and Schmidt, Harvard Business Review, May-June, 1973.

Total Authority Exercised
by Administrator

PARTICIPATIVE LEADERSHIP

Extensive Participation
by Subordinates

1   2   3   4   5   6   7

1	2	3	4	5	6	7
Administrator makes the final decisions and others are expected to accept them	Administrator "sells" the decisions to the other employees	Administrator proposes decisions which are subject to support and approval	Administrator presents problems, gets suggestions, then makes decisions	Administrator defines limits, then asks group to make decisions	Administrator permits subordinates to function freely within defined limits	Administrator is available as a resource person and advisor upon request

are expected to accept. This leader not only sets the goals for the group and makes the final decisions, but also discourages subordinate participation. At the other end is the extreme democratic administrator, who not only permits but actually encourages extensive participation by subordinates.

CONTRASTING LEADERSHIP PATTERNS

Within the three leadership methods just discussed, there are specific patterns which have distinguishable characteristics. A leader might, for example, be basically either autocratic or democratic and still exhibit certain characteristics included in the patterns described here. The contrasting patterns represent extremes, and most leaders function somewhere between. The study of these patterns can help administrators better understand the strengths and weaknesses of their own approach and help them to visualize the alternative approaches that could be considered.

An interesting distinction exists between *failure avoidance* and *success seeking* leadership. The failure avoidance strategy is based on the idea that one succeeds by simply avoiding failure. Accordingly, such a leader emphasizes adherence to rules and regulations. Change tends to be discouraged, because one measure of success is the smoothness of the operation and the absence of problems. Accomplishment of significant results often becomes hidden and neglected in the failure avoidance process. There is a tendency to accept relatively low productivity as long as it is above the failure level.

The success seeking style is just the opposite. Such a leader views success as relative and favors the highest possible level of achievement. Goal accomplishment is the principal task; and such a leader sees innovation problem solving, reasonable risk, and dynamic change as both sources and results of organizational vitality and success. A leader who stresses this style does not expect the operation to always run smoothly. Adherence to defined procedures and regulations is relatively unimportant if the expected results are achieved.

Another interesting contrast is the *integrated innovator* and the *detached director*. The integrator's procedure is socially oriented. Such a leader wants to be "one of the group" who exercises leadership as a fully involved member, strives for close and congenial associations, and attempts to move the group towards the desired goals by serving as the moving and directing force from within the group.

The detached leader takes the opposite approach. By assuming a distant boss—employee relationship, this type of leader directs the group toward the goals from an arm's length position. Such a leader may or may not be authoritative, but definitely does not integrate and use a socially oriented approach.

Two other opposite approaches in leadership involve *negative strategies,* which employ fear and threat in the motivation of the group, and *positive strategies,* which exhibit incentives and rewards as a means toward accomplishment. Leadership experts generally agree that even if the effectiveness of the two were equal, the positive approach would certainly be preferred. However, on some occasions, with certain individuals the hard-line negative approach becomes necessary in order to produce desired results.

Some leaders are *task-oriented* and others are *relations-oriented.* The task-oriented leader focuses on the completion of work with emphasis on well-defined projects or units of work. This kind of leader feels that the quantity and quality of work is the main consideration. It is the end to which all efforts are focused, and from the beginning, the emphasis is on the final result rather than the methods, processes, and relationships involved. Conversely, the relations-oriented person gives primary consideration to personnel. This is based on the idea that concern for individuals and relationships is a worthy end in itself, and in addition, it will produce the best overall results in productivity.

Another interesting difference in leadership styles is *functional* versus *formal*. Functional leadership depends greatly on highly workable relationships between the leader and others in the organization, which earn cooperation and support for the leader. By this method, the functional leader's authority is reinforced by the members of the organization. In contrast, the formal leader claims the authority that comes with the position, and utilizes the authority in a structured manner to enforce rules and policies. This formal authority enables the leader to have things done a particular way because "the boss says so."

LEADERSHIP MODELS

The process of reducing complex human behaviors into "leadership models" results in a substantial loss of individual detail. No person exactly fits any leadership stereotype, yet a description of leadership models provides guidelines by which one can analyze and understand one's own leadership behavior. Although leaders are in some degree prisoners of their personal heritage, few are so constrained that new alternatives are entirely closed to them. The particular models discussed here are *climbers, conservers, zealots, advocates, statesmen, philosophic leaders, experts, innovators, symbolic models, charismatic leaders, reformers,* and *administrators*. The basic characteristics of these models have been identified and explained in the literature on leadership.[1]

Climbers, as the name implies, are self-propelled in their quest for improved status. They are energetic in seeking out avenues of personal progress and self-aggrandizement. They tend toward empire building. When a frontal assault is blocked, the climber will likely regroup and then try to move in a different direction to increase the sphere of influence and recognition. Climbers tend to be abrasive to others, because of their aggressive approach. Many climbers, however, are effective leaders because they are "doers" who efficiently attack the situation.

Conservers are almost exact opposites of climbers. They tend to maintain the status quo. Conservers resist and even resent change, since it has an unsettling effect on the structured procedures and relationships. Conservers are more interested in security and stability than power and progress. They want to trim their management unit to a simplified, clear-cut package and then hold it intact. They prefer organizations that rely extensively on formal regulations and protocol.

Zealots have visions of greatness both for themselves and their programs, and they manifest an evangelistic zeal for the improvement of the organization—as they see it. They are generally aggressive, determined, and hard-driving. Unlike climbers, zealots have the interest of the organization primarily at heart. Unlike conservers, they are impatient and want to improve and innovate. The aggressiveness of zealots sometimes irritates people who do not share their visions. Opposition, however, means relatively little to zealots, who are more noted for aggressiveness than human relations. They are excellent instruments for stirring up an apathetic organization or getting a new one off the launching pad. They make better task force leaders than overall administrators, because they place their "sacred objectives" first and foremost, often to the neglect of broader and more far-reaching goals.

Advocates are concerned with improvement of the organization, especially the part they represent. They are tigers at fighting for their personnel and programs. Unlike zealots, who are basically loners, advocates are usually responsive to the ideas and influences of their superiors, peers and subordinates. Unlike climbers, who are ever self-serving, advocates will at times promote programs that do not benefit them personally, but have long-term favorable implications for the organization. Whereas zealots tend to take on all adversities, advocates usually engage in conflict only if supported by their colleagues. Externally, they defend their group or department in a partisan manner. Internally, they tend to be fair and impartial.

Statesmen are found in practically every organization. They have a strong inclination to intercede in conflict and politics, and they try to stand above parochial interests. They seek to reconcile conflicts and disagreements by pointing to the overall objectives or mission of the organization, or by emphasizing the fair and equitable side of the situation. Statesmen are sometimes located in the rank and file of the employees, and they perceive themselves as spokespersons for the group, usually in carrying messages to or negotiating with the management. Statesmen who are in administrative positions perceive themselves as spokespersons for the organization.

Experts are individuals who are recognized for their specialized knowledge. People look to them for expert opinion and professional guidance. What they say as teachers, lecturers, or writers takes on unusual significance. Recognition as an expert increases a person's influence in almost every respect. Each profession has its own group of experts who exert a strong influence within the profession and beyond it. Each organization also has individuals who are more or less recognized as experts and whose influence is felt accordingly.

Philosophical leaders place emphasis on philosophic ideas and ideals. Leaders of this kind can have significant influence on both goals and program results. Here again, each profession has its own philosophic experts, and each organization has personnel who exercise this kind of leadership.

Innovators have the ability to envision or develop better methods, techniques, and procedures. Some innovators are energetic doers who can bring about positive changes. Their approach is to search out or create better methods or products and apply them. Innovative leadership is an important characteristic among both teachers and school administrators. An adequate amount of it can make the difference between the educational program being alive and interesting or dormant and drab.

Agitators and *reformers* want people to turn against the present system or methods and either accept the proposed reform or search out or create a new or modified system. They are often associated with political, social, and religious unrest. They oppose the system, and their objective is to cause reformation to occur. Reform efforts are not limited to governments and churches. They go on often in less obvious settings, including the educational system. Even though reformation efforts are often distasteful, they sometimes produce constructive results, and there are cases when it seems that no other approach can bring about the desired changes.

Symbolic leadership has little application in the educational system; however, it is not totally lacking. Sometimes faculty members play a modified role of symbolic leadership, and occasionally a school board will have a member who is more symbolic than functional. International examples of symbolic leaders include the Queen of England and the Emperor of Japan (since World War II). Symbolic leaders derive their strength from tradition and association with the position. Whoever holds the position fills essentially the same leadership purpose regardless of the individual's characteristics or ability, assuming that the individual is respected and accepted by the followers. Many believe that symbolic leadership provides a stabilizing influence.

In terms of leadership, charisma is a kind of "personal magic." The *charismatic* leader captures the imagination of the followers, inspiring their loyalty and enthusiasm. Such persons lead and influence others by means of their personal appeal and direct motivation.

Administrative leadership is not a model in itself; it is a leadership function. Administrative leadership can have strong elements of any of the various models already discussed. The administrative leader provides a framework within which the other forms of leadership can be applied. The leader has a coordinating and supporting role in addition to implementing management procedures and providing direction toward the desired goals. The administrator is responsible for enhancing and controlling the environment within which others work.

It is often assumed that those in administrative positions make the greatest leadership contributions, but this is not necessarily true. Some people actually have more positive influence from nonadministrative positions. This is not meant to minimize the importance of administrators. The point is to clarify that nonadministrative positions can often be just as important in terms of overall contribution. Some seek administrative assignments while others prefer to apply their influence in different ways.

IMPORTANT LEADERSHIP CHARACTERISTICS

Although the traits discussed here are certainly not all-inclusive, they stand among the more important leadership characteristics necessary for successful administrators. These traits apply regardless of the particular leadership model one might resemble.

Ability

A person's capacity represents the limits within which ability can be developed. One becomes more able through normal growth and development, formal preparation, and a multitude of other experiences. Usually those who are selected to fill important positions are able individuals who have worked hard to develop themselves through education and practical experience. One's competence in the job is directly dependent upon the level of ability the person has developed, both in the general sense and in specific knowledge and skills.

Confidence

With the right combination of talent and preparation, a person can consistently experience success, which develops a self-awareness of competence and ability. With this awareness comes increased confidence, and this in turn, motivates a person to tackle larger and more significant tasks. The development of confidence at each new level helps to form a base for another step up the leadership ladder. Others in an organization recognize and appreciate well-founded confidence. This makes them feel more comfortable about the person in the leadership role. Conversely, when one loses confidence or displays false confidence, feelings of faith and support among colleagues usually falter.

Ambition

A key element in successful leadership is ambition, a trait that includes vitality, aggressiveness, and drive. The word *ambition* is used here in a positive context. It is not to be confused with false ambition or ambition with ulterior motives. The drive to work extra hours, indulge in difficult tasks, identify and solve problems, and consistently strive for better methods and more productivity are marks of an ambitious person. Ambition demonstrated in these ways is vital to the success of an organization. It is certainly an important element in leadership, and it can contribute to one's opportunities for advancement.

Willingness to Risk Failure

Too much talk about job security and pension benefits among many people leads one to believe that they are more concerned with security than opportunity. As one person stated, "some people seem more afraid of life than of death." A leader must be willing to take reasonable risks in the interests of success. An administrator who is self-protective and unwilling to accept calculated risks lacks the "crisp" approach that most people appreciate and desire. On the other hand, foolhardiness or reckless and irresponsible decision making are unacceptable. The appropriate balance is needed between risk taking and a fair chance for success. If those in leadership positions become too cautious, the organization will go flat. Conversely, if they take unintelligent risks, the consequences can be disastrous.

One of the most frequent risks by an administrator is possible loss of favor among colleagues when a decision is made that is right but unpopular. Fortunately, "right decisions" usually become popular, if the reasons behind the decisions are understood. At any rate, choosing between what is right and what is popular requires a leader to have the courage to choose what is right and then help others understand the reasons.

Another form of risk is speaking out forthrightly on issues. Truth and honesty are undermined by falsehoods and sometimes, by silence. As Emerson said, "All that is necessary for evil to prevail is for good people to remain silent."

Desire to Lead

Unless a person wants to be a leader, leadership likely will not happen. This is not to imply that desire alone will make an effective leader, but without it, a person is apt to lack the necessary persistence.

An athlete could never run a 4-minute mile without a strong desire. A sales manager cannot inspire employees to surpass last year's record unless the manager has a strong will to attain that goal. A school administrator cannot influence teachers and students to do better without personally feeling compelled in that direction. Every potential leader must want to succeed as a leader. Consistent desire for success is fundamental.

Integrity

Integrity is a complex concept and, therefore, difficult to evaluate. The superficial aspects of integrity are easy to appraise, but integrity in the deeper sense reaches far into a person's sense of values and relates to numerous other aspects of life: how the person deals with fellow beings, attitude and conduct on the job, fairness with one's employer, honesty as a neighbor, friend and family member, and finally, integrity with one's self. True integrity, in the full sense, is a deep-rooted characteristic; a significant element of one's personality. It is basic to fitness as an educational leader. It is honesty in all aspects of life.

Additional Characteristics

Following are additional characteristics that are important in educational leaders. Each administrator ought to try to cultivate and apply these traits.

1. A cooperative attitude and the ability to create congenial relationships.
2. A sincere interest in human service and in the positive development of individuals and of society as a whole.
3. Personality traits that are appealing to other people, along with character traits that induce respect.
4. A strong sense of personal responsibility and high moral standards in all areas of human relationships.
5. A keen insight into the kinds of educational opportunities that people need in order to achieve success, enrichment, and fulfillment.
6. The ability to work effectively with people of various ages, beliefs, and backgrounds, without interference because of race, sex, religion, or other differences.
7. The specific knowledge, skills, and insights necessary to administer the particular specialized area of education.
8. A basic conviction that all humans have worth and dignity and a determination to help them improve the quality of their lives.
9. The ability to think clearly and logically, to understand and analyze problem situations, and to arrive at intelligent conclusions.
10. Skill in communicating effectively with others, both orally and in writing.
11. Such personal qualities as warmth, patience, empathy for the needs and feelings of others, and a sense of humor, all of which contribute to the ability to get along.
12. Emotional and psychologic maturity. Successful leaders should understand themselves and others, be free from irrational prejudice, and be able to manage disagreement and opposition constructively.
13. The ability to be a self-starter: be able to clearly identify goals and move directly and forcefully toward them.

14. Integrity, honesty, and loyalty to the organization and to its goals and philosophy.
15. The ability to make difficult decisions without stalling or equivocating and then stand by them.
16. Both vision and practicality; have high goals and a clear vision of what might be possible in the future, while at the same time, maintaining a realistic sense of practical problems.
17. Flexibility in the sense of growing and changing with time, rather than clinging to outmoded views, attitudes, and practices.
18. A point of view that emphasizes cooperation and mutual support rather than competition and jealousy.

REFERENCES AND RECOMMENDED READINGS

1. Banovetz, J.M.: Leadership styles and strategies, *In* Managing the Modern City. Washington, D.C., International City Management Association, pp. 109, 118–121.
2. Blanchard, K., and Johnson, S.: The One Minute Manager. New York, Berkley Publishing Corp., 1984.
3. Drucker, P.: Management: Tasks, Responsibilities, Practices. New York: Harper and Row Publishers, 1973.
4. Frost, R.B., Lockhart, B.D., and Marshall, S.J.: Administration of Physical Education and Athletics, 3rd Ed. Dubuque, IA, William C. Brown, 1988, pp. 13–20.
5. Gordon, J.R.: Organizational Behavior, 3rd. Ed. Boston, Allyn and Bacon, 1991, pp. 338–395.
6. Hart, L.B.: Moving Up! Women and Leadership. New York, AMACOM, 1980.
7. Hitt, W.D.: Management in Action. Columbus, OH, Battelle Press, 1985, pp. 55–78.
8. Horine, L.: Administration of Physical Education and Sport Programs, 2nd Ed. Dubuque, IA, William C. Brown, 1991, Chapter 2.
9. Karabetsos, J.D., and White, H.R.: HPERD administrators—A profile. JOPERD, 60(4):25, 1989.
10. Parker, B.: School managers need charisma. Education Digest, 45:6, 1980.
11. Pierce, J.L., and Newstrom, J.W.: The Manager's Bookshelf, 2nd Ed. New York, Harper Collins Publisher, 1990, pp. 227–255.
12. Rosenbach, W.E., and Taylor, R.L.: Contemporary Issues in Leadership, 2nd Ed. Boulder, CO, Westview Press, 1989.
13. Sayles, L.R.: Leadership: What Effective Managers Really Do—And How They Do It. New York, McGraw Hill, 1979.
14. White, H.R., and Karabetsos, J.: A comparative analysis. Administrative characteristics of HPERD administrators. JOPERD, 58(7):18, 1987.

Part II
THE ART OF
ADMINISTERING

Chapter *4*

WHAT AN ADMINISTRATOR DOES

Just what is an administrator? In a general sense, an administrator is a person who gets things done through other people; one who gives direction to the organization and to the utilization of its resources. The administrator is responsible to shed light on the track and put steam in the boiler.

The term *administrator* is broad and can be used interchangeably with other terms. For example, all of the following are administrators: school principal, athletic director, police chief, hospital manager, or shop superintendent.

In the broad sense, the administrator is responsible for providing effective and consistent leadership for those activities needed to reach the organization's goals. The functions the administrator performs in order to accomplish this can be grouped into the following categories: (1) planning, (2) organizing, (3) staffing, (4) directing, and (5) controlling. At this point it should be stated that common in the thinking today is a dichotomy in education; those who teach and those who administer. This dichotomy dissolves when administrators share in the teaching and teachers share in the administrative function. All are educators who should be building and planning together for common purposes.

PLANNING

Long ago, Confucius added wisdom to the idea of planning when he said "a man who does not think and plan long ahead will find trouble right by his door."[9] Planning is put in perspective, however, by the fact that plans alone cannot make an enterprise successful; action is required. But, plans focus action on goals. Without adequate planning, action becomes a series of random activities and produces chaos.

The planning function involves establishing goals and arranging them in logical order from immediate to long-range. It includes deciding what to do, how to do it, when to do it, and who should do it. Planning provides the strategies to be followed to achieve the goals. It is like a recipe for the cook or a road map for the motorist. It results in a mapped-out course of where to go and how to get there. It involves getting people together and hearing their ideas so that the planning is done with them and not just for them.

The importance of planning can be illustrated more clearly by analyzing profit organizations than educational institutions, because profit organizations have the dollar and cent standard with which to measure success, whereas measuring educational success is less objective and less precise. Thune and House found some phenomenal results when they analyzed planning as it occurred in 6 different industries and 36 different firms.[7] Their results have useful implications for all kinds of organizations, including education. They compared companies that had formal planning approaches with companies that did not. They found the following to be true: (1) Firms that did formal planning were more successful than firms that planned informally. (2) Those companies that did formal planning performed more successfully after the formal planning approach was instituted. (3) On the average, sales increased by 38%, earnings per share rose 64%, and stock prices rose 36% within 2 years after formal planning began.

Planning should accomplish two broad objectives:

1. It should enable the administrator to foresee and control situations more effectively.
2. It should help an administrator shape the future of the organization.

One common element of all forms of planning is the time factor. Planning involves setting goals to be achieved within a certain time. Intermediate targets should be defined to serve as indicators that progress toward the goals is taking place within the desired schedule.

Flexibility, however, is crucial in planning, since planning deals with the future, and the future is not perfectly predictable. Sometimes, it becomes necessary to revise the plan before the final goals can be reached. It would be foolish to continue working with an obsolete plan; therefore, periodic review of the plan and timely updating is of utmost importance.

Planning is deciding in advance what to do, how to do it, when to do it, and who is to do it. Planning bridges the gap from where we are to where we want to go. Planning makes it possible for useful things to occur that would not otherwise happen. The following ten principles of planning stated by William Hitt have broad application.[8]

1. It is essential that those persons responsible for executing the plans be actively involved in developing the plans.
2. Planning logically precedes the execution of all other management functions.
3. Every plan should be viewed as a tool that can facilitate the accomplishment of the organizational objectives.
4. Planning should start with where we are, rather than with where we want to be.
5. It is important that the individuals involved in the planning process apply consistency in the premises for planning.
6. Ample flexibility must be built into the plan in order to accommodate unforeseen changes in the circumstance.
7. The plans for the organization should be closely integrated among the various levels.

8. The organizational plan should be clearly described and made available to the administrative and supervisory personnel at the various levels.
9. Planning has value, only if it is transformed into action that produces the desired results.
10. Plans should be reviewed periodically throughout the year and adjusted as changes in circumstances occur.

Management by Objectives

Although it is correct to say that management by objectives (MBO) combines selected aspects of all functional areas in administration, it is more meaningful to view it as a philosophy of administration—a way of operating an organization. Setting appropriate and meaningful objectives is of crucial importance in the MBO process. It involves mutual formulation of objectives by administrators at different levels, utilizing the participative approach, followed by mutual evaluation of performance toward the objectives, and a mutual understanding of the reasons for success or failure.

At regular intervals, the administrator and co-workers participate in deciding what results are to be achieved and what will constitute acceptable performance. The administrator then delegates responsibilities to subordinates, who must take the appropriate initiative at their levels to achieve the results agreed upon. The chief administrator gives overall direction to the setting of goals and the process involved in achieving them, but the subordinates take the main responsibility for what they have agreed to do. Periodically, program results are jointly measured and compared with the objectives.

Several potentially significant benefits can be derived from using the MBO approach. It usually insures that the motivation and sense of accomplishment of people up and down the administrative line remain high, because each person participates in determining the goals and how to achieve them. This helps to enhance each one's self-esteem. Furthermore, MBO enables management personnel at the different levels to understand the purposes and the plan of the organization. Also, the MBO approach focuses the thoughts and efforts of the employees on results instead of activities.

MBO is a subtle approach to helping people arrange and perform their activities in accordance with the plan. A further advantage is that it enables an administrator to evaluate subordinates on the basis of measurable results that relate to the objectives. Also, focusing on results makes decisions about salary and promotions more objective.

Management by objectives should not be viewed as a panacea or a solution to all management problems. In fact, it should not even be viewed as a complete management system. It is a framework within which management can be conducted and which will add a systematic approach to the utilization of resources at all levels toward these stated objectives. Every successful organization applies the MBO concept to some degree. Certainly organizations do not ignore the importance of setting objectives. But the MBO approach is highly focused and extensively involved in stating objectives and systematically applying resources toward their achievement. The advocates of the MBO approach claim that it offers the following benefits:

1. Forces detailed planning and facilitates the operational plan.
2. Provides direction for how the organization should be structured and clarifies roles and responsibilities.
3. Enhances participation by individuals up and down the line and thereby elicits comments and suggestions for effective action.
4. Provides a specific time frame and standards for evaluating results.

Listed below are the levels of objectives used in the MBO process:

Organization mission
Organization objectives
Department objectives
Division objectives
Individual performance objectives

The steps involved in the MBO plan are as follows:

1. Preparation for the MBO process. This involves education and orientation of individuals at the various levels.
2. Review and update of the organization's major objectives at the beginning of the MBO cycle.
3. Development of objectives at the subsequent levels within the framework of the major objectives of the organization—making sure that all of the objectives are properly aligned in hierarchal sequence and fit appropriately within the overall framework.
4. Interim reviews of all objectives and the progress being made toward their achievement.
5. Final review of all objectives at the end of the MBO cycle to determine the degree of success and to identify reasons and corrective actions in areas where the objectives were not achieved. The accomplishment of step 5 sets the stage for repeating the cycle.

It should be pointed that even though the MBO approach seems logical, there are many administrators who avoid it, because they believe it is too involved and too objective oriented.

Regardless of the techniques employed, planning is not foolproof, and sometimes good plans go awry. With adequate planning, however, an organization can better control its own destiny instead of being controlled by random events. Planning gives structure to the organization's program and the activities of the individual employees. A realistic plan that is well conceived and properly managed will usually succeed.

ORGANIZING

Organizing involves identifying the responsibilities to be performed, grouping the responsibilities into departments or divisions, and specifying organizational relationships. The purpose is to achieve a coordinated effort by the total organization. The primary focus is on definition of responsibilities and relationships. Among key questions are the following: (1) How many different tasks make up a particular job? (2) Which particular tasks fit together logically into one position? (3) Which positions fit together logically to form a division or department? (4) How do the divisions and departments fit together to form the complete organization?

In education, jobs and responsibilities are almost always grouped into divisions or departments according to specialty. Sometimes, however, a faculty member's specialty laps over two or more departments, thus causing a split assignment. Also, some staff positions, such as secretaries, financial managers, and facility supervisors do not relate to a particular educational discipline, so their placement in the organization is determined by other criteria.

Span of Control

One important question in organizing is how many employees should report directly to the particular administrator. Obviously, there is a limit to the number of persons an individual can supervise effectively. For years, management theorists and practitioners have analyzed this problem. Common sense indicates that the optimum span of control is contingent on the particular administrator, the subordinates, and the work being performed, and not on some magic number. The amount of time the administrator has for supervising employees is one important consideration. If a series of duties is required that takes time away from the supervisory function, then the span of control must be smaller. Other important factors include (1) the abilities of both the administrator and the subordinates, (2) the degree of coordination the particular kind of work requires, and (3) the frequency of new problems that arise within the administrator's realm and the potential difficulty of those problems. The effective span of control, then, varies with the situation. A common fault among administrators is to try to cover a span that is too broad. When this happens, the administrator can improve effectiveness by narrowing the span, thus relinquishing some of the control to others in the organization.

Delegation of Authority and Responsibility

Authority can be defined as the right to decide or to act within specific limits. From an administrative point of view, this includes the right to control people and situations and to allocate the organization's resources toward accomplishment of the objectives.

In an educational or business organization, the governing board represents the owners. The board grants authority to the chief executive, who in turn, delegates authority to others. When authority is delegated, an obligation is placed on the recipient to exercise it properly.

Delegating authority to a subordinate does not relieve the administrator of overall accountability. The administrator is still responsible for accomplishing the objectives of the organization and accounting for the use of its resources.

As an organization grows, it becomes increasingly difficult for one person to manage everything. Therefore, it is necessary to rely on subordinate administrators. Eventually, the administrator has to choose between: (1) losing command by trying to directly control too much (refusing to delegate) or (2) retaining orderly control by delegating authority and responsibilities (decentralizing). If a head football coach tries to coordinate all phases of the game, he does a mediocre job at best in all the different areas. A solution is to delegate the defensive responsibilities to the best qualified assistant and so forth. Through delegation the coach retains orderly control, in a general sense, over the various aspects of the program, while he gives up direct control of certain aspects.

Centralization and decentralization can be considered the extreme ends on a continuum with numerous intermediate points. Effective decentralization is dependent on: (1) the ability of the top administrator to delegate authority (and responsibility) to subordinates and (2) the ability of the subordinates to accept and handle it well (Chapter 5 includes additional discussion of the process of delegation).

STAFFING AND STAFF DEVELOPMENT

An organization is composed of people carrying out specific responsibilities that lead toward set goals. Effective staffing means filling the job positions with the right people at the right time. Personnel specialists can help in staffing by recruiting and screening people, but the ultimate responsibility for effective staffing rests with the administrator.

Position descriptions and specifications are essential in staffing. The descriptions detail the responsibilities associated with the various positions, and the specifications describe the personal qualifications required. Normally, the statement of qualifications includes the required educational level, professional experience, personality characteristics, rank, salary, and tenure status. Obviously, some positions are easier to write descriptions and specifications for than others, but regardless of the position, the best job description that can be prepared will be more useful than no description at all. Once it is clear what the job includes, it is easier to take an effective approach toward finding the right person.

Staffing

There are two general sources of personnel to fill positions—personnel from within the organization and applicants from outside. Promoting from within can be a positive morale factor, and it seems both logical and fair that first consideration should be given to the organization's own people. However, sometimes problems or situations prevent this approach. For example, it is unwise to advance a person who is not well qualified. This can result in low productivity and eventual failure for the individual. The result is undesirable for both the organization and the person. Also, promoting an unqualified employee can have a negative effect on morale. Furthermore, it is sometimes impossible to promote from within because of personality conflicts or jealousies.

The correct procedure is to attract the strongest applicants possible for a given position and then make an objective selection of the one who seems best prepared. If it turns out to be a stalemate between two applicants, and one is an employee of the organization, then why not promote from within?

Staff Development

A related function of staffing is personnel development or in-service training. This is discussed in more detail in Chapter 7, but it should be pointed out here that continued improvement of employees is an important function for two reasons: (1) to help employees perform their present responsibilities more effectively and (2) to better prepare them for promotion when the opportunity comes.

Staff development relates to the important concept that "the best way to get rid of a poor teacher is to make him into a good one." Although this is idealistic, it should be the first consideration and should receive an honest effort.

The staff development program should be evaluated periodically to determine whether it is meeting the needs of the organization. Simply having development programs provides no guarantee of effectiveness, and the time and cost involved in such programs can be substantial. The results of staff development activities should be reflected in measurable performance, both of the individuals and the organization.

An organization can offer the opportunities and provide the appropriate climate for staff development, but the individuals must seize these opportunities and turn them into the desired results. This requires employee motivation, and in the absence of adequate motivation, development activities will be unsuccessful.

In connection with staffing and staff development, William Hitt stated some useful principles, which are paraphrased below.[8]

1. A clearly stated organizational mission should be the beacon that guides the staffing function.
2. A human resource plan should be developed to serve as a road map in the staffing and staff development function.
3. Selecting the right people at the right time is essential to effective staffing. Mistakes in this regard are expensive.
4. The organization should provide an effective staff training program to meet the need for new knowledge and skills.
5. Long-term career development should not merely be "left to chance"; it should be systematically planned.
6. The primary purpose and final result of performance appraisal should be the improvement of job performance.
7. Each element of the staff and staffing development program should be evaluated periodically in terms of cost/benefit and contribution to organizational goals.

Staff Appraisal

Perhaps the most difficult aspect of the entire staffing function is performance appraisal. Many employees are threatened by performance appraisal, and administrators generally dislike making critical judgments about their colleagues. As a consequence, many administrators and employees alike have a negative perception of performance appraisal.

It is important to recognize that there are no perfect performance appraisal systems. But there are a number of useful guidelines for developing an acceptable system and thereby accomplishing the main purpose, which is to improve job performance. There may be secondary purposes, such as determining merit pay and promotions, but the primary purpose of a performance appraisal system should be the improvement of job performance. The benefit of this goal is the fact that it is shared by both the evaluator and the person being evaluated. The key to carrying out an effective appraisal system is to make it a joint effort between the staff member and that person's supervisor.

DIRECTING

Directing involves correct allocation of the organization's resources, leading employees in such a way that the comprehensive goals of the organization can be achieved, and providing an effective support system. The administrator accomplishes the goals through the work of other people.

Basic Human Needs

The literature on this subject indicates that social psychologists today generally agree with the hierarchy of needs presented many years ago by A. H. Maslow in one of the classic articles on the needs of employees.[6] Maslow included five needs in hierarchial order: physiologic requirements, safety and security, concern and affection, esteem, and self-actualization. It is believed that a person usually tries to satisfy these needs in order of their ranking and does not emphasize satisfying a higher need before the lower needs have been reasonably fulfilled. Thus, a person first acts toward physiologic needs and then focuses on safety needs, and so on. Each basic need in the hierarchy has several important aspects, and an administrator's understanding of these needs and their effects on behavior is important.

Physiologic needs pertain to the maintenance of the body; examples are food, drink, shelter, and relief from discomfort.

Safety and security needs refer to one's desire for freedom from threatening circumstances. The desire for safety and security encompasses both economic and psychologic aspects. People are especially concerned about such things as continued employment and a flow of adequate income. They also want to be free of potential expenses associated with long-term illness and property losses. Much of the social legislation and employee benefits of recent decades can be traced to the safety and security needs of people: social security, unemployment insurance, health and accident insurance, retirement benefits, and the like.

Concern and affection needs encompass the desire for friendship, compassion, and interactions with others. Humans are social beings who are desirous of associations with others and feelings of belonging. These needs are met on the job to some extent through belonging to an organization and the personal interactions that take place there.

Esteem needs encompass self-esteem and the esteem of others. Every individual wants to feel self-worth and self-respect, while also having the respect of others. This results in desires for positions and titles and feelings of achievement and approval. Esteem needs also comprise desires for prestige and recognition. The forms these needs take vary considerably among individuals.

Self-actualization needs are the desires one has for self-fulfillment and the achievement of one's potential. These needs are often less obvious than the other needs, and many people have not moved far towards fulfilling them. If each person's potential could be fully expressed, everyone would have a greatly enhanced quality of life.

It is obviously important for an administrator to be alert to the different kinds of needs that individuals feel and to help fulfill these needs to the extent that is possible on the job. This is a complex and important part of the *directing function*.

The two *lower order needs*—physiologic and safety and security—tend to be fixed or finite, and they are satisfied primarily through economic endeavors. One can actually overindulge in fulfillment of the physiologic needs by too much food or over emphasis on physical comforts. This also appears to be possible with safety and security needs. One can become so concerned about security that too little attention is given to other important matters. Furthermore, a person who becomes too secure can become apathetic. Also, when too much security is provided, individuals become excessively dependent. The needs for concern and affection, esteem and self-actualization, are not fixed or finite. As one increases fulfillment of these needs, they tend to enlarge. Thus, the higher order needs are never fully satisfied.

The employment relationship and the income one earns are used largely to obtain what is necessary to satisfy physiologic and security needs. A relationship can also exist between employment conditions and the satisfaction of higher order needs. People may, for example, use their earnings and free time to participate in private clubs, take on hobbies, buy goods and services for their own satisfaction, further their education, seek positions of status and leadership in private or voluntary organizations, serve society through charitable endeavors, and improve their personal skills and artistic abilities. The higher order needs, however, generally are satisfied by the meanings the individual attaches to personal experiences, and the individual's self-perception.

Whenever people work together, informal groups develop. The members of these groups are frequently in contact with each other in connection with their work: during lunch, at breaks, before and after work, and off the job at social gatherings. Being part of the group can provide satisfaction and fill certain needs. The group serves as a medium for conversation, socializing, and moral support. Certainly, there is some degree of psychologic security in belonging to such groups. Also, self-actualization of employees may be enhanced by belonging to the group.

It is helpful for an administrator to know as much as possible about the traits of the individual employees being supervised. With this kind of information and insight, the administrator is better prepared to work effectively with and for the employees in helping to fulfill their needs while working toward accomplishing the goals of the organization. (Related information is contained in Chapter 8, which deals with personnel management, and in the section on motivation in Chapter 6.)

People Emphasis versus Production Emphasis

One of the crucial issues in management is the question of a correct balance in terms of the emphasis on people as opposed to emphasis on production. Some would argue that such a choice is unnecessary because it doesn't have to be one or the other; the emphasis can be placed on both. It is a fact, however, that different administrators seem oriented more in one direction than the other, and circumstances sometimes influence the balance of emphasis. By its very

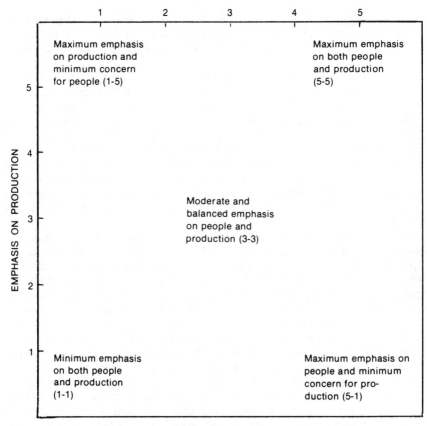

Figure 4-1. An example of a two-dimensional grid, pertaining to the relative administrative emphasis on people and production.

nature, education is people-oriented. It has to do with the development of the person. Education, however, also has a product (measurable knowledge and skills) that is at the focus of the total educational effort. To help in one's analysis of where to place the emphasis, a two-dimensional grid appears in Figure 4-1. Concern for people is represented on the horizontal axis, and concern for production on the vertical axis. Several leadership styles can be identified on the grid. Ideally, it should be the goal of the administrator to achieve style 5-5.

(1-1) Represents a weak administrative leader who shows little concern for either people or production.

(5-1) Represents a production-oriented leader who places high priority on production with little consideration for human factors.

(1-5) Represents a people-oriented leader who is concerned primarily with human factors and gives little emphasis to production.

(3-3) Represents a balanced leader who gives about average attention to both people and production.
(5-5) Represents an ideal administrative leader who shows a high level of concern for both people and production.

CONTROLLING

Recall the adage "a chain is no stronger than its weakest link." Management does not always know in advance which link of the operation is the weakest or when it will break. Therefore, controls are needed to ensure quality in all aspects and to detect potential or actual deviations from the organization's plan. The control function is to ensure high quality performance and satisfactory results while maintaining an orderly and problem-free environment. It involves the setting and achieving of performance standards and the application of the organization's policies and procedures. The control function is essentially a monitoring process for the purpose of identifying and handling weaknesses. It might also be viewed as an ongoing process of evaluation involving (1) defining standards, (2) measuring actual results against the standards, and (3) taking appropriate actions to prevent problems and overcome weaknesses. Also, it involves keeping a stern hand on the rudder during turbulent times.

Measuring Performance

Measuring performance is essential if the organization is to know whether its work is proceeding according to plan. With this in mind, two considerations stand out: how to measure and when to measure.

The question of how to measure has many answers, depending on the particular nature of the organization. Among the more widely used methods are personal observation, written and oral reports, statistical data, and personal conferences. All of these methods have the same general goal, that is, to supply the administrator with reliable information. Each method has its own strengths and weaknesses, so an administrator should not depend on information from any one source. Rather, information should be obtained to use in evaluation from various reliable sources.

The question of when to measure has no clear answer. Measurement in the form of observation and informal conversation goes on continuously, whereas the more formal methods occur only when planned, and they can happen as often or as seldom as the situation warrants.

At certain strategic times, special consideration is given to the effectiveness of the organization and its personnel. For example, at the end of each school year and each term, certain aspects are critically evaluated to determine what changes would be beneficial. Another strategic time is vacancy in a position. It is then appropriate to evaluate the effectiveness with which the job has been performed, the strengths and weaknesses of the one who vacated the position, whether the position should continue, whether the job description should be altered, and exactly what qualifications should be required of the one who will assume the position. Major financial and narrative reports also provide strategic opportunities for evaluation. In education, measurement focuses on the quality of the programs, student progress and achievement, and teacher effectiveness.

(Related information on this topic is contained in Chapter *18*, which pertains to evaluation methods.)

Taking Corrective Action

Measurement and evaluation can focus attention on deviations from accepted procedures and standards, and this should naturally lead to the next step—appropriate corrective action. In some cases, only minor adjustments are needed. But occasionally, evaluation results show a need for major changes. Thus, in one case corrective action might involve a change of procedure, a minor shift of resources, or a realignment of personnel so that the organization can regain its direction; some other case might call for a major reformulation of plans or a major shift of emphasis.

Behavior Aspects of Control

The objective of control is to get people to work more effectively toward the organizational goals, and especially to identify and eliminate weaknesses in that total process. The administrator, in exercising the control function, must consider how those who are affected by it will react.

Controls are often unpopular among those being controlled. Much of daily life is regimented by cultural norms, religious values, safety regulations, and family roles, to name just some of the restraining influences. The thought of additional controls can be distasteful, so the administrator must be prepared to deal effectively with negative responses.

A negative reaction can often be avoided or lessened if the manager is careful about interpreting and implementing control measures. Important in this respect are (1) the clear interpretation of organizational goals, policies, and procedures and (2) the education of employees about the goals and about the methods necessary to achieve them. Employees should understand that the goals and the processes used to achieve them make employment possible. If the goals are vague or inapplicable, it will be difficult for employees to generate enthusiasm toward them. It is important for employees to be able to see where their work contributes to the goals of the organization. This will help each one to know that measuring his or her performance is legitimate and necessary. Also, employees will better understand the reasons for adjustments when the evaluation results show a need for corrective action.

The administrator should encourage employees to participate in setting performance standards that are both challenging and obtainable. Management by objective (MBO), discussed previously, is one example of participation by employees in setting goals and evaluating progress. The value of this cannot be overemphasized because it is almost a certain guarantee of personal committment. Standards that are too low fail to motivate employees toward achievement, whereas standards that seem obtainable or too remote fail to stir enthusiasm and are likely to cause disinterest and discouragement. If the standards are to induce positive results, they must be challenging, realistic, obtainable, and mutually agreed upon.

REFERENCES AND RECOMMENDED READINGS

1. American Management Association: Workshop Notes on Management Responsibilities and Techniques. New York, NY, 1986.

2. Blake, R., and Mouton, J.: Corporate Excellence Through GMD Organization Development, 3rd Ed. Houston, Gulf Publishing, 1985.
3. Drucker, P.F.: Management, 2nd Ed. New York, Harper and Row, 1981.
4. Frost, R.B., Lockhart, B.D., and Marshall, S.J.: Administration of Physical Education and Athletics, 3rd Ed. Dubuque, IA, William C. Brown, 1988, pp. 21–40.
5. Herzberg, F., Mausner, B., and Snyderman, B.: The Motivation to Work. New York, John Wiley and Sons, 1959.
6. Maslow, A.H.: The theory of human motivation. Psychological Review, *50*(4):370, 1943.
7. Thune, S., and House, R.: Where long range planning pays off. Business Horizons, *13*:81, 1970.
8. Hitt, W.D.: Management in Action. Columbus, OH, Batelle Press, 1985, pp. 101–258.
9. Yutang, L., Ed.: The Wisdom of Confucius. New York: Random House, Inc. (The Modern Library), 1938.

Chapter 5

MANAGING TIME AND MAKING DECISIONS

Studies show that some administrators are plagued by the frustrating condition of more work to do and more people to see than they can satisfactorily handle. Although many administrators work longer hours than other employees and have above average energy and powers of concentration, they often feel the anxiety of unfinished tasks and unsolved problems. Underlying this is the concern that unfinished administrative work means delayed decisions and disrupted productivity of others in the organization. But these potential circumstances must be coped with effectively, because in order to manage others well, a person must first manage himself. Self-management is vital to administrative success.

Fortunately, there are outstanding examples of administrators in demanding positions who are able to organize their work in a way that leaves time for solid thinking about basic problems and for outside interest that make for a well-rounded life. Some, however, find it necessary to carry a problem-packed briefcase whenever they leave the office. An administrator who consistently faces this situation ought to consider whether the problem is *real* or only a symptom of something more basic. The basic problem might be *improper time management.*

Unfortunately, the busier a person becomes, the less time there is to analyze procedures and to plan better. Consequently, some administrators are always scrambling to keep from being overwhelmed by the mounting tasks of the job. Such a person, more than anyone else, needs sufficient time to identify weaknesses, improve administrative procedures, and grasp and implement the idea that the organization should be the slave, not the master.

TIME MANAGEMENT

Efficiency is the art of managing time and causing it to serve you fully and well. But managing time, like money, is an ongoing challenge, and the allocation of time should be in accordance with the priorities of one's responsibilities. There is an interesting example of a group of educational administrators who met to analyze their problems associated with time. They decided that each one should prepare a statement of the approximate number of days per year spent with each major area of responsibility. When they had finished, the total that some of them came up with exceeded the number of days in the year. One administrator counted 381 days. The group drew three conclusions: (1) They thought they were spending more time on certain responsibilities than was actually being spent. (2) They had failed to delegate enough of their responsibilities to subordinates. (3) They were spending too much time on certain unimportant aspects of administrative work; i.e., their use of time was not in accordance with the real priorities. Reportedly, every one of the administrators went home and immediately delegated certain responsibilities, and then realigned the allocation of time to better fit their priorities.[2]

Periodically, every administrator ought to go through this kind of analysis. It is an exercise that can be done independently or as a member of a group as in the preceding examples.

Another valuable exercise is to keep a detailed record for a week of exactly how your time is spent. This can be a real eye opener. Most people have analyzed their financial expenditures by keeping a record of everything that is spent, and many have improved their personal budgeting by this method. It is equally possible to improve the management of time by the same method.

Consider the example of one administrator who had a number of complaints from department heads about understaffing and heavy work loads and about the consequent lack of time for planning and supervision. One morning, each department head was handed a request to keep track on an hour-by-hour basis of how each day was spent, and then write an evaluation at the end of the day of how well the time was used and where improvements could be made. It was requested that each member of the department be required to follow the same procedure. After the evaluations had been completed, there were no more requests for additional staff. Instead, a general tightening up resulted, and the level of production increased. Figure 5-1 provides a sample form for recording and analyzing how a person spends time.

Control Your Schedule.   Parkinson's first law states that "work will expand to fill the time available." When the job pressures mount, the inclination of the conscientious person is to press harder and harder to get things done. This process can lead to a vicious circle which results in reduced time for planning. The consequent feelings of frustration and fatigue make working time less and less efficient. If you find yourself in this circumstance, take time at once to analyze your situation in a calm and collected manner. Arrive at a sensible plan for improvement; then apply the solution with confidence and composure. One important guide is that when you are under pressure of time, it is better to work smarter than harder.

Maldistribution of Attention.   Parkinson's second law states that "we tend to devote time and effort to tasks in inverse relation to their importance." Some administrators spend a disproportionate amount of time on relatively unimportant matters. There is a tendency to give prompt attention to items that are simple and uncomplicated, routine and repetitive, because with such matters success is easy and immediate. This can be described as an "activity trap" where one becomes so involved in activities that he loses sight of the more important aspects of the job. Realistically, a busy administrator cannot afford too much time dealing with $100 matters if $1,000 problems are being neglected. It is true that routine items such as parking privileges, janitorial ser-

NAME _____ DATE _____

Hour	Description of Time Use
8:00	_____
9:00	_____
10:00	_____
11:00	_____
12:00	_____
1:00	_____
2:00	_____
3:00	_____
4:00	_____
5:00	_____
Evening	_____
	_____

Summary and Analysis of How Time was Used (Hours spent)

Meetings _____

Telephone _____

Paper work (routine) _____

Special problems _____

Reports _____

Teaching _____

Research _____

Luncheons and social _____

Other _____

Figure 5-1. Example of a time analysis form.

vices, and food dispensers must receive attention by someone, but these matters should be kept in proper perspective. They must not infringe too much on the attention needed for the main objectives of the organization. Maldistribution of administrative time and energy is a potential weakness that needs to be constantly monitored. It involves the challenge of keeping first things first.

Inability to Discriminate. The term *discrimination* usually carries a negative connotation, but it also has a positive aspect. A person in an administrative position must be highly discriminating relative to (1) the number of people and the particular ones that are permitted to occupy time of the administrator in conferences, interviews, and telephone conversations; (2) the particular reports, surveys, and other written material that occupy time; and (3) the parts of the job the administrator handles directly as opposed to those responsibilities delegated. Unfortunately, many administrators are unable or unwilling to discriminate clearly between the more important and the less important matters to become involved with.

Long Conversations. Some people who aspire to administrative work are unsuccessful because they lack the ability to keep routine conversations short and to the point. Most conversations involving the administrator must be adequately thorough, yet relatively short. When the important business has been covered, the conversation should end. Another desirable element of conversation is one's ability to bring up the important points and lead the discussion to a conclusion without wasting time, and yet not cause the conversation to seem rushed. Furthermore, it is important for the administrator to play a proper role in each conversation and permit other people to do the same. One-way conversations are usually uninteresting and often unproductive; each conversation should result in an adequate exchange among those involved. The administrator is usually the one expected to give direction to the conversation and to keep it on track. Remember that a conversation always involves at least one person, sometimes more. The effective use of the other person's time as well as your own is also an important consideration.

Paper Handling. A certain amount of paper work is associated with administration, but it can easily be carried too far. For example, it is not necessary to make and keep on file a copy of every routine written communication. Neither is it usually desirable for two or more officers in the same organization to file the same kind of information. Furthermore, there is no need to put every kind of communication in written form. In short, an organization can easily become overburdened with too much handling and filing of paperwork. Many highly successful administrators "travel light" in this regard. The key is the ability to discriminate between what is necessary and what is not in terms of producing, handling, and filing written material.

Another important aspect of paperwork is expediency. An efficient administrator will have a consistent and highly structured approach to handling papers. The ideal is to handle each paper only once, but of course, this is not always possible. When you look at a particular written correspondence for the first time, try to decide what to do with it. Sometimes the decision is easy—discard it. In other cases it requires no action, but should go to the secretary for filing. Perhaps a telephoned response should be made immediately or maybe a quickly dictated reply would be better. Some papers should be passed on immediately to others in the organization, and a few papers require delayed attention—tomorrow, next week, or next month.

Some administrators can be labeled one-time handlers, some two-time handlers, and some multihandlers of paperwork. If you are a multihandler, you need to streamline your approach. Increased expediency of handling paperwork should be one of your immediate objectives. Specific information about how to cope with this problem appears in Chapter 7.

Excessive Travel.   Travel falls into two general categories: daily *travel within the vicinity of your work,* and *out of town trips.* Some people spend 2 to 3 hours per day traveling to and from work and running errands. If you are one of these people, you need to consider what you could accomplish on the job with a portion of this time and what changes could be made that would help you capture some of it. Often, not much can be done about commuting time unless you are willing to change the location of your residence on your work. Perhaps reducing unnecessary errands has more potential for saving time. Are you spending time delivering items that a secretary or other office employee could do? Or maybe your procrastination in handling matters on time requires too many hand deliveries that could be accomplished by mail if done a day earlier. Keep in mind that time spent traveling or running errands is time away from administrative duties.

Out of town travel has contributed to the downfall of many administrators. Some who enjoy business trips use various excuses to go when the need is truly doubtful. Or if the need is there, perhaps another member of the staff could fulfill it as well as or better than the chief administrator. A few administrators seem to believe that there is a direct relationship between time spent on business trips and job effectiveness. This is not consistently true.

Certainly, an administrator should not resist being away when there is a legitimate need to travel. If this were carried too far, one could easily lose touch with people and events with which contact should be maintained. But it is true that with some administrators less travel and fewer days away from the office would improve overall effectiveness.

Getting the Best Help from Your Secretary

Does your secretary feel "underutilized?"

If you have a top-notch secretary who spends a majority of the workday doing strictly clerical chores and not expected to do more demanding mental work, you may not be receiving the help you need to be as effective as you could be. Consider some areas in which you can use more valuable assistance:

Time Management.   A secretary can help you save precious time each day in several ways: help plan a schedule, make appointments, act as a barrier to interruptions by dealing with visitors and can enforce short meetings by entering when a visitor's allotted time is up. Also, by taking over some of your regular tasks, your secretary can free up your time.

Communication.   A good secretary can help you draft letters and answer phone calls. The secretary who knows the details of your dealings with others can handle many of the calls and draft replies to routine correspondence. In so doing, your communications will take you less time and stay more current.

Feedback. The secretary who is given certain responsibilities will be more interested in the business and will be able to spot problems as they arise, notice what is and isn't working well, and offer solutions. A good secretary who knows a great deal about the business of the office can help you make decisions faster and more effectively.

Organization. A good secretary sees the work flow, knows where bottlenecks develop or communication breaks down, and can suggest ways to keep up with the growing workload. This may mean devising and supervising more effective filing, record keeping, and paper handling. Also, this will allow you to concentrate more on other matters by spending less time dealing with crises which grow out of existing workloads.

Some Time-Saving Ideas

You might find it useful to make copies of a form such as the one shown in Figure 5-1 on which to record your activities of the day and the amount of time spent on each one. Evaluate the results at the end of each day and each week. Be analytic about how you could eliminate certain time-consuming activities and how you could improve the efficiency of your procedures. At the end of the year, it is valuable to reflect on the amount of time you spent in different categories of your job and to determine whether all aspects were in proper balance. For example, how much time was absorbed in travel? How much was used up with luncheons, receptions, and banquets? How much time did you spend handling paperwork, preparing or reading reports, and sitting in meetings? How much time was used in solving personality conflicts and dealing with emergency problems that should have been avoided? Did you have adequate time for serious thought and planning and for your own preparation and improvement?

You will probably be surprised to learn how many time-consuming activities in your schedule are unproductive in terms of what really matters. In connection with the analysis of how your time is used, ask what are the things that take time and contribute little; what would happen if these were not done at all. Ask whether you are giving the right kind of time for the truly important responsibilities. One of the differences between ineffective and truly effective administrators is that the effective person knows the limitations of time. An effective administrator does not believe that there are 24 hours in a day or even 8 hours for discretionary use of time beyond the basic requirements and recognizes that time is a peculiar resource which cannot be increased. Yet the really important things the administrator has to do take solid blocks of time, and if the right amount of time is given to them, effectiveness will be greatly increased. If there is one thing that can make an administrator more effective, it is knowing where time goes and how to better control and direct it toward truly important responsibilities.

Some administrators advocate the *open door policy*, which means that employees can come in without an appointment. It is true that such a policy can contribute to congenial relationships and a friendly atmosphere; but, in some cases, this is not the best way to improve accessibility to the administrator. Open doors often increase the wrong kind of communication—trivial and unproductive chatter. Interruptions are multiplied, and the administrator is frequently distracted from important matters. For administrators with demanding schedules, the open door policy is usually a poor one. Controlled access through a congenial but discrete secretary is usually better.

The *10-minute head start* technique for effective time management is worth considering. This is how it works. Whenever you leave the office, time your schedule so that you can leave 10 minutes earlier than necessary. This will provide a time buffer to cover unforeseen delays or unexpected phone calls. The benefits are that (1) it helps guarantee your promptness, which will have a positive influence on your image and the promptness of others, and (2) it removes tension and frustration caused by last minute rushing. Furthermore, it sometimes results in a little "gliding" time, which can be used constructively for thinking about the next important activity.

In order to organize yourself and your work effectively, you must apply the "talent for perspective" about yourself and your job and about your co-workers and their jobs. What should your job really entail: what should it include and what should it not include? Perhaps it would be useful to restate the description of your position in terms of duties, responsibilities, authority, and accountability. Ask yourself what are the educational and experience requirements and what is expected and needed by way of continued professional preparation? This kind of analysis will help clarify whether your job is really the same as the traditional description—the description that might be in the file or in the operational manual. Perhaps your perspective of the job is different from that seen by others in the organization. If so, these inconsistencies should certainly be resolved.

Once your job is seen in perspective, no matter how pressed you have been for time, it is usually safe to say that, with reasonably good organization, adequate delegation, and good relationships, your work will be manageable without an impossible work load or an excessive time requirement. This is a logical assumption because, for most positions, a predecessor was able to handle the job, and people in comparable positions are able to handle their jobs. It is safe to rely on the thesis that the problem of insufficient time usually lies within the person more than in the work situation. If the content of the job really is too much, it will become clear by means of perspective analysis, and this will help provide a basis for corrective action. On the other hand, if the job content is reasonable, then proper time management should serve as an effective solution. In such case, the focus should be on working smarter, not harder, in order to use the available time more efficiently.

CONTROLLING STRESS AND TENSION

Some administrators have oversized desks and stuffed briefcases, and they are sometimes thought of as ulcer-ridden bundles of complexities, obsessed with the idea of success and burdened with endless responsibilities. This picture is, of course, a grossly distorted version of an administrator. Yet, it cannot be denied that administrators often do feel the strain of their jobs and some suffer from tensions that rob them of both enjoyment and efficiency. (The problem of stress can also apply to athletic coaches.)

It is not possible to measure exactly the loss of efficiency emotional tension causes, even though psychologists are able to point to a considerable body of evidence that shows that efficiency suffers when one works under too much stress. Excessive tension can cut drastically into work accomplishments, and in extreme cases it can disable an administrator. Even a modest reduction in emotional stress can often produce a sharp upswing in imagination, foresight, and judgment, and this can add significantly to the effectiveness of the organization.

Some people are more susceptible to tension than are others. Some, in fact, generate their own private emergencies and remain more or less constantly on guard against their versions of disaster. This is a fatiguing approach to life, and such people do indeed find life an exhausting experience. Some of these people become administrators, and although they may be uncomfortable and perhaps unhappy, they are not always ineffective.

Knowing that too much tension can be destructive, what about too little tension? What happens to efficiency when people are too secure, too comfortable, and too complacent? Efficiency tends to decrease; people have to be motivated if they are to accomplish. As it happens, a sense of urgency and the pressures of disapproval or possible failure are pretty good motivators. Most people have to be at least a little bit apprehensive and keyed up to do their best work, and some are never so efficient as when they are half-scared. Emotional tension is not, therefore, an altogether undesirable thing. Tension becomes harmful only when it exceeds a reasonable level of tolerance or when it persists too long.

Too much tension can waste one's time in several ways. It can throw judgment out of kilter, so that it takes longer to reach correct decisions; and it may indeed prevent a person from making a decision at all. It can narrow one's perspective to a highly personal viewpoint and cause the objectives of the organization to become secondary or obscure. It can cause exaggeration of the importance of small problems at the expense of more important matters. It may cause an administrator to be unable to solve or lay aside the problems long enough to consider other items of importance. It can change a smooth, integrated thought process into a series of broken plays.

Sources of Tension

It is not likely that a person can alleviate tension unless the sources of it are identified and controlled. Following are possible causes of tension among administrators.[2]

1. *Inadequate command of the situation* can be both a cause and a result of tension. Tension can develop if a person is not holding things together, and problems develop faster than they are solved. Thus, the administrator becomes more of a problem solver than a forthright leader.
2. *Pressures resulting from lack of delegation* can relate to the situation explained in Item 1. If the administrator tries to give direct attention to too many responsibilities, it becomes impossible to cover them adequately. This can cause one to feel that the job is overwhelming.
3. *Waivering confidence* or distrust in one's own ability can cause tension to rise rapidly in pressure situations.
4. *Distrust of subordinates* can cause one to feel nervous about whether the responsibilities of subordinates are being done well.

5. *Insecurity* about whether others in high positions are displeased with your performance may be a product of imagination or caused by a lack of communication.
6. *A guilt feeling about having authority* causes some administrators to think they are not cut out to be separated from the rank and file, and they feel nervous about the authority and responsibilities they hold.
7. Other potential sources of tension are *problems at home, personal finances,* and *poor social relationships.* These can have negative influences on job effectiveness.

Controlling Tension

Unfortunately, the person who suffers from stress is in a weak position to control it. Once it develops, the person is less able to think clearly, analyze objectively, or command the situation. A good solution is to remain highly sensitive to the development of tension and try to nip the problem early before it becomes hard to handle. A person's supervisor can often be helpful in figuring out potential solutions, giving encouragement and building self-confidence.

Sometimes the best solution is to separate from the situation for a short while and do something that is filled with diversion and enjoyment. Also, jovial laughter can serve as a safety valve to keep yourself relaxed—some nonsense now and then is relished by even the wisest of persons. Inject humor and laughter into tense situations—they calm tempers and soothe jangled nerves.

Some people are able to reduce tension by simply adjusting their attitudes. This can be done by taking firm mental command of oneself and mental command of the pressure-causing circumstance. It can have an immediate result of increased confidence and better control.

DELEGATING RESPONSIBILITIES

The opposite extremes of delegation are well illustrated by a classic story that has often been told about two military situations. The first relates to an officer candidate in the Corps of Engineers who relied extensively upon delegation. He was asked the best way to get a heavy powerline pole upright in a hole. The candidate's response was, "Sergeant, take six men and put that pole up." The story showing the opposite extreme involves a captain who complained that the major who was his superior officer never let him run his company (Company B). When the captain was promoted to major and took the place of his former boss, his first comment was, "From now on Company B will be run my way." Both of these stories make their point by over simplification, because in between the two extremes lies a full range of delegation practices. Each administrator must decide whether he is going to function in the middle ground of delegation or toward one of the extremes.

When a person advances up the managerial ladder, there is a tendency to take along portions of the old job. This is illustrated clearly in the following example given by the American Management Association.[2] The chairman of a public transit authority has been elevated from a job where he was a hard-hitting front-line administrator. When promoted, he took his old job upstairs with him, including three telephones, through which he could bark orders to numerous employees down the line. Many of his meetings were interrupted by subordinates who had to consult him frequently for solutions to problems. He lived his job around the clock and made colorful copy for the press by taking personal charge of traffic jams or mishaps. But, the long range program of the traffic authority suffered. What was actually a double job of chairman and superintendent, left too little time for reflection on policy decisions, for the fundamentals of statesman-like conduct, and appropriate planning and preparation for the future. This example shows the time-eating effects of poor delegation.

Researchers have found that, in many cases, decision making would be vastly improved if the top administrator made fewer decisions. Often, others have more time to give adequate consideration to the influencing circumstances, and they are sometimes better informed on the specifics that should affect the decisions.[3]

It is a fact that one who cannot delegate effectively is incapable of a high administrative position. This inability forces some people to remain in nonadministrative positions or in positions at lower levels. Delegation involves the following:

1. Selection of competent personnel who can accept and handle delegated duties.
2. Clear definition of the responsibilities that are being delegated.
3. An adequate amount of freedom for the subordinates to handle the assignments their own way within the framework of correct procedures and sound practices.
4. Accountability for the results. A painful aspect of delegation is standing by and watching a subordinate struggle without interfering. One administrator who made a wise statement about accountability said, "I won't tamper with the fiddle and then hold you responsible for the music."

Confusion sometimes exists about the real meaning of delegation. It is different from simply assigning work to someone else. Delegation means that you pass on to a subordinate a portion of your *responsibilities*, along with the *authority* and the *accountability*. Some responsibilities are delegated with guidelines to define the framework within which they are to be conducted. In other cases, responsibilities are delegated with total freedom as to how to handle them.

In analyzing whether you delegate effectively, the following questions will be especially helpful.

1. Are you unavailable because you are almost always too busy? If so, are there valid reasons for this, or do you spend too much time doing things that someone else ought to do?
2. What would happen if you were suddenly taken out of circulation for a few days? Some administrators take pride in the idea that the place cannot get along without them. Such indispensability, however, (even if true) indicates an organizational weakness.
3. Is the operation slowed down and productivity diminished because others

must wait for you to fulfill all your responsibilities? Are others waiting for decisions that should have been made last week?

4. Are communication channels too rigid, requiring subordinates to channel too much information through you and not permitting them to cut across departmental lines, provided they keep you properly informed?
5. What does an analysis of your homework show? Does your briefcase bulge each night and on weekends with correspondence and reports?
6. Are there certain administrative matters that someone else could handle instead of you, even if not quite as well, or perhaps even better under the circumstances?
7. Are there responsibilities that someone could do at less expense than you, in view of the dollar value of your time?
8. Could a secretary or administrative assistant do many of the things you are doing, and would the additional freedom of your schedule more than compensate for the cost of the extra person through improved management and better results?

Why Some Administrators Fail to Delegate

Usually administrators understand the theory of delegation, but many are unwilling to apply it. Failure to delegate is usually inherent in the individual rather than the situation. Here are some interesting reasons gleaned from the literature that explain why some administrators resist delegating.[7]

1. *Fear of being found out.* Some administrators are not as well informed as they like others to believe. There is a tendency to defend against this by keeping others detached and uninvolved.
2. *Overdeveloped sense of perfection.* Such an administrator has the attitude that in order to have it done right, he has to do it. So he tries to do it all and the result is an organization that gets "gummed up" at the top level.
3. *A reluctance to admit that others know more about certain aspects of the operation.* If competent personnel are given ample opportunity for development, some will know more about certain responsibilities than the chief administrator. Some administrators find this hard to accept.
4. *Fear of not getting credit* Here, a fundamental insecurity manifests itself—the desire to get personal credit. This form of pettiness is found in high-ranking administrators as well as in lower-level supervisors.
5. *Fear of subordinates progressing too fast.* This can seem like a threat to an administrator who is afraid of "slipping."
6. *Fear of poor relationships.* Some administrators have such a strong desire to be well-liked that they avoid being firm in demanding that subordinates carry their share of the load.

An administrator cannot, of course, solve all the time problems by simply shoving projects off to subordinates. At the same time, one cannot hope to keep close tabs on every activity that occurs in the organization. A position in between is the best solution.

MAKING DECISIONS

Making decisions is one of the most important and most difficult functions of an administrator. Decisions involve judgments that are based on a combination of information and reasoning. They often involve breaking big tasks into their smaller parts and thereby simplifying the problem and the process. Teaching an individual to make good judgments is difficult; some say it is impossible. One can learn how to organize the steps in decision making, how to avoid certain mistakes and pitfalls, and how to gather, organize, and utilize facts. But even within the framework of all this, some are much better at making sound judgments than others.

In decision making, there are four possibilities, the first three of which result in error.[7]

1. Making the wrong decision about the wrong problem.
2. Making the right decision about the wrong problem.
3. Making the wrong decision about the right problem.
4. Making the right decision about the right problem.

This points out that identifying the *real problem* is a necessary step toward arriving at the best solution.

Difficult decisions are, to some degree, compromises because it is not usually possible to arrive at a perfect or ideal solution. Sometimes, however, it is a good idea to start by defining the ideal solution, and then strike as close as possible. The objective is to make the decision that has the best overall chance for success, and this usually involves compromising some points in order to strengthen others.

Obviously, "getting the facts" is an important part of decision making. But, effective administrators do not rely totally on facts. Actually, a decision starts with an opinion. Opinion plus important facts lead to understanding. Understanding enables one to identify the alternatives and to evaluate them accurately, and select the best one. This process can rightfully be termed "considered judgment," a process that results in a well thought-out conclusion.

In the military, *quick* and *accurate* decisions save lives, and there are other settings where such an approach can be beneficial. However, in the educational setting, *timely and accurate* is better terminology. The application of this concept is so important that it forms one of the basic ingredients of the administrative process. It is important to be abreast of situations and have readily available the best information on which to base correct decisions.

Some administrative decisions have little significance, whereas others have significant effects. It is necessary to clearly recognize the importance of the decision and its potential consequences. This requires a level of understanding and insight that some people lack.

Decisions are often labeled *right* or *wrong*; however, these are extreme labels. More meaningful terms are *strong* or *weak, appropriate* or *inappropriate, sound* or *unsound, good* or *bad* (or poor). In some cases, it is more descriptive to use a five-point scale: *poor, fair, acceptable, good, excellent.*

Many people with a good batting average for making decisions follow a structured approach toward identifying and defining the problem, considering all the important factors, and then arriving at a decision. Sometimes this procedure is not apparent to others; the decision maker may not even be aware of it himself. The following steps, if applied, will improve the probability of good decisions. Study these steps and attempt to build them into your pattern of thought. As with any new skills, early attempts might seem awkward, but gradually the process will become more natural.

State the Apparent Problem.   When a problem is first recognized, the solution often seems obvious; there is a tendency to plunge ahead to a quick decision. Unless adequate thought is given, you might find that you are only on the fringes of the real problem, and in some cases, you might even be looking at the wrong problem. Also, there is a tendency to deal with only the symptoms and not the underlying cause. To avoid this mistake, put the principle of definition to work. State the problem as it appears. Then think about it and perhaps discuss it with others. Knowing that the apparent problem might not be the real problem, go on to the second step.

Search Out the Important Facts.   In order to clarify the problem, it is important to examine the circumstances that surround it. You will need to judge how thoroughly this should be done, but as a rule, it is better to do too much than too little. In gathering information, remember the following:

> The individuals you involve will each see the situation from a different point of view, and their interpretations will be tilted in the directions of their philosophic beliefs, preferences, and personal needs. In light of this, you must keep each one's point of view in perspective.
>
> Once a person has taken a stand, there is a tendency to hold to it, especially if emotions are involved. Therefore, it is a good idea to get people's input without causing them to take a firm stand. Keep the alternatives open.
>
> It is pointless to try to change people's attitudes in the fact-gathering stage. Such an attempt would be premature.
>
> Discovering *why* the problem exists will help immensely in arriving at the best solution.

Define the Real Problem.   The most important part of decision making is to correctly define the *real* problem. Often, when all the needed information is gathered, the real problem turns out to be different from the one originally observed.

Obtain Expert Opinion.   An important element is to recognize your own limitations and seek assistance from experts when needed; experts who understand your kind of problem. In this regard, remember that the considered judgment of one expert is often more useful than the opinions of numerous nonexperts. The former is the application of intelligence, whereas the latter is the pooling of ignorance.

One advantage of consulting with an expert is that the interchange of ideas has a stimulating effect on the thought processes of both people, and this tends to have the influence of a third mind. The exchange often produces ideas that would not have occurred to either person in the absence of the interaction. Conversing with experts is not a means of letting others do your thinking, but rather a means of letting them help you think more clearly.

Sometimes the cost of consulting with an expert from outside the organization seems prohibitive. It should be remembered, however, that an expert brings special training and usually new insights into a situation. Often, not using the expert would be "costly" in time delays or wrong decisions due to improper analysis of the situation.

Two important guidelines are: (1) let your decisions be influenced by new facts and well thought-out judgments of experts and (2) avoid being influenced too much by self-appointed "specialists," half-baked opinions, and unproven theories. Nonexpert opinions are the cheapest kind of advice, and they are often worth even less than they cost.

Analyze the Alternatives. Carefully evaluate the strengths and weaknesses of each alternative, considering both the immediate and long-term effects. Sometimes, one alternative will stand out clearly from the others, which makes the solution relatively easy. In other cases, you might have to take the reverse approach and eliminate the alternatives one by one as you decide against them.

Select the Best Solution. In the final selection, keep the following in mind: (1) Too much haste can lead to an expedient compromise, which is less than the best solution. (2) Conversely, if a decision arrives too slowly it can lose its favorable impact, and in the meantime, the indecision can become a problem. (3) The right solution at the wrong time is often no better than the wrong solution at the right time—*timing* and *accuracy* are both very important. (4) The solution for a particular problem may be different for the short-term than the long-term, and sometimes it is necessary to deal with those two separately.

Implement the Decision. Laying the groundwork for acceptance of a decision is an important element. The people involved or affected by the decision should be adequately informed through the proper sources. Sometimes the stage is already set for acceptance, and nothing more needs to be done. In other cases, careful preparation is needed. In the absence of adequate attention, implementation can bog down, making the decision ineffective.

Obtain Feedback and Evaluate. The final step is evaluating the correctness of the decision, the effectiveness of its implementation, and whether some adjustments are needed. This step involves gathering information as to how people feel about the decision and whether it is living up to its expectations. You might discover the decision is not working well and that certain modifications are needed. Basically, sound decisions usually work well when people join together and make them work, whereas seemingly good decisions often fail when the people involved are not unified and supportive.

Remember these important steps toward decision making:

State the Apparent Problem
Search out the Important Facts
Define the Real Problem
Obtain Expert Opinion
Analyze the Alternatives
Select the Best Solution
Implement the Decision
Obtain Feedback and Evaluate

The accumulation of decisions creates a future state of affairs that will be different from the state of affairs that would exist if the decisions were different. This helps to understand that numerous small decisions can have a large and long-term impact. The accumulation of decisions sets trends and establishes precedent that influence both the present and the future. Second to none in this regard are the decisions relative to the selection of personnel, particularly faculty members, because these decisions influence both areas of emphasis and quality of programs over the long term.

Decisions can be categorized into *problem-solving* and *goal-oriented* decisions. Problem-solving decisions are generally of the routine type that are made to facilitate the day-to-day operation. Goal-oriented decisions are considered judgments that involve weighing of the anticipated results in terms of progress toward the organizational objectives. Both kinds of decisions are necessary for the effective functioning of the organization.

Sometimes decisions result from default, meaning that in the absence of a conscious or forthright decision a situation evolves to a particular result. This lack of conscious decision for whatever reason results in a course of action that might be different than would otherwise be the case.

An administrative office is a decision center that involves many decisions other than those made directly by the top administrator. For example, an effective secretary makes numerous decisions each day in the process of oral and written communications. Further, associates and assistants of the top administrator make decisions within their own realm of responsibility and also while acting for the top administrator. Well-qualified individuals who work in a "decision center" become oriented and educated to make decisions that are in accordance with the purpose and philosophy of the organization, thereby adding a unity of effort toward achievement of the organization's goals. This process is known as "internalization of the organization."

Avoid Procrastination and Half Measures

Business statisticians have found that among those who have failed in business, one of the most prominent reasons has been indecision: the lack of ability to make timely decisions that would have kept the business moving forward.

Most of us have a tendency to avoid making difficult decisions. It is enticing to wait for more information, to think it over longer, or hope a development will occur that would make the decision easier. But too much waiting can be detrimental. Rushing important decisions, however, or making them without adequate investigation and careful thought is also unwise.

Success is associated with people who are able to make accurate decisions quickly. Once a decision is made, it is important to stick to it, unless ample evidence to the contrary becomes available. In a nutshell, it can be said that highly successful managers make decisions *quickly* and change them *slowly*, whereas making decisions slowly and changing them quickly is a characteristic of unsuccessful administrators. Definite goals make it easier to reach sound decisions.

A related problem is the practice of taking half measures. A half measure is a form of temporary compromise which only postpones a more permanent solution. Those who practice half measures are like the person who writes a promissory note with great flourish and then says, "thank goodness that bill is paid." A bit of this kind of blind spot seems to be in all of us. Some administrators settle on half measures in order to stave off unpleasant action, or to settle on a compromise that will pacify those who resist forthright action.

It is true that a half measure is not always undesirable. Sometimes it can furnish a temporary solution and buy time that is truly needed to work out the best long-range solution. But a half measure is detrimental when used as a hedge against a full measure that is really needed.

Problem Solving

In practically all cases, the best approach to problem solving is to pursue the solution on a timely basis, with all of the information out on the table and with the concerned parties involved in a participative approach. In this approach, the administrator participates as mediator, facilitator, and team builder. The procedure involves the following steps.[7]

1. Clearly state the problem.
2. Let the applicable information identify the causes of the problem.
3. Determine the alternative solutions.
4. Evaluate the alternatives.
5. Determine a plan of action.
6. Implement the plan.

Creative Thinking in Decision Making

Everything starts with an idea and this makes creative thought the great power that it is. The process of creative thinking starts with seeing or sensing a problem or clearly analyzing a situation. One of the salient traits of a truly creative person is the ability to see problems and potential solutions more clearly than others see them. It has been said of Einstein that a part of his genius, like that of many other creative thinkers, was his inability to readily accept what seemed obvious.[10]

One who is satisfied with present situations tends to be blind to the need for change. Some measure of dissatisfaction with the present state of affairs is a prerequisite to any attempt at transformation or improvement. The creative person feels "constructive discontent."

The problem must be properly perceived and correctly defined. When it is, the very statement of the problem carries within it hints or suggestions as to how it may be solved. Improperly defined, the problem may appear insolvable.

After becoming aware of the problem in general, the creative thinker is capable of reorganizing and restructuring the problem in different ways so that all of the possibilities of solution can be seen.

Successful administrators are usually disposed to approach a problem with a highly analytic attitude. One would be ill-advised to do otherwise, yet in one sense, structured analytic perception is the enemy of creative insight. Analysis disassembles a whole into its parts. At a certain stage, this is necessary if progress is to be made, but in the course of analysis, certain attitudes that pertain to the phenomenon as a whole may be destroyed. What is needed, if there is to be a creative reorganization, is a free, spontaneous look at the whole situation in order to fully appreciate it. Such an approach encourages the use of imagination, which is so crucial in the reorganization of a problem.

People can be influenced to be more creative through "brainstorming" and stimulating discussions with other creative thinkers.

It is generally believed that certain characteristics of thought are possessed by people who think creatively.

1. The creative individual forms concepts more easily and quickly, and the concepts are more clear.
2. The creative person forms concepts that are more diverse and encompass a broader range.
3. The concepts formed by creative individuals are usually more flexible because they are formed in a mental environment that is relatively unstructured and permits free flow of thought.
4. The concepts of the creative individual tend to be more complex and far-reaching.

FACULTY PARTICIPATION

Faculty participation in decision-making is generally accepted as intrinsically good and as having positive effects on the educational function. But, it is reflected in varying degrees in actual practice, and often neither faculty nor administrators are very satisfied with the actual effectiveness of faculty participation. Being sympathetic to faculty frustrations about participation, many administrators seek ways to more fully integrate consultation with faculty into decision-making processes.

Rationale for Faculty Participation

The rationale for faculty participation in decision-making rests on the same reasons as employee participation in any organization, and also on reasons specific to the faculty role in education. Participation in decision-making is associated with employee satisfaction and esteem. Faculty expertise on the subjects on which decisions are made is perhaps the most fundamental factor supporting faculty participation. But, such participation also causes the faculty to be more supportive and cooperative in the full implementation of the decisions. Although participatory leadership models require a number of preconditions, these preconditions are met in the education environment more frequently than in most other organizational settings.

Challenges to Faculty Participation

Faculty historically have had the broadest role and greatest influence on matters of curriculum and personnel (especially tenure and promotion). Also, within the last two decades, faculty participation has become relatively well-accepted in institutional planning and the selection and evaluation of administrators at the various levels. Traditionally, faculty involvement in budgeting has been limited by both administrative resistance and faculty ambivalence. However, in many educational institutions and systems, faculty members are now more involved in budget planning, and they are gaining a better understanding of the technical basis and political dynamics of the budgetary process. Also there is evidence that the governing boards of educational systems and institutions are becoming more sophisticated about the importance of obtaining meaningful input from the faculty in the decision-making process.

Steps Administrators Can Take

The articulation of a set of shared values and goals is central toward participative decision-making. Thus, administrators increasingly see themselves as managers of a decision-making process, which requires shaping an environment of consultation with faculty, increasing the availability of information, and facilitating group deliberation. Frequent conversations with a broad spectrum of the faculty can make the administrator better informed and cause the faculty to feel that their views are valued and applied. At the heart of the participative process is the regular utilization of ad hoc and standing committees. The effective functioning of such committees should be an important element of the ongoing process of decision-making in the education setting.

REFERENCES AND RECOMMENDED READINGS

1. AAHPERD: Managing Teacher Stress and Burnout. Waldorf, MD, AAHPERD Publications, 1986.
2. American Management Association: Workshop Notes on Time Management. New York, 1986.
3. Arnold J.D.: Make Up Your Mind: The Seven Building Blocks to Better Decisions. New York, AMACOM, 1978.
4. Blanchard, K., and Johnson, S.: The One Minute Manager. New York, Berkley Publishing, 1984.
5. Boettinger, H.M.: Is management really an art? Harvard Business Review, *53*(1):54, 1975.
6. Braverman, J.D.: Management Decision-Making: A Formal/Intuitive Approach, 2nd Ed. New York, American Management Association, 1990.
7. Drucker, P.F.: Management, 2nd Ed. New York, Harper and Row, 1981.
8. Farber, B.A.: Stress and Burnout in the Human Service Professions. New York, Pergamon Press, 1983.
9. Gordon, J.R.: Organizational Behavior, 3rd. Ed. Boston, Allyn and Bacon, 1991, pp. 238–280.
10. Goslin, L.N., and Rethans, A.J.: Basic Systems for Decision-Making, 3rd Ed. Dubuque, IA, Kendall/Hunt Publ., 1986.
11. Horton, L.L.: What do we know about teacher burnout? JOPERD, 55(3):69, 1984.
12. Reynolds, H., and Tramel, M.E.: Executive Time Management: Getting 12 Hours Work Out of an 8-Hour Day. Englewood Cliffs, NJ, Prentice-Hall, 1981.
13. Virgilio, S.J., and Krebs, P.S.: Effective time management techniques. JOPERD, 55(4):68, 1984.
14. Whetten, D.A., and Cameron, K.S.: Developing Management Skills, 2nd Ed. New York, Harper Collins Publishers, 1991, pp. 94–155.

Chapter 6

ACHIEVING SUCCESS

It is especially useful for an administrator to be well informed about attitudes and methods that accentuate positive results. This chapter deals with that theme, with special emphasis on the topics of Formulas for Success, Traits to Emphasize, and Motivating Oneself and Others.

FORMULAS FOR SUCCESS

Many people, including some school employees and students, attain relatively low levels of success because they do not understand or do not apply the right formulas. It is important to know the ingredients of success, and even more important to apply the ingredients consistently. In the general sense, it can be said that success is achieved by discovering your best talents, skills, and abilities and applying them where they count the most. But once a person accepts a particular position or job then a delimiting influence exists. Thus, the challenge is high-level success within the framework of the circumstance. But, all else remaining equal, one of the most prominent factors in success is a positive approach.

Positive Thinking

An interesting psychologic law is known as the *law of attraction*. It means that a person's energy, actions, and achievements are attracted in the direction of one's thoughts. We do not always achieve all of our thoughts, but we are at least attracted in that direction. This implies that if you have positive thoughts leading toward worthy goals, your actions will be attracted in the direction of those goals, and you will utilize your energy in their accomplishment. If you think constructively, your actions will be constructive; if you think about the welfare of others as well as yourself, your actions will demonstrate this concern. The law of attraction suggests that each of us should purposely guide our thoughts toward well-defined and worthy goals. We should think positive, constructive, and humane thoughts, so that our energy will be used accordingly. This will help us in our efforts toward worthwhile achievements.

Another law known as the *law of positive expectation* means that if you expect good things to happen, it is likely that they will. The very fact that you expect it will cause you to dedicate your efforts in that direction. Others, who know that you expect it, will also help. Positive expectation truly pays off. Conversely, negative expectation has the same kind of attraction. If you expect negative results and psychologically condition yourself for them, and let other people know of your expectations, negative results are more likely to occur. An administrator ought to take advantage of these two laws by thinking positively and expressing positive but realistic expectations to others.

Norman Vincent Peale dwells on the importance of positive thinking in his book *Enthusiasm Makes the Difference.*[10] He explains the ingredients of the ADD concept; attitude, direction, and discipline.

A person's attitude is an outward expression of inward feelings. In order to be successful, one must think in terms of success. An administrator with an attitude toward mediocrity will encourage mediocrity. One with an attitude toward enrichment will enhance enrichment, and one with an attitude toward excellence will contribute excellence. Attitude can truly make the difference.

How is your attitude toward the positive progress of your organization or program? Do you think progress is important; do you think it is possible; and do you think that you're capable of giving adequate leadership toward its achievement? Next, how is your attitude toward the people in your organization? Are you really interested in their development and welfare or do you only have interest in yourself? Now would be a good time to clarify in your own mind the fact that one way to improve your organization is to improve the personnel. The organization will strengthen with the improvement of its people.

How is your attitude toward your work? Do you think of it as a good way to spend your professional life? Are you pleased with what you do and with the label that you carry? Do you radiate a proud attitude that is contagious to others?

The term *direction* in the ADD concept refers to being goal oriented. Having well-defined goals is one of the starting points toward significant achievement. Many people and many programs have reached low levels of achievement because there were no clear goals, or the goals were too meager, or the programs were not managed toward achievement of the goals. Most people (or organizations) who fail to accomplish much do so because they did not *plan* to accomplish much.

Many people's professional approach parallels the response given by a businessman when he was asked how he thought his business would do this year. He said, "It will do better than last year." When asked how it did last year he replied, "I don't exactly know."

Without knowing the direction you are headed for the future, how can you possibly know whether you are progressing toward your goals? More importantly, how can you reach your goals if you do not know what they are? People who do a good job are those who *plan* to do a good job. Clear direction helps to make the difference. Remember, "No goals are bad and meager goals are sad."

The third element of the ADD concept is *discipline.* It has been said, "We are what our habits make us." Habits are acquired slowly. Sometimes we do not realize that a habit is developing until it is already formed. To give some examples, ask yourself these questions. Which cigarette gives the smoker the smoking habit? Which bite of food makes a person 20 pounds overweight?

Which late appointment causes a person to become habitually tardy? The chains of a bad habit are too weak to be recognized until they become too strong to break.

Habits are formed through the practices one follows repeatedly. If you adhere to good work practices, you will develop, favorable work habits, and this is where discipline comes in. Each of us is actually two people. We are first the person that we know and others know, and second we are a much bigger person—the person that we should and could be. Plan for the kind of person you want to be; then discipline yourself accordingly. Without proper discipline, your plans for yourself and your program can never be achieved. Discipline is molding yourself into the kind of person you ought to be. It is probably the most important ingredient of self-realization.

More About Goals

Chapter 1 includes a discussion about goals and how goals can be structured and applied. The information presented here relates to that section, but the emphasis is on achieving success through the effective implementation of the right goals. It is true that a systematic approach to the application of goals can be a great asset to any administrator. Effective goal setting will help toward accomplishment of both short- and long-term projects, and it will benefit both the organization and the administrator.

Napoleon Hill, in his famous book *Think and Grow Rich,*[6] emphasized the vital importance of these three steps in connection with goals: (1) crystallize your thinking, (2) develop a plan, and (3) follow through with consistency. These elements are important in nonprofit organizations as well as in profit-seeking ventures.

Crystallize Your Thinking.   A person needs to determine which goals should be achieved—short-range, intermediate, and long-range—then state the goals in writing, clearly and concisely. Writing crystallizes one's thoughts because it is necessary to clearly understand a concept before it can be written. Once it is written it can be reviewed again and again and crystallized even more.

General and vague statements indicate lack of clear thought and exact purpose. A person must know precisely what he or she wants to achieve. This enables a vivid and crisp approach toward achievement.

Goal setting should involve creative and imaginative thinking, tempered by reality. There is no reason to state goals that are lowly, common, and unworthy. On the other hand, it is senseless to set goals that are clearly beyond one's reach or that fail to lead in the direction of one's long-range purpose. Setting realistic, and challenging goals is one of the administrator's most important single acts toward progress and long-term success. Setting goals helps turn theory into practice, thoughts into action, and energy into desired results. A plan of action based on clearly defined goals discourages procrastination, reduces indecisiveness, and increases efficiency.

Develop a Plan.   It would be largely unproductive to state goals without forming a plan to accomplish them. The plan serves as the blueprint or roadmap toward success. It always includes at least two basic elements: the tasks to be accomplished and the desired time schedule. A well-conceived plan will keep you on track and help you meet your timetable toward goal achievement. It will reduce floundering and the dissipation of energy and make success more likely.

In planning, one should recognize possible roadblocks and obstacles and have some ideas on how to get around them. The plan should take into consideration the strengths and weaknesses of those who will implement it and pinpoint the useful talents and skills each person possesses.

A plan is only a concept of action, and the action must be performed by people. This means that the effectiveness of any plan, regardless of how well conceived, is influenced significantly by the ability of the people who have to make it work. Some very good plans have failed because the people involved did not have the expertise to succeed. Conversely, some very able people have failed because the plan they attempted was unsound or ineffective. Although there is no such thing as a perfect plan, the plan for any educational endeavor ought to be relatively faultless.

When planning, it is important to involve those who will be affected and to benefit by their special knowledge and expertise. An example would be a teacher sitting in consultation with the principal or department head to formulate a plan for completing a facility remodeling project. Another example is a group of instructors meeting with the district specialist to develop a plan for the achievement of instructional goals. All teachers would be expected to represent their programs or departments. In this way, various points of view can be considered, and people are less likely to feel overlooked or isolated from the planning process.

Follow Through With Consistency. It is important to keep in mind the difference between *wish* and *desire*. A wish is a passive thought that may never result in significant action. It only expresses an idea of what you would like to happen. Desire, on the other hand, compels a person toward action, and if the desire is consistent and strong, the action will persist until the desired results are achieved.

In order to help ensure that your plans will remain valid, evaluate them regularly, with an open mind and adjust them as needed. As long as you are satisfied that your plan is sound, stick with it in spite of the obstacles you meet or what others may say. Dedication involves persistence, and persistence leads to accomplishment. Avoid floundering, vacillating, and procrastinating. Instead, move forward with confidence and determination. With this approach, your emphasis will be toward how things can be accomplished instead of why they cannot.

TRAITS TO EMPHASIZE

Leadership comes from individuals, and each individual has certain traits that are advantageous in the leadership role. Fortunately, the desirable traits of individuals can be strengthened within certain limits, and this affords the potential for self-improvement. The following discussions describe the traits that consistently contribute to an administrator's success. It would be well to give emphasis to the development of these traits in yourself and others.

Specialized Knowledge. Before a person can expect to accomplish important administrative goals, the specialized knowledge and skills must be developed that would logically make such accomplishments possible. Improvement of specialized knowledge and skills is fundamental to long-term administrative success. Sometimes, administrators find that more knowledge and skills are required than they have the ability to acquire, in which case, the best alternative is to engage other people as consultants or assistants who can help provide the necessary specialization.

Imagination. It is a basic truth that those things that finally become results started as ideas. When combined with clear purpose, desire, and persistence, an idea is the origin of success. Creative and ingenious ideas are trademarks of effective administrators. Imagination is the workshop where ideas and plans are created. Some leaders stress that a person can achieve anything, within reason, that is clearly imaginable. Once the mental concept is formed, the accomplishment is primarily a matter of follow-through. Unfortunately, two of our most basic limitations seem to be lack of imagination and lack of willingness to pursue with determination that which is imagined. As a person thinks of goals, it is important to be imaginative about how to achieve them. The mind needs to be constantly stretched toward improvement.

Desire. It has been proven many times that desire is one of the first requisites of success. It is the starting point for action. Yet many people encounter their first stumbling block at this point. Emerson stated it well when he said ". . . the implanting of a desire indicates that its gratification is in the constitution of the creature that feels it." This indicates that a person would not feel a desire unless capable of achieving it. It suggests that each of us has a built-in control that causes our desires to be modified by our abilities and aptitudes. To the extent this theory is true, whatever you sincerely desire you can achieve.

It is well known among coaches and athletes that, in order to run faster, you must either lengthen or quicken your stride or both. A similar approach is needed for one who wants to move faster and more steadily toward desired goals. Consistent desire toward worthy goals will cause one to lengthen and quicken one's strides in the right directions.

The following are six concepts or guidelines as to how desire can help to achieve your goals.

1. Be both definite and realistic about the level of achievement you desire.
2. Determine clearly what you are willing to sacrifice or the price you are willing to pay in terms of dedication and effort to accomplish your desire.
3. Establish a definite timetable on which to apply your plan and reach your goals.
4. Put in writing a clear plan you intend to follow. Think it through carefully to be sure that the plan is sound. Then implement it with confidence.
5. Read your plan periodically in order to refresh your memory of its content. Crystallize in your mind the procedures involved, and keep yourself motivated toward its achievement.
6. As you study the plan, try to visualize yourself already in possession of your desired accomplishments. Gaining this mental image is important to your success.

Enthusiasm. Enthusiasm is a form of emotional expression; a stimulating sensation for action. Enthusiasm can be influenced by overt circumstances such as potential reward, either tangible or intangible, or encouragement and support by others. It can change would-be drudgery into a pleasant and challenging pursuit. It can make the difference as to whether you feel stimulated to continue, can recover from setbacks, motivate others to assist with your plan, or sustain the necessary effort to ensure success.

Initiative. An administrator must exercise a sufficient amount of initiative in order to keep the different elements of the organization in motion and to initiate new projects and/or modifications of present projects. In this connection, it is important to recognize that often success goes to the person who is willing to act. This was illustrated well by a young writer who prepared a much needed document on a crucial issue. When colleagues criticized elements of the work, she replied, "there are several people who could have done better than me, but none of them did." Initiative caused the job to get done. While some of the critics might have had more ability, none of them caught the idea or exercised the initiative necessary to accomplish the task.

Persistence. Persistence is illustrated by the power of one's will. It is to a person what carbon is to steel. When applied to the aspects of one's aspirations and plans,persistence can make the difference between success and failure. Unfortunately, many people are lacking in this trait, and this keeps them from approaching their potential for achievement. Many have good ideas and formulate sound plans, but when the going gets tough, they falter. Lack of persistence deprives them of a full measure of success.

Faith is a cornerstone of persistence. It is a state of mind that may be induced or created, and it is a potentially strong motivational force. Every useful enterprise or accomplishment takes its first step toward success on the basis of faith: faith that it is worthwhile and faith that it can be achieved. Often, the dominance of a person's strong inner faith expresses itself overtly and affirms itself in actual accomplishment.

Self-Confidence. Confidence is influenced by a combination of adequate preparation and successful experiences. Positive thinking about one's ability to succeed can have a favorable influence on confidence. Self-confidence discourages and intimidates those who might oppose your efforts or resist the accomplishment of your goals. The confident approach will help you succeed, because it will help you to make fewer mistakes and recover more quickly from the mistakes you make.

Within the framework of reality and good judgment, you should never give serious mental recognition to the possibility of failure. Some setbacks will happen along the way, but a person must be able to take these in stride and handle them gracefully, and not let the temporary setbacks affect your positive thinking. Keep sight of your goals and pursue them with confidence.

Active Mind. The human mind represents one of the most unrealized potentials in our environment. The brain, which is the physical organism within which the mind works, is the most powerful instrument the world knows. It has been determined that there are between 10 and 14 billion cells in the brain, and this vast network represents a person's ability to understand, remember, analyze, interpret, and reason. This uniquely human power ought to be developed and applied effectively in every organization.

It is the power of the mind that has given us supersonic airplanes, probes into outer space, complex computers, electricity, power-driven engines, and all our other mechanical and technical devices. The power of the mind has enabled us to develop complex social and human aspects of civilization. All the elements of life that are uniquely human are related to the functions of the mind.

A person thinks by use of memory—the mental storehouse. Without memories we would have no sources from which to formulate thoughts and draw conclusions. We would be unable to recollect or to analyze and synthesize. Hunches, intuitions, and judgments are all products of the mind's storehouse of knowledge.

Our minds need to be continually developed through useful experiences in order to further load our memories with valuable information. This process results in an expanded supply from which new ideas and better conclusions can be drawn.

Open-Mindedness. In the book *How We Think*, philosopher-educator John Dewey provides a clear definition of open-mindedness.[3]

> Open mindedness may be defined as freedom from prejudice, partisanship and such other habits as to close the mind and make it unwilling to consider new problems and . . . new ideas.

Open mindedness is the willingness to try to understand different points of view, even though you may not agree.

Karl Jaspers, in his book *The Way to Wisdom*, states that human beings tend toward a "prison" of set opinions and convictions. This "prison" becomes the individual's reality and he or she tends to reject any ideas that contradict these opinions and convictions. Unless a person seriously attempts to break loose from the "prison," there is little hope for real progress toward becoming a truly educated and authentic person. We need to be sensitive to the fact that there are diverse views on every major subject—politics, education, religion, social services, leadership methods. We can become aware of these views simply by being attentive, that is, by reading, listening, and observing. In turn, this will give rise to some important questions, such as: Why does this person view the situation differently than I do? In all truthfulness is my own view on the issue any more valid than the opposing view? If we carry forward with this process, two things are accomplished. The process itself proves a degree of open-mindedness, and persistence with the process will finally generate a result that is characteristic of a truly open-minded person. It is a fact that an educator who is unable or unwilling to be open-minded runs the risk of contributing toward distortion of facts, diversion of truth, and perpetuation of misinformation.

Sixth Sense. The information present in one's mind has come from the accumulation of experiences. During these experiences, the five senses have been in operation, serving as receiver sets, which feed information and impressions into the mind. Some information is recorded in the conscious mind, some in the subconscious mind, and apparently some is not recorded at all, at least not in reproducible form.

The mind does not simply record and store information, it reproduces it in a different form. This is the formulation of thoughts, judgments, and conclusions, and it is sometimes referred to as the "sixth sense." The sixth sense uses the information stored in the brain, and through the process of analysis and synthesis, it creates ideas. A person with a strong sixth sense can produce ideas that are a far cry from the raw material from which they are created. The ability to create useful ideas is a great advantage to a person, whether the objective is to make a lot of money, manage an organization, invent and market a new product, or improve educational methods.

Everybody possesses the sixth sense in some degree, just as everybody possesses some amount of health, fitness, and basic intelligence. The development of the sixth sense to a high level is an ongoing process of mental self-improvement. This development follows the same principle as the development of strength or endurance: the application of progressive overload. In this case, it can better be termed "progressive mind stretching," a result of regular participation in mentally challenging activities. As the sixth sense develops, the subsequent "mind stretching activities" must be more complex in order to bring about further development.

The unique ability to create and produce ideas is one of the most distinguishing characteristics of humans as compared with other forms of life. it is truly a wonder and a blessing if developed thoroughly and used properly.

MOTIVATING ONESELF AND OTHERS

Motivation is the inner strength that releases itself in the form of energy and propels a person along the track of success. It is expressed in the form of desire and determination to reach one's goals. It provides willpower to resist temptations that would dissipate or misdirect energy; it keeps a person on track and moving forward.

Many administrators would agree that the effectiveness of their organizations would be greatly increased if they could discover how to tap the unrealized potential present in the human resources. Human motivation is the key factor in overall productivity.

External sources of motivation—the cheering of a crowd, slaps on the back, handshakes, certificates, medallions, and monetary rewards—are helpful; but these often have only temporary effects. Once their influence has passed, the person once again depends almost totally on internal motivation. This is based on one's inner thoughts, ideals, and aspirations, the sources from which the more permanent motivational energy originates and flows.

But, it is an error to depend too much on others for incentive. Creating and sustaining the necessary level of motivation is largely a "do-it-yourself" project. One of the greatest needs for sustained motivation is steady progress toward self-actualization. People must feel that they are growing, developing, and progressing in the areas of their particular interest. Musicians must make music, artists must paint, and poets must write if they are to be ultimately at peace with themselves. What individuals can be, they want to be.

It is true that most people will strive to live up to the expectations they know others have of them. Therefore, the expression of high expectation is an important element in motivation. Following are five other important elements.

1. Recognition and praise from peers, parents, and members of the public.
2. Ego reinforcement, which comes from a feeling of conquest or fulfillment.
3. Material gains such as money or material proof of achievement in the form of medals, certificates, trophies, and the like.
4. Emotional fulfillment or sensation derived from the achievement of a goal.
5. Fear of failure; a negative form of motivation that produces positive results.

Motivation means providing reasons for incentives that cause, or sustain, dedication toward a particular activity. Three of the dominant motivators are:

1. The need to feel important and recognized or the need for identity.
2. The need for refreshing change or new stimulation.
3. The need for a feeling of security.

There are two basic sources of motivation: external, provided by circumstances outside oneself; and internal, which comes from an inner drive. Internal motivation is potentially more powerful and more consistent.

It has been found that an athlete can train for months, go through several trial performances, get the proper rest and food, and have correct technique and knowledge of the activity, but without the internal motivation or will to excel the performances in competition will fall short of the athlete's true ability.

Tutko and Richards[12] in their discussion of the phenomenon of external and internal motivation explain that praise and punishment are two of the more common forms of motivation and that praise provides the best results. They suggest the following approach for correcting a problem: open with praise, make the correction or suggestion, end by complimenting.

John Wooden,[14] the legendary basketball coach at UCLA, used the positive-negative-positive approach. Says Wooden, "you will never motivate an athlete by alienating him." Wooden would demonstrate the desired behavior, quickly imitate the player's mistake, then follow with another demonstration of the proper way to do the skill. This seems to be a way of minimizing the alienation of the player by the coach, while being an effective way to constructively criticize and give positive feedback.

Motivational techniques are important points of knowledge for every coach, teacher, and administrator. The more techniques one knows and can effectively utilize, the better the chances of helping individuals reach their potential. The wise administrator understands that rewards are both intrinsic and extrinsic and knows how to motivate in both ways, yet keeps in mind that intrinsic motivation is usually better. The administrator needs to become well-acquainted with others in the organization, in order to know which motivational techniques will work best with each individual.

A Motivation Plan

Probably the best assurance of an organization's success is to have successful people. Productivity and achievement by people is what makes the difference. In light of this, the need for an effective plan for motivation becomes apparent.

Herzberg and Mausner[5] did some significant research on how employees feel about administrative techniques and work conditions. They found *motivation factors* and *maintenance factors*, with the motivation factors being those which bring forth initiative in employees and move them to a higher level of personal and organizational effectiveness. They listed the following as important among motivation factors: occupational achievement, deserved recognition, advancement, enjoyment of the work itself, opportunities for personal growth and enrichment, and responsibility.

The specific job conditions Herzberg and Mausner claim will motivate people to perform better are: (1) personal involvement in challenging tasks, (2) using abilities fully, (3) opportunities for testing one's knowledge, (4) discretionary control over one's own behavior and work conditions, (5) clear performance feedback, and (6) opportunity to interact with high-level administrators.

A timeless and classic example of motivation through goal setting is illustrated in the athletic achievement of Dr. Roger Bannister when he set out to break the 4 minute mile barrier, a feat that had been approached by several but accomplished by none. This example can serve as an excellent guide for others, including those in administrative positions.

It is generally accepted that Bannister was not the best physical specimen in the world at the time to accomplish this remarkable feat, but the right combination of important characteristics resulted in his success. Bannister claimed that the achievement was more dependent on psychologic preparation and self-motivation than on physical ability, although the physical ingredients had to be present. Through long hours of preparation he convinced himself that he could be the first human to ever surpass the 4-minute mile. He reasoned that if he could run the first three quarters in less than 3 minutes, he could certainly add the fourth quarter in 1 minute or less. He prepared himself both physically and mentally to hold that pace. When he hit the three-quarter mark slightly under 3 minutes, he knew almost for certain that he was only a quarter mile away from one of the world's greatest athletic achievements and one of history's great success stories—the mile run at 3:59.4.

Ironically, within the same competitive season, another man, John Landy from Australia, beat Bannister's time by running the distance in 3:58. It is unusual indeed, nowadays, for the mile to be won in a time slower than 4 minutes in a high-level national or international meet, and several athletes each year break this barrier. The world's record is now beneath the 3:48 mark, more than 12 seconds faster than the historic achievement of Bannister only three decades ago, and the present record is threatened often by modern-day superstars.

Both physiologists and psychologists contend that the 4-minute mark was more a psychologic than a physiologic barrier. Once the first person broke it, the barrier tended to dissolve in the minds of others, until now it is viewed more as a stepping stone than a barrier.

An interesting parallel situation has to do with the high jump. World class high jumpers flirted for over a decade with the 7-foot mark, and several of them surpassed 6'11". Finally, John Thomas, a 17-year-old high school student who was apparently unimpressed by the 7-foot psychologic barrier, cleared the bar at 7'1". Almost immediately, several other world class jumpers exceeded the 7-foot mark. Since then, numerous high jumpers have surpassed 7'6", and a few are now pointing toward the 8-foot "barrier."

The elimination of barriers such as the two mentioned can serve as a good lesson for administrators as well as people in other walks of life. It points out that in order to accomplish one's goals, the person must define the goals, determine a plan that will lead toward their accomplishment, and implement the plan systematically and with determination. If the goals are realistic in the first place, they can be achieved.

One word of caution in connection with all of this is do not try to take steps that are too big. A world record breaker like Bannister reaches the pinnacle of success by taking one step at a time. He had won many races at various levels of competition. With each improved performance, he reached a new level of achievement and put himself one step closer to his ultimate goal. By accepting each new challenge and planning toward it, Bannister used the stairstep approach until he finally arrived at the point in his preparation and progress that the 4-minute mile became the next step. By simply following essentially the same procedure that he had followed many times before in achieving lesser goals, he took one more step and crashed the 4-minute barrier.

All of us ought to apply this kind of approach in our own lives. First, we should reach levels of achievement that are within reasonable striking distance for us, and then use each new level as a base from which to take the next step. We should remain aware that each succeeding level is more difficult to achieve, and the risk of failure gradually increases.

Motivating others is a complex administrative technique. It seems to happen best when the motivator demonstrates consistency, as opposed to an erratic or moody approach. Methods that are sincere and genuine produce better long-term results than superficial or phony efforts.

It has been explained that the kind of motivation that serves the best and lasts the longest comes from within the individual. In view of this, a basic challenge of the administrator is to cultivate the self-motivation mechanisms of the other employees.

Who Motivates the Motivator?

One of the searching questions in the field of management is how those individuals who have responsibilities to motivate others stay motivated. Unfortunately, some administrators fall prey to the pitfalls of the uninspired. The result is diluted success, at best, and eventual failure. It is a fact that for an administrator, a rut is simply a grave that isn't covered over.

How many times have you observed a division or department head demonstrate a status quo attitude? How often have you seen people retained in leadership positions whose creative energy has evaporated and whose aspirations for progress have withered? In these cases, the potential motivator has lost motivation, and there is not much chance that such a person will have any inspirational effect on others.

It has been said that most of an administrator's responsibilities fall into two categories: "shedding light on the track" and "putting steam in the boiler." In order to put steam in other peoples' boilers, an administrator must keep his/her own boiler steamed up. A high level of self-motivation must be maintained and communicated to others. If this process is effective, it is like adding fuel to fire, causing it to produce more heat as well as more light.

What about you in particular? Do you have a burning desire for professional and personal success? Do you see yourself moving up, fulfilling a bigger and better purpose? Do you have enthusiasm for improvement and for opportunities to employ yourself in a larger capacity? Or has your ambition begun to settle? Are you gradually becoming complacent and more satisfied with mediocrity? Do you find it harder to approach your responsibilities with zest? Has it become more difficult to express optimism and enthusiasm to others? Are you reminiscing more and producing less? If the answers to these questions are yes, then you should not hold an administrative position. Your challenge is to improve your own attitude, revitalize your enthusiasm, and rededicate yourself. In short, you need to be motivated.

The following three danger signals can warn one whose motivation is on the decline. They are signs of administrative suicide which often develop at an undetectably slow rate.

1. Procrastination: the practice of putting off needed decisions, falling behind on important tasks, hesitating to take considered risks, and hoping the problems will take care of themselves.
2. Complacency: the inner urge to take it easy, the idea that you can glide more and do a little less, being satisfied with mediocrity instead of excellence. Related to complacency is the tendency to accept lack of initiative and originality among subordinates. As a result, the whole organization begins to settle.
3. Loss of purpose: lacking concrete plans or seeing insufficient reasons to develop and implement them. The executive who has lost a sense of purpose has outlived his usefulness as an administrator. There is no way that such a person can furnish adequate leadership to others and cause the programs of the organization to advance satisfactorily toward the goals.

One of the best sources of motivation for administrators is the satisfaction of achievement and service. Albert Schweitzer said, "The only ones among you who will be truly happy are those who have learned to serve." It is highly desirable for service to be the main component of one's motivation; but at the same time, it should be recognized that the majority of people also need other forms of motivation. Those who lean too hard for too long on the reward of service sometimes become discouraged and eventually develop the attitude that they have given too much and received too little. The potential development of such an attitude should be carefully monitored.

In addition to the satisfaction an administrator experiences in connection with the job, there are several self-motivating methods that administrators build into their lifestyles. For example, some read inspirational stories or thoughts written by or about highly successful people. Some listen to meaningful speeches by those who have experienced unusual success or who talk convincingly about the pursuit of achievement. Others find it both satisfying and inspiring to associate with successful colleagues or with individuals who demonstrate zest for life and high regard for achievement.

These methods might seem too time-consuming, but this need not be the case if you are selective about the motivational experiences you choose and if you use these as special interest pursuits or pleasure breaks from the routine of your work.

In addition, an administrator can be motivated by approval and encouragement from supervisors and by the approval and support of those within the organization. Regardless of the other sources of motivation, the administrator needs to have a strong inner drive, a clear sense of purpose, and consistent dedication to achievement. It is important to be a self-starter, a self-motivator, and a self-director. These are marks of professional maturity that many people never attain. It is a form of maturity that keeps one's focus on organizational goals and results, professional development and enrichment, and overall managerial efficiency.

REFERENCES AND RECOMMENDED READINGS

1. American Management Association: Workshop Notes on Employee Motivation. New York, 1986.
2. Butler, K., and Gems, G.: Motivation without competition? Strategies, 1(4):27, 1988.
3. Dewey, J.: How We Think. Boston, D.C. Health and Company, 1933.
4. Gordon, J.R.: Organizational Behavior, 3rd. Ed. Boston, Allyn and Bacon, 1991, pp. 130–160.
5. Hertzberg, F., Mausner, B., and Snyderman, B.: The Motivation to Work, 4th Ed. New York, John Wiley and Sons, 1985.
6. Hill, N.: Think and Grow Rich. Brooklyn, NY, Fawcett Crest Publishers, 1960.
7. Hitt, W.D.: Management in Action. Columbus, OH, Battelle Press, 1985.
8. Jasper, K.: Philosophy (II), Chicago: The University of Chicago Press, 1969.
9. Magnotta, J.R.: Positive motivational techniques. JOPERD, 57(8):78, 1986.
10. Peale, N.V.: Enthusiasm Makes the Difference. Englewood Cliffs, NJ, Prentice Hall, 1967.
11. Pierce, J.L., and Newstrom, J.W.: The Manager's Bookshelf, 2nd Ed. New York, Harper Collins Publisher, 1990.
12. Tutko, T.A., and Richards, J.W.: Psychology of Coaching. Boston, Allyn and Bacon, 1971.
13. Whetten, D.A., and Cameron, K.S.: Developing Management Skills, 2nd Ed. New York, Harper Collins Publishers, 1991, pp. 334–389.
14. Wooden, J.: They Call Me Coach. New York, Bantam, 1972, pp. 151–178.

Part III

MANAGEMENT
TECHNIQUES

Chapter *7*

MANAGEMENT SKILLS AND PROCEDURES

This chapter includes information about clear communication and correct techniques in connection with staff meetings, committees, and private conferences. The application of the guidelines set forth here can contribute significantly to one's effectiveness as an administrator.

COMMUNICATING EFFECTIVELY

The root of the word *communication* is commune, which means to share. Communication is the sharing of information, and it has two essential dimensions, speaking and listening. Unfortunately, there are several barriers to adequate communication, including different languages, different mind sets due to cultural environment, and restricted ability to speak or listen. Communication problems are not new; as illustrated by the fact that more than 2,000 years ago, Plato observed three reasons for poor communication: (1) people want to be right at all times, (2) people refuse to stick to the subject, and (3) people do not know how to listen.

In all aspects of verbal communication, it should be recognized that clear thinking is indicated by the proper selection of words. Words are the symbols that enhance our ability to think and express our thoughts.

The process of communication is illustrated by the following five steps. The total purpose is not accomplished unless all of the steps are completed.

1. Message conceived.
2. Message sent.
3. Message received.
4. Message understood.
5. Message applied or implemented.

For a busy administrator, it is important that all aspects of communication, from highly official to unofficial be performed effectively. Some important considerations that can help the administrator communicate better are as follows:

1. What information should be communicated and to whom and for what reasons?
2. How much explanation should be given?
3. Should the information be labeled confidential or restricted, or should no limits be placed on it?
4. Is it important for certain individuals to receive the information directly from the administrator?
5. Should certain persons receive it before others?
6. Through what sources should the information be passed, and how fast does it need to move?
7. What risk is there that the information will be misinterpreted, and what can be done to reduce risks?
8. Will certain individuals add their own versions, thus distorting the information?

Some communication can better be accomplished *orally*, whereas other messages should be in *written form*—memos, letters, directives, or reports. Still other information is transmitted by mood, expressions, and gestures.

Oral Communication

Important considerations of this form of communication are: (1) speak audibly so those listening do not miss words or phrases, (2) use correct volume and tone to make the words appealing and interesting, and (3) select words and statements that are easily understood. Placing the proper emphasis on words and phrases helps listeners to better understand the true meaning. Keep wordiness, unfamiliar terms, and meaningless jargon to a minimum. As a general rule, business conversations should be concise and to the point. Oral presentations should be well thought out, carefully organized, and should follow a predetermined plan.

The Power of Pause or Silence. Many administrators effectively use combinations of silence (often combined with facial and body expressions) more or less unconsciously. But conscious use of this technique can also add a subtle dimension to your communicative abilities. It can convey an attitude or opinion without making a commitment. Fast talkers avoid the pause, and as a result, they are more susceptible to repeating themselves, making misstatements, or overworking a point.

Since pauses can be as much a part of communication as words, administrators should strike a balance between the two in order to communicate with maximum effectiveness. A silence can have a cooling effect on an emotional situation. It can help to recapture the attention of those in a meeting or force a response from another person who wants to keep the conversation moving. Following a particular statement, it can give the statement special emphasis. During a negotiation, a period of silence or no reply places the pressure on the other person to keep the negotiation alive.

Written Communication

Good writing should be much like good speaking. Writing, however, should be even better because one has more opportunity to organize and express thoughts clearly.

A written communication should have a theme, which usually leads to certain conclusions. Some writing experts advocate stating the conclusions first and then developing the points that support those conclusions. Others believe that one should develop the theme and then state the conclusions. Whichever approach is taken, the main aspects are the theme and the conclusions. The theme must be developed logically and in as few words as possible, and the conclusions should be stated concisely and clearly.

Clarity is of utmost importance. One reason for vagueness and rambling is the lack of clarity in the mind of the writer. When a memo or letter doesn't come off exactly the way you had planned, carefully analyze the exact purpose of the communication. When the purpose is clearly in mind, take another look at the content and ask these questions: (1) Did I accomplish the purpose in a simple, clear and direct fashion? (2) Does the content contain any extraneous material that is unnecessary? (3) Are there any important points of information that need to be added?

Logical organization is basic to clarity. The thoughts in a memo or letter should proceed in a logical sequence, one flowing into the other from start to finish. The principle of logical organization applies to the total content as well as to the paragraphs, sentences, and even phrases. The ideas should run in a sequence that is easy for the reader to follow and absorb. Such sequence can be accomplished by thinking your letter through step by step. Even small changes in content and sequence will often make a big improvement in how well the content flows and how easy it is to understand. Clarity is not an accident; it's the end product of clear thinking.

Style is as important to writing as is organization. Keep your sentences and paragraphs "clean" and free of useless jargon. Use words and phrases that are clear and precise. Avoid words that might be unfamiliar to the reader or confuse the meaning of a statement. Be cautious about words that have generalized or relative meanings.

The tone of a memo or letter is influenced by the selection of words and phrases. Attention to tone can make the difference between whether the written message sounds rude or polite, reserved or enthusiastic, personal or impersonal, complimentary or critical.

Usually *memos* are used for written communication within the organization. Memos normally contain these elements: name of receiver, name of sender, date, subject, body, and signature (Figure 7-1).

A *business letter* format is normally used to send communications outside your own organization. Only on rare occasions is the letter format used within the organization. A business letter normally has the following elements: return address, date, inside address, salutation, body of the letter, complimentary close, signature, and special notations (if any). In preparing the letter, give special consideration to the theme, conclusions, communication efficiency, and tone (Figure 7-2).

A *proposal*, another form of written communication, is usually based on a substantial amount of thought and study, because acceptance or rejection is often influenced by how well it is prepared. A proposal normally includes a cover letter explaining its purpose and nature, recommendations, and justifications.

The telegram and registered or certified mail are sometimes useful methods

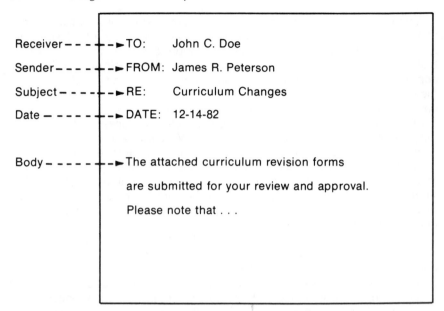

Receiver ─ ─ ─ ┼─ ─►TO: John C. Doe

Sender ─ ─ ─ ─ ┼─ ─►FROM: James R. Peterson

Subject ─ ─ ─ ─ ┼─ ─►RE: Curriculum Changes

Date ─ ─ ─ ─ ─ ┼─ ─►DATE: 12-14-82

Body ─ ─ ─ ─ ┼─ ─►The attached curriculum revision forms

are submitted for your review and approval.

Please note that . . .

Figure 7-1. Components of a memorandum.

of communication. The reason for using one of these methods is to ensure that an important message or material reaches the intended destination. At the destinations, the message must be signed for, ensuring that delivery was made.

A *written report* often consists of a combination of primary and secondary information, with primary being original and secondary coming from other written sources. Usually, a report includes a letter of transmittal, an introduction, the main body (presentation of data), a summary, and conclusions. Sometimes the summary and conclusions are placed at the beginning and sometimes at the end. A report must be well thought out, so that it contains the essential information arranged in logical sequence and stated clearly and concisely. It is important that the information be current, accurate, and pertinent. The readability of a report and the impressions it leaves often have a substantial influence on its acceptability and the results it generates.

The written communication should not be overworked because it becomes cumbersome if done too extensively, and it is a less personal approach than a direct conversation. On the other hand, written communication can be beneficial because the opportunity exists to make sure that it says exactly what is intended, copies can be sent to other individuals, and it can be referred to in the future if need be. The reader also has the advantage of being able to study written communications to make sure the full meaning is understood. Further, written communication is sometimes more efficient and convenient than oral communication, depending on the accessibility of those involved.

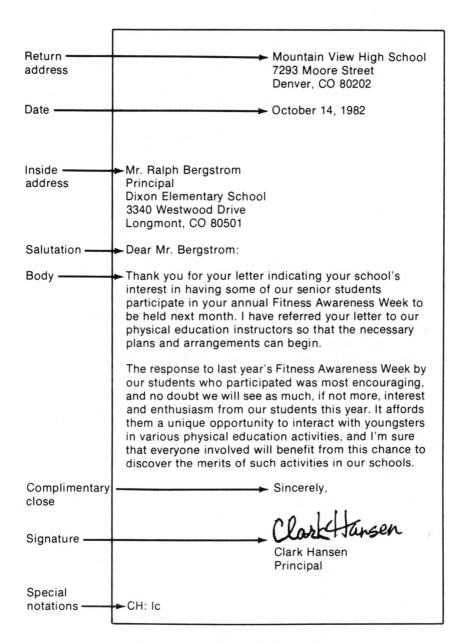

Return address → Mountain View High School
7293 Moore Street
Denver, CO 80202

Date → October 14, 1982

Inside address → Mr. Ralph Bergstrom
Principal
Dixon Elementary School
3340 Westwood Drive
Longmont, CO 80501

Salutation → Dear Mr. Bergstrom:

Body → Thank you for your letter indicating your school's interest in having some of our senior students participate in your annual Fitness Awareness Week to be held next month. I have referred your letter to our physical education instructors so that the necessary plans and arrangements can begin.

The response to last year's Fitness Awareness Week by our students who participated was most encouraging, and no doubt we will see as much, if not more, interest and enthusiasm from our students this year. It affords them a unique opportunity to interact with youngsters in various physical education activities, and I'm sure that everyone involved will benefit from this chance to discover the merits of such activities in our schools.

Complimentary close → Sincerely,

Signature → *Clark Hansen*
Clark Hansen
Principal

Special notations → CH: lc

Figure 7-2. Components of a business letter.

Mood

An administrator communicates either intentionally or unintentionally by mood. For example,the enthusiasm with which one greets a co-worker can send a clear message. Also, facial expressions, tone of voice, and the amount of attention given are methods of communication by mood.

Some administrators purposely use expression of mood as a form of language, whereas others show mood unintentionally or inadvertently. The primary danger of using this method of communication is the possibility of being labeled *moody, inconsistent,* and *unpredictable.* Administrators are generally more successful if they portray an even temperament and use a consistent approach.

Emotional Responses

People in administrative positions sometimes feel a need to put somebody in place, set the record straight, discipline a subordinate, or react firmly to a colleague. It is easy to become emotional in situations of tension and stress, and there is a tendency to make sharp and sometimes abrasive statements. Remember that once something has been said it is on the record, and it will never be completely erased. So be sure that you say what ought to be said and what you would want to say when not influenced by emotion. Keep in mind that the administrator is expected to be mature, objective, and composed.

When you feel emotional about a situation and want to lash out, try to hold back until you have had ample time to think it over. If you are going to respond in writing, follow the motto "write now, send later." In other words, after writing the memo or letter, put it in your desk drawer for a day or more while your emotions settle; then read it. If you honestly feel that it should be sent, go ahead; but there is a good chance you will decide to rewrite it or not send it at all. Be very cautious about coming out quickly with statements that you will wish later could be retracted. Even though you cannot always control what happens, you can control your response to it.

Listening

Listening is the other side of the communication coin. It is surprising what an administrator can learn about the organization and its people by just listening. Also, there is an important psychologic aspect to listening; being attentive to what others say is satisfying to them.

Careful listening is especially useful in the case of grievances. Often, when a person has thoroughly stated a grievance in the presence of the administrator, the problem is more than half solved. The remainder of the solution takes some checking and follow through, and this part is equally important.

There are many mind blocks to careful listening. Unfair prejudgments and stereotyping can prevent a person from effective listening. Anger or other emotional feelings can also get in the way, as can sloppy habits about paying attention. Good listening is more than just letting sounds pass through your ears. It involves concentrating on the meaning of what is being said and recording the important points in your mind (remembering). Here are some common pitfalls to effective listening that should be avoided.

1. Inadequate attention or divided attention.
2. Refusal to concentrate.
3. Over-emphasis on details. Do not try to memorize too many facts and figures; listen for ideas and concepts.

Listening cannot always be casual and relaxed. Serious listening requires precise attention and serious concentration. It is not just hearing words; it is also understanding statements, interpreting concepts, evaluating relative importance, and appraising intent. Often, effective listening involves "reading between the lines." Sometimes it involves interpreting what the person is trying to say or wants to say. It also involves watching expressions and gestures, recognizing emphases on words and phrases, and mentally attaching the correct meanings to the statements. It is said that some people listen but do not hear, others both listen and hear but do not understand. Effective listening includes *listening, hearing,* and *understanding.* One important kind of awareness is the ability to interpret the thoughts, feelings, and moods of others through their words, tones, facial expressions, and movements.

Additional Points

Physical proximity may be a very real factor in determining the frequency of oral communication, and hence the layout of offices is one of the important aspects of the communication system. Even the advent of the telephone has not very much diminished the importance of this factor, since a telephone conversation is by no means the equivalent of a face-to-face contact.

Manuals are sometimes used to communicate organizational practices that are intended to have relatively permanent application. Such manuals are often called administrative manuals or policy manuals. Two important uses of manuals are: (1) to acquaint new organization members with the written policies and procedures and (2) add consistency to the application of the organization's administrative methods. One inevitable result of the preparation and use of manuals is to increase the centralization of decision making, because a manual standardizes decisions that have previously been left to individuals.

A great deal of time can be saved if you learn to *dictate* correspondence instead of writing it in long hand before typing. To use a dictaphone properly, be sure to speak clearly and at a steady pace. If you expect the dictated material to be typed in final form, spell out unusual words and announce new paragraphs. If you wish to break into a letter with instructions, preface your remarks with the name of your secretary in order to separate the instructions from the text of the letter. If enclosures are to be included or a number of copies made, be sure to mention it. Finally, do not allow dictated letters to be sent with your signature without first reading them to check for mistakes, or have someone else do it in whom you have confidence.

To *use the telephone efficiently*, have the secretary screen the calls You might want to set aside specified times in the day for returning calls. Grouping similar activities such as telephone calls can help you make more efficient use of time. When speaking on the phone, identify yourself immediately, be courteous, get to the point quickly, but not in a hurried or abrupt fashion, and keep a pad and pencil handy to record information.

Using the telephone can help lay the groundwork for a future meeting. This mode of communication allows for an *exchange of ideas*, without the travel time of a face-to-face conference. A *conference call* among several people might accomplish as much as getting everyone together, and at a much lower cost in terms of both time and money. It is also possible, with the use of a *telephone speaker*, to link large groups together for a free exchange of ideas, so that everyone has access to the information. Telephone *message recorders* can sometimes be used to good advantage.

Reading

Reading administrative material is another important aspect of communication. Concentrate on what you are reading by avoiding distractions. Underline important statements or write notes in the margin or on a note pad as needed. Remember that some material should be read thoroughly in an effort to get the full meaning, whereas certain other material can be skimmed for broad concepts and high points.

STAFF MEETINGS

Administrators get involved with staff meetings of three different kinds:

1. Meetings with other administrators, such as a dean meeting with department heads; a superintendent, with principals; a department head, with area coordinators; or an athletic director, with head coaches.
2. Faculty meetings including all or a portion of the teachers in the administrative unit.
3. Meetings with nonteaching personnel.

Too often, staff meetings are viewed by those who attend as ineffective, and rightfully so. Thus, one important challenge to an administrator is the effective handling of staff meetings. This involves several considerations: (1) when and how often to call meetings, (2) whom to include in each meeting, (3) how long the meeting should last, and (4) which items should appear on the agenda.

On the wall of a business firm, a motto used to hang expressing the sentiments of the president. It said, "intelligence is no substitute for accurate information; enthusiasm is no substitute for experience; willingness is no substitute for ability." After a series of meetings one of the employees added, "and meetings are no substitute for progress."

Unfortunately, a high percentage of meetings are semi-failures, and often the reasons are lack of preparation and poor leadership. A successful meeting usually requires a strong leader who is dedicated to the participative process and knows how to implement it. It is the leader's job to see that the discussion moves toward the purposes of the meeting. The Standard Oil Corporation has in its administrative manual the following description of a meeting chairman. "He must plan, promote, lead, direct, inform, interpret, encourage, stimulate, referee, judge, moderate and conciliate."

Clear meeting objectives and time limits should be established and adhered to. If possible, the discussion leader should have a clock or a watch within view. With a time frame in mind and with a written agenda, the leader is obligated to move the meeting along at the appropriate pace, and to accomplish the purposes of the meeting within a reasonable time.

In the planning stages of a meeting, several important questions must be considered.

1. What are the purposes? This should be answered clearly in the opening remarks. If members begin to digress, restate the purposes of the meeting.
2. What is needed in the way of facts and figures? Should the leader present these or let someone else do it? Who is best prepared to do it?
3. Should certain information be copied and distributed either ahead of time or during the meeting?
4. Will there be any visiting experts? If so, are they fully oriented as to what is expected of them?
5. Would visual aids help? A picture can be worth a thousand words, but only if it is the right one and is used effectively.
6. Would a demonstration be useful? Sometimes a well-planned demonstration can make a point that people otherwise will not grasp.

Be especially cautious about expounding in tedious detail, monopolizing the discussion, or permitting anyone else to do so. A joke about one leader who droned on in a meeting illustrates the point. One of the members finally left the room. In the hallway, she met another sufferer who had escaped early. "Has he finished yet?" the first escapee asked. "Yes" said the other, "long ago, but the meeting is still going on."

President Eisenhower claimed he once received the following good advice from Sherman Adams: "Never neglect an opportunity to keep your mouth shut."

Tactfully silencing others requires gentle diplomacy combined with firmness. It seems to be a maxim that those who have the least to say take the longest to say it. But sooner or later, even the most long-winded person has to take a breath. When he does, the leader must come in promptly and take command of the discussion or pass it to someone else who will keep it moving.

An executive of a successful company stated this useful point:

> Every person on our staff has better ideas than mine, but my job is to get the jury to agree. Most of the decisions made in our meetings are based on compromises, because many of the good ideas are not compatible with each other. But occasionally, a diehard in the group, unwilling to bend, blocks the process of all the others. In such cases, I have to state a reminder that the purpose is *not to win a point but find a solution.*[9]

One wise administrator who found that too much time was being wasted in meetings made a rule that everyone who wished to present a problem had to prepare and submit a memorandum answering these questions: What is the problem? What is the cause of the problem? What are the possible solutions? Which solution do you recommend? As a result of this procedure, the number of meetings was drastically reduced because the solution usually became apparent without a meeting.

It is true that meetings are often held too frequently and last too long, but a positive side to meetings was illustrated well by one seasoned administrator. A younger person asked why there were so many meetings. The older person pointed out the window to two cars in the parking lot, one sparkling new and the other very old, and asked, "Do you know the difference between those two cars?" The younger elaborated on the numerous differences that were apparent. Then the older one replied, "The difference between those cars is meetings. Through dozens of meetings, administrators, engineers, and factory workers have been able to design and produce a vastly superior product. In the absence of meetings, that never would have happened."

Meetings can be highly useful for training, building group morale, decision making, grievance settling, creative brainstorming, encouraging group action, and gathering or disseminating information. Unless a meeting is really needed, however, it should not be held. According to a study made by the 3-M Company in 1980, meetings cost American industry over $35 million a year. During the last decade, the number has almost doubled, and the cost has tripled. So before you call your next meeting, ask yourself if it is really the thing to do. If it is, then go ahead; but do it right so that the meeting truly will be worth its time and cost. Be sure your meetings do not support the claim of one meeting critic who said, "You can accomplish work or go to meetings, but you can't do both."

A Written Agenda

Some meetings deserve a written agenda, whereas an agenda would give others too much structure. For example, an agenda should always be considered for a faculty or staff meeting, but often is unnecessary for a committee meetings. A good rule is "if in doubt, prepare an agenda."

An agenda offers several potential advantages. It forces decisions as to what should be included in the meeting; helps guarantee premeeting preparation; permits the arrangement of items into logical groupings and desired sequence; and provides an overview of what is going to be discussed, which gives each person a better opportunity to contribute the discussion. Time is usually more effectively utilized with a written agenda, because it helps the discussion move systematically from one item to the next.

COMMITTEES AND CONFERENCES

Committees and conferences can be among the greatest consumers of an administrator's time. Yet, guided group thinking is necessary for the proper conduct of any organization larger than a one-person shop. The potential fault lies not in the tool, but in its use or abuse. The ability to conduct an effective conference or give productive leadership to a committee is a necessary administrative skill.

A *business conference* is a meeting with one or more people for the purpose of analyzing a situation and receiving useful input or mapping out a plan to be enacted. A *committee meeting* between the administrator and a task force or standing committee is for the purpose of receiving information from the committee or giving direction to it.

The administrator should keep in mind that the judgment of experts is worth more than the opinions of nonexperts. The former is the collection of intelligence, while the latter is often the pooling of ignorance. Valuable administrative time can be wasted by listening to the opinions of people who are not qualified by background, education, or seasoned judgment.

An error that some administrators make is attempting to apply conference and committee techniques where they have little chance of success. Conferences and committees are no substitute for executive action. Following are three useful guidelines:

1. Usually it is necessary to involve members of the organization in conferences and committees in order to capitalize on their ideas and expertise and to allow them meaningful input into management.
2. On the other hand, it is important to avoid obtaining judgments and opinions and then failing to give them fair consideration. When this happens, co-workers recognize that they are only being taken through the motions—that the conference or committee procedure is phony.
3. Conferences and committee meetings may be highly formal or relatively informal. If the meeting is formal, an official record should be kept of the proceedings, decisions, and recommendations. In a less formal situation, there may be no need for a written record, although sometimes a brief memorandum of the high points of the discussion serves well as a matter of clarification and record.

Leading the Discussion

In the conduct of a conference or a committee meeting, the leader serves as the catalyst who draws out information and gives guidance to formulate a plan of action based on the specialized knowledge of those present.

The right psychology must be employed by the group leader in order to handle potential difficulties. For example, if the group consists of a mixture of higher and lower ranking employees, the lower ranking personnel may be reluctant to enter the discussion. One or more dominating personalities may intimidate others in the group. Perhaps one member talks too much but has relatively little to offer, or another leads the discussion astray.

It is important to have the members of the conference or committee say as much as they want without having the discussion become exhaustive. In this regard, the leader must exercise the right balance between thoroughness and expediency. It is undesirable to shut off any member's comment by a sarcastic or preemptory remark. This does not mean that one should avoid curbing or ending a certain line of discussion, but it should be done tactfully.

Unfortunately, some individuals have a tendency to use almost every kind of meeting for gripes and petty complaints. This has a deteriorating effect on the meeting's productivity. Such people are often excluded from important conferences or significant committee assignments because of this characteristic. When they are included, the discussion leader faces the challenge of letting them participate without allowing a disruptive or diluting influence.

The leader should avoid stifling a discussion when a disagreement is stated. In a situation in which the differences are so pronounced that the meeting does not seem to be progressing, it is helpful to work toward agreement on some generalities as stepping stones toward the specifics to be accomplished.

If the discussion is to be continued in a subsequent meeting, it is a good idea to end the meeting with a summary of what has been accomplished and where the next meeting will begin. The time and place of the next meeting should be set, and it should be clarified whether anyone is expected to do preparatory work prior to the meetings. If the purposes of the conference or committee have been accomplished, the leader should make this clear and should summarize the results and conclusions that have been reached.

The following are important characteristics of the conference or committee leader.

1. An ability to define the problem clearly and break it down into logical parts for analysis.
2. A quick mind to handle the interchange of ideas, and keep them flowing along the right track.
3. Tact in eliciting or controlling discussion as needed.
4. An open mind and a sincere interest in the opinions and judgments of others.
5. A sense of timing to know when to bring the discussion to a conclusion.

Some Additional Guidelines

1. Usually, it is awkward to have a leader of a committee whose direct supervisor is a member. Other participants might tend to side with "the boss," thus reducing the effectiveness of the group.
2. If the leader is one of high authority over the other committee members, it has the potential of squelching the free exchange of information.
3. Each participant in a conference or committee should be qualified to make a contribution. It is a waste of time to include unqualified people unless their participation is viewed as a developmental experience for them.
4. From the standpoint of economy, the following should be avoided:
   a. duplication of talents.
   b. involvement of those who cannot afford the time.
   c. a larger number than necessary to accomplish the purposes.
5. Simple rules of courtesy or protocol such as the following, are important:
   a. give sufficient advance notice.
   b. clear with the head of another department if a subordinate in that department is going to be involved.
   c. give proper recognition and introduction to participants from outside your organization.
   d. when a meeting must be cancelled, give prompt notice to all participants, together with an explanation.
6. Make a practice of starting on time so that everyone will learn to expect this and act accordingly.
7. Serious attempts should be made to keep meetings within business hours.
8. At the outset of each meeting, the leader should describe the intent, and the meeting should end with a summary statement that caps the discussion and states what is to happen next.

Divided Attention

Imagine yourself sitting in conference with an administrator for one hour and accomplishing only 30 minutes of work, with the other 30 minutes spent by the administrator conversing on the telephone or speaking with intruders. A co-worker who is in the administrator's office on legitimate business deserves a reasonable level of, if not undivided, attention. This is especially true if the person is there by appointment. Other signs of inadequate attention are when the administrator reads paperwork, reviews the schedule book, or writes notes not related to the conversation. Allowing such interruptions shows inconsideration for the person who has come to the office for a face-to-face meeting. It is inefficient and can be offensive to co-workers. Usually, an administrator will accomplish more overall by doing only one thing at a time and doing it well.

OFFICE MANAGEMENT

Office activities are integrated aspects of the overall function of the organization. Although a central office is usually needed, not all office work takes place in that location. Often, office work is decentralized in order to best serve the organization. Some of the usual aspects of office work are discussed in this section.

Receiving Visitors

The manner in which people are received when they come to the office has a significant influence on their impressions of the organization. When one considers that the receptionist has contact with many more people than does the administrator, the importance of this function becomes apparent. Consistent application of these guidelines will help assure the effectiveness of the receptionist.

1. A person who comes to the office should receive a pleasant greeting and immediate attention.
2. The receptionist should be knowledgeable about how to deal with routine matters and where to direct matters that can be handled better elsewhere.
3. Every person is important and should be treated with this in mind. Furthermore, every person's problems are important, at least to that person.
4. When possible, the receptionist should enhance the use of waiting time by providing information preparatory to the visitor's appointment.
5. The receptionist's function should not include idle conversation or entertaining of visitors. It is a business procedure that deserves the right balance of friendly formality and efficiency.

Organizing

One aspect of organizing is the definition of employee responsibilities and working relationships. This is covered in Chapters 8 and 12. Another aspect is office space utilization. The placement of furniture and equipment in offices is important from several points of view: attractiveness, efficiency, traffic flow, and intraoffice relationships. The challenge is to use the available square footage for optimum effectiveness. Intraoffice business relationships and the particular duties of each person should be clearly understood. Overlap or confusion about this will reduce efficiency.

Another aspect of organizing is the commitment of time. Appointments should be properly spaced to accommodate the necessary business, yet not cause any waste of time. Appointments should be clearly communicated so there is minimal chance of misunderstanding.

Office employees ought to be especially attentive to maintaining the established office hours. Doing otherwise detracts from efficiency and contributes to a poor image.

Paper Handling

Some individuals could be labeled *one-time paper handlers*, some are *two-time handlers*, and others are *multiple handlers*. Every employee in the office ought to strive toward being a one-time handler of paper work. This requires that when you first give attention to a task, you bring it to a conclusion and dispose of that particular matter. As you go through your mail, for example, complete as many items as possible at the time. Pass appropriate items to the secretary for handling. Items that can better be handled by other employees should be sent on to them immediately. Certain items require dictation which can be done at the time, or these items can be grouped together if you have a scheduled time for dictation. Items that must wait for one reason or another should be filed by a method that will bring them to your attention again on the appropriate timetable. Following are some additional procedures that you will find helpful:

1. In the file drawer of your desk have a folder for each month of the year, and use these for filing materials that should come to your attention at a later date. For example, if you receive paper work in June that should be handled in September, place it in the September file.
2. Also, have a folder on your desk labeled *immediate*, one labeled *tomorrow* and one labeled *next week*, and place papers in the respective folders for timely handling.
3. Keep file folders labeled with the names of people with whom you often do business. When an item comes across your desk that should be handled through conversation with a particular person, drop it in that person's file; then make it part of the agenda next time the two of you meet.
4. Certain items of paper work are marginal in terms of whether they should be placed in the office files. In order to safeguard against premature disposal and, at the same time, keep the files clear of unnecessary material, have a drawer that you view as a *temporary wastebasket*. Drop the items in the drawer and let them remain there for a safe period of time. After a certain period, say once each month, move these papers to a location that you view as a *semi-permanent disposal* and let them remain there for a longer time—several months. Any item that you have not needed during

this time will probably never be needed. This system keeps unnecessary papers from cluttering up the files.

Another aspect of paper work is the processing of forms. Every organization has certain standard forms to expedite management procedures. In most cases, the forms are prepared to furnish duplicate copies as needed. A purchase order is an example of a standard form. It is important to have an adequate supply of current forms, and office employees need to be knowledgeable about processing the forms properly. Recording complete and accurate information on the forms is of obvious importance. It is desirable to keep a copy of each standard form that is processed.

Record Keeping and Filing

Questions as to which records to keep and the methods of keeping them require some discriminating decisions. Some people are guilty of "keeping everything and being able to find nothing" whereas others are too casual about keeping records. The following questions are pertinent to the record keeping of any organization, and the answers will serve as useful guidelines for establishing a simplified, streamlined, and crisp approach.

1. Should typists routinely prepare a duplicate of correspondence and file it, or should only an original be typed unless a duplicate is specifically requested? Should file copies be on computer or hard copy?
2. How should office copies of standard forms be filed, and how long should they be retained?
3. Should all material kept on record be placed in file folders or should some be placed in loose-leaf binders or bound copy?
4. Which material should be filed in the secretarial office and which should be in a different place in order to provide the right balance of accessibility and confidentiality?
5. How should confidential records be protected, and who should have access to them?
6. How often should the files be cleared of unnecessary and obsolete material, and who should do this?
7. Which kind of filing system should be used?

Certain decisions, responses, policies, and procedures should be in writing. One reason for this is to reduce the chances of miscommunication or misunderstanding about what was said or decided. The written record can be referred to later, if the need arises. Examples that justify written records are financial agreements, contractual agreements, and policy statements.

Usually, the minutes of a meeting furnish an adequate record of the proceedings. Sometimes decisions and agreements that justify a written record are reached outside of formal meetings. In these cases, it is a good idea to follow-up with a letter or memo stating your interpretation of the important elements of the discussion. This helps to ensure that you and the others agree, and it provides a written copy for reference.

OFFICE AUTOMATION

Doing today's work with yesterday's tools is a pitfall that certainly applies to office management. Fortunately, many time-saving devices have been developed to enhance office work, such as computers and word processors. A letter can be composed and edited on the screen prior to being printed in hard copy or sent electronically to another office.

Preparing and duplicating written materials are among the more useful aspects of office work. These materials must be done on time, in correct form, and with acceptable quality. Frequent decisions are needed about which materials should be typed, photostatically reproduced, duplicated, or printed.

Dictation equipment can be useful if much written correspondence is to be done. A portable dictaphone to go along with a desk set is an added advantage. This combination of equipment makes it possible to dictate almost any time and place. In turn, the use of dictating equipment makes it possible for the typist to fit dictation conveniently into the schedule because it can remain in the machine until the preferred time.

Office equipment suppliers continue to develop improved products for the office of the future, and this is naturally a topic of interest to management experts. In one sense, the office of the future never arrives; although in another sense, yesterday's office of the future is already here. The competent manager will plan for the office of the future and implement it on a timely schedule. It will be more efficient, more economical, and more effective overall.

Two main lines of development are changing the way offices operate: electronic information processing and computer networking. Paper mania is largely disappearing from the processes of administration, where most of the information is transmitted electronically by a transparent interconnection that removes time and distance as critical factors in the sharing of information, both inside and outside the organization.

This process, often called "electronic mail," involves both voice and digitized print, making it possible to store either form of communication for replay if the party sought is not available at the moment of transmission. This innovation greatly reduces paper processes, paper storage, and paper mail. The "paperless office" that we have heard about for several years is finally on its way. Consequently, the era of an administrator having several file cabinets filled with paper is coming to an end.

The networking of computers for integrated office communications allows instant transfer of information and work from office to office, and from computer to computer, permitting the combining of several computers to share work on complicated problems for quick processing. Management will at least have the "total information system."

Putting together an up-to-the-moment status report, complete with graphics, is becoming greatly simplified. An administrator is able to call up such a report on the computer or make it available on a teleconference basis to several people inside or outside the organization.

However, a few changes are occurring in the work habits of administrators. For one, they will learn to type, at least well enough to handle a computer keyboard. This will not be much of a problem, because most of tomorrow's administrators are today's youngsters, and they are learning to use computers both at home and at school. Keyboard typing will be old stuff to them. Keyboards will become simpler and computer programs "friendlier." There will be no clerical stigma attached to typing on computer keyboards. It will be included in the state of the art.

However, improvements in voice recognition systems may come along fast enough to bypass keyboard typing for many administrators. This innovation exists today in primitive form. Within a few years, there may be a system sensitive enough to accept large vocabularies. If so, administrators will be able to dictate their correspondence directly into printed or electronically transmitted form.

The Paperless Office

A revolution is getting underway in the paper shuffling trade, and within a decade it will have eliminated a large portion of the paperwork currently involved in administrative procedures. The paperless innovations to watch for are these: laser disk data storage, fiber optics, and improved computer software. Here is how they will interact.

A *laser* disk is a smooth plastic disk that can be encoded with information that is read out by a laser beam. It can store incredible amounts of information: the equivalent of a small library on what looks like a 45 rpm record. In a few years, this method of storage will be as versatile as magnetic floppy disks are today. When this method becomes perfected, users will be able to readily pull up information, alter it, or display it in print or on a screen. The disks are capable of permanent storage, and duplicate copies can easily be made and stored separately for backup. Thus, entire vast paper files will be shrunk from room size to disk size.

Fiber optics will greatly increase capacity for communication and the recording of data, both voice and graphics, in digital form. Cables thinner than lamp wire will link office machines into coordinated networks for interchange of data and coordinated data processing.

Computer software will be designed to manage the fiber-optic networks and even to provide verification of signatures and time of entry. These will be as foolproof as advanced technology can make them and will become admissible as legal documentation. Software programs already exist with built-in verification that data have been received as sent without error, and these will be improved as time goes on. Obviously, the dividing line between hard copy (print) and soft copy (electronic) may become blurred. Deciding when and how to make a record of a communication or data within an organization or between organizations will be a matter of administrative protocol.

Some paper will still be in use, although much less than now. The biggest change is that once paper has served its fleeting purpose, it will be dumped, not stored. Offices will store information, not paper. Much space now devoted to file storage will be free for other purposes. What used to be the file and workroom might become the exercise room, where employees will loosen up after a few hours at their adjustable work stations.

Physical Arrangements

Automation is redesigning the environment of the office. Desks are becoming "work stations," which show resemblance to airplane cockpits. Computers and other freestanding equipment are being built in or set into the work station. Voice communication equipment is also being built in. The desk and chair is being adjusted to fit the user at the touch of electronic controls, much like the seats in a luxury automobile.

With noisy typewriters and copiers replaced by word processors and high speed laser printers, the only noticeable sound will be human voices. However, this will change as computer terminals become more talkative. Hence, office designers are coming up with new ideas for acoustical shielding. The "open office" design is being replaced thus most office workers will have at least a small private space to themselves with surrounding sound barriers.

Computers are becoming part of the administrator's standard traveling equipment, as they are much smaller and portable than in the past. These serve as work stations for the road with easy access back to the office via the nearest telephone or built in modem in the hotel room or in one's home.

Applying Controls

An important aspect of office management is keeping a tight rein on matters that must be controlled. For example, the issue of keys requires careful control and accurate record keeping; otherwise the security plan will deteriorate (Figure 7-3). Office supplies should be controlled at just the right level to avoid waste and still allow employees to feel that supplies are adequately available. Forms such as requisitions and budget adjustment forms should be available only to those who have official use for them. The right degree of control on the use of office machines—computers, word processors, typewriters, photocopiers, duplicators, and calculators—is needed in order to avoid misuse and breakage. It is useful to have a fee schedule per sheet or per hundred sheets when the machines are used by personnel from other departments or for nonofficial purposes. This can help pay for supplies, maintenance, and replacement. Controls are also needed on the availability and flow of official information.

POLICIES AND PROCEDURES

Standard policies and procedures are normally in writing, and the written form contributes toward their standardization. Nonwritten policies and procedures are less standardized. Other terms sometimes used for policies are *regulations* and *practices*.

Every organization of much size and complexity ought to have a set of written policies and procedures to serve as operational guidelines. Such statements can contribute to streamlining the organization and reducing confusion and misunderstanding. These statements should deal with information of significance. If too much detail is included, the organization becomes over-structured and loses the desirable amount of flexibility.

Ideally, policy and procedure statements should be concise, easy to understand, and should deal only with the matters of the operation that need to be standardized.

Many policies pertaining to a local situation are developed within the framework of higher authority. For example, the Constitution of the United States sets forth certain conditions that affect policies in organizations throughout the

```
                    REQUEST FOR ONE KEY

Issue one key to  _____      Faculty _____
                                           Staff   _____
Home Address  _____        Student _____
                                           Other   _____
Phone _____  Date _____            (explain)


I will not duplicate this key.             _____

                                                Position
I will not loan this key.

I will return this key when my need        _____  _____
    or employment terminates.              Office Address  Extension



                                           _____
                         Signature of Person to whom Key is Issued


                                                Do Not Write in
Key to fit  _____               This Space

Building  _____          Hook No. _____

                                           Date _____
_____   _____
Supervisor      Signature                  Issued by _____

                                           Posted by _____
_____   _____
Administrator   Signature                  Rec. by _____
```

Figure 7-3. A key request form. This is one kind of control that deserves exact procedures and accurate records.

country. Within this context, educators must comply with (1) the equal rights legislation as it applies to differences in race, sex, and age, (2) the concept of separation of church and state, and (3) the various conditions inherent in fair or due process. The State Code of each state contains various statements that influence the policies and procedures of the political subdivisions, including school districts and state colleges and universities. The State Board of Education establishes policies and procedures that apply to the local educational units. These include such items as the number of days school must be in session, teacher certification requirements, subject requirements, salary requirements, salary guidelines, and regulations pertaining to the school tax base.

Within the framework established by higher authority, local school officials establish local policies. As a general rule, the cliche "many hands (or heads) make work easy" is true in developing policies and procedures. Optimum involvement of people has two potential advantages: it results in useful input, and people feel better about adhering to policies and procedures when they participate in developing them.

Various approaches can be used successfully in preparing policy statements. One method is to identify the topics about which written statements are needed, and then assign a committee to formulate the statements in tentative form so that they can become finalized through approval of the administrator and/or employees. Another approach is for the administrator to draft policies and procedures and then go through the appropriate steps of having them reviewed by others in the organization. In schools, policies are often adopted from other schools or school districts where they have functioned successfully. This is a convenient method.

Policies and procedures should be viewed as guidelines and not absolute rules. The desirable amount of flexibility in connection with each policy might vary, depending on the topic and the related circumstances; but a strong element of consistency should exist. Policies and procedures should be viewed as dynamic in the sense that they should be kept current, undergoing changes as the circumstances justify.

Sample Policies and Procedures

Following are two sample policy statements, actually taken from a policy manual, which pertain to physical education and athletics.[5]

Policy Statement 1: Scheduling Facilities. The facilities of the department will be scheduled in accordance with the following priorities: (1) regular daytime classes and athletic practices and contests; (2) other activities sponsored by the department such as intramurals, extramurals, rehearsals, evening classes, and free play; (3) scheduled activities sponsored by other divisions of the school; (4) activities sponsored by student, faculty, and staff groups; (5) activities sponsored by groups not affiliated with the school.

Policy Statement 2: Grading. Because grades are important to students in several ways, the instructor is obligated to apply a sound system of grading. The instructor should do the following:

1. At the beginning of each course, clearly inform the students of the criteria for grading in that course.
2. Interpret for the students what each grade means in terms of quality and quantity of work or performance.
3. Be sure adequate information is obtained about each student and that accurate records are kept to support the grade.
4. Be especially careful in reporting grades in order to minimize the number of grade changes.

Other Topics for Written Policies and Procedures

Each organization varies in terms of the topics for which standard policies and procedures are needed; therefore, the following list would not apply totally to any particular situation. However, it provides insight about the topics for which statements are often prepared.

Class Conduct

Attendance records and class make-up procedures.
Student evaluation and grading.
Class attire for teachers and students.
Facilities, equipment, and supplies for class use.

Facilities

Priorities.
Procedures for scheduling.
Availability and restrictions for nonschool purposes.
Care of facilities.
Facility security—key acquisition and accountability.

Equipment and Supplies

Procedures relative to purchase.
Maintenance and care.
Checking out and in.
Responsibility and accountability.

Health and Safety

Safety regulations, particularly relative to hazardous areas and activities.
Reporting accidents, injuries, and sickness.
Availability and use of school nurse and physician.
Care and treatment of injured persons.
Student health services and insurance.

Personnel

Handling of contracts.
Tenure and dismissal procedures.
Sick leave, official leave, and vacation time.
Advancements.
Salary schedules and extra pay for extra service.
Retirement.
Definition of work load.
Teacher evaluation procedures.

Professional Development

Time and travel expenses for conferences, conventions, etc.
Advanced study and higher degrees.
Professional development leaves.
Additional remuneration.

In addition to the topics stated above, policy and procedure statements are often prepared on such matters as *committee work, in-house communication, financial management, nonschool relationships, conflicts of interest, and professional ethics.*

REFERENCES AND RECOMMENDED READINGS

1. Berko, R.M., Wolvin, A.D., and Curtis, R.: This Business of Communicating. Dubuque, IA, W.C. Brown, 1980.
2. Brown, H.M., and Reid, K.K.: Business Writing and Communication: Strategies and Applications, 2nd Ed. New York, Van Nostrand, 1985.
3. Gordon, J.R.: Organizational Behavior, 3rd Ed. Boston, Allyn and Bacon, 1991, pp. 286–330.
4. Hunt, G.T.: Communication Skills in the Organization. Englewood Cliffs, NJ, Prentice-Hall, 1980.
5. Jensen, C.R.: Policy and Procedure Manual, Revised Ed. College of Physical Education, Brigham Young University, Provo, UT, 1992.
6. Keeling, B.L., Kallaus, N.F., and Neuner, J.J.: Administrative Office Management, 8th Ed., Cincinnati, South-Western Publishing, 1984.
7. Mamchak, P.S., and Mamchak, S.R.: Complete Communications Manual for Coaches and Athletic Directors. West Nyack, NY, Parker Publishing Co., 1989.
8. Terry, G.R., and Stallard, J.J: Office Management and Control: The Administrative Managing of Information, 9th Ed., Homewood, IL, R.D. Irwin, 1986.
9. Tyson, C.H.: Communicating with self and others. (Address September 9, 1980), Vital Speeches, 47:16, 1980.
10. Whetten, D.A.,and Cameron, K.S.: Developing Management Skills, 2nd Ed. New York, Harper Collins Publishers, 1991, pp. 226–270, 452–479.

Chapter *8*

PERSONNEL MANAGEMENT

Personnel management is among the most important responsibilities of an administrator, because personnel compose the most important resource of the organization. This is particularly true in an educational organization, where the primary objectives have to do with the improvement of people. Underlying personnel management is the concept that if you can keep the right people in the right positions and provide them with an optimum amount of direction and support, they will cause the organization to succeed. Conversely, it is impossible to succeed in the absence of well-qualified personnel.

Aspects of personnel administration include the following: job analysis and descriptions, selection and hiring, contracts, benefits, orientation, supervision, staff productivity, tenure, grievances, termination, personnel files, professional ethics, professional improvement, teacher unionization, equal employment opportunities, and various additional personnel matters.

JOB ANALYSIS AND DESCRIPTION

Job analysis involves identifying the position, determining the responsibilities that go with each position, the qualifications that are required or desired for the position, and the overall value of the position to the organization. Critical job analysis often results in certain modifications and realignments of job responsibilities.

Written descriptions of the various positions in an organization serve a useful purpose by clarifying the personnel structure. Job descriptions should be written clearly and with enough specificity to cover the subject adequately, without spelling out every detail of the job. Some positions are relatively easy to describe, whereas others are difficult due to the diversification and unusual nature of the responsibilities.

Some of the jobs in educational organizations that need to be described are superintendent, principal, supervisor, specialist, dean, director, department head, teacher, coach, special facility manager, researcher, athletic trainer, secretary/receptionist, stenographer, typist, equipment manager, and issue room clerk. Not all of these positions would exist in any one organization; and in certain organizations, some jobs exist that are not named here. In two different organizations, a position with the same title might have a slightly different description; but usually the descriptions are similar. In order to provide representative samples, descriptions of two positions are included here: stenographer and swimming pool manager. In addition, descriptions of the following administrative positions appear in Chapter 12: superintendent, school principal, college dean, assistant dean, department head, and athletic director.

Stenographer

1. Takes shorthand and/or utilizes dictation equipment.
2. Types correspondence, minutes, tests, class materials, etc.
3. Answers the telephone and assists visitors, students, faculty, and others who contact the office.
4. Maintains budget records as assigned.
5. Maintains the office files and keeps complete and accurate records.
6. Proofreads correspondence, reports, etc.
7. Supervises part-time office employees.
8. Determines work priorities.

Swimming Pool Manager

1. Coordinates the selection, hiring, training, scheduling, and supervision of lifeguards.
2. Coordinates the maintenance and unkeep of all equipment and materials associated with the operation of the pools, with special attention given to safety equipment.
3. Coordinates the ordering and replacement of equipment and materials as needed.
4. Coordinates the scheduling of all activities in the swimming pools.
5. Coordinates the conduct of all competitive swimming, diving, and water polo meets held in the pools.
6. Posts and maintains regular office hours, during which time interested persons can discuss activities relating to the pools.

SELECTION AND HIRING

The wise administrator recognizes that an organization must have competent employees in order to succeed. Therefore, the most important decisions made by an administrator are those involving the selection of personnel. If these are consistently good decisions, the organization will be staffed with well-prepared and effective people, which will help to assure its success. An important guideline is to "hire the right people and provide them with success-oriented circumstances."

The exact procedures for selecting and hiring personnel vary with different organizations, but certain procedures are basic:

1. Usually files are established and maintained on prospective employees so that when a position becomes vacant, these individuals will receive consideration.
2. In most cases, a position vacancy form must be processed. This includes

a description of the position, the required qualifications, and eventually a list of all who are to be considered and the one finally selected.

3. An announcement of the vacancy is printed and/or posted in various sources and locations. The announcement includes the necessary information to attract the attention of potential candidates and an explanation of the procedures for applying.
4. Applications are received and handled in accordance with prescribed procedure.
5. After reviewing the applications, a few applicants are offered interviews, and from this group a final selection is made. The terms of employment are agreed upon and the person becomes officially employed. In some cases, the decision of whom to hire is made by the chief administrator; sometimes two or three administrators are involved; and in other cases, a search committee or selection committee is involved.

Procedural Steps for Employment of New Faculty Members

Typically, the following steps are taken in the selection and employment of a faculty member at a university.

- Obtain authorization to fill position by filing a position vacancy form.
- Prepare and distribute official announcement of the position vacancy with the essential information included.
- Receive applications and complete files of those who are legitimate prospects.
- Submit the files for review by the selection or search committee if such committee is utilized.
- Arrange for interviews of selected applicants. This involves travel arrangements and appointments with the interviewers.
- Select the most qualified applicant.
- Submit a "Request for Appointment," including recommended salary and rank.
- Obtain authorization to make an official offer.
- Send offer letter to the selected candidate.
- Send a copy of the candidate's reply to the vice president.
- Initiate a letter of appointment (contract) to be sent to the new employee.
- After the signed contract is returned, have official notice of employment prepared and sent to the new employee along with information about orientation procedures.

Assessing Applicants

Much useful information can be obtained from a well-prepared job application form. Such a form should include essential information about educational background and degrees earned, previous work experience, special or unusual achievements, and numerous other pertinent facts. The application becomes even more useful if it is accompanied by a personal resume or vita.

Assuming that an applicant's job performance in the future would be consistent with that of the past, recommendations from former employers may be excellent sources of information. One should be cautious about accepting letters of recommendation at their face value because (1) such letters are usually written by individuals of the applicant's choice, and (2) in writing letters of recommendation, people are often more complimentary than is justified. Letters of recommendation from reliable sources, however, can furnish some of the most valuable information for use in the selection process.

The best indication of potential success is immediate previous achievement in a similar position. Other indicators are much less reliable, but still useful. Among the other indicators are academic achievement, prediction tests, direct impressions of a candidate's potential, and success in other lines of work.

One of the most useful processes in assessing applicants is the personnel interview. The effective interviewer uses a "patterned approach" where the dialogue is guided by the interviewer, but the interviewee is encouraged to speak freely and in depth about relevant topics. The interviewer maintains control of the conversation to make certain that all relevant areas are covered systematically and within a reasonable time frame.

Common errors in interviewing include: lack of preparation, poor interviewing conditions, covering the content haphazardly, and invasion of privacy. An administrator who takes the interview process seriously will try to avoid these errors.

Figures 8-1 and 8-2 show examples of forms that can help to give structure to the selection process.

CONTRACTS

A contract is an official written agreement between two or more parties with certain conditions described. It is common practice for teachers, coaches and administrators to be employed under contract, whereas some other school personnel are employed under non-contractual arrangements, such as by time card at an hourly rate or by the month. A properly prepared and signed contract is a legal document, meaning that both parties are bound and are expected to adhere to the conditions of the contract, unless the parties mutually agree to a contract release or modification. Certain points of information are essential in a teacher contract, such as job title and/or rank, duration of employment, salary, fringe benefits (unless explained elsewhere), and the basic responsibilities.

Figure 8-3 shows an example of a typical contract. Most contracts include an attachment or enclosure that provides additional information about the specific conditions of employment.

BENEFITS

In educational organizations, employee benefits normally cost between 15 and 25% of an individual's salary but may run as high as 35%. It is assumed that the benefits are actually worth this much. Employees and prospective employees should be informed about the specifics of the benefits and their monetary value.

Normally, the two major aspects of the benefits program are retirement and insurance. Most professionals in education are enrolled in the state education retirement program, and these benefits are comparable from one state to another, even though they differ in some respects. Well-established private educa-

PROSPECTIVE EMPLOYEE RECOMMENDATION FORM

The below named applicant has given your name as a reference for a position in our school system. Your evaluation will be kept confidential. Please rate each category: (0) unobserved, (1) below average, (3) average, or (5) above average.

Date _____

To _____   RE: _____
                                         (applicant)

Address _____
                                    For _____
_____   (position)

	0	1	2	3	4	5	Remarks
1. Appropriate model for students							
2. Overall appearance							
3. Scholarship in major teaching areas							
4. Scholarship in minor teaching areas							
5. Rapport with students							
6. Ability to effectively organize							
7. Ability to effectively communicate							
8. Ability to motivate students							
9. Ability to control students							
10. Competency in teaching (coaching)							
11. Acceptance of responsibility							
12. Overall professionalism							
13. Overall ability to succeed							

How long have you known the applicant? _____

In what relation have you known the applicant? _____

Would you hire the applicant for this position? _____

Additional comments _____

_____

Signature _____   Title _____

Figure 8-1. Example of a prospective employee recommendation form.

INTERVIEW FORM

Name of Organization _____

After the applicant has left the room, complete this rating form. The rating categories are: (1) below average, (3) average, and (5) above average.

Date _____

Interviewer _____

Applicant _____   For _____
                 (name)   (position)

	1	2	3	4	5	Remarks
1. Personal appearance						
2. Ability to communicate						
3. Personality appeal						
4. Interest in the position						
5. Positive professional outlook						
6. Knowledge of subject area						
7. Knowledge of student characteristics						
8. Attitude toward students						
9. Philosophy of teaching/coaching						
10. Degree of appropriateness for the job						

Strengths: _____

_____

_____

_____

Weaknesses: _____

_____

_____

_____

Comments: _____

_____

_____

Figure 8-2. Example of an interview form for prospective teachers.

Letter of Appointment

Name and address   Date _____

of faculty member _____

_____

On behalf of the Board of Trustees and the President, I am
pleased to offer you a faculty position for the year beginning

_____ and ending _____. Your

salary will be $_____, to be paid to you in twelve equal

installments, commencing _____, and your rank or

title will be _____.

This letter is being sent to you in duplicate. If the terms of your
appointment are acceptable, please sign and return one copy within twenty
days of the date of this letter; otherwise this offer will lapse. We are required
to set this time limit in order that we may immediately recruit someone in your
place if we do not receive your acceptance within such period of time.

We are enclosing a memorandum relating to employment of faculty
members of this institution. Compliance with the terms of this memorandum
is a condition of your employment.

If you have any questions about this appointment, I suggest that you
confer with your dean, director, or other officer supervising your work.
Questions concerning payroll deductions, group insurance, and other fringe
benefits should be directed to the Benefits Office.

The Board of Trustees and the Administration are most appreciative of
the loyal service of the faculty of the University. We trust that the continued
spirit of cooperation and devotion to duty will improve even further the
quality of service to our students and our performance in our other duties.

Sincerely,

Academic Vice President

I hereby accept the appointment stated above this _____ day

of _____, 19__.

_____

Figure 8-3.   Typical letter of appointment for a college teacher. A high school teacher contract
would be similar.

tion organizations usually provide retirement benefits that are comparable to the state schools. The insurance program normally includes health and accident coverage and sometimes life insurance.

When a teacher applies for a new position, complete information should be obtained about the benefits associated with it. This can be done by a combination of the following approaches.

Information provided in interviews, the orientation sessions, or other conversations.
Information in the written contract, the policy and procedure manual, or other written documents.
Information obtained directly from the personnel office or from administrative officials.

Personnel benefits supplement, in a real way, the financial arrangements of the employment contract. The individual is provided a benefits package that would be very costly to the employee if obtained on an individual basis. A good benefits program helps in the recruitment and retention of competent personnel and enhances the morale of all employees. The following list of benefits is representative of those found in most organizations.

Retirement (including participation and Social Security)
Insurance—group life and medical
Workmen's compensation
Periodic medical examinations
Tenure
Leaves of absence—sick leave, maternity, emergency, professional development (conferences and workshops, travel study, sabbatical)
Credit union benefits
Legal services (under certain conditions)
Parking privileges
Free or reduced admission to special interest and entertainment events

It should be remembered by both employer and employee that benefits that have true value are as good as money in the bank. Many employees, however, would prefer increases in salary rather than an equivalent amount in benefits. The proportion of resources that go into salary as compared to benefits needs to be kept in proper balance for the overall good of the organization and the individuals.

ORIENTATION

The orientation of a new employee occurs through a combination of several approaches, including the interviewing process, study of the organization's policy manual, and conversations with other school personnel. In addition to these procedures, new employees usually go through formal orientation sessions. These can be viewed as an educational or professional development experience designed specifically to inform employees about policies, procedures, regulations, benefits, restrictions, and expectations that pertain to their positions. It is especially important that the orientation be well planned and effectively conducted. The manner in which the orientation is accomplished can have a significant influence on the employees' early impressions of the organization and its administrators.

SUPERVISION

Only a small amount of supervision is necessary and appropriate for employees who are highly responsible, dependable, and well prepared. A good employee has little need for a "boss." In such case, the "boss" needs only to provide general direction and support. This form of supervision is usually pleasant and relatively easy for both the supervisor and those being supervised.

On the other end of the scale are employees who need close and constant supervision. Such people may be incompetent in the sense that they are irresponsible and undependable. They violate rules of efficiency and effectiveness and take advantage of the employer. The practical way to deal with such people is to either bring about positive change or else replace them with more competent personnel at the earliest opportunity.

Some guidelines for a supervisor follow:

1. A supervisor should be viewed as both an educator and a motivator. The *educational* role involves teaching the employees how to better perform their responsibilities. The *motivating* function involves regular encouragement and meaningful challenge.
2. A congenial and business-like relationship is recommended. This contributes to pleasant working conditions and yet prohibits the employee from taking advantage of a relationship that might be too casual or chummy.
3. Each individual is different, and supervision therefore must be different. While some individuals may require little direct supervision due to their insight, understanding, and work ethics, others may have little feel for the circumstance or the assignments and therefore require constant guidance.
4. When a person has a split assignment, including regular work responsibilities mixed with some limited supervision, care must be taken to insure that the individual will perform with efficiency in both assignments.

STAFF PRODUCTIVITY (Figure 8-4)

In the literature on personnel relationships, two opposite views are often compared—the negative precept and the positive precept. The negative precept holds that the typical employee (1) dislikes work, tries to avoid it when possible, and must be coerced into performing adequately; (2) is not ambitious, dislikes job responsibilities, and needs to be supervised closely; (3) is naturally self-centered and indifferent or oblivious to organizational goals; (4) consistently resists change; and, (5) desires job security and economic rewards above all else.

The positive precept emphasizes that for the typical employee, (1) the expenditure of physical and mental effort in work is natural and rewarding; (2) self-direction and self-control can be expected; (3) commitment to specific objectives is associated with desire to achieve; (4) it is satisfying to accept

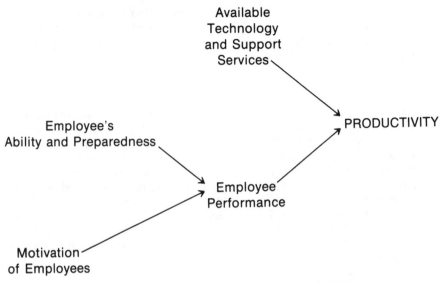

Figure 8-4. Factors contributing to employee productivity.

rather than avoid responsibility; (5) a substantial capacity exists for imagination, ingenuity, and creativity in solving organizational problems; and (6) most organizations only partially use the employee's potential.

Both the negative and the positive precepts have elements of truth, and certainly there are individuals and work groups who can be strongly identified with either of these extremes. Most people, however, fall somewhere between the two. Fortunately, professional educators typically tend toward the positive precepts. However, there are some unfortunate exceptions to this, and educational organizations sometimes employ nonprofessional individuals who may be more aligned with the negative precept. Any professional educator who is not strongly oriented toward the positive precept would be a poor representative of the profession and a bad risk for an educational organization.

An administrator must be alert to the kinds of precepts the individual employees exhibit and try to utilize that information in the motivating process. Often, positive changes can be brought about by encouraging positive precepts. The selection and hiring process provides the best opportunity for developing a high level of productivity. Well-thought-out decisions relative to personnel selection are crucial.

In addition, the total environment should be conducive to high-level productivity. There ought to be adequate facilities, equipment, and supplies; a climate that is relatively free of friction, apprehension, and frustrations; challenging assignments; and an atmosphere of encouragement.

Employee morale is another important factor in productivity, and the administrator is usually in a strong position to influence this. If good morale is to be attained, the administrator must have concern for the staff members and their welfare and must maintain an atmosphere of trust, honesty, and openness. Clearly stated objectives, consistency of procedures and overall administrative efficiency have positive influences on morale. A further discussion of this topic is included in the section on motivation in Chapter 6.

The crucial factor in education is student progress toward the educational objectives. Teachers are the primary facilitators of student progress. Therefore, teacher effectiveness must be viewed as the primary objective of administration.

Administrative practices and techniques have a direct influence on teacher productivity in several ways.

1. The administration must provide adequate facilities, equipment, and supplies. To provide less is to be ineffective.
2. Ample compensation is important not only because of the economic factor, but also because it sends a message about the perceived worth of the teacher.
3. Clearly defined and expedient administrative methods can contribute to the efficiency of everyone in the organization.
4. The administrative climate has a direct effect on the productivity of the teacher. Research indicates that teachers are highly motivated by a positive, congenial, and open administrative atmosphere. Conversely, dissatisfaction and absenteeism are common when the administrative climate is antagonistic and closed.

Practically all administrative efforts are pointed either directly or indirectly toward productivity of the organization's personnel.

TENURE

The rationale of tenure for teachers is based on the legitimate need to protect teachers from being dismissed for unjustified reasons, such as personal differences with a school administrator; legitimate participation in politics; making room for an administrator's friend or favorite; and practicing reasonable academic freedom, which might not be fully acceptable to certain administrators. Tenure contributes to stability of the faculty and to peace of mind for the individual employees.

Although most school systems in the United States operate under a tenure law, some do not. Where tenure laws do not apply, a "continuing contract" usually does. This means that a teacher's contract will be automatically renewed the next year unless the teacher is notified to the contrary before a specified date, in which case all aspects of correct due process should be followed.

New teachers are normally on a nontenured, or probationary, status for a period of 2 to 5 years (this time varies in different states) before becoming eligible for tenure. Coaches may receive tenure as teachers, but the coaching assignment is normally not subject to tenure.

The concept of tenure is clearly justified, and the results are generally positive. The tenure system has one glaring weakness, however; it gives a certain amount of job security to some teachers who have become unmotivated, outdated, and incompetent. Unfortunately, almost every school system has some teachers who have acquired job security at relatively high salaries and who could easily be replaced by more competent younger teachers at lower salaries.

The control or correction of these situations is an important challenge for school administrators.

According to the records of the National Education Association, states fall into four categories in terms of tenure laws.

Group 1 States with statewide tenure laws.

Alabama	Iowa	New Mexico
Alaska	Kentucky	North Carolina
Arizona	Louisiana	North Dakota
Arkansas	Maine	Ohio
Colorado	Maryland	Oklahoma
Connecticut	Massachusetts	Pennsylvania
Delaware	Michigan	Rhode Island
District of Columbia	Minnesota	South Dakota
Florida	Missouri	Tennessee
Hawaii	Montana	Virginia
Idaho	Nevada	Washington
Illinois	New Hampshire	West Virginia
Indiana	New Jersey	Wyoming

Group 2 Tenure laws that are less than statewide (exceptions noted).

California: Optional in districts with average daily attendance under 750 pupils.
New York: Certain rural districts not covered.
Texas: Law is permissive; all districts have the option of coming under the tenure provision.
Georgia: DeKalb, Fulton, and Richmond counties only.
Kansas: Kansas City, Topeka, and Wichita only.
Nebraska: Lincoln and Omaha only.
Oregon: Districts with an average daily attendance of 4,500 or more, and districts where tenure was in effect on August 24, 1965.
Wisconsin: County and City of Milwaukee only.

Group 3 Continuing contract laws with notification of termination required by a specified date (except as stated in group 2).

Kansas
Nebraska
Oregon
Wisconsin

Group 4 Annual or longer term contracts.

Georgia (exception stated in group 2)
Mississippi
South Carolina
Utah
Vermont

GRIEVANCES

For the overall good of the organization, it's important to keep gripes and complaints in perspective and in the proper channels, while still giving appropriate attention to them. These days it is common practice for an educational system to have a prescribed procedure for the handling of grievances. The procedure should be simple but effective. Ordinarily it involves the following:

1. Discussing the grievance with one's immediate supervisor and attempting to solve it at that level.
2. If this effort is unsuccessful, the grievance is taken to the next higher administrative level.
3. If the grievance remains unresolved, it will sometimes be taken one level higher, but more likely it will be placed in the hands of a grievance committee, composed of three or more staff members. This committee will study the situation and attempt to bring the matter to a satisfactory solution.

Grievances ought to be kept to a minimum because they use up time and energy that could better be spent on more productive matters. Effective control of grievances is closely related to the administrator's sensitivity and responsiveness to potential tension-causing situations, along with personality, good judgment, and implementation of sound procedures. However, it is not possible to totally avoid grievances; therefore, an organization must have a fair procedure for dealing with them. In the handling of grievances, the administrator's focus should always be on finding the best solution, not proving a point.

TERMINATION

Termination can occur by a natural process such as expiration or retirement, or by initiative of the individual or of the organization. Termination procedures ought to be spelled out in the policy manual, and they must be enforced in order to ensure that terminations occur in an orderly manner. Regardless of who initiates the termination or what reasons are behind it, the procedures should include the following: (1) sufficient advance notice; (2) written notification placed on file; (3) processing the termination form, which ensures proper checkout and clearances in terms of keys, equipment, library materials, and the like; and (4) final financial settlement.

PERSONNEL FILES

A file is kept on each member of the faculty, and files are usually also kept on other employees. It is important that personnel files contain as much useful information as possible, but not become filled with trivia or nonapplicable material. The files should be available only to those who rightfully have access to them and be treated with a high level of confidentiality. Most administrators would probably agree that individuals should be able to examine their own files upon request; however, this practice is usually governed by an organizational policy that spells out the handling and accessibility of personnel files. In large organizations, the trend is toward keeping personnel records on computer rather than hard copy.

PROFESSIONAL ETHICS

Professions adopt codes of ethics as recommended guidelines for conduct of those in the profession. The education profession has a code of ethics that has been set forth by the National Education Association (NEA) and the American Association of University Professors (AAUP). The American Alliance for Health,

Physical Education, Recreation and Dance (AAHPERD) has prepared a code of ethics, which is reprinted here by permission. All administrators, teachers, and coaches in physical education and athletics should be well informed about the contents of this code.

Preamble

Believing that the strength of our American democracy and its influence upon the course of events everywhere in the world lies in the physical, mental and moral strength of its individual citizens; believing that the schools of America possess the greatest potential for the development of these strengths in our young citizens; believing that the teachers of physical education have a unique opportunity, as well as a responsibility to contribute greatly to the achievement of this potentiality; believing that all teachers of physical education should approach this great responsibility in a spirit of true professional devotion, the AAHPERD proposes for the guidance of its members the following:

PRINCIPLES OF ETHICS

1. Inasmuch as teachers of physical education are members of the teaching profession, the AAHPERD endorses without reservation the Code of Ethics for Teachers, adopted by the National Education Association.
2. The aim of physical education is the optimum development of the individual. To this end teachers of physical education should conduct programs and provide opportunities for experiences which will promote the physical development of youth and contribute to social, emotional, and mental growth.
3. In a democratic society every child has a right to the time of the teacher, to the use of the facilities, and a part in the planned activities. Physical education teachers should resist the temptation to devote an undue amount of time and attention to the activities of students of superior ability to the neglect of the less proficient.
4. The professional relations of a teacher with pupils require that all information of a personal nature shall be held in strict confidence.
5. While a physical education teacher should maintain a friendly interest in the progress of pupils, familiarity should be avoided as inimical to effective teaching and professional dignity.
6. The teacher's personal life should exemplify the highest ethical principles and should motivate children to the practice of good living and wholesome activities.
7. To promote effective teaching, the teacher of physical education should maintain relations with associates which are based on mutual integrity, understanding, and respect.
8. The physical education teacher should cooperate fully and unselfishly in all school endeavors which are within the sphere of education. He should be an integral part of the school faculty, expecting neither privileges nor rewards that are not available to other members of the faculty.
9. It is an obligation of the teacher of physical education to understand and make use of proper administrative channels in approaching the problems encountered in education and in schools.
10. It is the duty of the physical education teacher to strive for progress in personal education and to promote emerging practices and programs in physical education. The teacher should also endeavor to achieve status in the profession of education.
11. Professional ethics imply that altruistic purpose outweighs personal gain. The teacher, therefore, should avoid using personal glory achieved through winning teams for the purpose of self-promotion.
12. It is considered unethical to endorse physical education equipment, materials and other commercial products for personal gain or to support anything of a pseudo-educational nature. Nor should a teacher profit personally through the purchase of materials for physical education by the school.
13. It is the responsibility of the teacher of physical education to acquire a real understanding of children and youth in order that he may contribute to their growth and development. To achieve this understanding, it is essential that an earnest effort be made to foster and strengthen good school-home-community relationships.
14. It is the duty of every teacher of physical education to become acquainted with and to participate in the affairs of the community, particularly those concerned with making the community a better place in which to live. The teacher should take an active interest in the work of the

various child- and youth-serving agencies, participating as a citizen, and as a leader of children, youth and adults.

15. Inasmuch as physical education will progress through strong local, state, and national organizations, the teacher of physical education is obligated to membership and active participation in the proceedings of professional organizations, both in general education and in the specialized field of physical education.

16. Institutions preparing teachers of physical education have an ethical responsibility to the profession, to the public and nation for the admission, education, and retention of desirable candidates for teaching. To meet this obligation, curriculum offerings must be in harmony with the highest standards of professional education.

17. Teachers of physical education should render professional service by recruiting qualified men and women for future teachers of America. The physical education teacher also has a professional obligation to assist in the learning, practice and understanding of student teachers in the field.[2]

PROFESSIONAL IMPROVEMENT

In the field of management, there is a sound bit of advice that states: "Hire carefully, dismiss sparingly, and cultivate to the maximum the talents and abilities of those who are employed." One approach to professional improvement involves the earning of a higher degree. There are also other kinds, such as attendance and participation at conventions, clinics, and workshops; meaningful research and writing; and the reading of professional literature.

It is essential for administrators to hold a long-range view of staff development. A return on investment may not be forthcoming this week, this month, or even this year, but over the long term, a well-planned program will produce substantial benefits, including (1) better qualified staff, (2) improved motivation and morale, (3) improved job performance, and (4) increased organizational productivity.

In allocating funds for professional development, administrators must be discriminating to make sure that the optimum improvement is gained for the amount of funds expended. In this regard, it is not good enough to simply respond to employees' ideas. It is also important to aggressively generate and implement development opportunities. In connection with each employee, especially the faculty, the concept of the individual development cycle presented in Figure 8-5 ought to be applied.

Figure 8-5. Diagram of an individual development program cycle.

Professional development opportunities have two purposes: (1) to prevent employees from becoming outdated and less competent and (2) to cause them to become better prepared and more competent. Professional improvement should be viewed as a valuable supplement to an individual's basic preparation and professional experience. It should be approached with enthusiasm and high expectations and viewed as an opportunity to improve both the individual and the organization.

In order for professional development experiences to be beneficial, they must be well planned (this usually involves a written proposal); approved and funded with enough lead time for adequate planning and preparation; and include an oral or written report of sufficient detail. In the case of professional development leaves, interim reports are also often required.

The use of lateral transfers or shifts in responsibilities is another means of fostering staff development. A person who remains in the same job for a lengthy period of time is likely to reach a "plateau" on the learning curve. When this plateau is reached, there is little opportunity for growth and little challenge in the job. The predictable result is boredom and deterioration in performance. To prevent this, the alert administrator will make use of lateral adjustments as an effective means for staff development and employee motivation.

Retrenching of Personnel

Sometimes an educational organization finds that the curricular emphases have evolved away form the competencies of certain faculty. Two acceptable solutions to this are either to replace the faculty members who have become outdated or to have outdated faculty members retrench themselves to fit the present and future curricular needs. Retrenching is usually done through the various professional improvement opportunities over a period of time. Occasionally, the need for new competencies is so pressing that, in order to meet the need, a person must go through extensive repreparation. Administrators should carefully monitor the need for professional retrenchment and try to provide attractive and timely opportunities to help the employees keep current with the needs of the program. A teacher who falls behind in educational methods and subject matter certainly cannot function effectively on the job, and this is a problem where prevention is better than cure. In this regard, it is important to remember the idea that "the best way to get rid of poor employees is to make them into goods ones."

TEACHER UNIONIZATION

Administrators typically oppose unionization of teachers because it emphasizes the labor versus management concept. This feeling of competition causes a barrier between teachers and administrators that detracts from a congenial working relationship. It contradicts the "happy family" environment that teachers and administrators have traditionally enjoyed. Some believe that unionization tends to damage the public image of the education profession.

In spite of these disadvantages, unionization among teachers has gained in popularity, and through collective bargaining, educators have gained some financial benefits. Whether unionization among teachers continues to be effective will depend largely on the public's attitude toward it and whether the union leaders and members act wisely.

EQUAL EMPLOYMENT OPPORTUNITIES

No discussion of personnel administration would be complete without reference to the laws pertaining to equal employment opportunities and affirmative action. The original equal employment opportunity act was Title VII of the Civil Rights Act of 1964, amended by the EEC Act of 1972. Educational institutions, at all levels, are under the jurisdiction of this act.

Title VII is the federal statute designed to provide all persons an equal opportunity for meaningful employment, regardless of race, religion, color, sex, or national origin. This law represents the federal effort to eliminate past patterns of discrimination in employment and to ensure that free and open access to employment will exist for all qualified applicants.

The basic concepts of Title VII are found in section 703, which outlines discrimination in employment and makes an employment practice unlawful when it:

1. results in a failure or refusal to hire any individual because of such person's race, religion, color, sex, or national origin;
2. results in the discharge of any individual because of such person's race, color, religion, sex, or national origin;
3. differentiates between individuals with respect to compensation, terms, conditions, or privileges of employment because of such person's race, color, religion, sex, or national origin;
4. limits, segregates, or classifies employees or applicants for employment in any way which would deprive or tend to deprive any individual of employment opportunities, or otherwise adversely affect such person's employment status, because of such person's race, color, religion, sex, or national origin.

Affirmative Action

Since January 13, 1973, all educational institutions (both public and private) with one or more federal contract(s) of $50,000 or more and 50 or more employees have been required to maintain a written affirmative action plan. Although the requirement to maintain a written plan does not apply unless an institution has a federal contract of $50,000 or more, federal contracts during any 12-month period that have an aggregate total exceeding $10,000 subject an institution to compliance with the executive orders and Office of Federal Contract Compliance Programs of the Department of Labor.

The basic authority requiring affirmative action is Executive Order 11246, as amended by Executive Order 11375. These orders require each federal contracting agency to include in every contract entered into by that agency, provisions that obligate the individual contractor, in part, as follows:

The Contractor will not discriminate against any employee or applicant for employment because of race, color, religion, sex or national origin. The Contractor will take affirmative action to ensure that applicants are employed, and that employees are treated during employment without regard to their race, color, religion, sex, or national origin. Such action shall include, but not be limited to the following: employment, upgrading, promotion, or transfer; recruitment or recruitment advertising; layoff or termination; rates of pay or other forms of compensation; and selection for training, including apprenticeship.

Additional Employment Regulations

Other federal government programs pertaining to equal employment opportunities include the following:

Law or Regulation

Equal Pay Act of 1963, with Education Amendments added in 1972	It declares that discrimination on the basis of sex is prohibited on pay scales and benefits. Equal skill, effort, responsibility, and similar working conditions are the criteria of determination.
Title VI of the Civil Rights Act of 1964	This section states that no person in the United States shall, on the grounds of race, color, or national origin, be excluded from participation in, be denied the benefits of, or be otherwise subjected to discrimination under any program or activity receiving federal financial assistance from the Department of Health, Education and Welfare.
Age discrimination in Employment Act of 1967 Amended in 1978	The Act declares that discrimination on the basis of age is prohibited against those in the age bracket of 40 to 70 in hiring, promotion, discharging, and benefits.
Executive Order 11246 Amended by EO 11375 of 1968	This action prohibits discrimination in all phases of employment on the basis of race, color, religion, national origin, and sex. Nondiscrimination requires the elimination of all existing discriminatory conditions. Requires Affirmative Action, including setting goals in achieving employment mixture.
Title IX of the Education Amendments of 1972 (Public Law 92-318)	This Title is designed to eliminate discrimination on the basis of sex in any education program or activity receiving federal financial assistance.
Rehabilitation Act of 1973—Section 503 and 504	Section 503 requires that organizations shall take affirmative action to employ and advance in employment the qualified handicapped. Section 504 prohibits discrimination against qualified handicapped persons in employment and in the operation of programs and activities receiving federal financial assistance.
Veterans Readjustment Act of 1974	This Act declares that employment openings are to be listed at Job Service, veterans should be given priority, and veterans are eligible for readjustment points.

Gender

Evidence seems to support the idea that men and women who have equal preparation can be equally effective in administrative positions. Furthermore, the legal framework has encouraged equal opportunities for women and men in the form of the Civil Rights Act of 1964 and the Title IX legislation of 1972.

Yet, a proportionately small number of women are in educational administrative positions, particularly in physical education and athletics. It was assumed by many that the strong trend toward the combining of men's and women's programs in the schools would result in a higher proportion of women in administrative positions. However, the great majority of physical education and athletic programs at all levels of education are presently administered by men. Undoubtedly, this is partly because more men are in the profession, and partly because men do not need to combine a profession with rearing a family as many women do.

Reif did a study entitled "Exploring some myths about women managers," in which he found that no significant differences exist between women and men that would limit the capacity of women to perform effectively in administrative roles. Leid[8] concluded that few, if any, significant differences exist between the leadership behavior of women and men, and the same kinds of preparation experiences apply equally well to both. Lied emphasized that with the same preparation for administrative leadership, men and women should be able to function with approximately equal effectiveness. It would appear that the framework is established for women to enter the field of administration more frequently than in the past. The psychology associated with women managers is more positive than ever before, and more women today are interested in managerial positions than in the past. This combination of circumstances will undoubtedly contribute toward a higher proportion of women administrators in physical education and athletics in the future.

ADDITIONAL PERSONNEL PROBLEMS

An administrator must guard against certain potential personnel problems. If these problems occur and persist, they can have a dragging effect on the organization. If they get out of hand, they can become disruptive.

Adverse Feelings

Part of one's leadership ability is being able to see through the eyes of others and understand their points of view. In this respect, an administrator must be sensitive to the potential of adverse feelings by others. One such feeling is frustration, which people express in various ways. A common response is either positive or negative aggression. For example, one person might express feelings of frustration through aggressive pursuit of positive goals, whereas another might strike out against a co-worker. Still another might resort to rationalization, such as when one tries to explain away a failure by blaming the boss or blaming "organizational policies." Some react to frustration with child-like behavior, such as an employee who, when denied a promotion, withdraws and pouts.

The administrator needs to avoid personal frustrations and help others to do the same. Feelings of frustration are unpleasant and contribute to unproductive uses of energy. When frustrations do occur, an administrator often can help others see that rationalization, regression, and negative aggressiveness are undesirable and usually counterproductive.

Unacceptable Relationships

Administrative positions are often thought of as lonely in the sense that the administrator cannot afford to be too friendly or appear too close to co-workers.

Chummy friendships with certain co-workers can create problems in the minds of other employees, causing them to feel suspicious or hurt. An administrator must show a strong element of consistency in the relationships with the various people in comparable positions within the organization. Yet it is desirable and certainly workable for an administrator to be generally friendly and congenial with all members of the organization.

Personal Neglect

Some people permit themselves to become physically or mentally deteriorated to the point that they are unable to perform their work. A reduction of energy or a loss of productivity due to deterioration or staleness has been the downfall of many administrators. No pat solution to this problem exists because it has various causes. Sometimes the culprit is the natural aging process and sometimes it is a pathologic ailment. Frequently, however, the deterioration or staleness is due to lack of exercise or diversion.

People who maintain a reasonable level of fitness function more effectively in all respects and have greater longevity. Many executives claim that they actually accomplish more in a day when they devote one hour to vigorous physical exercise. This causes the physiological systems to function more efficiently, thus decreasing the amount of rest required and increasing work output. It has also been found that exercise relieves emotional and mental stress. Many administrators are dedicated to the importance of periodic diversion from the work routine. The need for diversion varies with different individuals, but everyone has some need for it in order to keep the interest level high and avoid becoming stale.

Another potential problem is overweight. Most administrative work is passive. At the same time, administrators are often involved in luncheons, dinner meetings, and banquets. Under these circumstances, low resistance to food or lack of dietary discipline can cause a person to be overweight. It has been found that obesity can be a contributor to a variety of other health problems.

REFERENCES AND RECOMMENDED READINGS

1. AAHPERD: Managing Teacher Stress and Burnout. Waldorf, MD, AAHPERD Publications, 1990.
2. American Management Association: Personnel Management Workbook. New York, 1986.
3. Beach, D.S.: Personnel: The Management of People at Work, 5th Ed., New York, Macmillan, 1985.
4. Brigham Young University: Personnel Manual. Provo, UT, BYU Press, 1991.
5. Bucher, C.A.: Administration of Physical Education and Athletic Programs, 9th Ed. St. Louis, C.V. Mosby, 1987, pp. 188– 209.
6. Cayer, N.J.: Managing Human Resources: An Introduction to Public Personnel Administration, 2nd Ed., New York, St. Martin's Press, 1986.
7. Horine, L.: Administration of Physical Education and Sport Programs, 2nd Ed. Dubuque, IA, William C. Brown, 1991, chapter 4.
8. Leid, M.: Women as Leaders and Managers. M.A. Thesis, University of Illinois, 1977.
9. McGregor, D.: The Human Side of Enterprise. New York, McGraw-Hill, 1960.
10. Pierce, J.L., and Newstrom, J.W.: The Manager's Bookshelf, 2nd Ed. New York, Harper Collins Publisher, 1990, pp. 287–300.
11. Rosenburg, D., and McAleese, W.: FAIRPLAY: The teacher/coach role conflict. Strategies, *1*(5):15, 1988.
12. Whetten, D.A., and Cameron, K.S.: Developing Management Skills, 2nd Ed. New York, Harper Collins Publishers, 1991, pp. 510–530.

Chapter *9*

FINANCIAL MANAGEMENT

An administrative unit and the programs within it must be managed in a financially sound manner. The administrator and others in the department need to be held in high respect and credibility with those who control the finances of the larger organization. This means that budget requests should be based on accurate information and sound rationale. Expenditures should be made wisely and in accordance with the budgetary plan. Accurate financial records should be kept, and the program conducted in a manner that is cost-efficient. If these procedures are applied consistently, they will win financial support. Conversely, there are very few things that can cause an administrator more grief than the mismanagement of financial resources.

PRINCIPLES OF FINANCIAL MANAGEMENT

1. To the extent that values are accurately applied in budgeting, the budget truly represents the relative significance of the activities within the organization.
2. Administrators are often judged by their competence in financial management. Meticulous preparation and thorough justification of budget proposals and careful control of the expenditures reflect heavily on an administrator's image.
3. Regardless of who else is involved, the administrator of the given budgetary unit is immediately responsible for proper financial management.
4. As a general rule, those who furnish money for any enterprise have the right to know how it is spent. This is particularly true of the tax-paying public.
5. Funds for athletics should be allocated and accounted for in generally the same way as funds for other aspects of the school program. The revenue should go into designated funds, and the program should operate on an allocated budget, which is subject to the regular audits.
6. As much return as possible should be realized on any surplus funds that are on deposit either within the organization or in a bank or investment program. The principle of "return on your money" applies to organiza-

tional funds as it does to private funds. In some cases, this can be a substantial source of revenue.

7. In financial management, saving money is important, but spending money is also important. An important guideline is to obtain and spend the right amount in the right manner for the good of the program and to get the most for the money spent.

8. One aspect of financial efficiency is to stop doing some things in order to have additional resources to do other things that are more important.

PLANNING THE BUDGET

Budget planning and preparation are more complex processes than many people realize. Budget planning leads into all aspects of program planning, because the budget must be designed to finance the programs. In turn, the programs must be administered in accordance with the budget. Some guidelines for budget planning are as follows:

1. The budget should accurately represent the financial needs of the program in relationship to the stated program objectives.

2. Honesty in budget preparation is the recommended approach. Padding the budget will become apparent to alert financial personnel. This often damages the credibility of the administrator and may result in exaggerated budget cuts.

3. Accurate determination of enrollment, student credit hours, or other influencing factors is fundamental to effective budget planning.

4. The planning process should take into account anticipated income from all sources (both appropriated funds and revenue) and balance this with the anticipated expenditures.

5. The possibility of financial emergencies should be recognized and included in the budget. Sometimes funds are placed in contingency to cover unforeseen needs.

6. The budget should have the right balance of rigidity and flexibility—enough rigidity to give adequate structure and enough flexibility to accommodate unforeseen changes.

7. The budget should be prepared on a timetable that leaves ample opportunity for thorough analysis, evaluation, and review.

8. The budgeting process ought to involve all those in the organization who have administrative responsibilities.

9. The budget categories and the amount in each category should be correctly aligned to fit the financial needs of the different aspects of the program.

10. Usually, a detailed budget has a cover sheet that summarizes income and expenditures, so that the total budget picture can be seen at a glance.

Budget Preparation

Although the exact steps involved vary with different budgetary approaches, certain steps should be included in all approaches. They include the following: (1) clearly determine the objectives of the program the budget is to finance; (2) determine as accurately as possible the real financial needs of the program; (3)

prepare the budget in adequate detail so that it can be clearly understood; (4) present the budget through the prescribed administrative channels.

Each organization has its own version of budgetary forms. Within any particular organization, however, the forms are similar regardless of the budgetary approach used. Figures 9-1 and 9-2 are examples of budget preparation forms, showing the different categories. Although the forms may be similar, the procedures followed in arriving at the information vary significantly with the budgetary approach. The following section includes descriptions of the various approaches: conventional, PPBES, zero base, and cost analysis.

Conventional Approach

Conventional budgeting is a rather superficial and mechanical method, and yet, due to its simplicity, it is often used. It is also known as "line item," "shopping list," and sometimes, "incremental" budgeting, since each succeeding year usually involves an incremental increase from the previous year (often labeled cost-of-living or inflationary increase). Despite the weakness of this method, it is probably the most widely used approach. It is relatively simple, requires minimal work, and helps to preserve the status quo. With this approach, the person preparing the budget might be provided with a guideline figure—say a 5% increase over last year's budget. Last year's budget then becomes the starting point. The additional money is applied and other adjustments are made in accordance with informational judgment of how the money should be used. Under this system, the most mechanical approach is to apply the percentage increase to every category. Usually, however, based on changes in circumstances and projection of needs, the different categories are increased by various amounts. Some categories may even be decreased so that others can be increased disproportionately.

This approach has one clear weakness. The present status of the budget tends to be basically perpetuated without thorough analysis of productivity as related to expenditure, i.e., return on the dollar. It is assumed that last year's budget is accurate, and increases are tacked on each year for inflation. Thus, unnecessary programs and inefficient procedures may be retained year after year. It is conceivable that a budget item that should have been eliminated or drastically reduced 3 years ago is still in the budget and has received standard annual increases, while some other item that deserves considerably more emphasis has also received standard increases. This does not necessarily happen, but it can with the conventional approach.

Inherent in the conventional approach is a special need to *control waste*, because it encourages a tendency to make needless purchases toward the end of the fiscal year. Departmental personnel often feel that if the entire budget allotment is not spent, next year's budget will be dropped to match this year's spending. This is a foolish and wasteful approach to budgeting because, as the end of the fiscal year approaches, money is often spent on items that otherwise would not be purchased.

Ways in which this perpetual wasting can be controlled include requiring that purchase orders be approved by the principal and business officer during the last month of the fiscal year. Another method is to establish a reward system referred to as a "percent return rule." It simply means that a certain percentage

DEPARTMENTAL BUDGET REQUEST SUMMARY SHEET

Department _____

College/Division _____

Account Code _____

_____
Signature of Dept. Chairman

_____
Signature of Dean

Column	A	B		C		D		E	
Object of Expenditure	Cate-gory Code #	Present Budget		Request for Next Year		Program Improvement Request		Total Budget Request (C + D)	
		Amount	FTE	Amount	FTE	Amount	FTE	Amount	FTE*
1. Administrative salaries		$		$		$		$	
2. Full-time Faculty salaries									
3. Full-time Faculty Supplemental Earnings									
4. Part-time Faculty salaries									
5. Full-time Staff salaries									
6. Student Assistant salaries									
7. Student Wages									
8. Non-student part-time or temp. wages									
9. Payroll taxes, insur-ance, and retirement									
10. Equipment repairs and maintenance									
11. Rented–leased equipment									
12. Computer Services									
13. Capital Equipment									
14. Travel									
15. Supplies and other expenses									
16. Miscellaneous									
17. TOTALS		$		$		$		$	

* Full-time equivalent personnel

Figure 9-1. Budget proposal form for an instructional department, showing the different categories of the budget.

ATHLETIC BUDGET REQUEST SUMMARY SHEET

Account Code			(Sport)	

Object of Expenditure	Code #	Last Year	Present	Request Next Year
1. Administrative salaries				
2. Faculty salaries (coaches)				
3. Full-time Staff salaries				
4. Student Asst. Salaries				
5. Student Wages				
6. Payroll Taxes, Ins., and Ret.				
7. Telephone				
8. Vehicle Operations				
9. Repairs and Maintenance				
10. Capital Equipment				
11. Travel				
12. Supplies				
13. Postage and shipping				
14. Printing				
15. Programs				
16. Laundry				
17. Advertising				
18. Films				
19. Gear				
20. Award Jackets				
21. Recruiting (off campus)				
22. Coaches Clinic				
23. Scouting				
24. Grant-in-aid				
25. Grant-in-aid—Spring				
26. Books				
27. Training Table				
28. Tutoring				
29. Officials				
30. Guarantees				
31. Game Management				
32. Facilities				
33. Dues and Membership				
34. Insurance				
35. TOTALS				

Approvals:

Administrator

Director

Coach

Figure 9-2. Budget proposal form for an athletic program, showing the different categories.

of the total amount of the original budget (say 2%) can be carried over to next year's budget and placed in the unallocated category. This would mean that for a departmental budget of $150,000 as much as $3,000 could be carried over. This encourages tight control of funds and provides for some flexibility in next year's budget. Unfortunately, few educational organizations permit this procedure; although a few have implemented it.

Systems Approach (PPBES)

In order to coordinate the various steps involved in budgeting, a systems approach has emerged. It has been labeled PPBES (originally PPBS), which stands for *Planning, Programming, Budgeting,* and *Evaluation System.* Even though this method was first developed through noneducation agencies, the process has been adapted to education and is used extensively. The adapted process has also been referred to as "the Educational Resources Management System."

The most widely known PPBES system was developed by the United States Department of Defense during the 1960s, and in its evolved form, the system is still used by that agency.

By the late 1960s, the merits of this approach had become recognized in other agencies, particularly in the field of education. As demands by the public for accountability increased, many school systems across the country began using the PPBES.

The *planning* component of PPBES involves preparing goals (objectives) and defining expectations in terms of student accomplishments. The *programming* phase involves the selection of activities and events that will be included in the program for the purpose of accomplishing the goals. The *budgeting* component involves the preparation of a financial proposal that will enable the sponsorship of the program that has been planned. Of course, this must include all aspects of financial need such as facilities, equipment, and personnel. The *evaluation* aspect of the system involves a careful analysis of how adequately the budget fits the program, how well the program leads toward the goals, and how valuable the accomplishments are as related to costs.

The four phases constitute a complete cycle, with its different aspects having a logical sequence and a close relationship. The final step of the cycle (evaluation) logically lays the groundwork for the first step of the new cycle. One of the main advantages of the systems approach is the fact that it forces one to give adequate attention to all the important aspects of budget preparation and administration.

Sometimes explanations of the PPBES cause it to seem complex and cumbersome, but this need not be the case. It only involves the four steps that have been identified in proper sequence. With a large and comprehensive program each step is more involved, but regardless of the size of the program, the system still uses the same four phases.

Zero Base Budgeting

Zero base budgeting (ZBB) was developed at Texas Instruments Company in 1969 by a management team trying to find a better way to relate input to company objectives. It is a system of budgeting that focuses on the complete justification of all expenditures each time the budgeting exercise takes place. It does this by assuming that every element of the organization starts from zero and must justify its existence by its relative contribution to the organization's objectives. Its rapid increase in popularity can be attributed to three basic characteristics: the participative nature of the method by administrators at different levels, the merging effect it causes between budgeting and planning, and the crisp influence it has on decision making.

In effect, ZBB results in a thorough review of functions from the ground base (zero base) and proceeds in an upward direction. The method was developed to offset some of the undesirable features of the conventional budgeting technique. The most important difference is that ZBB avoids the practice of considering last year's budget as the base; and therefore avoids the question of how much is required next year to continue with a particular function. Rather, the question is whether funding should be allocated at all. This method denies the assumption that each aspect of the budget should be automatically continued.

Perhaps the foremost feature of ZBB is that it provides an avenue for budgeting and planning to occur jointly. Often these functions are performed too independently of one another. When program planning and financial planning proceed together from a zero base, relating the decisions about programming and financing becomes easier.

The specific steps to be carried out when implementing ZBB vary from one application to another. However, in a general sense, the following are common aspects of ZBB approaches[2]:

Definition and Goals.   Stating the goals (objectives) of the program is one important step. The goals influence the decisions involved in preparing the budget.

Program Planning.   The program must be planned in light of the goals. In the program planning phase, the following questions are important: What is the reason for doing it? What would happen if it were not done? Is there a better and more economical approach? Where does it fit in terms of priority? After the current aspects of the program have been scrutinized in this manner, new activities and approaches can be considered by the same procedure.

Identifying Alternative Decisions.   The previous step should result in a careful analysis of the relative value of the various aspects of the program. The purpose of this step is to identify and evaluate alternative approaches to accomplishing those aspects of the program that are considered important. For example, (1) scheduling athletic team air flights far enough in advance to take advantage of "super saver" rates; (2) having the school cooperate with the city on the construction of new tennis courts and having them lighted so that they serve both the school and the community; or (3) closing certain facilities during low-use periods so that money can be diverted to other aspects of the program.

Cost Analysis of the Alternatives.   This step involves cost comparisons of the alternatives. It would include questions such as the following: What are the relative costs of a team traveling with two vans as opposed to one bus? What would be the relative cost of playing more games at home and fewer games away, taking into consideration all of the financial factors, gate receipts, travel costs, guarantees, etc.?

Making the Decisions.   The information from the previous four steps brings the situation to the decision-making point. It is now time to decide two important questions. (1) Which functions should receive funding and which ones should not? (2) For those activities that will be funded, which of the alternative approaches is the best? The decisions must be realistic and in accordance with the information from the previous steps. It would be futile to go through the process and then make arbitrary decisions based on preferences that are inconsistent with the facts obtained.

If the ZBB approach is used properly, it will result in funding that fits the best plan for the accomplishment of the stated objectives. With the ZBB method, each aspect of the program has to be justified on a cost-benefit basis, and this has to be done each year (or each time the ZBB approach is used). Precedent, tradition, personal preference, and bias have no place in the ZBB method. It is a straightforward calculation of how much money can be justified in support of each function, when the functions are weighed carefully against each other, and in light of the stated objectives.

The ZBB method has specific advantages. For instance, it allows new programs to compete for funds against established programs. It increases decision flexibility with discretionary funds. It is especially useful in high-growth situations where program expansion is prevalent. Although cost reduction is not a required objective of ZBB, it is oriented toward cost reduction because the process naturally identifies and eliminates areas of the program that are overfunded or relatively ineffective in goal accomplishment.

ZBB is not a simpler method than other approaches, and there is no guarantee that its use will enable budgetary reductions. ZBB should, however, lead to an improved organizational climate as a result of the increased involvement and the direct participation by staff members. It should also result in better utilization of the funds toward accomplishment of the goals due to the careful interrelated analysis of objectives, programs, costs, and alternative approaches.

ZBB as a system is not a panacea, but it can be especially valuable to an organization that needs a "face lifting" in terms of budgetary procedures or one that needs to add rigor to its decision-making process. On the other hand, ZBB should be avoided by any organization whose budgeting approach is adequate and yet simpler and less time-consuming than the ZBB method. In other words, apply the adage that "if it isn't broke don't try to fix it." Also, ZBB ought to be avoided if the organization is involved in major changes in personnel, procedures, or organizational structure.

If zero base budgeting is used, an interesting question is how often the process should be repeated. Valid arguments for and against ZBB as an annual exercise are summarized as follows[2]:

FOR:

1. A different system would have to be used in off-years.
2. ZBB provides alternatives for budget modification during changing circumstances.
3. Administrators will become more proficient at using the system if it is done annually.
4. If the system is effective, then it would seem that annual implementation would be an advantage.

AGAINST:
1. The greatest benefit of the ZBB system accrues the first year and diminishes thereafter.
2. There would be a tendency to repeat the same decisions every year.
3. The process is time-consuming.
4. Good managers review programs critically on a continuous basis without ZBB.
5. ZBB is not needed every year, since programs and activities change little from one year to the next.

ZBB does a vast amount of analysis that is not normally a part of the budget exercise. It creates an atmosphere of rethinking, which can have a renewing effect on the organization, since it allows the organization no longer to be bound by budgetary precedent. However, many who try ZBB become disenchanted and look for some other "miracle cure" for their organizational problems. Such disenchantment may relate to failure to recognize that a budget system is a tool, not a manager. No system can substitute for poor management. No budget approach is any better than the people who operate it.

Cost Analysis

In education, cost analysis is a procedure whereby all expenses of the program are related to the total number of students served. In cost analysis budgeting, projected costs are computed on a per student basis. The total number of students is figured in one of two ways: the average daily *student membership* or the average daily *student attendance*. The membership represents all of the students enrolled in the school; whereas on any given day, the attendance is usually less than the membership. Most experts agree that the membership is the better measure of the two because teachers' salaries must be paid whether 95% or 100% of the pupils are in attendance. Also, school facilities, furnishings, books, and other costs remain approximately constant and do not fluctuate with average attendance.

If cost analysis is employed, a different formula (amount per student) applies at the different school levels because the nature of physical education and athletics varies at the different levels. The formula might allow for a certain dollar amount per student to cover the total expenses of physical education and athletics (and related programs), or it might provide specific amounts per student for physical education instruction, athletics, and intramural sports. In some cases, the school as a whole receives a set amount per student, and the principal assigns the amount for each phase of the total school program.

Although some room for variation exists within budgeting methods, the concept is consistent: the amount of allocation is based on the student population (either enrollment or attendance). This concept is based on the idea that there is a close relationship between educational costs and number of students. Under this method of budgeting, the best way to obtain more money in support of a program is to get an upward revision of the formula.

Sometimes, cost analysis is based on the production of student credit hours rather than on the number of students. In such cases, noncredit activities such as athletics and intramurals have to be budgeted on a different basis.

PRESENTING THE BUDGET

Several steps may be involved in presenting a budget, depending on the particular situation. In a high school, the proposal would logically go from the program director to the principal, to the superintendent, to the school board. In a university, the budget would pass from the department head to the dean, to the vice-president, to the president, and the board of trustees. At each step along the way, the budget proposal must be reviewed and approved. At any stage before final adoption, modifications might be required. These guidelines will help in the presentation process:

1. Provide sufficient copies of the proposal on time.
2. Be sure that the budget proposal is in the recommended format and that it is sound, accurate, and complete.
3. Have available all the information to justify the budget, such as (a) the objectives of the program; (b) evidence of previous success; (c) rate of student participation; (d) statistical data about the program that would be useful to the review personnel.
4. Consider involving other persons who can speak in favor of certain aspects of the proposal. The circumstances of the review indicate whether this would be appropriate.
5. Be thoroughly familiar with the content of the budget proposal and the rationale behind it.
6. Be precise and forthright in your presentation and responses. Avoid being vague or evasive.

SOURCES OF FUNDS

The most reliable source of funds is from *budgetary appropriation*. This method of funding adds stability and consistency and is clearly the preferred source.

In some situations, athletic *gate receipts* provide a source of revenue. In the public schools, gate receipts are relatively small; but in certain university programs, the gate receipts are substantial. It is strongly recommended that gate receipts go into the general fund, and that budgeted funds be used to finance the athletic program. This puts athletics on the same financial basis as other school programs, and it is a protective measure against abuse and in favor of stability in athletics.

Special fees constitute another source of income. Some schools require each student to pay an athletic fee in connection with registration. When this is done, students usually have free or reduced admission to athletic contests. Sometimes, a physical education uniform fee or a facility use fee is also paid by each student.

Several other sources of income are pursued with varying amounts of success by different educational institutions. These include the following: *donated funds* from foundations, companies, and individuals; *annual giving* by individuals through a fund-raising program or athletic booster club; *government grants* for area and facility development; *athletic guarantees* paid in connection with contests played away from home; revenue from *concessions, auto parking,* and *program sales* at athletic contests; and *special fund-raising* events, such as walkathons, marathons, and novelty athletic contests.

It should be noted that, in some states, the law prohibits the expenditure of tax dollars on athletics. In this situation, the athletic department should have the benefit of student athletic fees or help from athletic boosters (or other sources) to stabilize funding to ensure a healthy program.

EXPENDITURE OF FUNDS

Money is the exchange commodity that trades for goods and services. In education, the public has a right to expect a full measure of return on the money spent. In order to properly control expenditures and ensure accountability, it is necessary to be explicit about who is authorized to expend funds from a particular budget. The use of an authorized signature card, such as the one shown in Figure 9-3, gives a clear definition of who can expend funds.

In the case of educational budgets, the great majority of expenditures are for the payment of personnel and the purchase of equipment and supplies.

AUTHORIZED SIGNATURE CARD

_____

Account Code

_____ for
Authorized Signature

_____

Account Name

_____ whose signature appears
(Name—Print or Type)

above is authorized to expend from the above account code.

Restriction (if any): _____

_____

Approved by: _____
(Dean or Director)

Date: _____

Figure 9-3. A form for providing authorization to sign for expenditures against a particular financial account.

Occasionally, large amounts are paid to contractors in connection with construction projects. Relatively small amounts are expended for travel, leasing of equipment, student awards, and other ongoing expenses.

Payment of Personnel

Personnel are hired on *regular contract, special contract,* or *time card* arrangement. Full-time faculty and administrative staff are normally hired on an annual contract. Important elements in the contract are the title, the faculty status, the salary, the conditions of payment (such as monthly, for 12 months), and at least a general description of responsibilities. Some contracts are lengthy and definitive, whereas others cover only the essentials, although the latter sometimes have supplementary information enclosed.

A written contract with the proper signatures is a legal and moral agreement between the individual and the organization. Both sides should be anxious to live up to the conditions of the contract, whether the conditions are explicitly defined, implied, or reasonably assumed. Not all the conditions of employment can be described in a contract, but it should include the more important ones. In addition, it should be understood that the contract represents a "good faith agreement" between the two parties. Breech of contract without justifiable reason is both illegal and unethical. It ought to be strictly avoided. On the other hand, both parties should be open to reasonable negotiation when there is sufficient reason to modify an agreement. An example of a contract (letter of appointment) for a university faculty member appears in Chapter 8, Figure 8-3.

Special contracts are used for the employment of game officials and the accomplishment of special projects. A sample contract for game officials can be found in Chapter 16, Figure 16-2.

Clerical and support services personnel are usually hired on a time card arrangement. This involves processing a form that establishes a record of employment and spells out the essential conditions, including hours per week and the hourly pay rate. Once employment is established, time cards are submitted on the prescribed schedule, and each time card indicates the number of hours for which the person is to be paid.

Personnel must be hired and paid in accordance with the approved budget. Monthly budget reports are invaluable to the administrator as a method of checking that the amounts being paid each employee correspond with the agreements and the amounts that were allocated.

Purchases

The normal procedure for making purchases is to complete a requisition form, which is then followed by a purchase order. Sometimes a different form is used if the purchase is to be made from another division on campus or within the school district, as opposed to a purchase from a supplier or vendor. Figure 9-4 shows a purchase order, and Figure 9-5 is an example of a purchase requisition. The following is a discussion of some guidelines relating to purchasing.

When completing a purchase form, provide all pertinent information, including a complete and correct description of the item(s), the number desired,

PURCHASE ORDER

Date _____   Ship When _____

Ordered ⌐   ⌐
from   Ship to
Vendor └   └

Bill in Duplicate to: Requested by: _____
                                            **Authorized Representative
                                                or Principal**

                               Approved by: _____
                                            Program Director

                               Approved by: _____
                                            Purchasing Director

Account Number	Vendor No.	Purchase Order No.	

Invoice Number	Total Amount	Discount	Partial	Full	Net Amount	Approved for Payment

Quantity Ordered	Quantity Received	Description	Unit Cost	Est. Cost
		TOTAL AMOUNT		

Figure 9-4. Example of a purchase order or requisition. (Courtesy of Alpine School District.)

Date _____

School _____

Street _____

City _____

A/C No. _____

Quantity	Units	P.O. #	Index #	Description	Supp. A/C #	Code	Unit Cost	Total Cost

Approved By: _____   Received By: _____

Figure 9-5. Example of an intraschool district requisition form. (Courtesy of Alpine School District.)

color (if this applies), sizes, model number, and the recommended source of purchase, if there is reason to make such recommendation.

Place orders far enough in advance to make sure that the items are going to be available when needed and to allow the purchasing agent ample opportunity to properly investigate the various sources of purchase. Avoid rush orders because they are inefficient.

Order the right amount. Too much of a certain item in stock occupies valuable storage space, costs interest on the money invested in the items, and presents the risk of potential loss through fire, theft, or deterioration. Conversely, with orders that are too small, you sometimes lose the advantage of bulk rates, pay a high price on the next order due to inflation, and cause decreased efficiency because of frequent purchases and deliveries.

As a manager of public funds, you are obligated to search out and accept the best bargain. Of course, the best bargain is not always the cheapest price. Other important considerations are involved, such as quality of the product, quality of service, and convenience. However, when all else is essentially equal, the vendor who can provide the best price is the one that ought to be selected.

Avoid accepting substitutes by vendors unless you feel satisfied with the product and the price. Also, when items arrive, be sure they go through the proper receiving steps and are properly inventoried.

There are two kinds of organizational plans for purchasing, decentralized and centralized. With the decentralized plan, each school or department makes its own purchases directly from the vendors. The disadvantages of this system include the inability to buy in quantity having too many school personnel dealing directly with vendors, and the lack of control due to numerous people involved in the various aspects of the purchasing process. The greatest advantage is the convenience of quick buying to fill unexpected needs.

With the more commonly used centralized approach, all purchase are made through a central purchasing office. It is economical because it allows quantity buying and involves purchasing specialists who often have more leverage with vendors and experience negotiating with them. For these reasons, the centralized method is usually the better of the two.

Whenever the purchase is large enough to justify it, the normal procedure in purchasing is to obtain bids from different vendors. The purpose in *bid buying* is to obtain the best price possible for the specified product or for some acceptable substitute. In preparing a package for bid, one must provide exact specifications of the materials to be purchased. Incomplete or vague descriptions can contribute to inconsistencies among bids from the different vendors. The description must also indicate whether substitutions will be considered. An organization can consistently save money through the bid-buying process because it creates competition among vendors and affords the purchaser the opportunity of accepting the "best deal."

Often, large organizations have *direct buying* sources from which large purchases are made. Direct buying is making purchases from the wholesaler of the product and eliminating the retailer. Normally a substantial price advantage is gained with this method, while there is the disadvantage of the loss of service and convenience provided by a local retailer. Naturally, retail suppliers oppose this procedure because it eliminates their opportunity to do business. In each situation, the advantages and disadvantages of direct buying must be carefully weighed. If possible, information should be kept current as to which items can be bought from a local retailer at the same price as from the wholesaler. This can help to maintain a good relationship on the local level while saving money on larger items. An organization should not be coerced into doing business with local retailers at a higher cost unless sufficient reasons exist.

COMPUTERIZED BUYING

The computerized budgeting system for acquisition of physical education and athletic supplies is not apt to assist a single school or a small school district. For a large district, however, it can contribute to overall efficiency.

In the following explanation, the Beaverton School district in the state of Oregon is used as the model.

1. The school district established a comprehensive physical education and athletic request catalog by developing a master file with item specifications and estimated costs. This catalog lists the most often requested supplies and equipment for the physical education and athletic program.
2. The catalog is distributed to physical education teachers and athletic coaches through the school principals.
3. Individual coaches and teachers make requests from the catalog by specifying the identification number and quantity of each item. The requests are reviewed and totaled by department for each school.
4. Each school's request is then submitted to the central office where the requests are
   a. Reviewed for accuracy.
   b. Key punched and verified.
   c. Entered into the computer with all data necessary to produce a purchase request.
5. The bid document is reproduced in quantities to supply each vendor with two copies. Vendors indicate bid prices on items as specified. Substitutes must meet original specifications. Bid documents are returned to the central office by bid deadline.
6. Completed bid documents supplied by vendors are key punched to obtain updated vendor file names, addresses, vendor numbers, item numbers, and prices of all submitted items. The completed bid documents are processed to provide a vendor bid report, which lists by vendor each item in ascending bid price.
7. Selection is made of successful bids by product and unit price from the bid report.
8. Itemized purchase orders are produced and processed, and when the orders are filled, inventory records are established.

BUDGET REPORTS AND ADJUSTMENTS

In order to manage a budget effectively, it is necessary to receive periodic budget reports from the financial services division. Normally, these reports are provided on a monthly basis. The reports should include all of the financial transactions that have occurred during the reporting period.

The report can serve two purposes: as a check to make sure that only the correct entries have been recorded against the budget; with each report, the administrator can evaluate whether the expenditures are on the proper time schedule or whether the rate of spending is too fast. The budget must fit the approved plan, both in amount and kind of expenditures and the time frame over which the expenditures are made.

Each budget report should be carefully reviewed soon after it is received. Also, the report ought to be kept for a reasonable time for possible future reference.

Fortunately, the great majority of educational organizations have adopted a system of computerized (data process) budgeting. Among the advantages to this approach are the following:

1. Accuracy is increased and errors are more easily detected.
2. The budget report forms are simple and easy to understand.
3. The process is both fast and economical.
4. Numerous copies of a report can be produced, which can be convenient and timesaving.
5. The financial management process can be streamlined by eliminating certain steps.
6. By-products of the process assist in other aspects of administration, such as short cuts in purchasing procedures, improved inventory tracking, and availability of computer on-line budget information.

Sometimes it is necessary to transfer funds from one category to another, although this is not recommended as a common practice. For example, suppose a certain amount of money to pay the salary of a full-time secretary is in the staff salary category. Part way through the year, the secretary leaves, and a decision is made to finish out the year with part-time student secretaries. In this case, the remainder of the money would have to be transferred from the staff salary category to the student wage category. Ordinarily, educational organizations have a special form on which to process budget adjustments (Figure 9-6).

AUDITS

Financial audits are part of the normal procedures of almost all organizations. The audit usually involves two aspects: financial *procedures* and financial *expenditures*.

Many people think of audits in a negative sense, but this should usually not be the case. An audit should be a useful procedure for both the larger organization and the budgetary unit for which it is performed.

For the larger organization, the audit helps to monitor correct procedures and expenditures and to identify deviations or irregularities, if any exist. For the budgetary unit, an audit can be an educational experience for both the administrator and others in the unit. Recommended procedures and guidelines relative to expenditures that might otherwise remain vague can be made clear. An audit usually has a sharpening effect on the financial process, which contributes to overall efficiency.

There are *routine* audits and *special* audits. Routine audits occur periodically for the reasons just explained. They are part of the overall financial procedures

From _____ To: Budget Office

_____   _____

BUDGET ADJUSTMENT REQUEST
For School Year 198__-8__

I hereby request a transfer of funds for the following budget accounts:

DEPARTMENT	ACCOUNT NUMBER	INCREASE	DECREASE
_____	_____	$ _____	$ _____
_____	_____	_____	_____
_____	_____	_____	_____
_____	_____	_____	_____
_____	_____	_____	_____
_____	_____	_____	_____
_____	_____	_____	_____
_____	_____	_____	_____
_____	_____	_____	_____
_____	_____	_____	_____
	TOTAL	$ _____	$ _____

Approvals (authorized signatures):   Date:

_____   _____

_____   _____

Figure 9-6. A form for transferring funds from one budget category to another.

of most organizations. A special audit may be initiated by someone higher up in the organization or by the unit administrator. One reason for a special audit is to investigate a suspicion or accusation about misuse of funds or improper procedures. Also, special audits are sometimes done in preparing for a change of administrative personnel or reorganization of the unit. An audit should be viewed as a process that will enhance financial management and reassure that the financial records and procedures are correct.

FINANCIAL PITFALLS

Some people get into pitfalls because of either carelessness or dishonesty. The following guidelines for avoiding pitfalls should be helpful:

1. Keep adequate records of financial agreements and transactions. The following paper work must be kept on file: (a) personnel contracts or other employment agreements; (b) purchase requests; (c) a record of the essential information submitted on time cards; (d) contracts for athletic contests; and (e) memos, letters, and other written agreements that explain financial terms. It can be embarrassing and awkward to be unable to produce the necessary paper work in support of financial commitments or transactions.
2. Money can be collected only by designated personnel. This includes the sale of tickets and collection of student fees, among others. Those authorized to collect funds usually have clear instructions on how to handle and process the funds; and if much money is involved, the individual is bonded. Persons unauthorized to collect money ought to avoid doing so.
3. All collected funds should be deposited in a timely manner in the appropriate account, so that an official record is made and the funds, in turn, are utilized by the approved procedure and subject to financial audit.
4. Avoid having an unauthorized flow of petty cash, and if you have an authorized petty cash account, be sure it is tightly managed in accordance with correct procedures.
5. Avoid having cash in obvious places and never leave cash unsecured where it offers the potential for theft. In cases where much money is collected, deposits should be made frequently.
6. Follow the prescribed financial procedures of the organization in *all* cases, and have financial records subject to regular audit. Any deviation from this has real potential for getting an administrator into difficulty.

REFERENCES AND RECOMMENDED READINGS

1. AAHPERD: Budget Process. Maryland, AAHPERD Publications, 1990.
2. American Management Association: Financial Management. New York, 1990.
3. Brigham, E.: Financial Management: Theory and Practice, 3rd Ed. Hinsdale, IL, Dryden Press, 1985.
4. Bucher, C.A.: Administration of Physical Education and Athletic Programs, 9th Ed. St. Louis, C.V. Mosby, 1987, pp. 270–293.
5. Frost, R.B., Lockhart, B.D., and Marshall, S.J.: Administration of Physical Education and Athletics, 3rd Ed. Dubuque, IA, William C. Brown, pp. 217–230.
6. Horine, L.: Administration of Physical Education and Sport Programs, 2nd Ed. Dubuque, IA, William C. Brown, 1991.
7. Schick, A.: The road to PPB: The stages of budget reform. Public Administration Review, 25:253, 1966.
8. Van Horne, J.C.: Financial Management and Policy, 4th Ed. Englewood Cliffs, NJ, Prentice-Hall, 1986.

Chapter *10*

PUBLIC RELATIONS

It has been said that two forces are primarily responsible for social change: public opinion and the law, which is dependent on public opinion. This idea can serve as a useful guideline to school personnel in regard to the importance of public relations.

Public relations can be emphasized or neglected and can be positive or negative in terms of results; but, it cannot be avoided. Pertinent questions are how extensive the results will be and to what degree they will be favorable or disfavorable.

School personnel spend the public's money, while molding the public's most precious possession (the children) into products that must meet the public's approval. In view of this, members of the public have a right to know what is being done with the money and with their children. If the public feels dissatisfied and nonsupportive regarding the efforts of the schools, then the public has a right to bring about the desired changes. This is one of the basic reasons for the necessity of open and forthright communication between school personnel and the public. Without it, a school cannot serve its purpose well in a democratic society. Public relations should begin with the golden premise that the public has the right to know everything about the school system, and not just what school personnel want the public to know.

Successful business establishments have leaders who have learned to work effectively with the public. Although educational organizations have been generally effective in their public relations, educators have given less attention to it than is sometimes needed. Through public relations, educators can improve their effectiveness, thus winning broader and more favorable public support for their programs.

Those school personnel involved with athletics and physical education have greater public relations opportunities and responsibilities than most other school employees. For example, athletic events are of particular interest to the public and attract a relatively large amount of fan support and media coverage. The public invests considerably more in physical education and athletics than in other areas of education by way of facilities, including gymnasiums, swimming pools, playing fields, tennis courts, stadiums, racquetball courts, and the like. If adequate facilities of this nature are to be provided, the programs must be good enough to justify such a large expenditure, and the public has to be convinced of the value of physical education and athletics. They must be willing to pay the bill.

As part of public relations, it should be remembered that selling is not limited to people called salesmen, for we all have something to sell. To succeed, we must sell ourselves and our products well. In this sense, every teacher and coach in the organization should be involved.

DEFINITION AND SCOPE

People frequently interpret public relations to mean only radio, television, and newspaper coverage. The media is certainly one important aspect of public relations, but an overall public relations effort is much more inclusive. For example, in a school setting, public relations includes at least the following: (1) relations among school personnel, including both students and employees; (2) relations with parents; and (3) relations with the public in general. The avenues through which an effective public relations program is launched include (1) the mass media (radio, television, and newspapers); (2) direct conversation (face-to-face or by telephone); (3) written communications (letters, notices, reports, bulletins, and report cards); (4) the perception and image of the program that is communicated by students and faculty; and (5) the effective conduct of educational demonstrations, athletic contests, and other public events. All of this can be summarized by saying that public relations involves everything that influences the image of the school in the minds of the total public.

Organized public relations may range from the "hard-sell" campaigns of business or politics to the "soft" approach of nonprofit organizations and educational institutions.

An effective public relations program can be surprisingly simple. It need not contain "show business," gimmicks, or dramatic events. It can be a well-planned, normal, ongoing exchange of useful information among school employees, students, and members of the public. It should be a naturally integrated part of the school's overall efforts. This does not mean that there is never a need for special emphasis. Sometimes there is a particular reason to inform the public about certain issues or matters of special concern or to convince the public of a new and useful idea or particular need.

Public relations can be thought of as both an attitude and a process. As an attitude, it involves realistic optimism and positive thinking. As a process, it involves open and effective communication, with emphasis on the good and the positive. The purpose of public relations is to bring about a harmony of understanding between any group and the public it serves and upon whose good will it depends.

PURPOSES AND IMPORTANCE

Public relations in education has two main aspects: sponsoring excellent programs and effectively communicating that fact to the public. Certainly, the first aspect is more important, but both aspects deserve adequate attention. Among the specific purposes of school public relations are the following:

1. To inform the public as to the work and accomplishments of the school.
2. To establish confidence in the schools.
3. To rally adequate support for the educational programs.
4. To develop awareness of the importance of education.
5. To improve the partnership that should exist among the schools, the students, the parents and other members of the public.
6. To correct any misunderstandings that occur as to the aims and activities of the schools.

Public relations are pertinent to all areas of human activity—education, religion, business, politics, military, and government. It can be a powerful force which can sometimes make the difference between the success or failure of an institution. A good public relations program is not haphazard; it must be well planned and wisely implemented.

Although official polls show that the great majority of Americans are basically satisfied with the schools their children attend, they are still unwilling to give the level of support the schools need. Educational programs could be better if the public would channel more support to them. It is a dismal fact that people spend more for tobacco and twice as much for liquor each year as for education. Apparently, the tobacco and liquor industries do a much better job than the schools in terms of public relations.[4]

METHODS

An effective public relations program must have a strong element of consistency. It should involve an ongoing effort that keeps ahead of potential problems, as opposed to a crisis or "brush fire" approach. In public relations, "an ounce of care is better than a pound of cure."

Straightforward honesty is important, and the consequences of any amount of dishonesty are usually disastrous in terms of public relations.

A well-balanced public relations program includes a variety of approaches, several of which are described in this section. Of course, the total public relations effort extends far beyond these methods. It involves every kind of information and impression given to the public by school personnel, whether intentional or unintentional.

Parent-teacher *conferences* offer one of the best potentials for public relations. The effectiveness of this method depends largely on the nature of the conferences and how well they are conducted.

Another valuable approach is to *take students out* into the community on field trips, special interest tours, and educational visits to museums, historical sites, industrial and manufacturing plants, and the like.

One of the most useful means of public relations is through *handouts and notices* to students and parents. These can range all the way from report cards to informational materials and notices of programs and events.

It is important to publish periodic *reports* relative to the school's well-being (financial and otherwise) or about the personnel, programs, or special achievements. Reports about school deficiencies and special problems that need public assistance also can be helpful.

Report cards sent home to parents that include more description than the simple basics can serve as a good method of communicating important information about student achievement as related to expectations. Sometimes, certain other information can be appropriately enclosed with the report cards. This causes the information to receive more attention than if distributed separately.

Student performances on *youth fitness tests* are compared to state and national norms can be highly meaningful to the public. The awarding of fitness certificates and other forms of special recognition can be helpful.

Exhibits, demonstrations, and *open houses* have been used successfully in physical education programs. Parents like to see their children participate. Whenever demonstrations of this kind are given, they should portray interesting aspects of the school program rather than something "dreamed up" for the entertainment of the public.

Information can be transmitted to parents by use of mimeographed *bulletins* that are carried home by students. Such bulletins should contain pertinent information that is written in an appealing manner, so that they will have a positive image and parents will be motivated to read them.

Well kept *bulletin boards* can serve an excellent purpose. Useful information can be communicated through bulletin board displays.

Trophy cases are useful, particularly in connection with athletics. Much interest and pride can be instilled through the proper display of trophies.

Face-to-face *conversation* is one of the most effective implements of public relations. This can take place on the playing field and in the gymnasium with students, and on some occasions, with parents and other members of the public at athletic events, PTA meetings, service clubs, church meetings, and other such events.

In addition to worthy news items that are routinely provided to the media, special *feature stories* can be developed about new programs, outstanding teachers, or unique student achievement.

Valuable information for use by the media can be obtained from state and national organizations. For example, every state has a Department of Education with one or more *specialists* in the area of health, physical education, school recreation, and athletics. This state agency is capable of providing useful information in the form of news releases, news letters, and information bulletins. Certain national organizations can also be helpful. For example, the AAHPERD has a special public relations program known as PEPI (Physical Education Public Information), which provides a constant flow of information to the state PEPI representatives who, in turn, have the responsibility of providing it to the media and/or sending it on to local school personnel. Also, the President's Council on Physical Fitness provides facts and statistics that are of interest to the public.

Numerous *films* can be acquired on free loan or at reasonable rental rates from such agencies as the AAHPERD, the President's Council on Physical Fitness, the Athletic Institute, and West Glen Films at 565 Fifth Avenue, New York, NY. To give an example, the AAHPERD has two highly useful films entitled, "All The Self There Is" and "Every Child a Winner." These films illustrate the value of physical education in the total development of children and youth. Films like these can help members of the public better understand the objectives, values, and concepts of physical education. The other organizations mentioned have films on a variety of subjects.

Special opportunities for public relations exist in connection with *athletics*. These include the following:

1. The particular manner with which athletic events are presented: public address procedures, programs, adequacy of seating, ushering, cheerleading, half-time performances, and the conduct of coaches and athletes.
2. Athletic brochures: content, design, distribution.
3. Newspaper, radio, and television coverage: amount, type, and content.
4. Booster club activities: a booster club can be helpful if it has valid and clear objectives and is well managed. Conversely, a booster club that is not well managed can become a problem.
5. Promotion and ticket sales, and provision of parking privileges.
6. Public appearances by coaches at banquets, on television shows, radio interviews, and other public settings.
7. Awards and award presentations.

WHO SHOULD BE INVOLVED?

Some people think that public relations is the responsibility of a specialist who can give overall direction to the public relations effort and assist others in contributing their fair share; but a public relations specialist or even a staff of specialists cannot do the job alone.

Every school employee has a public relations responsibility. Each one, whether a coach, secretary, janitor, administrator, lunch room employee, or whatever, has the potential either for presenting a positive image and generating good will, or for doing the opposite. Each faculty member has public relations opportunities in connection with any particular phase of the program, and each one needs to contribute to the larger public relations effort of the school.

The better the employees are informed about matters of particular interest in public relations, the better prepared they are to give accurate information and to foster a positive image of the school. Well-informed employees can be a great asset.

The idea that "quality builds quality" applies well in education. The first consideration of quality should be personnel. If a school is staffed with high quality personnel, they will build quality into the other aspects of the program. An administrator should consider the public relations qualifications of each prospective employee, and this should play its rightful role in the selection of those to be hired.

Each individual in the profession has a responsibility to improve the public image of the profession. This can be partly accomplished by each one giving attention to the following:

1. Are you well groomed and attractively dressed or do you belong to the sloppy sweatshirt group?
2. Check your personal habits. Do you smoke in front of your students or anywhere in school? Are you seen in local bars? Do you use profanity? Have you let yourself become flabby and overweight through lack of exercise and self-control?
3. What about the quality of your teaching? Do you have your courses

planned in advance for the semester, with carefully planned objectives you want your students to reach, or do you improvise from day to day and on the spur of the moment?

4. Do you treat your students with kindness and understanding, but at the same time maintain discipline?

5. Are you well-read, or do you find the scholarly life a bore? Are you seen at concerts and public meetings in addition to athletic contests and other school events?

In addition to the public relations of employees, students can be effective ambassadors of the school. How they represent the school and what they say about it certainly has impact on the school's image. Focus is brought on certain students because of outstanding achievements in academics or athletics or because of popularity or social adeptness. These students have a greater than normal influence on the school's image.

Often, school personnel, programs, and procedures become topics of discussion in the home. The impressions communicated by the students have a significant influence on the minds of the parents. Parents view the attitudes of their children as reliable indicators of the success of the school programs. Parents also become emotionally involved and will, therefore, often accept their child's attitude at face value without seriously questioning the validity of it. For these and other reasons, the first front on which the public relations battle should be fought is the classroom. If the students believe in the program, the personnel, and the procedures, they will be a major factor in maintaining a high image and substantial public support.

The idea that "people listen better when others toot your horn" is an important consideration. Even with the same set of facts, what you say about your own program has less impact than what someone else says. Therefore, it is often useful to involve nonschool personnel in public relations efforts. For example, it could be beneficial to have a news article by a prominent physician about the health instruction program, the need for encouragement in the home of good health practices, or for emphasis on physical fitness. Sometimes, if a certain prominent citizen says that a facility or program is needed, the majority of others in the community will accept what is said.

A school-community public relations council can be a highly useful instrument if it functions properly. If can be a valuable source of ideas and can help implement them. It can serve as a barometer to measure effectiveness and also provide useful feedback for evaluation of the public relations effort.

The school public relations program depends on many people, including employees, students, and nonschool personnel. It is a complex effort that requires careful planning and continuous attention.

IDENTIFYING A PUBLIC

A public is a group of people who are drawn together by common interests, are located in a specific geographic area, or are characterized by some other common feature, including age, religion, sex, occupation, race, nationality, politics, income, social status, affiliation, or educational background. The more that can be known about a particular public, the easier it is to plan an effective public relations approach.[5]

In order to gather information about a public, various techniques may be used: surveys, questionnaires, opinion polls, interviews, and face-to-face conversations. Prevalent opinions in a particular public are often the result of influence in earlier life, but they are also influenced by more recent experiences and by the mass media.

Until recently, each neighborhood and/or community had its own school. The neighborhood school concept enhanced parental awareness and support. However, recent trends, including school consolidation, civil rights actions (busing of students to other neighborhoods), and other demographic and sociologic changes have altered the neighborhood school idea in many localities. This makes it difficult for school administrators to identify the public with whom they need to communicate, and it makes their public less accessible.

The several publics that must be considered in the public relations effort include: the present student body, past students (alumni), school employees (teachers, administrators, and others), parents, and other members of the general public. The methods of communicating effectively with these different publics vary both in content and procedure. It is important for the schools to have a sound plan that gives adequate attention to all segments of the population.

Sometimes the target group for certain information constitutes only a portion of the larger public, such as athletic fans, members of the PTA, particular ethnic groups, or parents of children of a certain age. It is important to define the population that the public relations effort is pointed toward. The "target" approach can greatly improve effectiveness.

COMMUNICATION

The art or act of communicating is one of our most effective measures for learning and it is of utmost importance in administration. Communication provides the thread that binds an organization together by ensuring common understanding. Effective communication is essential in good public relations; persuasive communication can sway or influence people's opinions.

Chapter 9 contains a major section about communication. Certain aspects of that section apply to the importance of communication in public relations; therefore, that section should be reviewed in connection with the present topic.

Listening is as much a part of good public relations as talking, and for some, listening is much harder. Listening can be highly informative; and it represents a show of respect for another person's point of view. Unfortunately, many people are better talkers than listeners.

Among public relations specialists, the following "Six C's" of communication have become popular. They can be effectively applied in the field of education, as well as in other fields.

Content. Communication should accurately state the intended message as clearly as possible. Correct content is fundamental to effective communication.

Clarity. Communication should be stated in a manner that will be easily understood. This will reduce the chances for misinterpretation, misunderstanding, and confusion.

Credibility. Communication should be based on accurate information from appropriate sources.

Context. Communication should fit the situation or the environment. It must be appropriate in terms of kind, style, and content.

Continuity and Consistency. Communication should flow with consistency and regularity in order to maintain open channels and mutual trust.

Channels. Defined and appropriate channels of communication should be used.

NEWS STORIES

News stories, whether in written or oral form, are generally of four types: pre-event, post-event, feature, or editorial. All these can be used effectively in the school's public relations program, and each one should receive ample consideration.

News stories are often generated by direct contact with news personnel. Ready access to useful photographs can often result in the publication of pictures along with printed material. Photographs attract special attention to news articles, and of themselves they can be highly communicative.

To establish good working relationships with the news media, consider the application of the following guidelines:

1. School personnel should become acquainted with the newspeople, and the newspeople should be encouraged to become acquainted with the school programs.
2. School personnel should become aware that a good story sent to the wrong department may be lost, since distinct differences exist between departments that handle sports news, political news, or social stories.
3. Coaches should have newsworthy information available for ready reference when they talk with news personnel regarding their sports.
4. The newsperson has an obligation to the public to give objective and accurate news coverage. Teachers, coaches, and administrators should expect to get the bitter with the sweet and should not consider it a personal attack.
5. Newspeople should be treated fairly. A story should not be given freely to other newspeople when a particular one has worked hard to obtain it. If both evening and morning news reports are available in the same locale, the big stories should be released at alternate times so as to ensure fair coverage. Dated releases may be used to achieve this end.
6. The attempt to "buy" favorable stories with gifts and favors beyond the usual and accepted practice should be avoided.
7. Careless and indiscreet statements to news personnel should be avoided. They often cause both embarrassment and damage.
8. Keep in mind that reporters have strict deadlines. Timely information must reach the media before deadlines to ensure that it will be included in a story. If the deadline is missed, the media may choose to forego the story rather than run it a day late.

PUBLICITY

Publicity means attracting public attention or public acclaim. It involves the attraction of public attention toward something such as a person, an event, or a program. It is usually done for promotional reasons. Publicity is one important aspect of public relations, but it is not synonymous with public relations. Normally, competitive athletics receives much more publicity than other school programs. Consequently, the publicity about athletic events is significant in the school's public relations effort. But, there are other activities and events that warrant publicity, including dance concerts, physical education demonstrations, and field days.

Publicity can be as unfavorable as favorable. It can be either overdone or underemphasized. It can accomplish the intent or miss the mark. Publicity can be done in the form of paid advertisements or through the reporting of newsworthy items and events.

HANDLING COMPLAINTS

Every organization that deals with the public will receive some complaints. This is especially true with education that involves people's children and is financed by public funds. A complaint involves one of two circumstances; a weakness or fault that justifies the complaint or a misunderstanding. A complaint left unresolved results in a continuing problem, one that is likely to grow and lead to other complaints.

From the public relations point of view, complaints should be handled in an open-minded and gracious manner. The one dealing with the complainer should avoid being defensive and abrupt. Try to understand his point of view and help him to understand yours. If the complaint is justified, then admit it and make the necessary corrections. If it is not justified, help the complainer to recognize that. This kind of objective approach will help soothe feelings and win support.

PRINCIPLES

1. A school system cannot avoid public relations. Relations with the public will exist in some form, good, bad, or indifferent.
2. The public relations program should be clearly defined, including purposes, procedures, responsibilities, and expected results. The better the program is understood, the better chance it has for success.
3. The public has a right to information pertaining to the school and all of its various programs. Educators should try to avoid operating in a world of their own, isolated from the public, to whom they owe their existence. However, it is a fact that the school officials must stay in control of the program and reserve the right to make the decisions and manage the program in a highly professional manner.
4. A vital function of public relations is to establish an open channel so that the public will be sufficiently informed to properly influence decisions.
5. While good public relations requires a well-conceived plan, flexibility and adaptability are necessary. It is important to adjust to changing circumstances and also to capitalize on unexpected opportunities.

6. The public is entitled to know the truth about school policies, finances, and programs. Hidden weaknesses fester and sooner or later erupt. If granted full knowledge of the facts, the public can often help in the solution of problems.
7. The way something is done is often as important as what is done. The particular approach can make a great deal of difference as to how a decision or a circumstance is accepted.
8. The most fundamental aspect of good public relations is a superior program for which there is absolutely no substitute. Educators should not expect public support of programs that produce inferior results.
9. Public education is a form of social institution, which is financed and maintained by the total public, not just those with children of school age. Therefore, educational programs must be designed and managed with the benefit of all of the people in mind.
10. One excellent means of public relations is through the students. Parents are especially interested in the attitudes and well-being of their children. A teacher may have 200 students in a day but is still Jane's coach or Billy's teacher in the minds of the parents.
11. Public relations whitewash wears off sooner or later, and then the facts become embarrassingly obvious.
12. Every well-planned public relations program is pointed toward a defined population. The population often has sub-populations who deserve special attention.
13. News stories and other reported information ought to be factual, relevant, free from bias, and appealing.
14. The public relations program should be a continuous, integrated phase of the overall school effort. Poorly planned, hit-and-miss efforts are only partially successful at best.
15. One of the most effective public relations approaches it person-to-person, teacher to student, student to parent, or teacher to citizen.
16. Some aspects of public relations need funding. If funding is inadequate, the success of the program is jeopardized. Adequate funding is just as necessary for public relations as for other aspects of the program.
17. Effective public relations specialists usually stay in the background instead of seeking the limelight; they keep abreast of the factors that affect the program, develop a wide acquaintance, and make helpful contacts.
18. A highly reputable image can serve several useful purposes, of which one is public relations.
19. A sense of humor, especially with some of it directed at yourself, can be helpful in public relations. Good, wholesome humor is a universal language.
20. Public relations, like other phases of the school program, requires both near- and long-term comprehensive planning.
21. School personnel who make sharp or abrasive statements or who criticize frequently or react defensively must gain control of these bad characteristics in order to become positive forces in public relations.
22. Selling is not limited to people called salesmen, for we all have something to sell, and in order to succeed we must sell ourselves and our products well.

EVALUATION

Regular, critical evaluation of the overall public relations effort is a method by which success is determined and improvements are made. This should include an ongoing process of error detection and correction. It helps to ask yourself searching questions about your public relations approach and give yourself honest answers. Clearly defined public relations goals that are attainable can serve as measures of success.

The school public relations program must be honest in terms of both intent and implementation. It must be continuous, positive, comprehensive, and sensitive to the particular public, and must communicate information that is useful and easily understood. The identification of weaknesses in any of these elements is good reason to adjust the public relations approach.

REFERENCES AND RECOMMENDED READINGS

1. AAHPERD: Citizen Survey Process. Waldorf, MD, AAHPERD Publications, 1986.
2. Frost, R.B., Lockhart, B.D., and Marshall, S.J.: Administration of Physical Education and Athletics, 3rd Ed. Dubuque, IA, William C. Brown, 1988, pp. 285–323.
3. Horine, L.: Administration of Physical Education and Sport Programs, 2nd Ed. Dubuque, IA, William C. Brown, 1991, chapter 10.
4. Jones, J.W.: Building Public Confidence in Your Schools: A Source Book of Proven Public Relations Practices. Arlington, VA, National School Public Relations Association, 1978.
5. Marston, J.: Modern Public Relations, 2nd Ed. New York, McGraw-Hill, 1985.
6. Nelson, J.E.: Communications—the key to public relations. JOPERD, 57(4):64, 1986.
7. Pangrazi, R.P.: A public relations dynamo. JOPERD, 53(9):52, 1982.
8. Rollof, B.D.: Public relations—objectives for physical education. JOPERD, 56(3):69, 1985.

Chapter *11*

LEGAL ASPECTS

Murphy's Law states "anything that can go wrong will go wrong." Some consider this to be a negative point of view, and not the attitude that should prevail. As a safety measure, however, constant awareness of Murphy's Law can help an administrator remain alert to potential pitfalls.

In a democracy, every person has a right to justice and fair treatment under the law. The growing concern for individual rights has taken precedence over the traditional concept of *sovereign immunity*. Teachers, coaches, and administrators are no longer held immune from liability under the law simply because they are employed in an educational system run by the state. As a result, educational personnel are obligated to pay particular attention to the protection, health, and welfare of students. This chapter is designed to help the teacher, coach, and administrator to better understand the legal aspects that pertain particularly to physical education and athletics.

Although physical education and athletics are among the more hazardous of the teaching areas, there is no reason to be apprehensive about providing a well-rounded program of meaningful activities. Generally, the courts are aware of the inherent risks in these activities and acknowledge the fact that the potential values exceed the risk expectancy, thus viewing most risks as being within the parameters of "reasonable risk." It is normally assumed that the programs are based on adequate knowledge of student needs and are conducted by competent and prudent instructors. One must recognize, however, that liability suits against administrators, teachers, and coaches are definite possibilities. Therefore, such personnel must (1) be well informed about the laws that pertain to educators, (2) use adequate caution and control in all the activities within their responsibility, and (3) always try to act wisely and prudently. The teacher/coach can meet legal obligations by carrying out the responsibilities of the job in the correct manner.

SELECTED LEGAL TERMS*

The following are definitions of some common legal terms, which may be encountered by educators and administrators in dealing with the legal aspects of managing physical education and athletic programs.

Act of God	Unavoidable incident due to forces of nature which could not have been foreseen or prevented.
Assault	Unlawful force directed at another person with the obvious intent and capacity to do harm. Assault may cause physical harm (criminal assault) or result in mental or emotional stress and apprehension (civil assault).
Assumption of risk	Participation or involvement in an activity or situation where an element of risk is inherent. Voluntary participation can be interpreted as an acceptance of risk. In physical education and athletics, an element of reasonable risk is normally assumed by the participant and his parents.
Attractive nuisance	A facility or situation that attracts participation and is hazardous. Examples are unsecured gymnastics equipment or trampolines, an unsupervised swimming pool, or playground equipment in poor repair. Whether a situation would be legally declared an attractive nuisance is influenced by the laws of the particular state, the age and competence of the injured person, and the various circumstances surrounding the incident.
Battery	Physical assault, resulting in injury.
Causative factor	The situation or factor that was obviously the main cause of an injury or incident.
Civil law	Civil action implies a noncriminal infringement upon the rights of a person, agency, corporation, or other. Tort and contract disputes are examples of civil suits. Civil law is different from criminal law.
Common law	That body of governing principles and rules of action derived from past practices, customs, and traditions.
Comparative negligence	A situation in which the injured party has contributed to his own injury by some type of negligence. This differs from contributory negli-

---

* Much of the specialized legal information in this chapter was furnished by Professor Linda Carpenter, Ed.D., J.D., of Brooklyn College.

	gence, because rather than acting as a complete block to legal recovery, the injured party's negligence simply reduces the recovery by a percentage equal to his comparative negligence.
Contract	A promise or set of promises. Three elements must exist to have a contract: an offer, an acceptance, and consideration (something of value contributed by each side such as money for a service rendered).
Contributory negligence	Applicable when an individual's action was not the primary cause of negligence but a contributing factor to the negligent act. A secondary or indirect cause of negligence.
Criminal law	That portion of the law which involves crime or illegal wickedness. A criminal action involves the breaking of a law, as in theft, battery, perjury, or murder. Different than civil law.
Damages	Monetary compensation awarded by the court in payment for loss or injury incurred.
Defendant	The party against whom relief or recovery is sought in a law suit. Opposite of the plaintiff.
Due process of law	The right of notice, the opportunity to be heard and defended in orderly court proceedings, and the right of appeal.
Equal protection of the law	The right of equal treatment by the law and law enforcement agencies for all persons under similar circumstances.
Foreseeability	The individual responsible for the negligent act could have and reasonably should have foreseen the danger that existed.
Immunity	Freedom or protection from legal action. Sovereign immunity refers to the protection of the government or the ruling body against possible suit or blame. It is based on the concept that "the king (or ruler) can do no wrong."
Injunction	A prohibitive ruling issued by a court directing a person or agency to refrain from performing a specific act.
In loco parentis	The purpose of acting in the place of a parent or guardian. It may be complete or partial. Teachers are considered to be in loco parentis to students during the time the students are under their supervision. The degree of this condition is influenced by the age of the students and the nature of the school.
Liability	Being responsible for a negligent act or other tort; having legal responsibility that was not fulfilled and resulted in injury.

Liability insurance	Insurance policies that provide protection against financial loss from liability claims.
Litigation	A lawsuit that is in process.
Malfeasance	An act that is illegal or improper and should not have been performed.
Mandatory legislation	Enacted legislation that must be observed. Opposite from *permissive* legislation.
Misfeasance	An act that may be legal, but was done in an improper manner.
Negligence	Not exercising the care or following the procedures a person of ordinary prudence would under similar circumstances. It can take the form of commission or omission.
Nonfeasance	Failing to perform an act that should have been done.
Permissive legislation	Legislation that legalizes an action but does not require or mandate it. Opposite from mandatory legislation.
Plaintiff	One who seeks to enforce the law by bringing legal action against another party. Opposite of the defendant.
Precedent	The utilization of a previous court decision in judging a similar court action with comparable circumstances.
Proprietary function	As pertaining to schools, a function different from the normal educational process, usually of a profit-making nature. Athletic contests that produce gate receipts are often classified as proprietary functions. Other examples are fund-raising events and renting or leasing out of facilities. It is the opposite of governmental functions.
Proximate cause	A situation or factor that was the cause or contributing cause of an injury or incident.
Prudent person	One who acts in a careful, discreet, and judicious manner in view of the particular circumstances.
Respondent superior	The responsibility of an employer for the negligent acts of his employees.
Statutory law	Law governed by statutes enacted by legislative bodies.
Tort	A civil wrong or injustice independent of a contract, which produces an injury or damage to another person or to property.
Wanton and willful act	An act against another person committed deliberately or with reckless disregard for safety.

TORT LAWS

The term *tort* is used to classify a group of civil wrongs, as opposed to criminal wrongs, which involve a violation of a specific law for which fines or imprisonment might be imposed. Negligence is a major tort; other torts are trespass, nuisance, and defamation.[5]

Disputes about contracts, although they fall within the category of civil rather than criminal wrongs, are not classified as torts. A person entering into a contract voluntarily accepts certain duties or responsibility, the violation of which might make the individual liable for legal action, is not taken voluntarily. Other characteristics, of torts are the following: (1) Torts are prosecuted by the injured person rather than by law enforcement officials. (2) An act may be both a tort and a crime, but not all torts are crimes. (3) To prove a tort, the injured party must demonstrate by a preponderance (more than 50%) of the evidence that the claim is justified. This last characteristic differs from a criminal case, in which proof beyond a reasonable doubt is required.

Under tort law, a person who causes injury to another, for which a legal liability exists, is frequently answerable to the injured person in money damages, although other forms of reparation are also used. People are not liable in tort for every accidental injury; a person is only liable for a tort when that person intentionally or negligently causes or contributes to an injury. The injured person (plaintiff) must prove that the injuring person (defendant) was the "proximate cause" of the plaintiff's injury. Proximate cause is an elastic legal term. Sometimes, to be considered the proximate cause, a cause need not be the immediate, or even the primary, cause only a contributing factor in producing the harm.

Tort law is common law or judge-made law. It has its most basic foundation in the concept of *fault*. For a fuller explanation of the concept of tort law, the reader should refer to one of the education law books in the references and recommended readings.

CONDITIONS OF NEGLIGENCE

One of the most important areas of tort law that an administrator should understand is negligence. In the legal sense, negligence is the failure to perform one's duties at the level expected of a responsible person under particular circumstances. Good intentions alone are no safeguard, because negligence denotes an unintentional failure to do what is reasonably expected. The fact that a teacher or coach is certified by the state indicates a level of expected behavior. When one falls short of these expectations and this failure contributes to damage to another person, the teacher can be declared negligent. Often, negligence is difficult to prove, and many individuals who are inclined to sue become discouraged when the legal grounds are weak or insufficient. In order for a person to be declared negligent, the following elements must exist:[6]

1. The defendant must have a *duty toward the plaintiff*. Teachers, supervisors, and administrators clearly have a duty toward the students entrusted to their care. In most states, a person does not have a legal duty toward a stranger, even when the stranger is in dire need of help. To encourage aid when needed, some states have passed "Good Samaritan" laws.
2. The plaintiff must have been *harmed* by the tort or wrong committed by the defendant. This could be in the form of property damage, personal injury, or damage to one's character or reputation.

3. The individual having a "duty" must have breached that duty by an *act of omission* (nonfeasance) or an *act of commission* (misfeasance). This means that a person who does nothing when something should have been done is often as liable as one who responds incorrectly.
4. The breach of duty must have been directly related to the damage done by the plaintiff. In other words, the breach of duty was the proximate cause of the damage.

These four elements pertain to legal negligence, and all of them must exist in order to justify legal action. Sometimes nonlegal negligence is committed by a teacher, but if no tort results (due to the lack of one or more of the four elements, such as no "harm") the teacher's behavior might be the rightful subject of administrative action but is not a matter for the courts.

SITUATIONS OF POTENTIAL NEGLIGENCE

Several conditions are frequently found in teaching or coaching situations that, if unattended, could injure a student and cause the teacher to be guilty of negligence. It is important to understand these potential hazards and deal effectively with them.

Faulty Equipment

Acting both as instructor and supervisor, the teacher or coach must prevent students from using defective equipment. For example, requiring or even permitting students to climb a dangerously frayed rope would be grounds for negligence, if the rope should break and cause injury. The same would be true of permitting students to use faulty gymnastic apparatus, a trampoline with a damaged bed, or defective playground equipment.

In addition to the duty to prevent the use of defective equipment, the duty exists to periodically inspect the equipment with the intent of discovering any defects.

Attractive Nuisances

Hazardous equipment that may attract students, such as bows and arrows, climbing ropes, trampolines, and scuba equipment must be safely secured or made inoperative in order that students not be attracted to use it in the absence of proper supervision. A swimming pool that is unsecured or lacking supervision is an attractive nuisance.

Inadequate Supervision

Negligence could result from permitting people to swim in an outdoor area during a lightning storm, permitting children to play in an area too close to traffic where one might spontaneously dart in front of an automobile, or permitting play on a field where the surface is too hard and rough or otherwise unsuitable for the particular activity.

Poor organization can also constitute negligence. When students are required, encouraged, or even permitted to participate in a school activity, a reasonable amount of organization and order is expected.

Other Hazardous Situations

Poor selection of activities can contribute to negligence where there is a likelihood of collisions among participants, or inappropriate rough-and-tumble or tackle activities. Inadequate provision for individual differences, as in a mismatch in a combative activity, can also result in a problem.

Lack of provision for protective equipment and procedures could be declared an act of negligence. Examples would be to permit students to participate in tackle football, fencing, ice hockey, or lacrosse without the proper protective equipment.

THE JURY'S INTERPRETATION

A jury decides whether a person in a particular situation acted reasonably in performing a duty to protect from harm. What an educator thinks is reasonable might be considered unreasonable, and thus negligent, by a jury of noneducators.

Reasonable-Person Test

The duty of care is the major question decided by the courts. In all states except Illinois, the duty of care required to avoid tort liability is that which a reasonable person of ordinary prudence would exercise for the safety of others in the circumstances. In Illinois, the standard of the duty owed has been lowered to the imposition of liability only for willful or wanton misconduct.

The test to be applied in most situations is what the particular individual should have reasonably foreseen and done. This standard is often referred to as the *reasonable-person test*.

The reasonable-person test also allows courts and juries to adapt society's views of reasonableness as they change from time to time and place to place. A child is not held to the same degree of "reasonableness" or responsibility as an adult. Therefore, if a child's duty were in question, the test would be whether a reasonable child of the same age, intelligence, and circumstances would have acted in the same way. It is important to recognize that the law does not require that all possible harm be removed, only that which can be done so reasonably.

DEFENSES TO THE CHARGE OF NEGLIGENCE

Some of the factors or conditions that help to keep a person from negligence are considered in the following paragraphs. Each of these defenses should be carefully considered when a liability suit is a possibility.

Lack of Legal Duty or Proximate Cause

Sometimes a plaintiff will try to establish liability against an individual who has no legal duty that is related to the damage. In the absence of legal duty, liability normally does not exist.

Even though an individual breached a duty and was involved in the chain of events associated with damage done to another person, the associated individual might be free of liability due to lack of proximate cause. In other words, a clear and direct linkage must exist between the action of the defendant and the damage done the plaintiff. There has to be evidence that the defendant actually contributed to the cause of damage.

Assumption of Risk

Certain situations, such as physical education activities and competitive athletics, have inherent dangers. Dangers also exist in industrial arts, chemistry, home economics, driver education, and traveling to and from school. In fact, some element of risk exists in many of the activities of life; but in most cases, the potential benefits justify a reasonable risk. Different activities have different levels of risk, and students, with the aid of their parents, have a certain amount of freedom to pick and choose the activities in which they participate. For example, football, rugby, and skiing are high-risk activities, and for this reason, some people avoid them. Damages that result within the limits of a known, reasonable risk do not constitute liability. Participants should be informed of the typical risks involved in an activity. "Consent forms" are often used, and these will be discussed later.

Contributory or Comparative Negligence

In some cases, the person who sustains damage was a party to the problem. Perhaps on the plaintiff's own initiative, more risks were taken than were necessary, disobeying warnings or safety regulations, or perhaps emotional behavior caused unwise acts. In such cases, the injured person contributed to his or her own damage and therefore is guilty of either contributory or comparative negligence. Different states deal with this situation differently. In some states, the type of contributory negligence system used bars injured plaintiffs from recovery if they contributed in any way or to any degree to their own injuries. Other states (increasing in number) have adopted a system of comparative negligence in which is diminished by the percentage that the injured person was at fault for the injuries. Whichever system is used, the defense, if successful, can reduce the size of the judgment.

Act of God (Nature)

Some acts or conditions of nature cannot be foreseen or controlled by humans, and for these acts, no person can be held responsible. Examples are a student being struck by lightening or someone being injured due to an unforeseen cave-in of the earth's surface.

Sovereign Immunity

In its governmental role as an educational agency of the state, a school system is sometimes protected from suit under the concept of sovereign immunity; however, sovereign immunity is decreasing today, and more school systems are susceptible to suit. Under some circumstances, the school serves as a proprietor or profit-making agency, and under these conditions, the sovereign immunity concept does not apply. Included in the proprietary function are activities where admission is charged, such as athletic events, exhibits, and concerts; and properties owned by the school district and rented or leased to companies or individuals. Often, schools are not subject to suit in connection with their governmental education roles, but they can be sued in connection with their proprietary roles.

PREVENTING A LAWSUIT—BEFORE AN ACCIDENT

Waivers and Permissions

Permission forms that involve a parent's consent to a student's participation in athletics or intramural activities often contain a clause that releases the school and its employees from liability for any injury that happens while students are participating in the activity. Such permission forms have limited, if any, legal effect. In spite of this, such forms may have a psychologic influence on the parents and decrease the likelihood of their bringing tort suits against schools. Some reasons for waiver and permission being legally invalid are as follows: (1) It is impossible to release a future tort because of the unpredictability of future events. (2) Parents cannot sign away the rights of a minor child. (3) Children, being minors, cannot release the school from possible tort claims. (4) The waiver or form is usually unspecific as to the rights being waived or all risks involved in the activity.

Although the typical permission or waiver forms (Figures 11-1 and 11-2) are

NAME _____
            Last   First

I hereby apply for the privilege of trying out for the _____ team, 19___

I recognize my responsibilities if I try out for the above sport. I will make it a point to so govern myself that my connection with the sport will bring honor to it and to the school, and expect to be asked to withdraw from the team in case I do not.

If extended the above privilege I will:

   I. Practice and train consistently as advised by the coach.

   II. Follow the prescribed training rules during the school year.

   III. Make a serious endeavor to keep up my studies.

   IV. Do all in my power to help keep athletics desirable.

   V. Make it a point to abide by the rules and regulations of the student body.

   VI. So conduct myself at other schools that I will bring credit to my team.

I have read the eligibility rules of the Utah High School Association. I am presently eligible according to these regulations.

Signed _____
                              Student

Figure 11-1. Student request for participation.

NAME _____
 Last   First

I hereby apply for the privilege of trying out for the _____
team, 19___

I recognize my responsibilities if I try out for the above sport. I will make it a point to so govern myself that my connection with the sport will bring honor to it and to the school, and expect to be asked to withdraw from the team in case I do not.

If extended the above privilege I will:

  I. Train consistently as advised by the coach.

  II. Not smoke during the school year.

  III. Make a serious endeavor to keep up my studies.

  IV. Do all in my power to help keep athletics desirable.

  V. Make it a point to abide by the rules and regulations of the student body.

  VI. So conduct myself at other schools that I will bring credit to my team.

I have read the eligibility rules of the Utah High School Association. I am presently eligible according to these regulations.

Signed _____
                              Student

Figure 11-2. Athletic permission and waiver form. (Courtesy of the Provo School District.)

not legally binding, it is still a good idea to use them. The completion of such forms should bring to the attention of the students and parents that risk is involved, and that you wish them to understand that they are making a decision as to whether the student should participate. Thus, both parents and child are aware that they are assuming some risks by participation in an activity.

It is also a good idea to obtain other information on the permission form. Data pertaining to the notification of parents and other emergency information ought to be obtained. The severity of a situation may be lessened if the parents' wishes as to medical attention are known and followed in the event of an injury to the student.

Adequate Supervision

Negligent supervision is the cause of most school-related lawsuits. The major questions are as follows: Did the teacher properly recognize, report, or correct an unsafe condition? Did the teacher fail to or wrongfully instruct students? Did the teacher arrange student participation in an unsafe way? Did the teacher aid a student in need? Underlying the total situation are two basic questions: (1) Did the teacher have a duty to supervise the student in the situation that caused the injury? (2) If there was a duty to supervise, did the teacher breach that duty?

As a physical education teacher or athletic coach, you must be careful to observe some simple principles of supervision. First, do not create danger by your own conduct. This type of situation would be created by instructing students to participate in a dangerous and unsafe activity. Second, avoid foreseeable perils that are created by others.

The school has a duty to supervise school grounds during normal operating hours. Such supervision may also be required before and/or after school hours, depending on circumstances surrounding the use by students. If students are known to misuse the equipment or engage in misconduct or if the conditions are unsafe for unsupervised play, then supervision is necessary.

Transportation

Athletes or other students require transportation, and sometimes the use of private vehicles is the most convenient and economical method. Whenever possible, however, students should be transported by common carrier. A common carrier is insured and bonded, and the drivers are trained to handle passenger vehicles. Many school buses are owned by private drivers or companies who are contracted by the schools. Privately owned school buses are desirable common carriers, because the initial liability rests with the driver/contractor rather than with the school district or teacher.

Coaches have been found negligent for the following reasons: (1) the coach transports athletes in his or her own automobile, (2) the coach permits student athletes to return home in student-driven automobiles, (3) the coach drives a bus loaded with students when unlicensed to do so and unspecialized as a driver of such a vehicle.

Unfortunately, the laws governing the transportation of students are inconsistent from state to state. Every teacher, coach, and administrator should be well informed about the applicable state laws, and within the framework of this knowledge, apply caution and good judgment.

PREVENTING A LAWSUIT—AFTER AN ACCIDENT

Treatment of Injuries

When a student is injured, the teacher or supervisor is placed in a precarious position. A teacher could be liable for not administering first aid when needed or for administering it incorrectly.

In the case of athletic trainers or coaches who act as athletic trainers, several guidelines are especially important.

1. Confer sufficiently with the team physician relative to the prevention of injuries.
2. Be well prepared to perform emergency care for injuries commonly incurred in athletics.

3. Obtain medical advice and approval for any medically-related treatment beyond first aid.
4. Keep accurate records of injuries, treatments given, and authorizations by medical personnel.
5. Have a medical doctor or emergency medical service at all contests that involve contact sports.
6. Have accurate and up-to-date medical records on each athlete and use that information properly.
7. Permit athletes to return to practice and competition following serious illness or injury only after securing medical approval.
8. Be adequately concerned with the provision and use of properly fitted protective equipment for each athlete.
9. In all actions relating to injury or illness, carefully apply the "reasonable person" concept (act prudently).
10. Be especially cautious about assuming responsibilities that officially or logically belong to the team physician.

Accident Reports

An accurately written report should be prepared as soon as possible after an accident, to serve as a record of the facts. Every educational system or institution ought to have a well-designed accident report form, along with the requirement that the form be completed and signed by the supervisor and the victim, or a witness in the place of the victim. In many school situations, accident reports are available to the plaintiff as well as to the defendant.

CONTRACTS

A contract is a legally binding agreement representing both sides and explaining certain conditions. It is assumed that contracts are entered into voluntarily, in a spirit of agreement and with a legal purpose in mind.

Teachers, coaches, and administrators enter into various kinds of contracts. Among these are employment contracts, supplemental contracts for extra duties, contracts with suppliers and construction personnel, and contracts with other institutions.

When an institution offers an individual an employment contract, the offer remains valid for a reasonable time, until a specified date, or until the offer is withdrawn. If the potential employee signs the contract, the individual and the institution become legally bound to the conditions of the contract, and neither party has the legal right to violate or change them unless the explicit permission of the other party is obtained. A similar situation exists with a contract involving an institution and a supplier or construction company; or between two educational institutions, such as a contract for an athletic contest.

Although teacher contracts are usually signed annually, the contract has a different meaning if the teacher is on tenure. Tenure is the right to hold a position indefinitely unless just cause exists for termination. Tenure, and the stability it provides, has both strengths and weaknesses. It may bring out better performances in teachers and make teaching a more attractive profession; but in some instances, schools get stuck with teachers who have lost their motivation or whose incompetence went undiscovered during the probationary period.

Most public schools handle coaching assignments with a separate contract, which is supplemental to the basic teaching contract. This permits flexibility in assigning coaches and changing their assignments without altering the basic contract. This practice is also followed in college situations; but, usually college level coaching assignments are included in the basic annual contract. A few coaches are given multi-year contracts, but this is the exception, not the rule.

CURRENT ISSUES

Athletics: A Right or Privilege?

Athletics are subject to the requirements of the 14th amendment to the Constitution of the United States and federal civil rights statutes. To be in compliance with the law, a school may not discriminate among students; neither may a school district discriminate among schools and leagues.

Although in certain states, athletics have been established and maintained by statute, participation in athletics by any given student has been held by the courts, in most cases, to be a privilege.

The rightful suspension of a student athlete from participation has been held to be valid by the courts. In some cases, when the student athlete might suffer career losses by disciplinary expulsion from varsity sports, the courts have required prior hearings.

Student Records

The Family Education Rights and Privacy Act of 1974 (FERPA) is the federal regulation that governs the release of educational records. Under FERPA, the methods of administration, rather than any requirements concerning content of student records, are stated.

This federal law creates the right of eligible students (over 18 years of age), and parents in the case of ineligible students, to see, inspect, reproduce, and challenge the accuracy of their education records. It also requires the student's (or parent's) written permission before the disclosure of personally identifiable information to nonprivileged parties. This final provision has implications for teachers and coaches. When college coaches and prospective employers request specific information, the school personnel must be aware of all the restrictions on the release of such information.

Statutes Governing the Handicapped

The Rehabilitation Act of 1973 prohibits discrimination against the handicapped in all federally aided prorgams. The Education for All Handicapped Children Act of 1975 (PL-94-142) provides federal funding to aid state efforts in providing appropriate education to the handicapped. In addition, each state has specific statutes dealing with the handicapped with regard to participation in physical education, intramurals, and interscholastic or intercollegiate sports. More is said about this in Chapter 15.

GUIDELINES TO APPLY

1. The protection and welfare of the students should be a top priority in conducting all school programs, particularly physical education and athletic activities.
2. Administrators are responsible for giving leadership to the development and implementation of sound policies, procedures, and safety regulations. This includes posting safety regulations in proper places, a *standardized system* of emergency care in the case of accidents, and a standard procedure for reporting accidents.
3. Teachers, coaches, and administrators should have adequate liability insurance, preferably provided through the school system. If no such provision exists, adequate coverage should be obtained from another source.
4. Up-to-date knowledge about emergency medical care is an important aspect of the professional development of school personnel, particularly those in the areas of high risk.
5. Due to the differences in laws of the various states, educators should become well acquainted with the liability laws of the particular locales in which they work.
6. A teacher, coach, or administrator who consistently acts with prudence in daily procedures on the job and gives special attention to prudent conduct during times of injury or emergency will greatly reduce, if not eliminate, the chances of legal involvement.

If an accident takes place under your supervision, a few simple procedures will help to strengthen your case if a suit is brought.

1. Correctly follow all procedures established for first aid, transportation, and notification.
2. Make a record and include as much information as possible about the accident, including names of students involved and witnesses.
3. If the student violated a rule, document this, along with a lesson plan of the instruction and the student's attendance in class that day.
4. Discuss the matter only with the parents, official medical personnel, school officials, and school legal counsel.

REFERENCES AND RECOMMENDED READINGS

1. Adams S.H., and Bayless, M.A.: A liability checklist. JOPERD, *56*(2):49, 1985.
2. Alexander, K.: Legal relationships, student teacher/university. JOPERD, *57*(6):65, 1986.
3. Baley, J.A., and Matthews, D.L.: Law and Liability in Athletics, Physical Education and Recreation. Dubuque, IA, William C. Brown, 1989.
4. Blucker, J.A., and Pell, S.W.J.: Legal and ethical issues essential for Professional preparation curricula. JOPERD, *57*(1):19, 1986.
5. Carpenter, L.J., and Acosta, R.V.: Negligence. JOPERD, *53*(2):51, 1982.
6. Carpenter, L.J., and Acosta, R.V.: Violence in sport. JOPERD, *50*(4):18, 1979.
7. Carpenter, L.J.: Courtside: Negligence—who pays? Strategies, *2*(3):13, 1989.
8. Carpenter, L.: Courtside: Constitutionality. Strategies, *4*(1):9, 1990.
9. Christiansen, M.L.: How to avoid negligence suits. JOPERD, *57*(2):46, 1986.

10. Clement, C.P.: Law in Sport and Physical Activity. Madison, WI, Brown and Benchmark, 1990.
11. Current Issues in Sport Law: NASPE, Waldorf, MD, AAHPERD Publications, 1987.
12. Dougherty, N.J.: Intramural liability. JOPERD, *56*(8):45, 1985.
13. Figone, A.J.: Seven legal duties of a coach. JOPERD, *60*(7):71, 1989.
14. Frost, R.B., Lockhart, B.D., and Marshall, S.J.: Administration of Physical Education and Athletics, 3rd Ed. Dubuque, IA, William C. Brown, 1988, pp. 381–402.
15. Horine, L.: Administration of Physical Education and Sport Programs, 2nd Ed. Dubuque, IA, William C. Brown, 1991.
16. Lehr, C.: Courtside: Test your liability quotient. Strategies, *1*(5):26, 1988.
17. Maloy, M.C.: Law in Sport. Madison, WI, Brown and Benchmark, 1989.
18. Nygaard, G., and Boone, T.H.: Law for Physical Educators and Coaches, 2nd Ed. Scottsdale, AZ, Gorsuch Scarisbrick Publishers, 1989.
19. Osinski, A.: Legal responsibilities of lifeguards. JOPERD, *59*(5):73, 1988.
20. Rafes, R.: Nine guaranteed ways to increase your liability. JOPERD, *58*(7):108, 1987.
21. Wade, S.C., and Hay, R.D.: Sports Law for Educational Institutions. Westport, CT, Greenwood Publishing Group, 1988.

Part IV
PROGRAM
ADMINISTRATION

Chapter *12*

ORGANIZATIONAL ELEMENTS

Organizations are created to help people accomplish collectively what they could not achieve individually. According to the scriptural account, Moses met numerous obstacles in leading his people out of Egypt to the Promised Land. Contributing to the problems was his lack of organization; he had not established a hierarchy of authority and responsibilities. Moses' father-in-law, Jethro, apparently being a perceptive person, recognized this lack of organization, so Jethro offered the following appropriate advice for Moses. "Hearken now unto my voice, I will give thee counsel . . . thou shalt provide out of the people able men . . . and place such over them (the people), to be rulers of thousands and rulers of hundreds, rulers of fifties and rulers of tens. . . ." (Exodus 18:17–21.) Essentially Jethro was saying "we must get organized."

Today, more than 3,000 years later, leaders are still saying we must get organized, because lack of organization generates chaos, contributes to friction and ill relationships, diminishes confidence, and causes overall poor utilization of organizational resources. Conversely, good organization creates order out of chaos, thus facilitating achievement of the organization's goals. Further, good organization builds morale and confidence in the organization and its leadership.

The importance of organization is further emphasized and clarified by Koontz and O'Donald in the following statement.[9]

Organizing involves the establishment of an intentional structure of roles through determination of the activities required to achieve the goals of the enterprise and each part of it, the grouping of these activities, the assignment of such groups of activities to a manager, the delegation of authority to carry them out, and provision for coordination of authority and informational relationships horizontally and vertically in the organization structure.

The process of designing an effective organization includes at least the following.

1. Determination of the programs and activities required to achieve the goals of the organization.
2. Grouping of these activities.
3. Assignment of a manager over each group of activities.

4. Delegation of authority and clarification of responsibilities for each manager.
5. Provision for coordination of the different units.

We have established the idea that a well-designed organization has structure and orderliness. But, it is possible for such structure to become static unless balanced with an appropriate amount of flexibility and spontaneity. This adds a fluid characteristic to an otherwise rigid organization.

William Hitt has provided ten useful principles to enhance the design of an organization.[6]

1. The key activities that are necessary in order to accomplish the organization's goals must be clearly defined.
2. These activities should be grouped on some logical basis.
3. The responsibilities of each division, department, unit, and job should be clearly defined.
4. Authority should be delegated as far down in the organization as practicable.
5. Responsibilities should always be accompanied by an equal amount of authority.
6. The number of persons reporting to each manager should be reasonably small to accommodate an appropriate span of control.
7. The organization should be designed to provide the right mixture of stability and flexibility, thus making it a well-structured, fluid enterprise.
8. The organization should be designed for perpetuation and self-renewal.
9. The structure should be evaluated on the basis of its contribution to the organizational goals.
10. The leaders of the organization should be responsive and accommodate new needs and changing circumstances.

Noted organizational specialist, Peter Drucker emphasizes that "structure follows function." This means that the functional aspect of an enterprise should determine the structural characteristics. This is reasonable because the only purpose of structure is to accommodate and enhance function.[3]

Organization is a means to an end, rather than an end itself. Sound structure is a prerequisite to a healthy organization, but it is not health per se. The test of a healthy enterprise is not the beauty, clarity, or perfection of its structure. It is the functionability of the organization.

Some elements of organization can be explained with diagrams (organization charts), whereas other are better explained by defining responsibilities associated with positions and the flow of authority and accountability within the organization. In order to help the reader better visualize the full scope of organizational structure, this chapter is separated into three sections: (1) examples of organizational patterns; (2) explanations of selected administrative positions; and (3) the connection between physical education and athletics and related fields.

PATTERNS OF ORGANIZATION

There is no such thing as an ideal organizational pattern to fit all situations. Different ones have advantages and disadvantages. To some degree, the structure of an organization must be tailored to fit, and no two situations are exactly alike. Also, the personnel of an organization have some influence on which pattern will work the best. Management experts emphasize that the main ingredient of an organization is people; therefore, peoples' personalities, interests, competencies, and relationships have a significant influence on which kind of structure is preferred.

The organizational pattern illustrates lines of authority, responsibility, and accountability. It describes the proper administrative channels and the interrelationships of personnel and programs. Having the organizational pattern clearly defined and well understood can expedite administrative procedures and enhance overall effectiveness.

The sample organization charts presented here are for administrative units that include physical education and athletics. A careful review of these charts will help provide a clearer concept of how different educational organizations can be structured effectively.

One of the disadvantages of the traditional "line of command" organization is that it emphasizes the line of authority. Many educators feel that the line of authority should be deemphasized and that nonauthoritative relationships should receive more emphasis. Some feel that their positions or the positions of their programs on the chart fail to give a true picture of them in terms of significance and total contribution. For these reasons, many educators prefer a circle chart or some other method of defining the organization rather than a line chart.

Line Organization (Figure 12-1)

This form of administration is characterized by a clear and direct line of authority. The most basic feature is a chain of command to be followed from the top (highest executive) to the bottom (lowest level employee). The simplest way to explain the line of authority is that those at the top or in the superior position "make the rules" and those positioned at the subordinate levels "follow the rules."

Line-Staff (Figure 12-2)

This form of administrative organization is much the same as the line organization. It still contains a prominent and direct line of authority. The added dimension of this pattern is the presence of advisors (staff) who assist the executive. A staff person is an advisor or special assistant to the administrator and is out of the line of authority. Strict observance of the staff role seldom exists, however, because the staff person usually is delegated some amount of decision-making power. In the absence of the administrator, staff personnel often have the "authority" to make and implement certain decisions.

Functional (Figure 12-3)

The functional type of organization contains many of the same characteristics as the line-staff organization. The superior–subordinate and administrator–advisory relationships are still evident.

This type of organization has some unique characteristics. For example, em-

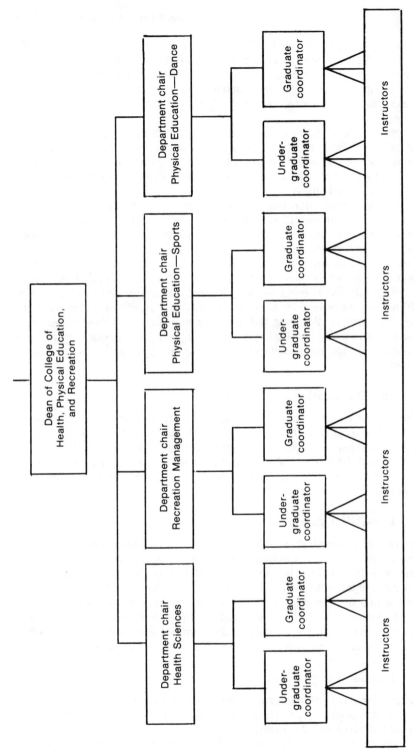

Figure 12-1. An example of a straight line organizational plan of a college within a university.

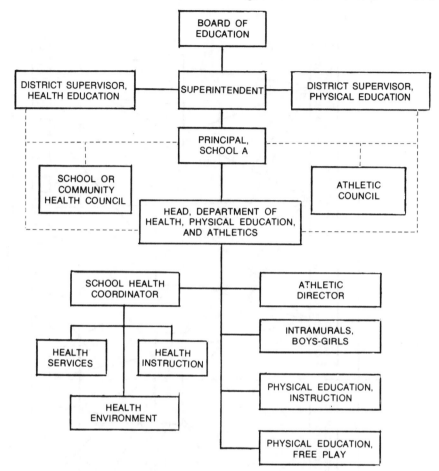

Figure 12-2. A chart showing a line-staff organizational pattern in a secondary school. (Courtesy of Alpine School District.)

ployees may be subject to the decisions of several superiors. This changes the way in which authority is exercised. There is no direct chain of command, and as a result, employees must work through two or more decision-making channels. Also, it provides the opportunity for subordinates to communicate on certain occasions with top level executives, without giving the appearance of "going over the head of someone." This pattern encourages the active participation of lower level employees in administrative matters.

Circle (Figure 12-4)

This organizational pattern is employed most often in business or in higher education. Responsibility and authority from the chief administrator flows outward to the various subdivisions. The vice-presidents (or assistant superintend-

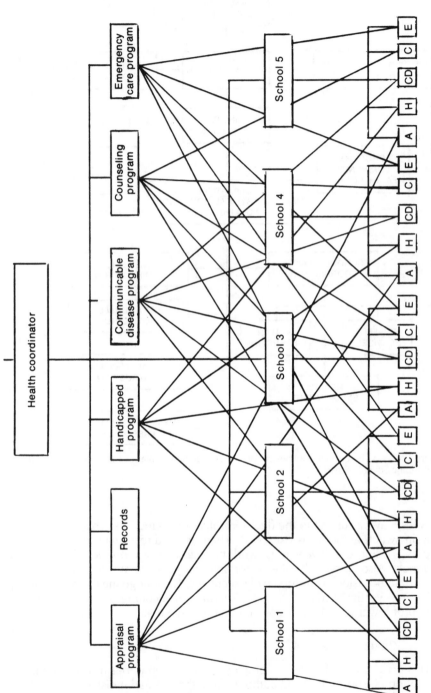

Figure 12-3. An example of a functional organization structure for a public school health program. (Courtesy of Provo School District.)

Integrated activities include such things as:
1. Curriculum development and management.
2. Student advisement and student records.
3. Cooperative use of personnel, space, and resources.
4. Mutual support and overall cooperation.

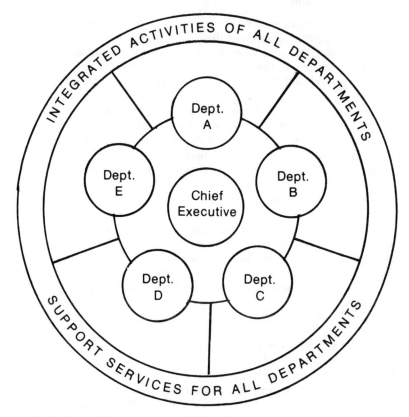

Support services include such matters as:
1. Facility planning and management.
2. Supply and equipment management and issue.
3. Learning resources and support.
4. Computer and media services.
5. Research services.

Figure 12-4. A diagram showing a circular pattern of organization.

ents) all have the same level of authority, and all are equally accountable to the chief administrator for their assigned responsibilities.

ADMINISTRATIVE POSITIONS

The most crucial features of an organization are its people, their assigned duties, and their functional relationships. Much insight into organizational relationships can be obtained from knowing the basic responsibilities associated with each administrative position. Following are descriptions of certain administrative positions in the schools.

Superintendent

Typically, local school systems are known as districts, and all of the schools within a district are managed under the administrative leadership of a superintendent. In general, the superintendent's responsibilities are to give direction to the district educational system in accordance with state laws, regulations, and guidelines, and with the directions and counsel provided by the district school board.

The school board is the local governing authority to which the superintendent is responsible. The superintendent is the chief administrator for the school district and is the one who manages the educational system in accordance with the actions and wishes of the school board.

The superintendent performs the following specific functions:[10]

1. Prepares the agenda for meetings of the school board and meets with the school board.
2. Finalizes the hiring, fosters the development, and provides for the evaluation of all school district employees.
3. Provides leadership to the board of education and the professional staff in defining, clarifying, and modifying educational goals and programs consistent with sound educational practices, democratic ideals, and community expectations.
4. Plans for, manages, and evaluates negotiations with organized employee groups in the district.
5. Maintains and strives to improve communications within the school district and between the school district and the community.
6. Plans and supervises the budget development process to ensure that budget recommendations made to the board reflect prudent planning, efficiency, and sufficient budgetary support of district programs and priorities.
7. Continually assesses the general climate and conditions in the schools through informal visits in schools and in classrooms. Formal and informal conversations with the administrators, teachers, and students, regular administrative staff meetings, meetings with the officers of the district education association, and open agenda meetings with the school faculties.
8. Investigates concerns raised by district residents directly or through members of the board of education.
9. Carries out other responsibilities that are required by law, contractual agreements, and board policies.

A school superintendent should be a well-prepared educational administrator and not a political appointee. The professional requirements of the position vary considerably among school districts. Some districts are small and have meager educational programs, while other districts have large and complex school systems. Typically, a small district would require that the superintendent have a master's degree and several years of successful experience. The superintendent of a large system would be expected to hold a doctorate degree and be a highly regarded and reputable educator.

The professional staff of the superintendent's office often includes associate or assistant superintendents, with one in charge of each of the levels of education—elementary, junior high school, and senior high school; and supervisors or specialists of particular areas, such as physical education and athletics, music and art, and special education. A business manager and legal specialist are also important staff positions. The kind of staff and its size vary with the complexity of the school district. Some operations amount to little more than the superintendent and a secretary, whereas others consist of a large and highly specialized staff.

The superintendent's span of control and direct administrative contacts usually involve the associate and assistant superintendents, supervisors and specialists, and the principals of the various schools within the district.

School Principal

The principal is the chief administrator of a particular school and the one directly responsible to the superintendent. In general, the principal's responsibilities are to provide effective administrative leadership for all aspects of the school program. Typically, this involves the following:[10]

1. Participation in the selection and hiring of teachers and other personnel in the school.
2. The assignment of teacher loads and the utilization of facilities in connection with the teachers' assignments.
3. Supervision of curriculum development and management of the curriculum for effective results.
4. Administrative leadership of noncurricular activities and programs.
5. Definition of the role of student government in the school and the administrative supervision of it.
6. Supervision of the school's teaching process.
7. Budgetary planning and management in connection with all aspects of the school.
8. Management of the community relations program within the broad framework of the district public relations effort.
9. Professional development and enrichment experiences of school personnel.
10. Administrative leadership toward desirable student values, behavior, and discipline.
11. Supervision of the school's planning function, both short-term and long-term, with respect to goals, faculty, facilities, and programs.

The requirements of a principal's job vary with the size of the school. The job of principal of a school of 200 would be much less demanding than that of a school of 2,000, even though the two jobs would include the same elements. The principal is responsible to the superintendent or, in some cases, to an associate or assistant superintendent, as designated.

College Dean

Typically, a university is divided into several colleges or schools, with each college encompassing several departments related in subject matter. The dean is the chief administrator of a college or school. The heads of the several departments report to the dean, and the dean, in turn, reports to one or more vice-presidents. The basic administrative responsibilities of a dean require the following[1]:

1. Coordinate and facilitate personnel matters such as
   a. selecting and appointing new faculty members;
   b. determining faculty and staff salaries;
   c. dealing with rank advancements, leaves of absence, terminations, and retirements; helping determine faculty assignments and evaluating faculty loads and effectiveness;
   d. receiving and evaluating student and faculty suggestions and complaints;
   e. supervising and working effectively with the heads of the several departments.
2. Oversee the preparation and management of college and departmental budgets.
3. Review and act on proposals for program and curriculum changes.
4. Review and act on department head's recommendations relative to classified personnel, part-time faculty, and student assistants.
5. Appoint and supervise college committees as needed.
6. Serve as the liaison between the college and other colleges and schools and between the college and the central administration.
7. Serve as the focal point of relationships between the college and nonuniversity organizations and agencies.
8. Supervise nondepartmental functions of the college such as centers, laboratories, and institutes.

Associate or Assistant Dean

A dean may allocate a variety of responsibilities to associate or assistant deans. Among the more logical responsibilities to delegate are the following:

1. Review and evaluation of faculty assignments and loads.
2. Supervision of assigned college committees.
3. Supervision of service aspects of the college closely related to academic programs.
4. Management of the college budget and/or portions of it.
5. Coordination of facility scheduling, management of equipment, and ordering of textbooks.
6. Interview and selection of student assistants and part-time faculty.
7. Supervision of nondepartmental units and programs.

Department Head

Department heads are key members of the administration because they manage programs at the grassroots level. They are the "front line" administrators who work directly with the faculty and students. The basic responsibilities of a department head include the following[1]:

1. Coordinating student advisement and supervising of progress toward completion of student requirements.
2. Determining the need for faculty and formulating recommendations for such to be considered by those in higher administrative positions.
3. Reviewing faculty salaries and participating in recommending salary adjustments.
4. Preparing class schedules and arranging for facilities and equipment in support of classes.
5. Coordinating faculty assignments, generally supervising faculty involvement, and evaluating faculty productivity and performance.
6. Providing recommendations relative to faculty advancement, leaves of absence, terminations, and retirement.
7. Organizing and supervising departmental committees.
8. Supervising departmental staff members in addition to faculty (clerical personnel, student assistants, and others).
9. Preparing and managing the departmental budget.
10. Coordinating curriculum and program planning and modifications.

Athletic Director

Many of the responsibilities of an athletic director are similar or equivalent to those described for department heads, except directing athletics does not involve matters relating to class instruction, such as curriculum, scheduling classes, and ordering textbooks. It does involve the following responsibilities not included in the description of department chairmen.

1. Scheduling athletic contests.
2. Conducting athletic contests.
3. Promoting and selling tickets.
4. Implementing rules of athletic eligibility.
5. Providing and managing athletic areas and facilities, and acquiring and caring for athletic equipment.
6. Providing sports medicine needs.
7. Dealing with the sports media.
8. Coordinating the total public relations effort with regards to athletics.

The complexity of an athletic director's position varies greatly from a high school or small college program to a major university program. In the latter case, there is a much greater amount of public interest (and pressure) and, therefore, much more public relations involvement, large crowds to accommodate and control, high-pressure game situations that must be properly managed, and extensive financial involvement. The basic elements of an athletic director's position, however, are essentially the same as described, whether the program is large and complex or small and relatively simple.

RELATED FIELDS

In a general sense, this book pertains to the combined areas of physical education and athletics. The relationships that exist between these two phases of the school program are apparent. Physical education and athletics are so interrelated that they are often combined into one administrative unit. In many universities and in some large high schools the two areas are separated for administrative convenience; but in most of these cases, there continues to be a close relationship. Physical education is also closely related to other phases of the school program, including *health education, recreation*, and *outdoor education*.

Health Education

Traditionally, health and physical education have been closely associated. In fact, the differences between them have often been too indistinct for the good of either, particularly health education.

In the broad sense, health encompasses the total field of medical science, in addition to some aspects of psychology, sociology, and physical education. Only some aspects of this total field apply to the school setting, and those align closely with physical education.

Even though health and physical education should remain closely associated and strongly supportive of each other, the days are gone when health education can be viewed as part of physical education or supplemental to it. Health should be a separate phase of the curriculum under the leadership of a health education specialist. The American Alliance for Health, Physical Education, Recreation and Dance has published a position statement concerning a comprehensive program of health instruction. It includes the following (reprinted with permission):

1. A program of health education should be unified and organized in such a manner that there is scope and sequence from kindergarten through grade 12.
2. A program of curriculum development should be undertaken that will stress (a) the identification of specific courses with content, learning activities, and evaluation requirements, and (b) coordination and integration with other subject areas.
3. The health curriculum should be jointly developed by school personnel, curriculum specialists, individuals from public and voluntary health agencies, and national and state consultants.
4. Health teachers should be specialists in health education and have a genuine interest in this field.

Within the framework of the above statements, there are several procedures that involve health in the areas of physical education and athletics, including the following:

1. A required medical examination before participation in vigorous sports.
2. Medical services available at school athletic contests where injuries or emergencies are probable.
3. Written permission from a physician after a serious illness or injury before a student can return to physical education or athletic activities.
4. Prescribed procedures for the emergency care of injuries and illnesses in connection with physical education and athletics.

5. The qualification of teachers and coaches to administer emergency care when needed.
6. The provision of adaptive and corrective physical education activities based on health records or medical recommendations.
7. The provision of a healthful and safe environment in locker rooms and physical education facilities.
8. Ample emphasis on physical fitness throughout life as a method of perpetuating optimum health.

In some schools, health education receives little attention beyond that provided by the physical education teachers. In such cases, the physical educators ought to make an honest effort to provide useful health instruction and encourage sound health practices. Health and physical education are too important and too closely related for us to allow either area to be neglected.

In order to help the reader better understand the proper position and role of health education in the schools, the following information has been included. It is an excerpt from the official position statement of the Society of State Directors of Health, Physical Education and Recreation and is printed with the permission of the Society.

Health Program

The Comprehensive School Health Program encompasses School Health Education, School Health Services, and Healthful School Living. Health Education has the purpose of imparting health knowledge and cultivating desirable attitudes, habits and practices. School Health Services undergird the total educational program by identifying and securing correction of, or compensation for, individual health problems. It also provides protection, guidance and opportunities for health learning experiences. Healthful School Living is the provision of a safe and healthful school environment. In addition, this phase provides many opportunities for the reinforcement of school health education and school health services.

The ultimate goal of the Comprehensive School Health Program is to help every young person to achieve his full potential through becoming responsible for his own personal health decisions and practices, through working with others to maintain an ecological balance helpful to man and the environment, and through becoming a discriminating consumer of health information, health services and health products.

ABOUT ADMINISTRATION AND ORGANIZATION

The State Education Agency, in cooperation with appropriate school and health personnel and representatives of official, professional and voluntary health agencies, has the responsibility for establishing goals, objectives, standards and evaluative criteria for the comprehensive school health program.

Every school should formulate and implement health policies, consistent with modern medical and educational concepts and practices, designed to assure each pupil:
—appropriate health education.
—effective school health services.
—safe and healthful living conditions at school and at school-sponsored events.

School health policies should be formulated to facilitate maximum cooperation and coordination within each school and school system, and between the school and the community.

The Comprehensive School Health Education Program should include a planned, sequential series of experiences in health education at each grade level. Time allotments should provide:
—in the elementary school, at least two hours per week of health instruction and other educational activities, which are designed to promote valid health practices.
—in the middle or junior high school, the equivalent of a daily period of direct health education for at least two semesters.

—in the senior high school, the equivalent of a daily period of health education for at least two semesters, one of which may include driver education.

ABOUT CURRICULUM

The Comprehensive Health Education Program should consist of planned learning experiences which will assist students to achieve desirable understandings, attitudes and practices related to critical health issues including, but not limited to, the following: emotional health and a positive self-image; appreciation, respect for, and care of the human body and its vital organs; personal fitness; health issues of alcohol, tobacco and drug use and abuse; health misconceptions and quackery; effects of exercise on the body systems and on general well-being; nutrition and weight control; boy-girl relationships, preparation for marriage, and wholesome family life; the scientific, social and economic aspects of community and ecological health; communicable and degenerative diseases including venereal diseases; disaster preparedness; safety and driver education; choosing professional medical and health services including insurance programs; and health careers and, also, the health aspects implicit in career education. The interrelationships of these topics with one another and with other phases of the school health program make it essential that they be taught and administered as one broad and comprehensive curriculum. Special health problems or emphases should be treated within this comprehensive context and not dealt with in piece-meal fashion.

The curriculum should be directly related to the needs, problems and interests appropriate to the growth, development and maturity level of each student involved.

The scope and sequence of the comprehensive school health education curriculum, grades K-12, should be planned and organized so as to avoid both serious omissions and unnecessary duplication and repetition.

ABOUT SCHOOL HEALTH SERVICES

The State education agency and public health department have a responsibility for cooperative planning between themselves and with other appropriate agencies and professional organizations to develop and implement policies and standards which can be adapted for use in local communities. Similar coordination by community agencies at the local level should be effected.

Careful follow-up procedures are indispensable if school health appraisals are to contribute to the health and education of children and youth. Therefore, the findings of the health appraisals should be used for making adaptations in the school program, interpreting health status to pupils and parents, and motivating and securing correction of remedial defects.

ABOUT HEALTHFUL SCHOOL LIVING

School authorities, in cooperation with health departments and other appropriate agencies, are responsible for providing and maintaining a safe and healthful school environment which will help ensure a wholesome physical, social, emotional, intellectual and moral climate.

Supervisory responsibility for maintenance of school buildings, grounds and equipment should be delineated. Provisions should be made for periodic inspection by qualified personnel. Hazards and defects should be corrected quickly.

In schools where food services are provided, the facilities, time schedules, and menus should contribute to good nutrition, nutrition education, and the development of an appreciation of related social values. The school lunch program should be flexible enough to complement other curricular areas rather than detract from these instructional programs.

A properly equipped health service unit, with separate rest and isolation rooms for boys and girls, as well as adequate personnel to provide supervision and care, should be available.

All school personnel should have periodic health examinations.

ABOUT PERSONNEL

Well-defined, specific standards for certification of teachers and school health personnel (consistent with standards developed by national professional organizations) should be established by the respective state certification agencies.

Every elementary and secondary school should have a school health coordinator, appointed from the faculty or staff and responsible to the principal. This coordinator should receive special training and should facilitate coordination and communication among those who are involved in the Comprehensive School Health Program.

Elementary teachers should have specific preparation which will equip them with the competencies and understandings essential for effective health education, including special abilities in observing the health status of children and in using appropriate referral and follow-up techniques. Teachers of health education in the secondary schools should be certificated in health education.

The elementary teacher and the teacher of health education in secondary schools should receive assistance from a health education specialist or supervisor who is an outstanding instructional leader. The supervisor should also provide the liaison with health agencies and other community groups that will tie school and community health education together in a consistent fashion.

All teachers and administrators should seriously recognize their unquestionable role as an exemplar before their students. For a teacher or an administrator to teach one thing and be a living example of a conflicting way of life, practice, or point of view is to negate such instruction in the eyes and minds of many students. In this day, when hypocrisy and communication gaps are widely discussed, all school leaders should exemplify the healthy, active, quality life which they promote for their students.

Recreation

Physical educators should recognize the tremendous contribution of organized recreation in providing opportunities for participation in physical education activities. At the same time, those concerned primarily with recreation programs should feel highly supportive of physical education because it teaches skills and develops interests that are useful in recreational pursuits.

Schools become involved in recreation in three ways: (1) education for the worthy use of leisure time; (2) the provision of recreational activities, such as intramurals, club sports, and free play, as part of the school program; and (3) involvement in supporting, co-sponsoring, or sponsoring public recreation programs.

The worthy use of leisure has been recognized as an important function of education for a long time. This is evident by the fact that in 1917 it was stated as one of the seven cardinal principles of education. Several aspects of the school curriculum contribute to this objective, such as photography, art, music, drama, literature, and industrial arts, but a good physical education program can be one of the main contributors. One of the primary common interests of physical educators and recreation leaders is the development of physical skills and positive attitudes toward active participation throughout life. The present emphasis placed on lifetime sports and sports for all is especially important in the worthy use of leisure time.

The out-of-class *school recreation* program includes special interest clubs, hobby pursuits, and special events, which relate to several aspects of the curriculum. But the noninstructional physical education activities make an important contribution in the form of intramural sports, club sports, and free play.

As part of the enabling legislation of almost all states, school districts are permitted to sponsor and manage public recreation programs over and above their normal educational responsibilities. Few school districts function as the sponsoring agency for the public recreation program (only about 2%); but many are involved as co-sponsors or cooperative sponsors of public recreation.

School systems have a large amount of both indoor and outdoor facilities. By putting these facilities to effective use, they need not be duplicated in the form of community centers, playgrounds, or athletic fields. School personnel represent a valuable source of leadership that sometimes can be available in recreation programs during the summer and on a limited basis during the school year. School districts are usually not able to adequately manage a balanced recreation and park system, however, because in addition to the recreational facilities and activities that are closely related to the school program, a complete recreation program must involve nonschool facilities, such as golf courses, aquatic facilities, and picnic areas, and sometimes such specialized facilities as boating areas and marinas, winter sports areas, zoos, aquariums, natural areas, preserves, museums, and cultural centers. In other words, even though many aspects of recreation are closely aligned with school programs and facilities, some aspects are not. A school district dedicated to doing a good job in sponsoring recreation can make a significant contribution so long as the school's recreation efforts are supplemented by other local agencies to round out the complete scope of recreational opportunities.

Professional recreation and park planners have strongly encouraged recreational use of school facilities and school use of recreation facilities. This approach has been advanced under the "park–school" and "community school" concepts. The *park–school* is a facility that consists of one or more school buildings constructed on or adjacent to a park site. The *community school* is a concept in which the school is conceived as an agency that makes maximum use of its facilities and other resources to serve both the educational and recreational needs of the community, serving people of all ages. It is a "lighted schoolhouse" concept.

Effective implementation of cooperative school and community use of facilities must involve joint planning. This means that each recreation and education facility or area is originally planned and constructed for joint use by the two agencies. Even though this approach is a valuable one, not all recreation and park needs can be satisfied by this method. Following is a portion of the position statement of the Society of State Directors of Health, Physical Education and Recreation. This information will help to explain how recreation opportunities should fit into education. It is printed with the permission of the Society.

The Recreation Program

Social, economic, and other developments taking place in this final quarter of 20th Century American life highlight recreation as a major cultural force. The school must help prepare each individual to use his free time in constructive, creative and satisfying ways. Furthermore, schools must accept a major responsibility for providing personnel and making maximum use of their facilities and equipment in a broad, coordinated school-community program of recreation for students, parents and other community members.

ABOUT ADMINISTRATION AND ORGANIZATION

Schools have a basic responsibility to help the community develop awareness and understanding of the recreational needs of its children, youth and adults.

The "community school" concept recognizes the school, augmented by other community resources, as a center of the community's civic, cultural and recreational activities. Elementary schools are natural neighborhood centers. Secondary schools may serve a larger area of the community. This concept should be interpreted, supported and strengthened in and for the community by school personnel.

All government agencies having a vital role in recreation, including the State department of education, should give direct attention to cooperative planning and action through an interagency council. The State director of health, physical education and recreation and staff, working with and through the chief state school officer and the state board of education, should provide leadership in the development of the recreation program by:

—establishing and maintaining cooperative working relationships with other state and local agencies, colleges, and universities, professional and voluntary agencies, and other interested individuals and groups.

—cooperating with state and local leaders in studying pertinent recreation problems and developing recommendations that may be widely disseminated for implementation and evaluation.

—becoming informed on trends, problems and successful practices and maintaining communication with and providing consultation services to school districts, other agencies, and organizations.

ABOUT PROGRAM

The school curriculum should offer many opportunities for developing attitudes, understandings, knowledge and skills that will lead to the wise use of off-the-job hours.

Schools should provide planned experiences beyond the classroom, including outdoor education, in order to ensure maximum articulation between learning and recreational activities.

Opportunities for children, youth and adults to participate in a variety of the physical, aesthetic, cultural and social aspects of recreation should be provided under school auspices.

ABOUT RECREATION PERSONNEL

State departments of education should provide leadership to help increase the supply of qualified recreation personnel and should work closely with colleges, universities, and professional recreation associations in helping upgrade opportunities for preservice and in-service education of persons working in recreation programs—professionals, paraprofessionals, aides and volunteers.

Policies and procedures relating to the qualifications of recreation personnel employed by schools should be established by State departments of education.

General areas of professional preparation should include:

—the recreation major who has selected the field of recreation as a career.

—education majors who have selected recreation as a minor to prepare themselves for part-time work in recreation in addition to other education responsibilities.

—other majors who have selected recreation as a minor in order to prepare themselves with a better understanding of the impact of leisure on modern society.

Outdoor Education

Physical education contributes to the skills and attitudes involved in outdoor education. In turn, outdoor education relates to outdoor recreation, because much of what is learned in the educational process is subsequently applied in recreational pursuits. Outdoor education, or at least some aspects of it, is often administered as part of the physical education program. Some examples are camping, hiking, mountain climbing, skiing, archery, marksmanship, and orienteering.

Outdoor education includes *two* major categories: education *in* the outdoors and education *for* the outdoors. The two categories are closely related and they complement each other. The former category occurs in an outdoor environment, whereas much of that included in the latter category may take place in an indoor setting. The following will give additional insight into the two categories.

Education In the Outdoors. This entails direct outdoor experiences, involving observation, study, and research in outdoor settings such as school sites; park and recreation areas; camps; school or community owned forests, farms, gardens, zoos, sanctuaries, and preserves; state and federal land and water; and private outdoor resources.

Education For the Outdoors. This entails the learning of skills and the development of appreciation for activities such as the following: camp and survival skills; casting and angling; shooting and hunting techniques; boating and

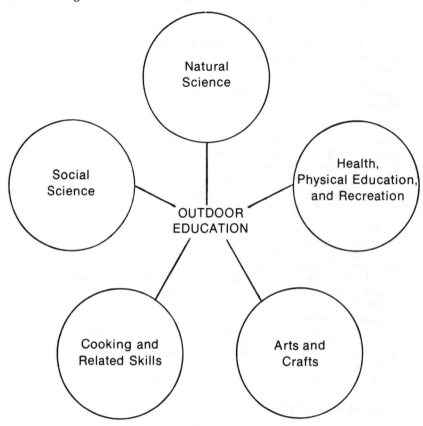

Figure 12-5. Topics that are often integrated with outdoor education.

small craft techniques; aquatics—swimming, water skiing, skin and scuba diving; archery; winter sports; mountain climbing; hiking and bicycling; use of compass—mapping and orienteering outdoor photography; and outdoor cooking.

Outdoor education should not be separated from other subjects, but should integrate them as much as possible. Figure 12-5 shows the relationship between outdoor education and other school topics.

REFERENCES AND RECOMMENDED READINGS

1. Brigham Young University: Personnel Manual (with Position Descriptions). BYU, Provo, UT, 1991.
2. Bucher, C.A.: Administration of Physical Education and Athletic Programs, 9th Ed. St. Louis, C.V. Mosby, 1987, pp. 23–45.
3. Drucker, P.: Managing the Results. New York, Harper and Row Publishers, 1964.
4. Frost, R.B., Lockhart, B.D., and Marshall, S.J.: Administration of Physical Education and Athletics, 3rd Ed. Dubuque, IA, William C. Brown, 198, pp. 247–266.
5. Gordon, J.R.: Organizational Behavior, 3rd. Ed. Boston, Allyn and Bacon, 1991, pp. 508–560.

6. Hitt, W.D.: Management in Action. Champaign, IL, Sagamore Publishing Inc., 1984.
7. Horine, L.: Administration of Physical Education and Sport Programs, 2nd Ed. Dubuque, IA, William C. Brown, 1991, Chapter 3.
8. Kaufman, J.E., and McBride, L.G.: Health and leisure—Are they strange bedfellows? JOPERD, 56(11):37, 1985.
9. Koontz, H., and O'Donnell, C.: Management: A System of Contingency Analysis of Managerial Functions, 2nd Ed. New York, McGraw-Hill Book Co., 1986.
10. Provo School District: Job Descriptions of School Administrators. Provo, UT, 1991.
11. Sandefur, J.T., and Oglesby, B.E.: The dean and the department head: A special relationship. JOPERD, 53(5):4, 1982.

Chapter *13*

THE INSTRUCTIONAL PROGRAM

The essential mission of the educator should be to improve the quality of life through the provision of creative and meaningful experiences. Also it is the mission of an educator to help people to succeed, not cause them to fail. A superior physical education program will involve adequate concern about what students do in tennis, swimming, and creative dance. But, in addition, it will involve much greater concern about what these activities do to the students.

Any program ought to be tailored for the situation and the particular student body. The modifications of the instructional program that are made from time to time should be based on the principle of retaining those practices and educational experiences that have proven valuable and modifying those that are judged deficient. The two extremes of "change for the sake of change," and "blind worship of the old and traditional" should both be avoided.

Care should be taken to avoid a program that attempts to do some of everything, with nothing done well; repeats the same experiences year after year without regard for progression or expansion into new areas; and treats all students alike, with no serious attempt to meet students' individual needs.

In the design and management of the program, the following considerations should receive serious attention: (1) appropriate class size to enhance effective instruction; (2) appropriate length of class periods and adequate instructional time per week; (3) the use of competent teachers, assigned in accordance with their strengths; (4) provision of adequate facilities, equipment, and supplies; (5) adequate variety to meet the students' needs and interests; and (6) involvement of the right sequence of progressions to lead effectively toward educational goals. Figure 13-1 shows the fundamental importance of the physical education instructional program.

CLASS SCHEDULING

The introduction of computers into education has increased the potential for efficiency in scheduling. The extensive development of loop films, video tapes, recordings, and programmed learning modules makes it possible for certain instruction to occur separately from teaching stations and faculty. The trend

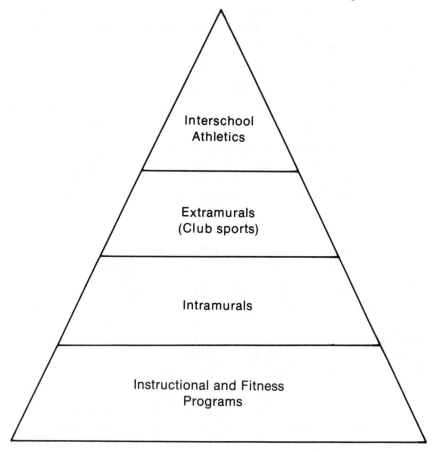

Figure 13-1. Hierarchy of the elements of a physical education/athletic program based on skill level and the usual number of participants. The instructional program forms a base on which other elements of the total program can be built.

toward combining men's and women's programs and emphasizing coeducational classes has also had an influence on class scheduling.*

Traditional vs. Modular

Traditional scheduling is the assignment of a given number of students to an instructor for a certain time slot (class period). Usually each class period occupies an equal amount of time. Typically, one teacher instructs the class for the entire semester.

---

* Much of the specialized information about programs and curriculum in this chapter and Chapter 14 was furnished by Professor Joyce Harrison, who is a recognized curriculum specialist and author of the textbook on Curriculum Design in Physical Education.

Time	Monday	Tuesday	Wednesday	Thursday	Friday
8:00- 8:55	Biological Science --
9:00- 9:55	Social Studies --
10:00-10:55	Study ---
11:00-11:55	Industrial Arts ---
12:00-12:55	Lunch ---
1:00- 1:55	Physical Education --
2:00- 2:55	Geometry --
3:00- 3:55	Chemistry ---

Figure 13-2. A student's class schedule, using the traditional scheduling method.

Traditional scheduling has certain benefits. It enhances the opportunity for developing close teacher–student rapport, and it is the simplest method of scheduling. It also has some disadvantages. The number of students in the class usually remains constant regardless of the subject matter that needs to be covered at various times during the semester. The time period remains constant, when in some cases a longer or shorter period would be beneficial. Traditional scheduling seldom involves homogeneous groupings of students. Figure 13-2 is a simple example of traditional scheduling.

Some variations of traditional scheduling are as follows:

Physical education can be scheduled less frequently (two or three times a week), with each session of instruction lasting two class periods. This results in proportionately more instructional time, because less time is utilized in dressing, showering, taking attendance, and other nonteaching activities.

Within the framework of traditional scheduling, *team teaching* can capitalize on the expertise of different teachers.

With *modular or flexible scheduling*, the school day is divided into short periods of time called modules (mods). Each module is the same length, usually 15 to 30 minutes. Modules can be combined to provide the desired length of time for different instructional units. The instructional periods for a particular subject may vary in length from one day to the next, meaning that a student or a teacher may have a different schedule each day of the week. Once established, the weekly cycle usually remains the same throughout the term. In a highly flexible system, however, an instructor may request class length and frequency on a weekly basis. In such cases, students and teachers pick up new schedules prior to the beginning of each week (or other time cycle). This kind of scheduling requires the use of a computer along with careful planning and coordination among teachers. It is not a frequently used method, but it does function effectively in certain situations. An example of a student's class schedule using a modular or flexible system appears in Figure 13-3.

CLASS SIZE

Class size is influenced by several factors: regulations and policies issued by higher authority, the size of each teaching station, the nature of the subject or

TIME	M	T	W	Th	F
8:00	English	Indep.	English	Social Studies	English
8:30		Study		Indep. Study	
9:00	Indep.	Math	Guidance	Math	Social
9:30	Study		Social Studies		Studies
10:00	Math	English	Math	English	
10:30	Indust. Arts		Indust. Arts	Typing	
11:00	Boys' Chorus	Typing	Boys' Chorus	Physical	Math
11:30	Indep. Study		English	Education	
12:00	L	U	N	C	H
12:30	Social Studies	Social	Indep.	Indep.	Guidance
1:00		Studies	Study	Study	
1:30	Physical Education	Indust.		Indust.	Physical Education
2:00			Physical		
2:30		Arts	Education		English
3:00					Boys' Chorus

Figure 13-3. A student's class schedule for one week, using flexible scheduling with 30-minute modules. (From Organizational Patterns for Instruction in Physical Education. Reprinted by permission of the American Alliance for Health, Physical Education, Recreation and Dance, 1900 Association Drive, Reston, VA 22091.)

activity, and the number of students that must be accommodated with the facilities and teachers available. A tennis class with only four courts available would have to be smaller (maximum of 16 students) than a soccer class, which would have the use of two regulation soccer fields.

A modern dance class in a studio 30 × 40 feet would have to be restricted in size as compared with one taught in a studio 40 × 50 feet.

Class size is also influenced by the nature of the activity. For example, a class of 25 in modern dance or ballet would be large for one teacher to handle effectively; whereas in ballroom or folk dance, one teacher can handle 40 or more students. In beginning swimming, an optimum ratio is one teacher for about 15 students; whereas, in certain field games, a teacher can manage as many as 30 students effectively.

Another factor is that some teachers handle larger groups better than others. In fact, some prefer relatively large classes because their teaching methods involve pairing or grouping of students and then assisting the students as they teach each other. Conversely, other teachers dislike this method and prefer individual coaching. A few small classes can be justified, provided there are oversized classes to compensate. The important point is to strive for an optimum average class size, with each particular class adjusted in accordance with the influencing circumstances. The average class size recommended by the AAHP-ERD, and the President's Council on Physical Fitness is 35 (or smaller if circumstances permit). Adaptive physical education classes should have no more than 20.

TIME ALLOTMENT

Individual states prescribe minimum instructional time. For *elementary schools*, the AAHPERD recommends that pupils should participate in an instructional program of physical education for at least 150 minutes per week, in addition to time allotted for free play during recess and noon hour. The instruction should occur on a daily basis. The Society of State Directors of HPER recommends a daily instructional period of at least 30 minutes, exclusive of time for dressing, showering, and free-play periods.

For *junior high school* and *high school* students, the President's Council on Physical Fitness recommends physical education for one standard class period per day, 5 days per week. The Society of State Directors of HPER recommends at least 300 minutes per week spread over 3 or more days.

Whatever the arrangement, the use of time is more important than the amount. As little time as possible should be spent in dressing, showering, roll call, and other matters that relate to instruction and exercise, but do not produce the intended results. The important question is what is accomplished toward the educational goals rather than how much time is spent.

TEACHING STATIONS

A teaching station is the area assigned to a teacher for a class. One method of calculating the number of teaching stations needed for a *secondary school* is illustrated in Table 13-1. The table is based on a school of 1,000 pupils with each pupil having 30 periods per week, five of which are for physical education (one period daily). The result is seven teaching stations needed for physical education. In addition to the method illustrated in Table 13-1, the following formulas are useful:

$$\text{Number of sections to be offered} = \frac{\text{total number of students}}{\text{anticipated class size}}$$

$$\text{Number of teaching stations needed (classes per class period)} = \frac{\text{total number of students}}{\text{class size} \times \text{number of periods/day}}$$

$$\text{Number of teachers needed} = \frac{\text{number of sections}}{\text{number of periods taught/day by each teacher}}$$

Figure 13-4 is a chart that shows teacher assignments correlated with teaching stations and class periods. In order to assure efficient use of staff and facilities, a two-way chart such as this should be constructed. In the chart, the teaching

TABLE 13-1. Plan for Calculating the Number of Physical Education Teaching Stations Needed for 1,000 Pupils in a Secondary School (Willgoose, C.E.: The Curriculum in Physical Education, 3rd Ed. Englewood Cliffs, NJ, Prentice-Hall, 1979, p. 170. Reprinted by permission of the publisher.)

Plan	Example
1. Divide the anticipated enrollment by the desired average class size. This will give the number of sections needed.	$\dfrac{1000 \text{ students}}{30 \text{ pupils per class}} = 34 \text{ sections}$
2. Multiply the number of sections by the number of periods per week physical education is offered.	$34 \times 5 \text{ periods} = 170$
3. Multiply the resulting number by 1.25 to allow for a utilization factor.	$170 \times 1.25 = 203$
4. Divide the resulting figure by the number of teaching periods available in the school week (30 periods).	$\dfrac{203}{30} = 6.7 = 7 \text{ teaching stations}$

stations appear horizontally across the top, and the time periods are shown in the vertical left hand column.

To calculate the number of teaching stations required for an *elementary school*, proceed as illustrated in Table 13-2.

In this example, an elementary school of approximately 500 girls and boys would require two teachers of physical education. Each would teach 25 30-minute periods a week, aside from any intramural supervision or program planning.

Few schools have all of the teaching stations that are needed to conduct a complete program. When necessary, certain activities can be taught in multi-purpose rooms, little-used hallways, unoccupied classrooms, or on theatre or auditorium stages.

CLASS PERIODS		GYMNAS-IUM #1	GYMNAS-IUM #2	WRESTLING ROOM	OUTSIDE FIELD	SWIM. POOL
	1	Smith	Hansen	Shaw	Jones	Black
	2	Smith	Black		Jones	Moss
	3	Black	Hansen	Shaw	Jones	Moss
LUNCH	4	Smith	Black	Shaw		Moss
	5		Hansen		Jones	
	6	Smith	Hansen	Shaw	Black	Moss
	7	Smith	Hansen	Shaw	Jones	Moss

Figure 13-4. A scheduling form for coordinating periods with the assignment of teachers and facilities (teacher and station assignments).

TABLE 13-2. Plan for Calculating the Number of Physical Education Teaching Stations Needed in an Elementary School (Willgoose, C.E.: The Curriculum in Physical Education, 3rd Ed. Englewood Cliffs, NJ, Prentice-Hall, 1979, p. 171. Reprinted by permission of the publisher.)

Plan	Example
1. Estimate the enrollment by counting the number of grades and number of classes in each grade.	A school with 6 grades of 3 classes per grade = 18 classroom groups
2. Decide on length and number of class periods.	A total of ten 30-minute periods per day = 50 periods per week
3. Decide on the number of periods per week for pupils	5 periods per week
4. Calculate number of teaching stations:	
Teaching stations = 18 classroom groups $\times \dfrac{\text{5 periods per week}}{\text{50 periods per week}} = \dfrac{90}{50} = 1.8$	

STUDENT GROUPING

Placement of students into classes should reflect more than administrative expedience. Classes are learning groups, and students should be assigned to these groups according to their learning needs. Scheduling students into classes can be accomplished in a variety of ways. Among the more prominent reasons for logical student grouping are the following:

1. To safeguard the health of participants.
2. To group pupils for effective learning.
3. To equalize competitive conditions.
4. To facilitate progress and achievement.

Being in a group with persons of similar physical characteristics and skills ensures some success, a chance to excel and to be recognized, a feeling of belonging, and security. Consequently, this enhances the overall development of the individual. Following is useful information when considering the best methods of grouping[3]:

1. The need for grouping students homogeneously for instruction and competition has long been recognized, but the inability to scientifically measure such important factors as ability, maturity, interest, and capacity has served as a deterrent from accomplishing this goal.
2. The most common procedure for grouping today is by grade or class.
3. The ideal grouping organization would take into consideration all factors that affect performance—intelligence, capacity, interest, knowledge, age, height, weight, and so on. To utilize all these factors, however, is not administratively feasible at the present time.
4. Some form of grouping is essential to provide the type of program that will promote educational objectives and protect the student.
5. On the secondary and college levels, the most feasible procedure appears to be to organize subgroups within the regular physical education class proper.
6. Classification within the physical education class should be based on such factors as age, height, and weight statistics and other factors such as interest and skill that are developed as a result of observation of the activity.
7. For those individuals who desire greater refinement in respect to grouping, utilization of motor capacity, motor ability, attitude, appreciation, and sports-skills tests may be used.

Eight different methods for grouping students are presented here. Sometimes grouping is based on a combination of two or more of these methods.

Grade Level—The most common method; the general age characteristics are similar, but maturity and skill level may vary widely.

Height-Weight or Age-Height-Weight Exponent System—Useful in athletics, especially contact sports, and in junior high where physical maturity varies considerably.

Ability or Skill Level—May be determined by skill in a specific sport or by general motor ability; provides for instruction on the student's skill level. Highly skilled students can move quickly to advanced skill development.

Physical Fitness—This is especially beneficial for students with low fitness because they can benefit from a different kind of program geared to their individual needs.

Interest—It increases students' motivation to be in groups where others share their interests and adds an important social dimension.

Competency—Based on previous competencies passed in a given activity or in a sequence of activities.

Instructional Method—Students can choose the teaching method they prefer.

Sex—Preferred for some vigorous and contact sports or activities of primary interest to one sex or the other.

FACULTY UTILIZATION

The *traditional* method is to assign a teacher to a class, for which the teacher is to be responsible during the term. This is the simplest pattern and offers the advantage of the teacher becoming well acquainted and establishing a good rapport with the students. The main disadvantage is the lack of flexibility in utilizing the strongest attributes of several teachers.

The *team teaching* method is one in which two or more teachers share the responsibility for a particular class. The purpose is to capitalize on the strengths of each teacher. The two basic styles of team teaching are *topical* and *differentiated*. With the topical approach, members of the teaching team provide instruction on a particular topic or activity in which they are highly specialized. For example, during a term, the swimming specialist might teach a 4-week course on swimming, then a gymnastics specialist would teach gymnastics for 4 weeks, then a tennis specialist would teach a 4-week course of tennis. The *differentiated* method involves a master teacher and two or more supporting teachers. The master teacher is "the expert" who directs the class, gives overall leadership to the learning process, and supervises the supporting teachers. The supporting teachers work with subgroups in specialized phases of instruction.

Assignment of Teachers

The main element in a successful educational environment is a competent and concerned teacher. Teachers should be assigned to classes on the basis of their qualifications and proven success and not on preference or convenience. Teachers of potentially hazardous activities, such as swimming, gymnastics, and skiing, should have the specialized knowledge necessary to conduct the activities at a reasonably safe level. In such cases, certification by national agencies associated with the sport is highly desirable.

The several methods of staffing for physical education in *elementary schools*, with each method having advantages and disadvantages, are as follows:

Physical Education Specialist. Have one or more specialists in the school teach all of the physical education classes. Advantages are (a) expertise in physical education subject matter and methods, and (b) knowledge about motor learning at the various stages of development. Disadvantages are (a) the specialist does not know the students as well as the classroom teacher, and (b) teaching the same subject all day can become monotonous.

Rotating Specialist. A specialist assists classroom teachers by team teaching with them at least once a week and providing leadership and program ideas for the instructional periods when the specialist is not there. Advantages include (a) specialist is knowledgeable about physical education subject matter and methods; (b) a specialist understands motor learning; and (c) through in-service workshops, master lessons, and coaching, a specialist can improve the classroom teacher's physical education techniques. Disadvantages include (a) specialists often must travel to two or more schools; (b) some classroom teachers do not work effectively with the specialist; and (c) the specialist is unable to become well acquainted with the pupils, due to limited contact.

Classroom Teachers Trade Assignments. One teacher instructs physical education for another, who in turn teaches something else for the first teacher. The main advantage is that teachers can teach in areas of preference and expertise. The main disadvantage is the problem of having teachers who are prepared and willing to do the trading that is needed.

Classroom Teacher Teaches Physical Education. The advantages include (a) the teacher can integrate physical education with other subject matter; and (b) the teacher is familiar with the students and knows their personalities and abilities. The disadvantages include (a) lack of expertise in teaching physical education; and (b) no opportunity for a break from the routine of supervising the same students every period of the day.

Several important considerations relate to staffing classes in *secondary schools*.

1. Is it better for a physical education instructor to teach only physical education, or is it better to teach some classroom subjects? Most teachers and administrators would agree that a combination of classroom and physical education subjects is better.
2. Is it desirable for a teacher to instruct in the physical education program several hours during the school day and then have a heavy coaching assignment after school? It is generally agreed that this is too much. A better combination is some classroom teaching along with physical education instruction and coaching.
3. Is it appropriate to perpetuate the belief that a successful classroom teacher or a successful athletic coach can get by with an inferior job of physical education instruction? This attitude should be unacceptable. The idea should be enforced that teaching 30 students in physical education is just as important as teaching 30 students in English or mathematics or coaching

30 students on the athletic field. Any teacher who views it differently ought to be prohibited from teaching physical education.
4. Secondary school physical educators should be generally informed about the instructional programs in physical education that precede those in the secondary schools in order that the subject matter and teaching methods fall into sequence and build progressively onto what the students have already learned. In the absence of this kind of preparation, the idea of graduated levels of instruction fails.

Teaching Loads

In *colleges and universities*, it is generally accepted that a teaching load should not exceed 12 class hours per week of lecture courses, 15 class hours of teaching techniques courses, or 18 class hours of activity courses.

In *secondary schools*, it is recommended that class instruction per teacher not exceed 5 clock hours per day, or 1500 minutes per week. Six clock hours per day or 1800 minutes per week should be considered an absolute maximum, and this should include any after-school responsibilities. A daily load of 200 students per teacher should be the maximum. Finally, each teacher should have at least one free period daily for consultation and conferences with students.[9]

The number of hours per day or week is not an absolute measure of teaching load because other factors must be considered. If a person teaches a different kind of class each hour, more preparation is required as compared with teaching multiple sections of the same class. The correct balance between these two extremes is important because the necessity of too many preparations contributes to inefficient use of the teacher's time; whereas, teaching too much of the same subject can make the material routine and dull.

Another consideration is the length of the class periods. A large number of short class periods are more difficult to teach than a smaller number of longer class periods, because more classes require more preparations and contact with more students. For example, six 40-minute classes would be more demanding than four 60-minute classes, even though the total minutes of instruction are the same.

In addition to the time spent in class, a teacher needs time for planning and preparation, student consultation, and consultation with administrators and parents.

Another factor is that many physical educators have extra duties after hours: coaching athletics, conducting intramurals, coaching cheerleaders and marching groups, and serving as advisors for activity clubs. Two prevalent methods are used by schools to compensate teachers for performing extra duties. One method is *extra pay* for extra work, and the other is to give the teacher *released time* from the normal school day. Whichever method is used, the arrangement should be fair and equitable both for the school and the individual. (Extra duties are also discussed in Chapter 15).

SPECIAL INSTRUCTIONAL METHODS

Learning packages, independent study, and learning contracts can work effectively with individual and dual activities and physical fitness programs.

These approaches work better with mature students and students who are highly motivated.

In the *learning package* approach, a description is provided of the procedures that must be followed and the achievement levels that are expected. The student then takes an individualized approach to completing the requirements, at which point credit for the learning package is given.

The *independent study* approach involves a tailor-made program for a particular individual. Once the individual has accomplished all aspects of the prescribed program, credit is given.

With the *learning contract* approach, the student and teacher agree upon the objectives the student will accomplish and the time frame (which is sometimes flexible) within which the accomplishments will occur. The conditions of agreement are described in writing, and this becomes a *contract*. When the student completes the conditions of the contract, credit is given.

All the individualized study approaches must involve the following to some degree: (1) stated behavior objectives (expected outcomes); (2) preassessment and postassessment (and sometimes, intermediate assessments); (3) a clear understanding by both teacher and students of the requirements, the methods of evaluation, and the system for awarding credit and grades.

HANDICAPPED STUDENTS

The Rehabilitation Act of 1973 prohibits discrimination against the handicapped in any federally aided program. Furthermore, the Education for All Handicapped Children Act of 1975 provides federal funding to aid state efforts in providing an appropriate education for the handicapped.

This second law, known as Public Law 94-142, is intended to ensure an appropriate public education for all handicapped students. In part, the law enables ". . . specifically designed instruction, at no cost to parents or guardians, to meet the unique needs of a handicapped child, including classroom instruction, *instruction in physical education* (emphasis added), home instruction and instruction in hospitals and institutions." The portions of the law that apply the most to physical education are Sections 2, 3, and 4. The provisions that apply directly to physical education are the following:

1. Search for handicapped students.
2. Identify the population that needs service.
3. Provide the least restrictive educational environment.
4. Prepare an *individualized education program* for each handicapped child identified as having special needs.
5. Do an evaluation of the progress of each student at least annually.
6. Conduct a fair hearing for students, or parents on behalf of their children, to establish the needs of the student if there are any questions (grievances) regarding the individualized education program.

Components of an Individualized Education Program

In order to develop the individualized education program in compliance with the requirements of Public Law 94-142, the following components must be included for every handicapped child requiring special education and related services.

A statement of the child's present levels of educational performance, including academic achievement, social adaptation, prevocational and vocational skills, psychomotor skills, and self-help skills.

A specific statement describing the child's learning style.

A statement of annual goals that describes the educational performance to be achieved by the end of the school year under the child's individualized education program.

A statement of short-term instructional objectives, which must be measurable intermediate steps between the present level of educational performance and the annual goals.

A statement of specific educational services needed by the child (determined without regard to the availability of those services), including a description of:

  a. All special education and related services that are needed to meet the unique needs of the child, including the type of physical education program in which the child will participate.

  b. Any special instructional media and materials that are needed to implement the individualized education program.

The date when those services will begin and length of time the services will be given.

A description of the extent to which the child will participate in regular education programs.

A justification for the type of educational placement that the child will have.

A list of the individuals who are responsible for implementation of the individualized education program.

Objective criteria, evaluation procedures, and schedules for determining, on at least an annual basis, whether the short-term instructional objectives are being achieved.

Least Restrictive Environment

The continuum of physical education placement is represented by Figure 13–5. As one of the basic principles (indicated on the diagram), students should be placed in the environment that will allow them to function best—the least restrictive environment. The physical education teacher is the person best equipped to make the judgment as to the kind of physical education setting in which the student belongs. In making such judgments, teachers should remember that handicapped students are first and foremost people—who have the same basic needs, desires, and interests as the nonhandicapped. The handicapped are much more like others than they are different.

The concept of least restrictive environment means that each handicapped child should be placed in the most normal situation possible. The physical education administrator should be knowledgeable about each situation, so that if called upon, the administrator can provide an accurate report on the status of the individual in question. The administrator must also be aware of how effectively teachers in the department are working with the handicapped students.

As can be seen on the continuum of physical education placement, there are five levels. Four of these involve the assistance of a teacher other than a physical

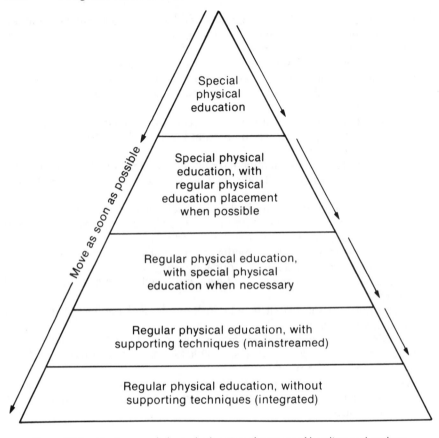

Figure 13-5. Continuum of physical education placement of handicapped students.

education teacher in a regular class. Public Law 94-142, if applied correctly, might enable a school to hire a specialized staff member to assist those handicapped students requiring special attention.

MARKING (GRADING) STUDENTS

Every teacher should develop effective methods of marking students (the term marking is preferred over the term grading). A student's marks determine to some extent whether the person will secure a good position of employment, be admitted into college, win a scholarship, be eligible for lower automobile insurance rates, or gain prestige among classmates. Marks represent to the student and the parents an indication of success in school. Because of the importance placed on them, an accurate system for determining and reporting marks is imperative.

Purposes of Marking

Marks serve different purposes for students, teachers and guidance counselors, parents, and school administrators. A mark should indicate whether the student has met the standards on which the mark is based and performed as compared to the requirements and expectations. A mark must be accurate and justifiable and have a strong basis, or it loses its value to the student. It may even destroy the student's interest and incentive and result in a negative attitude toward the subject and the teacher.

Teachers and guidance personnel may use marks for guidance and counseling. If accurately determined, marks can help the teacher predict how successful a student might be in certain pursuits and may also help the teacher evaluate the effectiveness of the teaching.

Parents are usually eager to learn of their children's success in school and desire to know the reason for the lack of success. Marks that are properly obtained, reported, and interpreted will furnish desired facts. As a result, guidance from home may help overcome deficiencies.

Also, marks are essential to administrators, who interpret them as symbols of progress and indicators of accomplishment. Since marks become permanent records of achievement, they are also used as a basis for promotion and scholastic honor awards. It is essential, then, that marks be established on a solid, equally fair basis, and that they be accurately reported and interpreted.

Criteria for Useful Marks

Marks should be *valid*. They must truly represent the quality and quantity of pupil achievement for which they purportedly stand.

Marks should be *reliable*. They must accurately and consistently represent the same results for each student.

Marks should be highly *objective*. Different teachers, given the same data on a student, should arrive at the same mark. This characteristic is dependent upon a clearly defined marking system.

Marks should be assigned on the basis of *definite standards*. The standards should not differ for each pupil nor should they fluctuate widely from one year to the next.

Marks should be capable of *clear interpretation* with regard to what they signify. If the significance of an A is not evident in terms of quality and quantity of achievement, then the grade lacks meaning.

Marking should involve an element of economy of the teacher's time and effort. Since marking is just one of the teacher's many tasks, only a reasonable amount of time can be justified for it.

Marks should be *timely*. Final marks are recorded only at the end of semesters; but for purposes of incentive, students should be frequently informed of their progress and present standing.

Methods of Reporting Marks

Some of the several methods of reporting student achievement are as follows:

Five-Letter.   This is the most frequently used method. The teacher determines the criteria for each grade: A, B, C, D, E (F). Each student is given a letter mark based on performance in the class. The mark is reported, and sometimes an interpretation accompanies the mark telling what it means in terms of level of performance.

Pass or Fail. In this system, a standard of acceptability is established. If the performance is up to the standard, the student passes; if performance is below the standard, the student fails. Sometimes satisfactory or unsatisfactory are terms used in place of pass or fail.

Percent. With this method the student is given a percentage score as a mark, with 100 percent representing excellent performance. Percentages can then be converted to letter marks in order to make them more meaningful in the school system. Usually it is assumed that 90 to 100% = A; 80 to 89% = B; 70 to 79% = C; 60 to 69% = D; below 60% = F.

Accumulative Points. In this method, the student is awarded points for performing the various activities throughout the unit of instruction. Each student's class standing is determined and reported on the basis of accumulated points.

Contract. Through agreement between the student and the teacher, it is decided which projects the student will complete, and this agreement becomes a contract. The particular conditions of the contract define a predetermined grade that will be received if the student completes all the conditions.

Descriptive Statement. This method consists of a short paragraph explaining the student's status and stating the student's strengths and weaknesses in the subject. The statement is reviewed by the teacher, student, and parent in reaching an understanding of the student's progress. Some schools include with the regular report card a sheet showing comparative physical fitness test scores. An example of such a form is shown in Figure 13-6. Items and columns can be altered from this model to fit any specific situation.

A POSITION STATEMENT

The author firmly believes that every student is a unique individual with differing physical, mental, emotional, and social needs. Students have varying abilities, aptitudes for performance, and rates at which motor skills are perfected. Regardless of the differences, however, *every student, including the handicapped,* has the need and the right to benefit from well-planned physical education experiences.

Physical education is an important part of the development of the whole person. Even though the emphasis is on the development of physical fitness and motor characteristics, good physical education experiences also contribute to social, psychologic and mental development. Without an effective physical education program in conjunction with the academic subjects, it is impossible for students to achieve the well-rounded development they need and deserve. An effective program:

1. Enhances growth and development, including physical fitness, motor skills, and desirable physique and postural characteristics.
2. Contributes to one's health and well-being.
3. Has potential for enhancing self-image, psychologic adjustment, and social adeptness.
4. Develops desirable lifelong recreational interests and skills.

In a statement of beliefs, the Society of State Directors of Health, Physical Education and Recreation added clarity as to the conditions that should exist

COMPARATIVE PHYSICAL FITNESS TEST SCORES

Student's Name _____ Grade _____

School _____ Teacher _____ Date _____

Physical Fitness Test	Student Score	Class Avg.	School Avg.	District Avg.	Natl. Avg.
Sit-ups					
Pull-ups					
Shuttle run					
Standing Long Jump					
50 yd. dash					
Softball Throw					
600 yd. run/ walk					
Push-ups					
Set-ups					
Rope Climbing					
Trunk Flexion Standing					
Trunk Extension					
Forward Roll 40 feet					
Backward Roll (Pass or Fail)					
Vertical Jump					
Agility Jump					

Note: Any column left blank indicates that there are no average scores available.

Figure 13-6. A report card for selected physical fitness skills.

relative to the physical education instructional program. The author concurs with this statement, and thinks that every physical educator ought to be familiar with these beliefs. It is printed with the permission of the Society.

Class Instruction

ABOUT ADMINISTRATION

Physical education is essential for all students, boys and girls, from pre-kindergarten through grade twelve. The daily instructional period for elementary school pupils (Pre-K, K-6) should be at least 30 minutes in length, exclusive of time allotted for dressing, showering, recess, free and/ or supervised play periods, and noon hour activities.

The minimum instructional class period for pupils in secondary schools should be a standard class period daily, except where the length and frequency of the class periods are altered to offer students a more comprehensive program. Where modular or flexible scheduling is used care should be taken to involve students in some combination of at least 300 minutes of physical education per week spread over three or more days.

All pupils, including those participating in varsity athletics, sports clubs, dance clubs, and the like, should be involved each year in the instructional phase of the physical education program.

Physical education should be adapted for those pupils who have special needs. To the extent feasible, such pupils should take part in regular classes. Special classes should be scheduled for pupils who are severely handicapped or who are otherwise unable to participate successfully in the regular program.

—A physician's recommendation in consultation with teachers, parents and the student should be the basis for assignment to special classes. The physician should work with the physical education teacher in determining the activities which should be prescribed for each child who requires adaptive physical education.

—Students may need adaptive physical education because of poor coordination, lack of strength or similar deficiencies.

—The services of teachers with special preparation in adaptive physical education should be available to every school.

All pupils from pre-kindergarten through twelfth grade, should be scheduled for physical education according to their physiological development, ability, interests and individual needs.

Credit in physical education should be required for graduation from high school. Standards should ensure satisfactory achievement based upon reasonable objectives for each individual student.

Class size in physical education should be consistent with the activity being taught. Effective physical education instruction requires both large and small groups.

All students should wear physical education clothing which permits freedom of movement and safe participation. Showering should be encouraged whenever class activities are sufficiently vigorous to cause perspiration. Appropriate instruction and supervision should be provided to ensure safe, healthful practices in dressing and showering.

Differences in abilities and interests will create at times separation or grouping within a coeducational physical education class in elementary and secondary schools. In addition to the social values gained, coeducational physical education classes provide instructional flexibility, make maximum use of the talents of instructors and offer students a wider variety of activities.

Physical educators should be alert to changing patterns of school organization, methodology, and educational technology so that the educational potential of new practices and innovations may enhance the physical education program.

ABOUT PROGRAM

Class instruction in physical education should provide a planned, balanced, varied progression of activities based upon needs, abilities and interests of boys and girls at all developmental levels.

The elementary school physical education program should provide instruction in sequential experiences including basic and creative movement, rhythms and dance, relays, games, sports skills, stunts, tumbling, apparatus, swimming, outdoor activities, and other activities which meet the objectives.

The middle school and junior high school program should include rhythms, various types of dancing, aquatics, gymnastics, stunts, tumbling, individual and dual sports, team games, special conditioning activities and outdoor recreation.

The senior high school program should emphasize lifetime sports and carryover activities as well as the involvement, knowledge and understandings necessary to provide insight and motivation for a lifetime of vigorous physical activity. The achievement of personal physical fitness during the school years and the maintenance of fitness throughout adult life should become the goal of every student. Every effort should be made to allow senior high school students the opportunity to select activities appropriate to their own needs and interests.

In addition to the necessary space, indoor and outdoor facilities, equipment and supplies for conducting the instructional program in physical education, good teaching requires an adequate collection and proper use of books, periodicals, audiovisual materials and other teaching aids. Innovative use of modern technology is encouraged whenever it can contribute to improved instruction.

Evaluation of the curriculum by both students and teachers should be continuous. Evaluation should be used to assess student progress toward stated goals, to provide guidelines for adjusting current programs and planning new ones, and to indicate needs for instructional improvement. Evaluation is an important means of interpreting the program to students and adults in order to improve community understanding of the values and outcomes of physical education.

ABOUT PERSONNEL

Certification standards for physical education personnel, consistent with general certification requirements, should be established and periodically reviewed by each State department of education. Increased interest and involvement in certification on the part of professional associations and teacher preparation institutions should be encouraged and welcomed.

Elementary classroom teachers should have a clear understanding of the contribution good physical education makes to the education of boys and girls, including the relationships of physical growth and development to the general educational progress of all pupils.

Elementary classroom teachers should have sufficient preparation and laboratory experiences in the basic skills, methods, and content of physical education to enable them to conduct an effective program under the guidance of a physical education specialist or supervisor, and to relate the experiences in physical education to ongoing classroom instruction.

Whenever possible, elementary pupils should receive the major part of their physical education instruction from a specialist in elementary school physical education having a major in physical education with strong emphasis in movement education and elementary school physical education. The elementary school physical education specialist should work directly with classroom teachers to coordinate the physical education program with other classroom activities and to foster mutual reinforcement in assessing and helping individual pupils.

Secondary school physical education teachers—both men and women—should have a major in physical education and should be able to demonstrate leadership and teaching skills in the wide variety of activities outlined in the preceding section on Program.

Teachers who work with students who have special needs or characteristics, e.g., inner city, disadvantaged, pre-school, handicapped, ethnic or non-English speaking, should be specially selected and prepared. The tremendous personal and social benefits of physical education for such students should be maximized through the program.

All teachers of physical education should be provided with assistance from supervisors or resource persons who are qualified by education and experience to provide professional leadership and guidance in physical education. In addition, clinics, workshops, and other in-service opportunities should be provided for both classroom teachers and specialists.

Teacher aides, when utilized, should work under the direct supervision of a certificated physical education teacher and only in a supportive and supplementary capacity.

LICENSING

As the educational programs related to physical education and athletics become more refined and more specialized, the trend toward "licensing" continues to grow. Licensing includes both accreditation of programs and certification of specialists.

Teacher certification within each state is already established. Recently there has been a strong push to have athletic trainers certified by the National Athletic Training Association (NATA). Some institutions have established athletic coaching certification procedures, wherein an individual who completes certain requirements at the institution is provided a certificate verifying that he or she is professionally qualified to coach athletics in the schools. Others offer specialized programs in commercial physical education, and some have established a certification procedure in connection with this specialty. Accreditation of various professional preparation programs has been gaining ground in colleges and universities; and although program accreditation specific to professional education is still infrequent, it seems unlikely that it will escape the growing trend. Program accreditation can serve a worthwhile purpose provided the criteria and procedures are carefully worked out and properly applied.

IMPACT OF TITLE IX

Title IX of the Education Amendment Act of 1972 has had a major impact on the various aspects of physical education. This law is based on the principle that all activities in educational programs have equal value for both sexes. Therefore, the governing regulations state that physical education classes may not be conducted separately on the basis of sex, nor may participation in physical education programs be required or refused on the basis of sex. This concept has caused dismay in the minds of many administrators and teachers, because for many years, separate instruction in physical education skills has been offered, beginning sometimes as early as midelementary school. (See also the section on Title IX in Chapter 15, which explains its application to athletics.)

With respect to *physical education courses*, Section 86-34 of the law states that an institution or agency may not ''. . . provide any course or otherwise carry out any of its education program or activities separately on the basis of sex, or require or refuse participation therein by any of its students on such basis, including health, physical education, industrial business, vocational technical, home economics, music, and adult education courses.'' The following specific conditions apply:

1. The law does not prohibit grouping of students in physical education classes and activities by ability as assessed by objective standards of individual performance, developed and applied without regard to sex.
2. The law does not prohibit separation of students by sex within physical education classes or activities during participation in wrestling, boxing, rugby, ice hockey, football, basketball, and other sports if the purpose or major activity involves bodily contact.
3. When use of a single standard of measuring skill or progress in a physical education class has an adverse effect on members of one sex, the recipient shall use appropriate standards that do not have such effect.
4. Portions of classes in elementary and secondary schools that deal exclusively with human sexuality may be conducted in separate sessions for boys and girls.

(See also the section on Title IX at the end of Chapter 15.)

SAFETY CONSIDERATIONS

The teacher or supervisor of a class or activity is fully responsible for seeing that the activity is conducted with optimum safety and in a prudent manner. This involves providing a safe environment in terms of facilities and equipment, adequate supervision, and the proper selection of activities for the particular group or individual. It means especially that a student should not be allowed to engage in activities against a physician's recommendation. Sometimes, be-

Physician's Recommendation

This is to certify that I have examined _____

from _____ school and have found the following

abnormal condition _____

_____

    Therefore, I **recommend that participation** in physical education be as checked below:

_____ **Normal program—all activities**

MODIFIED PROGRAM

_____ **Relaxation and rest**

_____ **Mild exercises, done** lying or sitting on mat

_____ Nonvigorous **games** or dance

_____ **Body building exercises** modified as to need

_____ **Other (specify)** _____

Duration: for _____ weeks, for _____ months, until next examination

Date: _____ Signature _____ M.D.

Telephone _____ Address _____

COMMENTS: _____

_____

_____

_____

_____

Figure 13-7. Example of a physician's recommendation for modified physical education or excused absence.

cause of health reasons, a physician will prescribe modified activity or excused absence for a student. Such a recommendation should always be honored. Figure 13-7 shows an example of a physician's recommendation form.

    Another important consideration is the possibility of an accident. In case of an accident to a student in a class or other supervised activity, the person in charge should follow these procedures:

REPORT OF ACCIDENT

NAME_____ ACCIDENT DATE_____

HOME ADDRESS_____ TIME_____ A.M._____ P.M._____

PUPIL; PARENT; OTHER (Specify)_____

SEX: M F GRADE_____ AGE_____ SCHOOL_____

☐AUDITORIUM   ☐CORRIDOR   ☐LABORATORIES   ☐SHOWERS
☐GROUNDS   ☐DRESSING ROOM   ☐POOL   ☐STAIRS
☐CAFETERIA   ☐GYMNASIUM   ☐REST ROOM   OTHER (Specify)_____
☐CLASSROOM   ☐HOME ECONOMICS   ☐SHOP

NON-SCHOOL:☐HOME   ☐TO AND FROM   ☐BICYCLE   ☐TRAFFIC

NATURE OF INJURY

☐ABRASION   ☐BURN   ☐LACERATION   ☐SHOCK (E1)
☐AMPUTATION   ☐CONCUSSION   ☐POISONING   ☐SPRAIN
☐ASPHYXIATION   ☐CUT   ☐PUNCTURE   OTHER (Specify)_____
☐BITE   ☐DISLOCATION   ☐SCALD
☐BRUISE   ☐FRACTURE   ☐SCRATCH

PART OF BODY INJURED

☐ABDOMEN   ☐BACK   ☐ELBOW   ☐FINGER   ☐HEAD   ☐MOUTH   ☐TOOTH
☐ANKLE   ☐CHEST   ☐EYE   ☐FOOT   ☐KNEE   ☐NOSE   ☐WRIST
☐ARM   ☐EAR   ☐FACE   ☐HAND   ☐LEG   ☐SCALP   OTHER (Specify)_____

DESCRIPTION OF THE ACCIDENT

_____
_____
_____
_____

Teacher or supervisor in charge:_____

Present at scene of accident: Yes_____ No_____

Witnesses: Name_____ Address_____

           Name_____ Address_____

IMMEDIATE ACTION TAKEN

First aid treatment by_____ Sent home by_____

Sent to school nurse by_____ Sent to physician: Dr._____

Sent to hospital: Name_____

Name and relationship of person notified_____

Number of school days missed_____

Signed: Principal_____ Teacher_____ Supervisor_____

Figure 13-8. Example of a student accident report form.

1. Administer appropriate first aid (all physical education teachers and athletic coaches should know correct first aid procedures).
2. If additional care is needed, see that the student is properly escorted to the student health center or the hospital or doctor's office. Call an ambulance if such service is needed.
3. As soon as possible after the accident, complete an accident report form in detail, with the appropriate signatures, and have the copies distributed as directed on the form. Figure 13-8 shows an example of an accident report form.

Hazardous Activities

Because of the equipment involved and the nature of the activities, weight training, gymnastics, skiing, swimming, and certain others present more than a normal amount of hazard. Teachers of these activities are expected to have thorough knowledge of the hazards, teach safe procedures, and provide the supervision that is necessary to ensure safe practices.

Swimming Pool Safety and Sanitation

Since swimming areas require more attention to safety and sanitation than most other areas, specific regulations are described. Since these are examples, they may not exactly fit a particular situation or suit everyone's preference. They can, however, serve as useful-guidelines for swimming areas in general. Also, these particular regulations provide additional insight into the kinds of safety rules needed with other hazardous activities.

General Regulations

A thorough soap shower must be taken before putting on the swimsuit and entering the pool.

Running, tag, and other forms of dangerous play on the decks are prohibited.

Street shoes may not be worn in the pool area.

Instructors and lifeguards should teach and encourage people to use the most sanitary practices while in the pool or on the deck.

Only one person at a time is permitted to be on a diving board.

A diver is required to be certain that the water area is clear of swimmers before diving from the deck or the board. Swimmers should stay clear of the water in the vicinity of the diving boards.

Double bouncing is prohibited on the diving boards.

Wrestling, throwing, or pushing people in the pool is not permitted.

Admission to the pool will be refused to any person having a contagious disease, infectious condition, or any other condition that in the judgment of the lifeguard or instructor should prohibit participation in swimming activities, either for the person's own protection or the protection of other participants.

Food and drinks should not be allowed in the swimming pool area.

Participants should be discouraged from calling for help except when help is actually needed.

No one is allowed to enter the pool except when an authorized lifeguard is on duty. It is assumed that all swimming instructors are qualified as lifeguards.

Nonswimmers and weak swimmers are required to remain in shallow water where they can touch the bottom of the pool.

Lifeguard Requirements

In order to qualify for employment, a lifeguard must hold a current American Red Cross, YMCA, or Canadian Senior Lifesaving Certificate.

Preference will be given to those who hold current Water Safety Instructor cards or YWCA Leader Examiner Certificates.

Successful experience in lifeguarding is highly desirable, but not required in all cases.

Official lifeguard uniforms must be worn at all times by lifeguards on duty. Such uniforms may not be worn under any conditions by other people in the swimming pool area.

A lifeguard must remain on duty at the assigned station until a replacement arrives.

Lifeguards are required to be on the job 100%, meaning that they are not permitted to read books, carry on nonbusiness conversations, or participate in other activities that detract from their effectiveness as lifeguards.

One lifeguard must be on duty at all times when the pool is open; and there must be one lifeguard for every 50 participants in the pool area.

Lifeguards must never leave the pool unguarded even for a short time.

Each lifeguard should be situated in the most advantageous position to cover the assigned area of the pool.

Whistles will be used sparingly to attract attention, so they will not become commonplace. Whistles may be used by lifeguards only.

When a lifeguard is in doubt in terms of a person's danger, the guard should assume that the person is in serious trouble and act accordingly.

Lifeguards should be on the watch for weak swimmers, tired swimmers, or other persons who may find themselves in difficulty, and should control the activities of these people in order to prevent them from getting into danger.

Lifeguards are responsible for being thoroughly familiar with emergency procedures, know how to use the available emergency equipment without hesitation or fault, and should assist the Pool Manager in making certain that the equipment is in position and operable at all times.

Lifeguards should stress that the best procedure for safety is prevention. It is a duty of lifeguards to help educate people in safe practices and to make sure they follow such practices.

Emergency Procedures

In the case of a potential drowning, begin resuscitation *immediately*. Do not stop until relieved by a competent person. Treat for shock.

Have someone call the emergency number immediately. The nature of the emergency should be explained, so that the emergency personnel will come fully prepared to handle the situation.

Have the pool cleared of people (because lifeguards will be occupied with the victim) and keep people away from the victim.

After the emergency procedures have been handled, have the proper authority (administrator) notified of the situation.

As soon as the more urgent matters have been handled, but within no more than 12 hours following the accident, complete an accident report and be sure that *all* pertinent information is included.

REFERENCES AND RECOMMENDED READINGS

1. AAHPERD: Physical Activities for the Mentally Retarded. Waldorf, MD, AAHPERD Publications, 1986.

2. AAHPERD: Physical Education and Recreation—For the Visually Impaired. Waldorf, MD, AAHPERD Publications, 1986.
3. AAHPERD: Physical Education and Sport for the Secondary School Student. Waldorf, MD, AAHPERD Publications, 1986.
4. AAHPERD: Required: Quality Daily Physical Education. Waldorf, MD, AAHPERD Publications, 1987.
5. AAHPERD: The Role of the Teacher/Coach in Secondary Schools. Waldorf, MD, AAHPERD Publications, 1988.
6. Auxter, D., and Pyfer, J.: Principles and Methods of Adapted Physical Education and Recreation, 6th Ed. St. Louis, C.V. Mosby, 1989.
7. Blakemore, C., Hawkes, N., and Burton, E.: Drill to skill: Teacher Tactics in Physical Education. Dubuque, IA, William C. Brown, 1991.
8. Bucher, C.A.: Administration of Physical Education and Athletic Programs, 9th Ed. St. Louis, C.V. Mosby, 1987, pp. 50–87.
9. Camaione, D.N.: A method for determining instructional load credit. JOPER, 50(5):58, 1979.
10. Colvin, N.R., Colvin, G.T., and Kammenui, E.J.: Minimizing teacher stress. JOPERD, 53(10):54, 1982.
11. Cotten, D.J., and Cotten, M.B.: Grading: The ultimate weapon. JOPERD, 56(2):52, 1985.
12. Depauw, K.P.: PE and sport for disabled individuals in the United States. JOPERD, 61(2):53, 1990.
13. Espiritu, J.K.: Quality physical education programs—cognitive emphases. JOPERD, 58(6):38, 1987.
14. Graham, G.: Physical education in U.S. schools, K-12. JOPERD, 61(2):35, 1990.
15. Grosse, S.: Sport Instruction for Individuals With Disabilities: The Best of Practical Pointers. Waldorf, MD, AAHPERD Publications, 1991.
16. Harrison, J.M., and Blakemore, C.L.: Instructional Strategies for Secondary School Physical Education, 2nd Ed. Dubuque, IA, William C. Brown, 1989.
17. Kneer, M.E.: Ability grouping in physical education. JOPERD, 53(11):10, 1982.
18. Laray, B., and DePaepe, J.: The harbinger helper. Why mainstreaming in physical education doesn't always work. JOPERD, 58(7):98, 1987.
19. Loughery, T.J.: Quality daily physical education programs. JOPERD, 58(6):35, 1987.
20. Miller, G.A., Dowell, L.J., and Pender, R.H.: Physical activity programs in colleges and universities—a status report. JOPERD, 60(6):20, 1989.
21. Mueller, L.M.: What it means to be physically educated. JOPERD, 61(3):100, 1990.
22. Norton, C.J., Ed.: Secondary school physical education today: Problems and possibilities. JOPERD, 58(2):19–34, 1987.
23. Schack, F., Cranfield, P., and Marsallo, M.: Physical education, mainstreaming, and you! JOPERD, 4(3):14, 1991.
24. Trimble, R.T., and Hensley, L.D.: Basic instruction programs at four-year colleges and universities. JOPERD, 61(6):64, 1990.
25. Willgoose, C.E.: The Curriculum in Physical Education, 4th Ed. Englewood Cliffs, NJ, Prentice-Hall, 1985.

Chapter *14*

CURRICULUM DEVELOPMENT AND MANAGEMENT

The school curriculum must be based on sound values that are in harmony with the philosophy of the particular school system. The curriculum should be efficient in leading students toward educational goals. A review of Chapter 1 will help in understanding the importance of goals and working toward them, and a review of Chapters 2 and 3 will help in understanding the importance of sound values on which to base the curriculum. Further, it is helpful to remember that the end of our efforts is not to engage students in activity; that is a means. The end should be the development of human potential in all of its aspects.

ELECTIVE VS. REQUIRED PHYSICAL EDUCATION

Part of the philosophy of a given institution or school system is whether to have required or elective physical education. Physical education has long been a required subject. A strong case can be made for maintaining this status at the elementary and junior high school levels. However, the case weakens slightly at the high school and college levels, where the students are better prepared to make sound judgments relative to electives. At any level, an effective physical education program can be easily justified whether required or elective.

Changing from a required to an elective program does not necessarily mean lesser status or a reduction in faculty or student enrollment. It does, however, change the nature of the program. An elective program defines the activities to be offered, and students select those in which they desire instruction. Following are some pros and cons of required and elective physical education.

For Required

1. Mandatory enrollment facilitates efficient scheduling.
2. Physical education might not be emphasized by the particular administration or might deteriorate if not required.
3. Students take so many other required courses, they would not have time for physical education as an elective.
4. All students need daily vigorous activity for emotional release, physical fitness, and total development.
5. Students look at required subjects as being more important than electives.

Against Required

1. A required program does not motivate teachers to meet student needs and interests.
2. Physical education classes may become irrelevant and time-wasters.
3. Students resent requirements and so do parents.
4. Required classes are counter to the principle of individualized education.
5. Many students lack motivation toward required participation.
6. Some students learn to dislike physical education when it is required and want nothing to do with it in later life.

For Elective

1. Student choice of activities increases enthusiasm for participation.
2. Elective programs increase possibilities for meeting individual differences among students.
3. Elective programs increase student freedom and responsibility for making their own decisions and increase the possibility of carry-over into later life.
4. The drive for activity will cause students to enroll voluntarily.
5. Elective programs often better utilize community facilities, thus reducing expenses to school districts.
6. An elective program motivates teachers to do a better job because students will enroll only if the classes are interesting and useful.

Against Elective

1. Those who need physical education the most will not take it.
2. Elective physical education is harder to schedule and tends to result in less efficient use of facilities.

Each state and territory of the United States has legislation that describes the educational requirements. A district or institution may enact requirements beyond those of the state, but a district may not require less. Based on information from the AAHPERD a summary of the requirements for physical education in the various states and territories is presented in Table 14-1.

CURRICULAR GOALS

In order to clarify the discussion, let us first look at some commonly used definitions of what a curriculum is.

1. All of the planned experiences a student undergoes through his participation in a school's instructional program or a particular area of it.
2. An orderly sequence of courses and/or experiences offered by an educational institution to create an environment in which the objectives of the program can be achieved.
3. A systematic set of educational experiences designed to efficiently produce the most important learning and behavior needed for successful living.
4. All of the instructional and extra-instructional activities sponsored by a school. (This is a broader definition than normally accepted, because it includes both instructional/and noninstructional programs.)

TABLE 14-1. Physical Education Requirements in the States and Territories of the United States

States that Require Physical Education in the Public Schools Grades 1 Through 12 (the amount of the requirement per week varies with the different states).

Alabama	New York
Alaska	North Dakota
Arkansas	Ohio
California	Pennsylvania
Colorado	Rhode Island
District of Columbia	Tennessee
Illinois	Texas
Iowa	Vermont
Louisiana	Virginia
Massachusetts	Washington
Missouri	West Virginia
New Hampshire	Wisconsin
New Jersey	Canal Zone

States and Territories that Require Physical Education at Least 8 out of 12 Years

Connecticut	New Mexico
Delaware	North Carolina
Florida	Oregon
Georgia	South Carolina
Hawaii	South Dakota
Kansas	Wyoming
Kentucky	Guam
Maine	Puerto Rico
Minnesota	Virgin Islands
Montana	

States and Territories with a Physical Education Requirement of Less Than 8 Years

Idaho	Mississippi
Indiana	Nevada
Michigan	Utah

States and Territories that have no Physical Education Requirement

Arizona
Nebraska
Oklahoma

The goals (purposes, aims, objectives, and expected outcomes) for which the curriculum is designed must be sound and easily understood. The Board of Education in Calgary, Canada provided a useful concept of purpose when it described physical education as "an integral part of the total education program which contributes to the physical, mental, social and emotional development of the child through the medium of carefully selected physical activities carried on under skilled leadership and in adequate facilities." Additional direction was provided from the same source with five specific statements of purpose. The goals of physical education stress the development of the following:

1. Physical skills which will enable participation in a wide variety of activities.
2. Physical fitness and soundly functioning body systems for an active life in his/her environment.
3. Knowledge and understanding of physical and social skills, physical fitness, scientific principles of movement, and the relationship of exercise to personal well-being.
4. Social skills which promote acceptable standards of behavior and positive relationships with others.
5. Attitudes and appreciations that will encourage participation in and enjoyment of physical activity, fitness, quality performance, a positive self concept, and respect for others.

The AAHPERD gave its version of the goals of physical education with the following statement:[6]

Physical Education is that integral part of total education which contributes to the development of the individual through the natural medium of physical activity—human movement. It is a carefully planned sequence of learning experiences designed to fulfill the growth, development, and behavior needs of each student. It encourages and assists each student to:
Develop the skills of movement, the knowledge of how and why one moves, and the ways in which movement may be organized.
Learn to move skillfully and effectively through exercise, games, sports, dance, and aquatics.
Enrich understanding of the concepts of space, time, and force related to movement.
Express culturally approved patterns of personal behavior and interpersonal relationships in and through games, sports, and dance.
Condition the heart, lungs, muscles, and other organic systems of the body to meet daily and emergency demands.
Acquire an appreciation of and a respect for good physical condition (fitness), a functional posture, and a sense of personal well-being.
Develop an interest and a desire to participate in lifetime recreational sports.

A carefully planned curriculum indicates that those responsible have clear direction, and it helps the students understand where they are going in their educational programs and how to get there. In today's complex and changing society, the casual or nonchalant approach to curriculum planning just is not good enough. The approach must be thorough, timely, and precise. It requires educators who are truly experts and who are dedicated to providing effective educational experiences.

FRAMEWORK FOR THE CURRICULUM

Among the most important purposes of education in a democratic society are (1) to ensure the development of the type of personality required to perpetuate and maintain the desirable features of a society; (2) to teach the individual to constructively evaluate issues and to influence the social order by contributing to useful changes; and (3) to develop individuals to their fullest potential so they can function effectively within society, both currently and in the future, through intelligent self-direction and group deliberation and action.

In the past, meaningful statements have been set forth that have served as guidelines for the direction of education and for the placement of emphases. For example, in 1918, the Commission on the Reorganization of Secondary Education stated the seven cardinal principles of education:[10]

1. Health.
2. Command of the fundamental processes.
3. Worthy home membership.

4. Vocational preparation.
5. Civic education.
6. Worthy use of leisure.
7. Ethical character.

These principles have been looked upon in the past as guidelines toward sound education. They are still often referred to by professional educators.

In 1938, the Educational Policies Commission[11] set forth four comprehensive educational aims: (1) self-realization, (2) human relationships, (3) economic efficiency, and (4) civic responsibility. Like the cardinal principles, these aims have had significant impact, and they are still considered by educators to be meaningful goals of education in America.

In 1966, the American Association of School Administrators stated the imperatives in education. These are guidelines that should be at the forefront as curricula are developed and modified, instructional methods revised, and organizational patterns reshaped to meet current educational needs.

1. To make urban life rewarding and satisfying.
2. To prepare people for the world of work.
3. To discover and nurture creative talent.
4. To strengthen the moral fabric of society.
5. To deal constructively with psychological tensions.
6. To keep democracy working.
7. To make intelligent use of natural resources.
8. To make the best use of leisure time.
9. To work with other peoples of the world for human betterment.

More recently, the Institute for Educational Management at the United States International University at San Diego, California, was asked to study the most pressing needs of youth. The institute prepared a set of guidelines, which state the following.[15] All youth need to

1. Develop saleable skills.
2. Develop and maintain good health and physical fitness.
3. Understand the rights and duties of the citizen of a multicultural democratic society.
4. Understand the significance of the family for the individual and society.
5. Know how to purchase and use goods and services intelligently.
6. Understand the influence of science on human life.
7. Develop an appreciation of literature, art, music, and nature.
8. Be able to use their leisure time well and to budget it wisely.
9. Develop respect for other persons.
10. Grow in their ability to think rationally.
11. Learn how to make urban life rewarding and satisfying.
12. Discover and nurture their creative talent.
13. Be able to deal constructively with psychological tensions.
14. Learn how to make intelligent use of natural resources.
15. Know how to work with other peoples of the world for human betterment.

STEPS IN CURRICULUM PLANNING

Accomplishments in curriculum design and revision almost always occur as a result of careful planning. In the long run, changes left to chance seldom succeed.

The logical steps in curriculum development begin with establishing a curriculum committee with well-defined purposes and clear direction to do the following:

1. Study the local conditions and attitudes that should influence the curriculum.
2. Study and clarify the philosophy and goals of physical education in the particular school system.
3. Become well informed about opportunities and limitations relative to resources—facilities, teachers, and equipment.
4. Thoroughly evaluate the present curriculum in terms of both strengths and weaknesses.
5. Recommend curriculum changes along with the justification for them.
6. Assist with the implementation of approved changes, including dissemination of information to teachers, students, and public, and in-service training of the staff as needed.

Those responsible for curriculum development must be both planners and doers, and they should be well aware of the expertise available through national, state, and local organizations and institutions. Curriculum personnel should be diligent about keeping abreast of useful research and curricular trends and innovations. Sources of valuable information include the AAHPERD (publications, staff specialists, position statements, conferences, conventions, and workshops), the state association of HPERD (conferences, conventions, and publications), the President's Council on Physical Fitness and Sports, specialists from the State Department of Education, and college professors who are curriculum specialists.

Curriculum committees take different forms in different situations. For example, a large high school might have a curriculum coordinating committee and several subcommittees representing different areas of the school program. In such a situation, each subcommittee would study the curriculum content in its particular area of responsibility and recommend revisions. The coordinating committee would consider recommendations from the subcommittees, help the subcommittees identify weaknesses and possible solutions, watch for curricular conflict, duplications, and voids, and give broad leadership to curriculum development for the school.

In addition to the curriculum committee and/or subcommittees in a particular school, the school district often has a curriculum coordinating committee with two important functions: (1) to serve as a resource body for the curriculum committees in the various schools of the district, and (2) to coordinate the curricular content of the different schools.

The curriculum coordinating committee ought to have representation from the administration, faculty, student body, and community (through the PTA or the school board). An administrator can provide insight into such matters as budget, facilities, faculty resources, and the like. Teachers can represent the grassroots professional level because they work daily with students and are in close touch with what will and will not work. Students can provide information regarding their interests and the relevance of learning experiences. A representative of the public can help interpret the usefulness of curricular content in a practical sense as viewed from outside the school.

The local educational system must be compatible with the basic philosophic values that exist in the locale and comply with the needs and interests of the residents. The curriculum must be consistent also with government legislation and regulations.

CURRICULUM TRENDS AND PATTERNS

A curriculum must have a strong element of stability, and yet it should be gradually improved and updated based on changing circumstances and new information. Rapid change for the sake of change, and blind worship of the old and traditional are extreme approaches, and both should be avoided. Also, it should be remembered that excellence is never obsolete. Some of the current trends in curriculum development are the following:

1. Greater emphasis on physical education at the elementary school level, with concentration on perceptual motor learning and movement education.
2. Increased attention to the individual needs and interests of students, resulting in (a) more student involvement in learning methods, (b) student's choice of activities rather than school-imposed activities, (c) equal opportunities for both sexes, (d) emphasis on physical fitness activities and lifetime sports, and (e) increased use of audio-visual media for instruction.
3. More flexibility in scheduling in terms of time, space, student grouping patterns, and staff made possible by the utilization of computers.
4. Increased accountability for the effectiveness of the curriculum and instructional methods. Failure of students to attain minimal proficiency in basic skills—reading, mathematics, sports—has resulted in lawsuits by parents and students. Some states have already passed laws requiring teachers and educational institutions to be accountable for their teaching effectiveness. The use of appropriate performance objectives and effective evaluation are becoming more common as a result of this trend.

Physical educators should be aware of the various curriculum patterns that are common in the schools and the characteristics of each. Some of the more prevalent patterns are as follows:

1. The *separate subjects* pattern.
   The traditional pattern of curriculum organization.
   Teaching of separate subjects—history, English, physics, physical education—for a set amount of time each day.
   Little attempt made to relate one subject with another.
   Tendency for students to learn isolated facts and skills without perceiving

them as being related.

Physical education sometimes left out due to lack of time.

2. The *broad-fields* pattern.

Seeks to eliminate sharp lines between subjects: physical science, rather than physics, chemistry, and geology; fine arts rather than music, art, and drama.

Helps students see relationships between specific subjects.

Provides for fewer subject-matter areas and, therefore, longer time periods for each of the broader areas.

Physical education can be combined with health, safety, and recreation, although health is often combined with the biologic sciences. Experience indicates that both health instruction and physical education are more successful when taught as separate subjects; however, the two subjects logically belong in the same curriculum group.

Requires administrative flexibility in scheduling.

3. The *correlated* (integrated) curriculum.

Seeks to utilize relationships among subjects without destroying the identity of any one subject, i.e., science, English, and physical education can be combined in the following way:

Students go on bike, canoe, or pack trips involving physical fitness and the study of geology, astronomy, biology, and photography. Students write reports on their findings. All activities are cooperatively planned by teachers and students.

More common at the elementary school level.

4. The *experience* (problem-solving) curriculum.

Seeks to organize learning experiences around situations and problems that confront students in everyday life.

Based on a humanistic approach to teaching: respect the individual and specific needs.

Has advantage of being highly relevant to youth.

Results are doubtful because of large time blocks involved and *lack of continuity* in learning basic skills, which in this method are taught as they are needed.

More common at the elementary school level.

Movement education in physical education seems to be a way of relating this philosophy to physical education.

Interests, needs, and purposes of children determine the educational experience.

Activities are planned cooperatively by students and teacher. Problem solving is the dominant method.

Teachers need a broad background in order to serve as resource persons.

Administrative efforts must be flexible to meet facility, transportation, scheduling, equipment, and budgetary needs.

SELECTING CONTENT

Determining the content of the curriculum from kindergarten through twelfth grade (and through college) is a complex task. The curriculum must have (1) the proper sequence of learning experiences, (2) the proper breadth and scope,

(3) the right kind and amount of emphasis at the different stages of child development, and (4) be practical in terms of weather conditions, facilities, equipment, time, and faculty resources. Sources of information that can be useful in selecting curriculum content include the following:

1. Teachers' opinions based on their own orientation, their professional preparation, and their evaluation of the students' needs and interests within the framework of what is feasible under the circumstances.
2. Information from questionnaires completed by parents and/or students.
3. Consultation, oral or written, with known experts in the field, whose information and judgment on curriculum matters are respected.
4. Information produced and judgments made by a curriculum committee composed of representation from the administration, faculty, student body, and public.
5. Curriculum content recommended in curriculum guides and textbooks on curriculum.

Since the amount of school time that can be allotted to any particular topic is limited, those determining curricular content should be highly selective. Well-defined criteria such as the following can aid in the selection process.

1. Is the activity consistent with the stated goals of physical education for the school? Will it contribute significantly and consistently to the goals?
2. What are the strengths of the activity, be it physical fitness, lifetime sports skills, social interaction, character development, or the development of useful knowledge, attitudes, and appreciations?
3. Is the activity suitable for the particular student level (state of development), and does it fit properly at this point in the overall curriculum sequence?
4. Is the activity relevant, meaningful, and interesting to students, and do students relate to it, have an interest in it, and see a need for it?
5. Does the activity contribute to a logical sequence of curricular content?
6. Is the activity safe, or under what conditions can it be made safe at an acceptable level?
7. Does the school have the resources—faculty, facilities, equipment, or budget—to sponsor the activity?
8. Is the activity compatible with the local situation; is it within the limits of what the public would perceive as acceptable, useful, important, and appropriate?

Additional criteria could be listed for a particular situation. Proposed curricular content must measure up when compared to these basic criteria. However, it should not be assumed that each criterion has the same value in the selection process. It is often a good idea to weight the criteria so that each one carries the influence that it logically deserves. Table 14-2 provides an example of how certain activities were evaluated against selected weighted criteria.

SEQUENCE OF CONTENT

Programs are often planned so that every student experiences at least a minimum of exposure to (1) team sports, (2) individual and dual activities, (3)

TABLE 14-2. An Example of a Structured Approach to the Evaluation of Different Sports that Could be Included in the Curriculum. (Courtesy of Professor Jacqueline W. Asbury, Lynchburg College.)

Activity (Girls)	Safety		Basic Skills		Physical Fitness		Total Involvement		Social Interaction		Leisure Time Skills, Development		Total
	1–5	29%	1–5	21%	1–5	18%	1–5	15%	1–5	9%	1–5	8%	
Senior High Girls													
Tennis	4.3	124.7	3.7	77.7	3.8	68.4	4.3	64.5	3.1	27.9	3.5	28.0	391.2
Basketball	3.2	92.8	4.0	84.0	4.3	77.4	3.9	58.5	4.6	41.4	4.2	33.6	387.7
Folk Dance	4.6	133.4	3.2	67.2	2.8	50.4	3.1	46.5	4.3	38.7	4.3	34.4	370.6
Square Dance	4.6	133.4	3.1	65.1	2.5	45.0	3.4	51.0	4.3	38.7	4.3	34.4	367.6
Modern Dance	4.6	133.4	3.2	67.2	2.6	46.8	3.4	51.0	3.8	34.2	4.3	34.4	367.0
Soccer	3.1	89.9	4.0	84.0	4.7	84.6	3.9	58.5	3.6	32.4	1.8	14.4	363.8
Floor Exercise	4.1	118.9	4.6	96.6	3.5	63.0	3.1	46.5	2.3	20.7	1.8	14.4	360.1
Volleyball	4.6	133.4	3.8	79.8	2.7	48.6	3.7	55.5	3.3	29.7	1.4	11.2	358.2
Swimming	3.4	98.6	3.2	67.2	3.1	55.8	4.2	63.0	4.7	42.3	3.7	29.6	356.5
Softball	3.6	104.4	3.8	79.8	3.8	68.4	3.6	54.0	2.9	26.1	2.6	20.8	353.5
Badminton	4.3	124.7	3.6	75.6	2.8	50.4	2.7	40.5	2.9	26.1	3.9	31.2	348.5
Tap Dance	4.6	133.4	3.0	63.0	2.7	48.6	2.9	43.5	2.7	24.3	4.3	34.4	347.2
Activity (Boys)													
Senior High Boys													
Basketball	3.5	101.5	4.3	90.3	4.5	81.0	4.0	60.0	4.0	36.0	4.1	32.8	401.6
Speedball	3.9	113.1	3.7	77.7	4.0	72.0	3.8	57.0	3.6	32.4	2.1	16.8	369.0
Soccer	2.9	84.1	4.2	88.2	4.1	73.8	4.0	60.0	3.9	35.1	2.8	22.4	363.6
Volleyball	4.0	116.0	3.4	71.4	3.0	54.0	3.9	58.5	3.7	33.3	3.6	28.8	362.0
Flag Football	3.0	87.0	4.0	84.0	3.7	66.6	4.0	60.0	3.9	35.1	2.7	21.6	354.3
Softball	3.5	101.5	3.9	81.9	3.0	54.0	3.4	51.0	3.6	32.4	3.8	30.4	351.2
Calisthenics	4.2	121.8	2.3	48.3	4.1	73.8	3.8	57.0	2.2	19.8	2.8	22.4	343.1
Square Dance	4.5	130.5	2.6	54.6	2.0	36.0	3.9	58.5	3.9	35.1	3.0	24.0	338.7
Running	4.2	121.8	1.9	39.9	4.2	75.6	3.9	58.5	1.7	15.3	3.4	27.2	338.3
Modern Dance	4.5	130.5	2.7	56.7	2.8	50.4	3.3	49.5	3.3	29.7	2.6	20.8	337.6
Wrestling	2.7	78.3	4.2	88.2	4.5	81.0	3.1	46.5	2.4	21.6	2.0	16.0	331.6
Badminton	4.2	121.8	3.1	65.1	2.8	50.4	3.0	45.0	2.5	22.5	3.3	26.4	331.2
Jogging	4.3	124.7	1.6	33.6	4.0	72.0	3.6	54.0	1.5	13.5	3.4	27.2	325.0

rhythms, and (4) aquatics. Although a minimal exposure may be required, students are usually encouraged to explore activities beyond the minimal level, particularly in areas of the students' primary interests.

Curriculum sequence is the order in which the learning experiences occur. The sequence should be logical and related. One of the weaknesses of physical educators has been a failure to provide a graduated sequence of instruction. Too often, the same basketball unit, for example, has been taught repeatedly without offering new learning experiences. The content of the physical education program should be organized into a continuous flow of experiences through a carefully planned, graduated sequence of skills, knowledge, and fitness levels from preschool through high school and into college. The sequence should be developed in light of the students' needs and interests and built progressively toward the attainment of challenging physical education goals. The following discussion is an overview of recommended program emphasis at the different school levels.

Preschool and Kindergarten

The *emphasis* should be on freedom of movement and basic skills, with attention centered on gross motor patterns (running, walking, crawling, climbing, pushing, pulling, and dodging), balance and stability, gross hand/eye coordination, and the development of self-awareness and expression through movement. The *orientation* should be toward the child as a unique individual with particular physical, mental, emotional, and social needs. The *activities* should emphasize spontaneous movement in an environment that provides opportunities and freedom to explore and create movement patterns. There should be an abundance of vigorous large-muscle activity.

Primary Grades (K-3)

The *emphasis* should still be on fundamental or basic movement patterns, but they should be more continuous and unified. Attention should be given to (1) movement and performance awareness, (2) simple, organized activity concepts, (3) basic rules of safety, and (4) the development of flexibility, agility, balance, and coordination. The *orientation* should still emphasize the child as a unique individual. The *activities* would concentrate on large-muscle development, movement exploration (stunts, tumbling, and creative movements), rhythmic activities (singing games and simple creative and folk dance patterns), and games of low organization or student initiation.

The following activities are recommended for students in the lower (primary) grades:

Throwing and catching with medium and large balls
Informal ball handling
Relays
Catching and fleeing
Tag games
Jumping and hopping games
Tumbling skills
Dodging and darting games

Balancing skills
Rope jumping
Playground equipment activities
Body flexibility exercises
Rope climbing and swinging (within safe limits)
Basic rhythmic games and simple dances
Basic soccer-type skills

Intermediate Level (4–6)

The *emphasis* should be on the development and refinement of motor skills, physical fitness, the use of correct body mechanics in basic skills, and the development of activity related concepts, such as rules and basic strategy. The *orientation* should be on a combination of individual development and the individual as a member of the group (social interaction). The *activities* should include a logical sequence of experiences in movement education: basic and creative movements, rhythmic and dance activities of a basic nature, vigorous sports and games of low organization, basic aquatic and gymnastic skills, physical fitness activities and tests, and motor skills.

Some of the specific activities recommended for students in the upper elementary grades are listed:

Dodgeball games
Kickball games
Relays and races
Strength and flexibility exercises
Physical fitness activities and tests
Track and field skills
Gymnastics skills
Tumbling activities
Soccer
Basketball
Volleyball
Softball

Note: In all of the above, the proper progression is especially important.

Junior High School

The *emphasis* should be on (1) the development and maintenance of physical fitness, (2) the development of a wide variety of specific activity skills, (3) a basic knowledge and appreciation of a variety of activities to serve as a base for intelligent choices relative to out-of-class participation, and (4) the development of self-awareness and self-confidence. The *orientation* should be on the individual as an emerging adult in society who needs broad exposure and significant challenges. The *activities* should emphasize the development of a diverse range of human talents and interests, which would form a base for choices and contribute toward a feeling of fulfillment and success. The student's frequent awkwardness should be de-emphasized and the need for social interaction, group involvement, and vigorous participation should receive ample

TABLE 14-3. Sequence of Physical Education Activities for Junior High School

	Autumn Program	
Grade 7	*Grade 8*	*Grade 9*
Power volleyball skills	Soccer skills and team play	Power volleyball
Soccer skills	Indoor racquet skills	Speedball
Field hockey skills		Football (flag)
	Early Winter Program	
Stunts and tumbling	Basketball team play	Advanced outdoor
Basketball skills	Folk dance	challenges
		Social dance
		Concepts of
		physical
		education
	Late Winter Program I	
Wrestling skills or	Wrestling skills or Self	Circuit training
Aerobic dance	defense	Floor hockey
	Late Winter Program II	
Gymnastics	Gymnastics	Gymnastics
	Spring Program	
	Computerized AAHPER test administered—2 weeks	
Track and field	Track and field	Paddleball
Outdoor and racquet	Team handball	Climbing
skills		Softball

emphasis. Team sports are of obvious importance. The program should also include challenging aquatic activities, graduated stunt, tumbling, and gymnastics skills, combative activities for boys, intermediate level dance activities, outdoor education skills, and graduated fitness activities and tests.

Table 14-3 shows a sample program covering the different seasons of the year for grades 7, 8, and 9. It is similar to actual junior high school situations. Even though it may not be an ideal program for any particular situation, it will furnish some useful ideas.

Senior High School

The *emphasis* here should be shifted more toward lifetime activities, some vigorous and some less so. Also important is the development of knowledge, understanding, insight, and motivation toward "the active life." Emphasis should continue on graduated physical fitness activities and tests. A reasonable amount of group activities should be included with emphasis on the development of self-confidence, individual initiative, character, and responsibility to one's self and to others. The *orientation* should be toward the individual as a capable pursuer of activities appropriate for the student's needs and interests when given options to choose. The *activities* should include a wide range of graduated participation opportunities in lifetime sports, physical fitness, combatives and self-defense, aquatics, gymnastics, creative and social type dance, vigorous team sports, and challenging outdoor activities.[17]

College

The *emphasis* in college should be much the same as in high school except with more orientation toward lifetime activities in all of the different aspects of the program (team sports, individual sports, aquatics, dance and outdoor skills) and physical fitness, with concentration on the underlying concepts and the ability to design and follow through with a lifetime individualized fitness program. The orientation should be toward the students' needs to gain insight into their future as nonstudents in terms of (1) physical fitness needs, (2) the aging process, (3) potential participation opportunities outside of the school, and (4) the scientific and social concepts that should serve as a basis for selecting from the available activity options. During the course of all this, the selected *activities* should promote the idea of active participation for the pure joy of it. The "enrichment of life" concept should be carefully interwoven into the whole program.

PROFESSIONAL EMPHASIS

No profession can be successful unless its practitioners are able to relate its services to the current needs of individuals and society. This requires timely changes in preparation and emphasis. Traditionally, those who majored in physical education took a generalized curriculum that emphasized a combination of physical education teaching and athletic coaching. But, during recent times, the body of knowledge has greatly expanded, and there has been an upsurge in the number of specialties.

During the last few years, there has been a significant increase in the emphasis on *athletic training*. This has resulted largely from a combination of two trends: (a) pressure from outside the schools (including lawsuits) to have more and better athletic training offered in the schools, and (b) the significant expansion of athletic competition for girls and women. To accommodate the increased need for athletic trainers, many universities have added athletic training certification programs.

The concept of movement education has become well established as the core of the physical education program at the *elementary school level*. Much information has been gained about the need for physical education at this level, and there have been vast improvements in elementary programs. However, physical education at the elementary level is still lagging.

Three relatively new subjects areas, *motor learning, biomechanics*, and *sports psychology* are already quite well developed. The growth of these subjects has had a strengthening influence on professional preparation programs because they encompass substantial and useful bodies of knowledge. Additional development of these subjects will undoubtedly occur during the foreseeable future.

Some universities have instituted an athletic *coaching emphasis* or a coaching major, which is different from the physical education teaching major or the traditional teaching/coaching combination. Typically, the coaching major is designed for one who desires to coach athletics and teach subjects other than physical education. Many school administrators have encouraged this because there is a need for a pool of athletic coaches that extends beyond the physical education staff. Some physical educators do not want to coach and some are not successful at it. Some athletic coaches do not take physical education seriously, whereas they would be serious about teaching a classroom subject.

Also, a few universities now offer a major in *athletic administration* (on sports management). Usually this specialty is offered only at the graduate level for the express purpose of preparing competent managers to work in athletic programs and organizations. Thus far there has been a very limited demand for such programs, because traditionally, the great majority of the administrators and managers have come up through the ranks.

Commercial physical education is another area in which some universities are offering majors. This has been encouraged by the upsurge of employment opportunities at spas, racquet clubs, fitness centers, golf courses, and the like.

SUBSTITUTES FOR PHYSICAL EDUCATION

Practically every educational system has requests for substitutions for participation in the physical education instructional program, including athletic teams, ROTC, and marching band. These requests should always be evaluated on the basis of the following questions: (1) Does the proposed substitute contribute satisfactorily to the objectives of physical education? (2) If not, what special contribution does it make toward student development that would justify this substitution? Unless the answers to these questions are acceptable, the substitute should be denied.

REFERENCES AND RECOMMENDED READINGS

1. AAHPERD: Elementary Curriculum: Theory and Practice. Waldorf, MD, AAHPERD Publications, 1986.
2. AAHPERD: Fitness in the Elementary Schools. Waldorf, MD, AAHPERD Publications, 1986.
3. AAHPERD: Focus on Dance IX—Dance for the Handicapped. Waldorf, MD, AAHPERD Publications, 1986.
4. AAHPERD: Guidelines for Elementary School Physical Education. Waldorf, MD, AAHPERD Publications, 1988.
5. AAHPERD: Guidelines for Middle School Physical Education. Waldorf, MD, AAHPERD Publications, 1986.
6. AAHPERD: Guidelines for Secondary School Physical Education. Waldorf, MD, AAHPERD Publications, 1986.
7. Berg, K.: A national curriculum in physical education. JOPERD, 59(8): 70, 1988.
8. Brassie, P.S., Pease, D.A., and Trimble, R.T.: A formula for credit hours and instructional levels. JOPERD, 53(1):54, 1982.
9. Cipriano, R.E.: Curriculum development. JOPERD, 55(9):50, 1984.
10. Commission on Reorganization of Secondary Education: Cardinal Principles of Secondary Education. Washington, D.C., US Government Printing Office, 1918.
11. Educational Policies Commission: The Purposes of Education in American Democracy. Washington, D.C., National Education Association, 1938, pp. 9, 24.
12. Gabbard, C., and Miller, G.: Intermediate school game curriculum. A balance of the traditional and the contemporary. JOPERD, 58(6):66, 1987.
13. Graham, G., Hold/Hale, S.A., and Parker, M.: Children Moving: A Teacher's Guide to Developing a Successful Physical Education Program, 2nd Ed. Mt. View, CA, Mayfield Publishing, 1989.
14. Harrison, J.M., and Blakemore, C.: Instructional Strategies for Secondary School Physical Education, 2nd Ed. Dubuque, IA, William C. Brown, 1989.

15. Institute for Educational Management: Imperative Needs of Secondary Youth, International University, San Diego, CA, 1980.
16. Kelly, L.E.: Instructional time—the overlooked factor in PE curriculum development. JOPERD, 60(6):29, 1989.
17. Melograno, V.: The balanced curriculum. Where is it? What is it? JOPERD, 55(9):38, 1982.
18. Michaud, T.J., and Andres, F.F.: Should physical education programs be responsible for making our youth fit? JOPERD, 61(6):32, 1990.
19. Pangrazi, R., and Dauer, V.: Dynamic Physical Education for Secondary School Students—Curriculum and Instruction. New York, Macmillan Publishing Co., 1988.
20. Pangrazi, R., and Dauer, V.: Dynamic Physical Education for Elementary School Children. New York, Macmillan Publishing Co., 1989.
21. Pangrazi, R., and Hastad, D.: Fitness in the Elementary School. Waldorf, MD, AAHPERD Publications, 1989.
22. Seefeldt, V.: The Value of Physical Activity. Waldorf, MD, AAHPERD Publications, 1986.
23. Siedentop, D., Mand, C., and Taggart, A.: Physical Education: Teaching and Curriculum Strategies for Grades 5–12. Mt. View, CA, Mayfield Publishing, 1990.
24. Sterne, M.L.: Conception to realization. JOPERD, 62(1):35, 1991.
25. Trimble, R.T., and Hensley, L.D.: Basic instruction programs at four-year colleges and universities. JOPERD, 61(6):64, 1990.

Chapter *15*

THE SCHOOL
ATHLETIC PROGRAM

It has been said about *work* that what one receives for doing it is less important than what the work causes the person to become. This concept also applies to participation in athletics. Fortunately, most educators recognize that what is achieved in the win-loss column is of only transitory importance, whereas the experiences that contribute to the development of the individual have long-term significance for both the person and society. In spite of the validity of this concept, however, it must be tempered by the idea that most of the values accrued from athletics can be achieved just as well or better while winning than while losing. After all, one of the obvious reasons for athletics is to achieve excellence, and winning is a natural product of excellence.

Some of the ingredients of a successful athletic program are obvious, but much is relatively unapparent. The obvious portion and the most important in the minds of the fans, involves the competitors and coaches. However, forming the base and providing the support are such things as (1) school pride and tradition, (2) the philosophy that underlies the program and is integrated through it, and (3) support from the larger organization.

VALUE OF ATHLETICS

Educators have supported competitive athletics for many reasons. Some concentrate on the entertainment value, and who would deny that athletics can have this effect. Some cite the goodwill with the alumni, and a prominent athletic program surely builds alumni loyalty. Others refer to the importance of successful athletics in promoting a fund-raising program, and there is evidence of a direct correlation between the success of many fund-raising efforts and the success enjoyed on the athletic field. All of these reasons are persuasive, but they are not the most important.

The principal reason that educators ought to support competitive athletics is that athletics can be among the most effective ways we have of teaching some profound principles of life. Following are several examples.

Conditioning and the Law of the Harvest

We have all heard of the law of the harvest: "whatsoever ye sow, that shall ye also reap."

This principle is illustrated in the conditioning of athletes. Imagine, for example, a photograph of a highly conditioned athlete racing to victory in a distance event. The caption might well read, "victor paid price." Successful athletes do "pay the price" through the hard work of conditioning, both physically and mentally. This is nowhere more evident than in individual sports, such as swimming, wrestling, gymnastics, golf, and track.

Teamwork

Team sports teach teamwork more effectively than practically any other medium. Team sports such as basketball, football, baseball, and soccer have the greatest attraction for the athletic spectator because these sports move fast and are particularly entertaining. Team sports are, however, a means of teaching some useful lessons.

For many, teamwork means the thrill of the well-executed play, with each member of the team performing an assigned task with diligence and precision. Can anything compare with the excitement we experience when what started out to be a run up the middle for short yardage turns into a game-winning 80-yard touchdown due to teamwork, where every player carried out his assignment to perfection? The same lesson is taught by a precisely executed pass by a wingman in soccer for a quick goal or by a stunning assist on the basketball court.

Teamwork by definition requires a united effort; and sometimes, a majority willing to perform quietly and effectively in the background, as for example the linemen in football. The names of the quarterback, running backs, and receivers are well known, but the hard-working linemen who provide pass protection and blocking are less known. Careful watchers of the game realize how important they are and when even one of them lets down, the total effort is frustrated. A group of players who fail to learn the importance of team play will never be successful.

Preparation

Even a person unfamiliar with athletics can sense the importance of training and preparation. An individual or team who has failed to train—to practice and prepare—will be a witness to their own shortcoming. Imagine, for example, the negative effect of lack of preparation in a wrestler whose skill is good enough to carry him through to victory, but in the third period his muscles become unable to respond due to lack of conditioning. The opponent, who is less deserving in terms of skill and potential, becomes the victor. It is not uncommon to see a young athlete in the 400 meter run who has less speed and less potential for that event emerge as the champion in the final stretch due to superior preparation.

Opportunities occur in life on which we can capitalize if we are prepared. We must be ready to pick up the ball and run with it all the way to the goal line. Such opportunities sometimes come with bewildering speed at unexpected times and places. The variations are endless, but the question is the same. Will you be prepared? The importance of preparation was notably emphasized by Abe Lincoln during his younger years when he said, "I will work hard to prepare myself, and perhaps some day my chance will come."

Extra Effort Determination

One of the most exciting characteristics of an athletic contest is the opportunity it affords the players to demonstrate the significance of extra effort. Who has not thrilled at the gymnast or golfer who refuses to crack under extreme pressure; the tennis player who is in the fifth set of a close match, when even the mildest lack of determination can result in a loss; the cross-country runner who consistently grinds out 5 to 10 miles a day in a training program; or the powerful and determined running back who can carry tacklers with him by force and determination for an extra two yards?

This kind of extra effort applies to almost all activities of life. Many people fail because of half-hearted efforts, and many others, less talented, achieve success and distinction because of their extraordinary determination. There is more of everything for the one who makes the extra effort—more success, more achievement, and more satisfaction.

Playing by the Rules

Athletic participation can teach the importance of playing by the rules. A maximum effort is hoped for, but the effort must be within the area marked out for the play of the game. A brilliant defensive effort by a basketball player is of no value if there is a foul in the process. A swimmer can put in an excellent performance but end up being disqualified because of an illegal turn. The football player who tackles improperly or blocks from the wrong angle, can incur a severe penalty that will nullify any gain the team has made.

In all activities of life, if we fail to observe the rules, we bring a penalty of some kind upon ourselves and our team.

Defenses Against Discouragement

Another important lesson athletics can teach is how to withstand stress and potential discouragement. We have all seen teams that slowed down or stopped when things went wrong. Crowds headed for the door midway through the second half, acting on their judgment that the team had stopped trying, that it was discouraged, and so were they. We have also thrilled at the opposite—the team that never stops trying, never concedes defeat until the last second has expired.

Competitive athletics have great entertainment value, build loyalty in the alumni, promote fund-raising programs, and contribute to the morale of the student body. The most important contribution of athletics, however, is teaching the essential lessons of life—the lessons that make the difference between failure and success.

GOALS FOR THE PROGRAM

Interschool athletics is generally considered an integral part of the total educational process, which has as its aim the development of physically, mentally, socially, and morally fit individuals. Athletics can serve as a vital educational training ground, incorporating the following worthy goals:

1. To nurture and properly channel the competitive urge that is inherent in all of us.
2. To engender in youth the will to win by fair and honest means.
3. To promote pride in successful effort for the sake of accomplishment.
4. To build team spirit and desire on the part of those who engage in sports, and to work with each other in a cooperative effort.
5. To teach self-discipline and self-control.
6. To build morale and mold character.
7. To develop sound minds and bodies through mental and physical preparation for competition.
8. To encourage spectators and nonparticipants to take an interest in and appreciate the values of competitive sports.
9. To stimulate a continuing institutional interest and loyalty among students, alumni, and friends.

The program should be designed to develop:

Loyalty to purpose
Respect for discipline
Capacity to lead and direct
Respect for rules and authority
Ability to act effectively under stress
Capacity for self-discipline in the interests of accomplishment
Determination to overcome obstacles
Sportsmanship—the "Golden Rule" in practice
Enduring relationships with teammates
Health, strength, and bodily vigor

AREAS OF RESPONSIBILITY

Coaches provide the direct leadership for the athletic teams, but certain school administrators also have important responsibilities.

School Superintendent (Or College President)

The school superintendent has the following duties in connection with athletics (in an institution of higher education, the president would have the same responsibilities): to (1) clarify and communicate the role of athletics in the particular school system; (2) establish and communicate the athletic responsibilities of the various personnel; (3) evaluate the accomplishments of athletics in terms of its contributions to the educational goals and the welfare of the educational system; (4) maintain a high level of leadership in the athletic program; (5) establish a framework of policies for the provision and use of athletic facilities; (6) make sure an effective program of public relations is maintained; (7) give leadership to the budget and determine methods by which the program should be financed; (8) assume appropriate policies in connection with such matters as the safety of athletic participants, the balance of athletic opportunities for boys and girls, and the scope of the total program; and (9) be accountable to the governing board for all aspects of athletics within the school system.

School Principal

The principal shares with the superintendent some of the responsibilities indicated; however, through cooperation with the school athletic council (if one exists) and the athletic staff, the principal is concerned with more specific problems and procedures. These include: (1) certifying the eligibility of players; (2) defining responsibilities of athletic personnel; (3) supervising the faculty members involved; (4) giving administrative leadership in terms of crowd control and ethical behavior; (5) making and enforcing policies relative to the use and care of facilities and equipment; and (6) selecting and hiring athletic staff members. At the college or university level, these responsibilities are performed by designated middle level administrators, such as a college dean and/or the athletic director.

Athletic Director (and Assistants)

The athletic director is responsible for the direct administration and close supervision of the athletic program. Among the director's major responsibilities are (1) scheduling and contracting contests; (2) arranging for officials; (3) establishing travel schedules and enforcing travel policies; (4) monitoring athletic eligibility; (5) making certain that the program is conducted in compliance with the rules; (6) preparing for athletic contests and providing administrative supervision; (7) providing adequate athletic training and medical services; (8) preparing and administering the budget; (9) properly reporting accidents; (10) providing leadership to public relations; (11) supervising coaches; (12) evaluating the coaches, helping them improve their procedures and effectiveness.

Often an *associate* or *assistant athletic director* carries a portion of the administrative load. Also, large programs, particularly at the university level, include a *business manager*, who is responsible primarily for financial matters; a *sports information director*, whose responsibilities include working with the news media; and sometimes a *special events director*, who has the responsibility for promotion and management of the athletic contests, the sale of tickets, and the supervision of facilities.

Some of those in administrative positions also have coaching assignments. When the athletic director is also a coach, the director must be objective and fair in providing balanced administrative support for the total program. Too often the administrator/coach has used the administrative position to provide disproportionate support for a particular sport at the expense of other sports. Whether or not the athletic administrator should have a coaching assignment cannot be clearly answered. Often, that person's coaching expertise is needed. It is a matter that should be handled with discretion and good judgment.

Typically, administrators of athletics are former coaches who decided to become administrators when the opportunity arose. An athletic director's job requires many of the same skills and competencies as other administrative positions. Experience as a coach may give an administrator added insight, but a successful coaching career does not guarantee success as an administrator.

Athletic Coach

Coaching involves a unique combination of teaching and managing. Unfortunately, some people have the idea that a coach is not a teacher. Yet, some of the most sophisticated and individualized teaching methods are applied in athletics. If athletics is to be justified in the educational system, it must be conducted in an educational manner and contribute toward educational goals. Athletics are co-curricular in nature, and they tend to have broad appeal beyond the confines of the school; but at the core of the program is a professional educator (the coach) working with students in a school setting for the purpose of accomplishing the objectives of the educational system. Normally, the coach should be required to have the same kind of basic professional preparation as other members of the faculty, and hold faculty status. The coach is responsible for (1) maintaining a wholesome educational environment; (2) establishing effective teacher/student relationships; and (3) producing acceptable educational results.

Sometimes a coaching assignment is given to a person who is not competent in the particular sport. This diluted approach, which may be the only alternative, results in the supervision of students in a self-teaching exercise without the benefit of a subject specialist to guide effective learning experiences. Students would learn little about English in a class that was simply supervised by a nonspecialist. The same is true of athletics. If a sport is to flourish and if the students are to develop a high level of proficiency in it, the coach must be a well-prepared specialist.

The professional preparation of athletic coaches is just as important as the preparation of biology teachers, English teachers, or counselors. The best coach is the one who has had the best preparation. Generally, a coach needs three basic kinds of information: (1) thorough knowledge about of the sport, its rules, skills, techniques, and strategy; (2) adequate understanding of people, particularly the age group being coached; and (3) knowledge about the physiologic and psychologic preparation for athletic competition. The coach's success depends to a large extent on specific knowledge and the ability to apply that knowledge effectively. In addition to these specifics, high values and strong leadership are the key elements in success.

Athletic Council Members

Athletic councils (or committees) are prevalent in colleges and universities, and many exist in the secondary schools. Generally, they are advisory in nature, with their advice flowing to the chief administrator of the educational system. For example, a university athletic council is typically advisory to the university president, vice-president, dean, athletic director, and coaches; whereas a school district athletic council is advisory to the superintendent, principals, athletic directors, and coaches. In some cases, the council is more than advisory and gets involved in making and enforcing policies. Whatever the case, the role and perimeters of the council should be clearly defined.

An athletic council is composed primarily of nonathletic personnel. It is designed to give others in the school system (and sometimes representatives from the community and alumni) an opportunity to exert a positive influence on the athletic program. This helps to keep athletics in proper perspective and integrated with other aspects of education.

At a university, the council normally includes representatives from the administration, the athletic department, the booster group, the alumni, the student body, and the faculty/staff at large. At the secondary school level, the council includes selected members from the administration, the board of education, the athletic staff, the faculty, the student body, and the public (or boosters).

GOVERNING ORGANIZATIONS

Descriptions of several selected organizations involved in promoting, coordinating, and regulating athletics at various levels are in Chapter 20. It is recommended that, in connection with this section, the reader review those descriptions.

High School Leagues

For high school athletics, local leagues are formed to enhance scheduling, provide league championship competition, and implement useful policies and procedures. In some cases, a district or regional organization encompasses several leagues. Such organizations serve essentially the same purpose as local leagues except on a broader scale. They are the next step of competition.

High schools are classified for purposes of athletic competition on the basis of selected criteria, with size of student body being the most influential factor. In a state with four classifications, the divisions might be 1-A, 2-A, 3-A, and 4-A, with 4-A designating the larger schools. The divisions are aligned in various ways and given different labels, depending on the state. Divisions are determined primarily by school population, with geographic location also being a consideration.

State championships are sponsored in a variety of sports in most states. In a few of the larger states, it is not practical to complete all of the competition necessary to determine the state champions; therefore, regional championships are the highest level of competition.

Championships beyond the local league are sponsored under the auspices of the State High School Athletic Association. The two kinds of high school athletic associations are (1) those affiliated with the State Department of Education and (2) those that are unaffiliated (volunteer and not established by law). Most of the state athletic associations are of the second kind—voluntary in nature.

When the state association is affiliated with the Department of Education, membership in the association is automatic for all public schools, with private and parochial schools having the option of joining. In a voluntary state association, each school or at least each school district has a choice of whether to belong. In practically all cases, schools choose to belong because of the advantages, which include the following:

1. Eligibility for participation in regional and state championship athletic events.
2. Enforcement of regulations for the conduct of athletics.
3. Sponsorship of a classification plan for high schools.
4. Certification and assignment of athletic officials.
5. Enforcement of athletic standards.
6. Published bulletins and newsletters.
7. A final authority for the resolution of questions, controversies, and appeals.

Member schools have some obligations in return, which include compliance with all regulations of the association, cooperation, support, and loyalty.

College Athletic Conferences

Colleges and universities (including junior colleges) are organized into athletic leagues (usually called conferences), through mutual agreement of the member institutions. The conference is usually governed in accordance with a written constitution and a regulatory code.

The conference is administered under the jurisdiction of one or more governing boards known as a Conference Council and/or President's Council (most conferences have both). If the conference is large enough to employ an administrator, this person is known as the Conference Commissioner. The large university conferences have a conference staff of employees.

Some institutions do not belong to conferences. They remain disaffiliated or unattached, and are known as independents. Institutions such as Army, Boston College, Marquette, Navy, Notre Dame, Pittsburgh, Rutgers, and Tulane are just a few that feel it is better to remain independent.

In addition to belonging to athletic conferences, colleges and universities are affiliated with the appropriate national governing organization. For intercollegiate athletics, this means affiliation with one of the following: National Junior College Athletic Association (NJCAA); National Intercollegiate Athletic Association (NIA); or the National Collegiate Athletic Association (NCAA). Within certain of these national organizations, the member institutions are classified into divisions according to their athletic prominence or to their emphasis on athletics. These national organizations are made up of colleges and universities, not of athletic conferences, but conferences sometimes become affiliates of the national organizations.

Advantages of Leagues

When a high school or college acquires membership in an athletic league (or conference), the school is obligated to fulfill all requirements of the particular league.

Most athletic personnel agree that the ideal size of a high school league is six to eight schools. College leagues function especially well with eight or ten schools. This size permits a complete round of competition in football and certain other sports, and it permits a home and home arrangement in sports like basketball. In addition, this size of league enhances championship meets in individual sports such as track, swimming, and wrestling.

League schedules are usually prepared by an individual or a committee and are subject to approval by the appropriate representatives of the member schools. Nonleague contests are arranged by the officials of the two schools involved. Important considerations in selecting nonleague opponents include (1) schools of approximately the same size and with similar athletic programs and facilities; (2) schools that provide natural rivalries; (3) schools that have positive relationships with each other; and (4) schools that are in locations that afford interesting trips without excessive travel.

REGULATIONS AND RULES

The athletic governing organizations establish and enforce regulations for member schools. Among the purposes of the regulations are (1) to standardize athletic programs and procedures; (2) to protect student athletes and school personnel against possible abuses of athletics; and (3) to help keep athletics in the proper perspective in the educational setting. The regulations are especially valuable in protecting students, coaches, and administrators against exploitation.

Some of the regulations apply to individuals, whereas others apply to schools. Regulations that apply to individuals often deal with the following: (1) age of the athlete; (2) completion of a minimum number of units with an acceptable grade point average; (3) current registration for a specified number of units (minimum full-time student status); (4) parental permission to participate when applicable; (5) amateur status; (6) disaffiliation with non-school teams during the athletic season; and, (7) adherence to transfer rules.

Regulations that pertain to schools typically relate to the following: (1) conditions governing athletic events; (2) limitation of the number and value of athletic awards; (3) use of official athletic contracts; (4) exchange of eligibility lists; (5) control of postseason games; (6) limitation of the number of contests and the length of season; and (7) specified number of practices prior to the opening contest.

Eligibility

The standards or requirements for athletic eligibility are defined by the particular governing organizations. For example, a university affiliated with an athletic conference and with the NCAA must make sure the eligibility requirements of both are strictly enforced. At the high school level, the local league might have certain eligibility regulations in addition to those of the State High School Athletic Association.

The eligibility standards should be reasonable and functional and lived by impeccably. Individuals and institutions are expected to police themselves, although each governing organization has a penalty system for eligibility violations.

Athletic coaches and administrators must be well informed and in total compliance with eligibility rules. Athletes and their parents must be provided with the pertinent information on eligibility.

Recruiting

Recruiting is not (or should not be) an element in high school athletics, but at the college and university level, recruiting has become an important aspect of success. Many, including some athletic directors and coaches, feel that recruiting has become both dominant and distasteful. They would like to deemphasize its importance, but do not know how.

Athletic personnel need to be well informed about the precise regulations associated with recruiting. Administrators beyond the athletic department level must also adhere to recruiting and all other regulations.

WOMEN IN COMPETITIVE SPORTS

Competitive athletics for women has developed slowly. Different leaders and different segments of society have had difficulty agreeing on the involvement of women in athletics. Early advocates of athletics for women experienced a long and hard struggle and met with little success. During recent times, however, athletic competition for women has escalated rapidly, and that trend is continuing.

Women first entered international Olympic competition in 1900 with 12 entries in two events. This milestone turned out to be an exception rather than a rule, because during several subsequent decades, there was little expansion in opportunities for women. Some momentum was gained following World War II, but still not much happened.

About 1970, controversy arose about the tremendous differences between athletic opportunities for men and women. The mode of the time emphasized equal rights and equal opportunities regardless of race, creed, or gender. A strong base was laid during the early 1970s, and during the last half of the decade, athletics for women entered a new era. There were several forces behind the movement, probably the most prominent being the passage of Title IX of the Educational Act of 1975. Subsequent interpretations of the Title IX regulations have had unusual significance in the athletic world. (See the last section of this chapter for specific information about the application of Title IX to school athletic programs.)

ATHLETICS IN JUNIOR HIGH SCHOOLS

The questions of whether junior high schools should sponsor interschool athletic programs and, if so, to what extent and under what conditions have received much attention and are still controversial.

Athletic programs in junior high schools should be conducted under the same sound principles and procedures expected at the senior high school level. The main differences ought to be that the younger students are generally less prepared physiologically and psychologically for intense competition and that there is less justification to emphasize specialization in athletics at this early age. Therefore, the junior high school program ought to be less intent (more fun oriented), less restricting in terms of specialization, and less demanding physiologically, mentally, and emotionally.

SOURCES OF FUNDING

For the majority of athletic programs, the main source of funding is the appropriated budget. Supplemental sources, which vary in significance in different situations, include (1) gate receipts; (2) donations; (3) concessions; (4) parking fees; and (5) revenue from special projects sponsored by the booster club, student body, or members of athletic teams. It is usually preferable to have all forms of revenue associated with athletics deposited in the school's general fund and, in turn, have the athletic program managed exclusively on a planned and approved budget. The alternate approach is filled with potential hazard, because if the program depends directly on a variety of nonbudgeted sources, large variations can result in the amount of funding from year to year. Obviously, this would be disruptive in terms of planning and continuity. Also, if the program depends heavily on nonappropriated sources, it is easy for athletic personnel to become obsessed with producing revenue instead of providing high quality educational leadership. Outside interests that help with nonappropriated funding sometimes become too involved in athletic policies and procedures. More information about the sources of funding is provided in Chapter 9.

Within the basic philosophy described, sponsoring certain fund-raising events can be desirable for two reasons: (1) they can provide funds for some *extras* in the program that otherwise would not be possible; and (2) special fund-raising events can have a *rallying effect* for the program. Here are some ideas that have proven effective in both high school and college programs:

1. *Jog-a-thons (mini-marathons) or swim-a-thons.* Funds can be raised either from the participants paying entry fees or soliciting sponsors who pay a specified amount per mile covered by the participant (or per lap in the case of swimming). Sometimes events of this kind produce several thousand dollars profit.
2. *Athletic youth camps.* These have become common at colleges and universities, and often a portion of the revenue goes to athletics. Some high schools have also become involved.
3. *Celebrity golf tournaments.* Two potential sources of income exist here: (a) golf enthusiasts pay a specified fee to play in a foursome with a celebrity; and (b) if the field of participants justifies it, admission tickets can be charged.
4. *Special food events* such as breakfasts, chicken frys, and hot dog dinners are often sponsored. The tickets are priced to produce a profit. Arrangements can usually be made to have the food contributed by local merchants.
5. *Raffles* are sometimes held in conjunction with the events described in number 4. The items given away are usually donated by local sporting goods vendors and other merchants. Sometimes a large item like a set of golf clubs is given as the grand prize.
6. *Novelty athletic events* such as the Harlem Globetrotters, donkey softball or basketball and varsity vs. alumni games are often successful.
7. Also, concession stands, and the sale of printed programs, souvenirs, and folding chair seats are possibilities.

ATHLETIC AWARDS

We like to think the joy and satisfaction of participation in school athletics is sufficient reward for time and effort spent. An athletic letter or other similar award is meaningful, however, because it is a symbol of achievement and represents a standard of excellence. In spite of the desirability of a well-managed awards program, some problems are associated with it, especially the following: (1) having clearly defined criteria, which are fair and equitable; and (2) the question of how much the program costs the school and whether this money could be better spent in other ways. Fortunately, the National Federation of State High School Athletic Associations and its counterparts at the intercollegiate athletic level place an upper limit on the monetary value of athletic awards. The rationale is to preserve amateurism; however, such organizations are also concerned about budgetary and other problems if limits were not imposed.

Some Guiding Principles

1. Awards should serve as symbols of achievement and have little monetary value.
2. The primary goal of student athletes should be the joy and satisfaction derived from participation and accomplishment, of which an athletic award is a symbol.
3. Opportunities should be provided for an ample number of students to earn awards, yet the criteria should be high enough to make the awards meaningful.
4. Good citizenship should be considered along with athletic participation and achievement.
5. No distinction should be made between awards for different sports or for different levels of achievement, because the lesser awards then become meaningless, perhaps even unwanted.
6. An award should be given for recognized academic achievement, such as academic all-conference and academic all-Americans.

Specific Requirements (Criteria)

The requirements for earning an award should be specific but simple. The following are suggested, and they apply equally well to boys and girls in the appropriate sports. The criteria are skeletal, and not all sports are included, but the list provides a sampling of the kind of criteria recommended.

Football. Participation in at least one third of the quarters played by the team in the total schedule.

Basketball. Participation in at least one third of the quarters played by the team in the total schedule or participation in the state tournament.

Baseball. Participation in at least one fourth of the innings or one third of the games played by the team in the total schedule or participation in the state tournament. Exception: Pitchers may be recommended for letters without an established requirement of participation. Base coaches may also be recommended for letters.

Track. Score an average of two points per meet for the dual meets or qualify in the district or state meet.

Swimming. Score an average of two points per meet for the dual meets or qualify in the district or state meet.

Tennis. Participation in at least one half of the matches played by the team in the total schedule.

Cross Country. Participation in at least one half of the meets on the team's schedule and finishing among the first seven in the school in half the meets.

Soccer. Participation in at least one third of the halves played by the team in the total schedule.

Wrestling. Score an average of one point per match in the dual meets, or score two or more points in the district or state meet.

Service Letter. May be awarded to a student who has been faithful in practice and participation for at least 2 years and has completed the sport season during the senior year without having reached the required standards, either because of injury or lack of skill.

Manager's Letter. May be awarded for a minimum of one full season of service as team manager.

ADDITIONAL REMUNERATION FOR COACHES

Athletic coaches in the public schools put in many after-school hours. There should be a reasonable trade-off for the extra time or a sound formula for additional compensation.

In some cases, coaches are allowed free periods in exchange for the after school hours. Sometimes the plan involves a combination of free periods and extra compensation. The most common is to provide extra compensation. Whatever plan is used, it must be equitable in view of the professional preparation and experience and the amount and kind of extra services performed.

A relatively unstructured, unsophisticated method would be to offer the coach a flat salary for extra services. This figure would usually relate to merit and the quality of the prior years' work. However, a more exact approach might involve a multiplier, which relates to base salary and also includes steps for years of service. Such a method is based on the concept that the teacher should be fairly compensated for the fractional amount of time spent and in accordance with the base salary schedule. As the teacher's base salary increases, the extra compensation should increase a proportional amount.

The following formula provides a method of calculating extra compensation. This method can be used with other subjects besides athletics, such as for a language teacher who works extra hours with the language club or the forensics teacher who coaches the debate team.

$$\frac{\text{Number of hours per day in the extra activity}}{\text{Number of hours in the school day}} \times \frac{\text{Length of the extra activity per year (weeks or months)}}{\text{Length of the normal school year}} = \text{Time Index}$$

For example, the wrestling coach spends 2 hours per day with the team; the workday is 8 hours. The wrestling season lasts 4.5 months, and the school year lasts 9 months.

$$\frac{2}{8} \times \frac{4.5}{9} = \text{Time Index} = .125$$

If the coach's base salary were $25,000, the extra compensation would amount to $3,125 ($25,000 × .125 = $3,125).

PRINCIPLES FOR THE CONDUCT OF SCHOOL ATHLETICS

The following important principles for the conduct of school athletics help form the basis of a solid athletic program (paraphrased from principles stated by the NCAA):

1. **The Principle of Institutional Control and Responsibility.** The educational institution should control its athletic program in compliance with applicable rules and regulations. This responsibility includes the actions not only of its staff members, but also of other individuals and organizations engaged in activities directly affecting its athletic interests.

2. **The Principle of Ethical Conduct.** Individuals employed in or associated with the conduct of athletics (including participating student-athletes) deport themselves with honesty and good sportsmanship at all times so that their behavior reflects, not only for themselves as individuals but for the institution they represent, the high standards of honor and dignity that should characterize wholesome competitive sports in the educational setting.

3. **The Principle of Sound Academic Standards.** Maintaining athletics as a vital part of the educational process, with the athlete as an integral part of the student body, requires that principles of sound academic standards be followed. Student athletes shall be regularly matriculated, degree-seeking students. They shall be enrolled in at least a minimum full-time program of studies. They must maintain satisfactory academic progress and be in good academic standing.

4. **The Principle of Rules Compliance.** Each institution should comply with all rules and regulations of the athletic organization with which it aligns. The responsibility for compliance with rules extends to members of an institution's staff, to student athletes, and to other individuals and groups representing the institution's athletic interests.

5. **The Principle of Amateurism.** Individuals participating in school athletics shall be amateurs whose primary motivation for engaging in sports is the educational, physical, mental, and social benefits and for whom participation is an avocation. Thus, regulations are designed to afford student-athletes protection from professional and commercial exploitation.

6. **The Principle Governing Eligibility.** Eligibility for athletic participation should be based on compliance with all rules and regulations. These requirements should be designed to: a) assure proper emphasis on educational objectives and academic achievement of student-athletes, b) prevent exploitation of student-athletes and c) promote competitive equity among educational institutions.

7. **The Principle Governing Playing and Practice Seasons.** Limitations are established on numbers of contests and on length of playing and practice seasons to assure that students participating in athletics are able to be an integral part of the student body and to make satisfactory progress toward their designated degrees.

8. **The Principle Governing Post-Season Competition and Contests Sponsored by Non-Collegiate Organizations.** Reasonable restrictions on competition that occurs outside the school must be properly controlled to prevent unjustified intrusion on the time student athletes devote to their academic programs and to avoid commercial or professional exploitation.

Important Concepts

1. The primary objective of athletics should be the positive *development of the individual participants*. Lack of focus on this objective would be inappropriate at an educational institution. There are other potential benefits, but they should be secondary to the welfare and development of the student athletes. This implies that it would be unjustified for an institution to exploit an individual athlete in order to gain any other benefits.

2. There are *no virtues automatically inherent in athletics*, but participation in athletics has unusual potential for positive results. Whether positive development actually occurs depends upon the quality of the experiences and the caliber of leadership. High quality leadership is of paramount importance.

3. A single event, whatever the score, is of *transitory importance*, while the influence of the event on the character and development of individuals is of significant consequence. What the event does for the development of the individual is far more important than any immediate aspect of the event itself.

4. Even though losing a portion of the contests is inevitable, there is *no particular virtue in losing*, and practically all of the values of athletics can be accomplished at least as well while winning as losing. Even at best there will be enough losses to learn the lessons associated with losing. Recall the rich man who said, "I've been rich and I've been poor—and rich is better." In athletics, you win some and lose some—and winning is better.

5. *It's better to lose with winners than win with losers*—meaning that pure athletic ability should never take precedence over individual character and worthiness. The ultimate is to have student athletes who have the right combination of character and athletic ability. Strive to have teams that are composed of individuals who are winners both in athletics and in life.

6. A school athletic program should be *integrated into the educational system* and contribute to the school's overall objectives in much the same manner as academic programs. Athletics should be part of the mainstream of campus life and highly compatible with it.

7. The athletic program ought to *focus on excellence*—excellence of programs and excellence of individuals. Winning and excellence are closely related but are not synonymous. Excellence can be demonstrated in some respects while losing, and while winning some forms of excellence can be seriously lacking. Emphasis on the development of excellence in the broad sense helps keep athletics in proper perspective in the educational setting. Winning is a natural product of excellence, and constant pursuit of excellence is the best assurance of a winning program.

8. The main purpose of *amateur athletics* is development of the individual, and the main purpose of professional athletics is the production of a profit. Interschool athletics should be based on the spirit of nonprofessionalism, so that participation is regarded as important for its own sake and for the personal development and enjoyment that it brings.

9. The program should be as broad based as possible, thereby providing opportunities for many individuals in a variety of sports, with reasonable season limits placed on each sport in order that a student's life will not be dominated too much by a single sport.

10. Athletics should be viewed as part of the broad program of physical education. Ideally, the total program should constitute a pyramid of four phases with athletics at the apex. Other elements of the pyramid include club and extramural sports, intramural activities, and the instructional and fitness program (See Figure 13-1).
11. All-around physical fitness, lifetime skill development, and recreational participation are important aspects of the broad program of physical education. Members of competitive teams should not be deprived of these important opportunities.
12. Athletics should be viewed as an integral part of the total educational program and conducted in a manner that can be justified on an educational basis. Integrated throughout the athletic program should be the important concepts of fair play, ethical conduct, and good citizenship.

PRECAUTIONS

Athletic leaders and school administrators must constantly safeguard against certain bad practices and false values. Among these are (1) over-emphasis on winning at the expense of other important values; (2) over-glorification of star athletes; (3) disparagement of nonathletes; (4) presenting school athletic contests as public spectacles instead of education-related events; (5) distortions in the educational program, such as lowering standards to meet eligibility requirements; (6) putting coaches under undue pressure to produce winning teams; (7) improper balance of opportunities for male and female athletes; (8) yielding to community pressures in ways that are inconsistent with sound educational practices; (9) selecting coaches because they were outstanding performers and not because they have desirable leadership traits and are competent educators. The school athletic program is part of an educational institution; it should not become an athletic foundry.

A POSITION STATEMENT

Chapter 13 contains a position statement from the Society of State Directors of Health, Physical Education and Recreation on the physical education instructional program. The Society has also stated its beliefs regarding interschool athletics, and the statement is printed here with permission of the Society. It would be advantageous for a potential school administrator to be familiar with these beliefs.

Interscholastic Athletics

A well-directed interscholastic athletic program should be made available to all boys and girls who are interested and sufficiently skilled. This area of physical education allows students to participate in competition characterized by variety teams, leagues, conferences, regular season schedules, specialized coaching, and high quality of performance.

ABOUT ADMINISTRATION

The interscholastic athletic programs should be provided for and financed by boards of education with funds accountable through the general school budget. The program should be administered by school officials.

Interscholastic athletic leagues or conferences should be confined to pupils in grades 9–12.

If elementary school, middle school or junior high interscholastic sports programs are deemed necessary, AAHPER guidelines for such programs should be followed closely.

The rules and regulations of the National Federation of State High School Associations should be used as guidelines in administering the interscholastic athletic program.

The standards and guidelines of the National Association for Girls and Women in Sport may be used in administering the interscholastic sports program for girls, where considered appropriate.

State Departments of Education should be represented on the boards of control of all state high school athletic associations.

The health and welfare of pupils should be the first consideration in planning an interscholastic athletic program. To protect and promote the health and welfare of competing athletes, the following conditions should be met:

—Policies for the protection of athletes should be based on the best medical knowledge available.

—Policies should include procedures to assure adequate medical examination plus ongoing medical supervision of all athletes. A minimum of one medical examination should be required each year. Preferably this should be given immediately prior to the sport season. Re-examination should be required after any serious injury or illness before the pupil returns to participation.

—Coaches should understand and recognize the physical capacities of individual players. Coaches should be ever alert to note signs of undue fatigue or injury, thereby guarding the health and well-being of all participants both in practice sessions and in contests.

—High quality protective equipment should be provided and carefully fitted for every participant.

—Equitable competition between teams or individuals should be assured by the use of standardized classifications and eligibility requirements.

—Playing seasons should be of reasonable length and should be preceded by an adequate period of conditioning and instruction in fundamentals. No post-season or all-star games should be permitted.

—Contests should be confined to small geographic areas with no interstate competition except between schools located near state borders.

—Practice periods should be of reasonable length and geared to the physical condition of participants.

Awards should be simple, of little monetary value, and provided by schools rather than outside agencies.

ABOUT PROGRAM

The interscholastic athletic program in all high schools should provide maximum opportunity for both boys and girls to participate in a variety of individual, dual and team activities and should provide for differing levels of size and ability.

The high school athletic program should provide full opportunities for girls to compete in interscholastic athletics in accordance with their needs, abilities and interests. The girls' athletic program should be under the general supervision of a woman physical education teacher.

Interschool games and contests should be administered and conducted so as to enhance wholesome social relationships among community members and students, rather than to foster conflicts or extreme behavior based on unreasonable rivalries.

Interscholastic boxing should not be permitted.

ABOUT PERSONNEL

Coaches should be certificated teachers, members of the school staff and well prepared for assuming their coaching responsibilities. Certification of coaches is highly recommended.

Athletic directors should be competent administrators and educators with a rich background in interscholastic athletics. It is recommended that athletic directors acquire specific preparation for their position through formal courses or regular in-service work.

Games and contests should be officiated by qualified personnel who are certified by the appropriate governing body or officials association.

IMPACT OF TITLE IX

Information was provided in Chapter 13 about the application of the Title IX regulations on the physical education instructional program. This section contains parallel information about interschool athletics and intramural activities.

Section 86.41 of the law pertains to interschool and intraschool athletics. It states "that an institution or a district must develop and operate athletic programs according to the following specifications."

1. *General.* No person shall, on the basis of sex, be excluded from participation in, be denied the benefits of, be treated differently from another person or otherwise be discriminated against in any interscholastic, intercollegiate, club or intramural athletics offered by a recipient, and no recipient shall provide any such athletics separately on such basis.
2. *Separate Teams.* Notwithstanding the requirements of paragraph (1) of this section, a recipient may operate or sponsor separate teams for members of each sex where selection for such teams is based upon competitive skill or the activity involved is a contact sport. However, where a recipient operates or sponsors a team in a particular sport for members of one sex but operates or sponsors no such team for members of the other sex, members of that sex must be allowed to try out for the team offered unless the sport involved is a contact sport. For the purposes of this Part, contact sports include boxing, wrestling, rugby, ice hockey, football, basketball, and other sports the purpose or major activity of which involves bodily contact.
3. *Equal Opportunity.* A recipient which operates or sponsors interscholastic, intercollegiate, club, or intramural athletics shall provide equal athletic opportunity for members of both sexes. In determining whether equal opportunities are available the Director will consider, among other factors:
    (i) whether the selection of sports and levels of competition effectively accommodate the interests and abilities of members of both sexes
    (ii) the provision of equipment and supplies
    (iii) scheduling of games and practice time
    (iv) travel and per diem allowance

Unequal aggregate expenditures for members of each sex or unequal expenditures for male and female teams will not automatically constitute noncompliance with this section. But such inequality will be considered when assessing equality of opportunity for members of each sex.

REFERENCES AND RECOMMENDED READINGS

1. Bucher, C.A.: Administration of Physical Education and Athletic Programs, 9th Ed. St. Louis, C.V. Mosby, 1987, pp. 182–263.
2. Conn, D., and Maloy M.: Organizing Policy for Interscholastic Athletics. Madison, WI, Brown and Benchmark, 1990.
3. Hall, K.G.: Qualifications for secondary school athletic directors. JOPERD, 60(9):65, 1989.
4. Hasbrook, C.A.: Female coaches—Why the declining numbers and percentages. JOPERD, 59(6):59, 1988.
5. Kinder, T.M.: Organizational Management Administration for Athletic Programs, 2nd Ed. Dubuque, IA, Eddie Bowers Publishing, 1990.
6. Lapchick, R.E., and Slaughter, J.B., Eds.: The Rules of the Game: Ethics in College Sport. New York, American Council on Education and Macmillan Publishing Co., 1989.
7. Magnotta, J.: Why teachers won't coach. Strategies, 3(5):19, 1990.
8. Olson, J., Hirsch, E., Breitenbach, O., and Sanders, K.: Administration of High School and Collegiate Athletic Programs. Dubuque, IA, William C. Brown, 1988.
9. Sage, G.H.: High school and college sports in the United States. JOPERD, 61(2):59, 1990.
10. Squire, D.R., Saunders, J.M., and Dempsey, C.: Guide to Title IX and Intercollegiate Athletics,

2nd Ed. Washington, D.C., Squire, Saunders and Dempsey and National Collegiate Athletic Association, 1991.
11. The National Council of Athletic Training: Checklist for safety in sports. Strategies, 2(4):24, 1989.
12. U.S. Department of Education Office of Educational Research and Development: Light and Shadows on College Athletics. Washington, D.C., U.S. Government Printing Office, December 1990.
13. Yiannakis, A.: Sports marketing and fund raising. JOPERD, 55(9):20, 1984.
14. Zeigler, E.: Defining athletic success. Strategies, 1(1):17, 1987.

Chapter 16

CONDUCTING ATHLETIC EVENTS

School athletic contests today attract more attention from educators, students, alumni, and members of the public than ever before. And, since the business of the schools is education, the athletic events should be conducted in accordance with sound educational objectives and procedures. Athletic events should be sponsored primarily for the benefit of the students and for the overall good of the educational system.

Athletic competition has tremendous potential for individual development; but, the extent to which the potential is achieved depends greatly upon the quality of leadership. Athletic competition is neither innately good nor bad. It is only a potent medium that can produce positive results when conducted under high quality leadership; however, under poor or improper leadership, negative results are more likely.

Athletic events generate public enthusiasm and sometimes controversy because (1) athletic competition is dramatic in nature and, therefore, stimulates the emotions of both participants and spectators; and (2) athletic contests attract the attention of a relatively large segment of the public, and some members of the public become almost obsessed by athletics. Athletic events have a significant influence on the school's public relations.

SCHEDULING

Athletic events, especially those which attract a large number of fans, should be scheduled and announced well in advance. This can be beneficial in scheduling facilities, promoting the events, and avoiding competition or conflict with other activities. Also, scheduling in advance affords an advantage in the selection of preferred opponents.

Usually the contests that involve many fans and have financial implications are scheduled by written agreement, with all of the important elements specified. Such an agreement is referred to as an *athletic contract*. Written agreements reduce the possibility of misunderstandings and protect against default or unwarranted changes. Contracts are usually not used in connection with nonrevenue sports because many coaches feel that they can work just as well using less formal agreements. Even in these cases a simple contract or letter of agreement would be recommended.

Figure 16-1 is a sample athletic contract. Contracts range from less complex to more complex than the one illustrated, depending on the significance of the event and the particular conditions associated with it.

In scheduling events, realistic limits should be placed on their number and the length of the season. There is a tendency for the competitive seasons to become longer and longer and include more and more contests. Reasonable limits must be enforced for the good of the participants and the school program.

Following are some guidelines for scheduling athletic events:

1. Maintain membership in a reputable athletic league made up of schools similar to yours that sponsor similar athletic programs.
2. Facilitate scheduling by aligning men's and women's programs with the same athletic league.
3. Maintain membership in appropriate state, regional, and national athletic organizations. These organizations facilitate scheduling by the classification of schools according to the nature of their athletic programs.
4. Carefully select nonleague opponents to give the athletic schedule variety and interest. Contests should be scheduled within a reasonable distance due to the time, expense, and hazard of travel.
5. Involve coaches in the scheduling process. The advantages are that (a) it is a morale factor for the coaches; (b) their contacts with other coaches can often facilitate scheduling; and (c) coaches should be involved in determining the caliber and location of the competition.

MANAGEMENT

A host of duties must be handled in connection with an athletic event. The best way to identify and keep track of these duties is to prepare a checklist and review it to make sure that all the duties are handled effectively and on the proper timetable. It is desirable to identify the person responsible for each duty; however, since this varies from one situation to another, such identification does not appear on the sample checklist that follows.

Some athletic administrators prefer to have a separate checklist specific to each kind of athletic event, such as a checklist for basketball games and a different one for football or track. If this method is preferred, the checklist presented here can serve as a useful guide.

Normally, the athletic director does not perform all the functions on the checklist but is responsible for seeing that they are handled properly.

ATHLETIC CONTRACT

THIS AGREEMENT, Made and entered into this _____day of
_____, 19 ___, stipulates:

FIRST: That the _____ teams representing
the below named institutions shall play a game of _____
at _____ on _____, 19 ___ at
_____ p.m.

SECOND: That in consideration of playing the above named game, the
administrator of the _____ program shall pay
the administrator of the _____ program the
sum of _____
_____
_____

THIRD: That the officials for games shall be settled at least _____
_____ before the contest and the expenses of the same
shall be _____
_____

FOURTH: If either institution refuses to play except for some breach of
this contract, the administrator of the program of the institution refusing to play shall forfeit to the administrator of the other program the
sum of _____
_____

FIFTH: That this game shall be played under the rules of the _____
_____ Conference, and the _____
(national governing organization).

For _____ (institution)   For _____ (institution)

_____   _____
Faculty Representative   Faculty Representative

_____   _____
Director Athletics   Director Athletics

Figure 16-1. Example of a contract form for an athletic contest between two schools. This model contains useful elements from actual contracts, but it does not duplicate any particular one.

Before Game Preparations

Check When
Completed

_____ Contract completed
_____ Facilities officially scheduled
_____ Eligibility records checked
_____ Medical examinations completed
_____ Permission slips obtained
_____ Game officials scheduled and contracted
_____ Equipment available and in good repair
_____ Facility prepared (lined, cleaned, etc.)
_____ Media coverage arranged
_____ Courtesy arrangements made for visiting team
_____ Tickets printed and ready for distribution
_____ Programs printed and ready for distribution
_____ Arrangements made for concessions
_____ Ushers assigned
_____ Game statisticians assigned
_____ Police arrangements made
_____ Parking areas available and properly prepared
_____ Parking area personnel assigned
_____ Scoreboard in working order
_____ Public address system ready
_____ Spectator area properly prepared
_____ Half-time arrangements made
_____ Decorations completed
_____ Scorers, timers, judges, and announcer selected and scheduled
_____ Physician's presence arranged (game format)
_____ Written time schedule and contest procedures distributed to those who need them.

Game Responsibilities

_____ Supplies and equipment on hand
_____ Tickets and ticket takers available
_____ Ushers present
_____ Contest programs on hand
_____ Officials' quarters ready
_____ Visiting team's quarters checked and courtesies provided
_____ Flag-raising ceremonies arranged
_____ Intermission (half-time) program set
_____ Players' benches in position
_____ Physician present
_____ Scoreboard working
_____ Guards for dressing rooms on duty
_____ Concessions open
_____ Cheerleaders and pep band ready
_____ Police personnel on duty
_____ Rest rooms open, clean, and policed as necessary

_____ Extra equipment guarded
_____ Media personnel arrangements completed
_____ Game statisticians ready
_____ Game management personnel prepared—announcers, timers, scorers, etc.

After-Game Responsibilities

_____ Payment of officials
_____ Payment to visiting school
_____ Equipment repair and maintenance
_____ Storage of equipment
_____ Deposit of ticket receipts and concession income
_____ Financial statement prepared
_____ Proper use of game statistics
_____ Proper attention to any lingering problems

Progress has been made toward developing computer software for the conduct of track and swim meets. Computerization makes it possible to have the meet organized in the computer prior to the date of the meet, including time schedule, entries, heat and lane assignments, records for each event, etc. At the time of the meet, the names of athletes are simply entered into the plan. Immediately after the completion of each event, reliable and detailed results are run and readily available to all concerned, including the media.

Also, software packages have been developed for analyzing defensive and offensive strategies in football and certain other team sports. Further, individualized strength and conditioning programs for athletes have been computerized. All of the computerized programs mentioned above are still relatively unsophisticated, but undoubtedly during the foreseeable future, these programs and other similar programs will become refined and will be applied extensively.

CONDUCT OF SPECTATORS AND PARTICIPANTS

In the highly competitive environment of athletics, sportsmanship and proper conduct require special monitoring, both of participants (including coaches) and fans. In the educational system, this responsibility lies in the hands of those in leadership positions—the coaches and administrators. The coaches have the primary responsibility for the conduct of the athletes and themselves, whereas the conduct of spectators is primarily a responsibility of the administrators. Coaches and administrators would be well advised to hold a hard line against misconduct of both participants and fans. This problem can escalate rapidly if not strictly controlled, and there is no justification for it. The AAHPERD guidelines for crowd control include the following:

(1) Provide separate seating areas for the supporters of the two teams; (2) have uniformed police officers inside and outside the facility when needed and appropriate; (3) ban alcoholic beverages, mechanical noise makers, and undesirable signs; (4) provide free faculty passes to encourage faculty to attend athletic events; and have the faculty interspersed throughout the spectators; (5) place continuous emphasis on sportsmanship and proper self-control among both athletes and coaches; (6) provide adequate lighting of parking lots and areas adjacent to the athletic facilities; (7) carefully plan spectator flow in and out of the seating areas; (8) have an adequate number of

ushers or supervisors located throughout the facility; (9) provide adequate divisions or barriers between spectators and playing area; (10) play restful music over the public address system after the contest.[1]

In addition to these suggestions, Hardy[1] has stated some applicable ideas interested readers might want to pursue.

Sometimes, brief remarks by a school administrator, athletic representative, or student body officer can be helpful, in which the idea is clearly communicated that athletic events will be permitted only under desirable behavior of participants and spectators. Those unwilling to accept and support this should not attend.

GAME OFFICIALS

Poor officiating can be one of the primary sources of negative behavior of athletics fans and unethical conduct by coaches and players. Good officiating, therefore, should be viewed as important in itself and also as an effective method of controlling related problems. Of course, no official is capable of doing a perfect job, particularly in the eyes of partisan fans, coaches, and participants. A strong effort should be made to obtain well-qualified officials and get the players, coaches, and fans to recognize that the officials deserve their understanding and support. To gain experience, a new official often starts with high school junior varsity games. Another starting place is preseason practice games. This provides varsity game experience with less pressure than league games. A prospective official is usually required to pass written and practical certification tests.

Game officials should be selected and assigned by the appropriate representative of the athletic association, conference, or league, not by a representative of either of the schools. A sample contract for game officials is shown in Figure 16-2.

CHEERLEADERS

Cheerleaders, like players, are representatives of the student body, chosen as a result of their skills and general ability to lead. By nature of their positions, they have an excellent opportunity and important responsibility to promote good will and sportsmanship. Cheerleaders can exert a significant positive influence on other students and on fans in general.

Good sportsmanship is conduct that expresses appropriate self-control, courteous relations, and graceful acceptance. Sportsmanship can be shown in athletic contests, pep rallies, student assemblies, and many other school settings. Good school spirit is a reflection of sportsmanlike attitudes and behavior. If a school is to succeed in one of its prime functions—good citizenship—student groups must radiate proper conduct. Sportsmanship is one form of good citizenship in action.

The World Cheerleaders Council has the slogan "You never get a second chance to make a good first impression." Following are some important guidelines for cheerleaders that are advocated by the Council:

1. Stimulate and control crowd response.
2. Choose the right cheers at the right time.

Contract For Athletic Officials

Date _____ 19 ___

This is an agreement to officiate as _____ by

_____ at the _____school
       (name)

on _____ 19 ___. The _____
      (date)   (sport)

contest between _____and

_____ will begin at _____.
                                            (time)

The fee for this activity will be _____. Mileage will pe paid at

_____ ¢ per mile both ways. Other officials who will be working with

you are:

_____   _____
      (name)   (position)

_____   _____

_____   _____

You will be expected to report _____minutes prior to

the contest. In case of postponement, you will be informed of such by

_____.
      (time)

_____   _____
(Director of Athletics)   (Official)

_____   _____
(Address)   (Address)

_____   _____
(Telephone number)   (Telephone number)

Return one copy and keep one for your records.

Figure 16-2. A sample form for contracting game officials.

3. Be certain that words used in a cheer are not suggestive in a negative sense and do not inflame an audience.
4. Use gestures that are synchronized, pleasing to watch, and easy to follow.
5. When booing develops, divert the crowd's attention by starting a popular yell.
6. Do not conduct a cheer that competes with or disrupts the visiting cheerleading squad.

7. Select positive cheers.
8. Develop a large repertoire of desirable and timely cheers to use at appropriate moments.
9. Always maintain enthusiasm and composure especially in trying circumstances, remembering your responsibilities for leadership.
10. Give encouragement to injured players and recognition to outstanding performances regardless of team affiliation.
11. Always show friendliness to rival cheerleaders.

Cheerleaders should have the following objectives:

1. To develop a wholesome and enthusiastic school spirit.
2. To develop loyalty to the school and team regardless of the outcome of the game.
3. To promote a cooperative spirit between the student body, faculty, and school administration.
4. To promote the kind of sportsmanship that will help students acquire the basic attributes of good citizenship.

ATHLETIC TRIPS

In scheduling athletic trips, the following considerations should be taken into account. A trip should not involve excessive distance or time; transportation arrangements should be adequate and safe; and an ample amount of responsible leadership should be provided. The mode of transportation to use—vans, school bus, or commercial carrier—has both safety and legal implications with respect to the choice of vehicle and driver. Occasionally, sufficient reasons exist to cancel an athletic event, such as adverse weather or prevalent illness among team members. Leagues should establish clear guidelines as to what justifies cancellation and the procedures that should be followed.

The best approach to thorough planning and effective arrangements for an athletic trip is the utilization of a checklist, such as the example that follows:

Check When
Completed

_____ Confirm game details with the host school by letter or telephone.
_____ Make travel arrangements by common carrier or other approved mode.
_____ Plan travel itinerary, including food and lodging arrangements.
_____ Draw check from school fund to cover the expenses and cash the check.
_____ Secure and distribute or sell the tickets provided for the visiting school.
_____ Send itinerary to parents and secure the signed permission slips for all athletes, as required by the school's policy.
_____ Inform the athletic groups, student groups (band, cheerleaders), and adult groups (athletic booster club, parents of players) of itinerary.
_____ Pack game equipment and assign student manager to guard the baggage. Include athletic training supplies.
_____ Load equipment; inventory the items.

_____ Load athletic team personnel; check roster.
_____ Check team personnel before leaving each stop.
_____ Unload personnel and equipment at contest site.
_____ Contact host staff immediately on arrival.
_____ Assign student manager to guard clothing and equipment during the contest.
_____ Have travel vehicle prepared to leave immediately after the contest.
_____ Secure the contract payment.
_____ Account for equipment and personnel before departing.
_____ Account for equipment and personnel on arrival.
_____ Write courtesy follow-up letter to the host school.
_____ Confirm all matters that apply relative to insurance.

USE OF FACILITIES

Facilities used for athletic practices and competition are also used for other activities, such as physical education classes, intramurals, and free play. In view of this, at least three important guidelines pertain to facilities:

1. Enter requests for facilities for both contests and practices well in advance, and make certain that the requests are complete and clearly communicated. Early requests are especially important in connection with interschool athletic contests.
2. Be reasonable and considerate in terms of others' needs for the facilities. Unfortunately, some athletic coaches become greedy and inflexible about facility use. Practically all school sports facilities should be multipurpose in nature, and each of the different uses should be held in proper perspective and correct priority.
3. Every teacher or coach has a responsibility to make sure the facilities are used appropriately (and not abused). Also, each one has a responsibility for leaving the facility in as good a condition as possible for subsequent users.

The best way to avoid conflicts in scheduling facilities is to have well-defined priorities and clearly described scheduling procedures which are strictly enforced. In addition, each teacher or coach should be encouraged to avoid infringing on the scheduled time of others and to consistently contribute to a congenial and mutually supportive relationship in terms of facility use. It is a good practice to prepare a schedule form for each teaching station prior to the beginning of each term.

ATHLETIC ELIGIBILITY

It is necessary for all schools to honor and respect the eligibility regulations of the athletic league and the state and national athletic associations to which they belong. Some schools have other regulations in addition to those of the league and the associations. It is generally agreed that a student who fails to make normal progress toward a degree or a diploma should not be allowed to participate. Figure 16-3 is a sample of a high school eligibility certificate.

ATHLETIC ELIGIBILITY CERTIFICATION

This is to certify that the students listed below are eligible to represent

the _____ High School in the following

athletic contest _____

to be played at _____ on the

_____ day of _____.

FACULTY REPRESENTATIVE _____

PRINCIPAL _____
(Signature)

COACH _____
(Signature)

Names of Contestants			Uniform Number		Birth Date	Class
Last Name	First	Initial	Home	Away	Mo. Day Yr.	
1.						
2.						
3.						
4.						
5.						
6.						
7.						
8.						
9.						
10.						
11.						
12.						
13.						
14.						
15.						
16.						

Figure 16-3. Sample form for certifying eligibility of student athletes.

SAFEGUARDING THE HEALTH OF ATHLETES

The National Federation of State High School Athletic Associations and the American Medical Association's Committee on the Medical Aspects of Sports have issued a joint statement that the athlete has the right to optimal protection against injury to the extent this can be assured through proper conditioning, careful coaching, good officiating, proper equipment and facilities, and adequate medical care. Periodic evaluation of each of these factors should help provide a safe and healthy experience for players. The five major areas of the joint statement follow:

1. *Proper Conditioning.* This helps to prevent injuries by hardening the body and increasing resistance to fatigue. Coaches and athletic administrators should:
   —Give prospective players directions to follow and activities to perform for preseason conditioning.
   —See that there is a minimum of three weeks of practice before the first game or contest.
   —Take precautions to prevent heat exhaustion and heat stroke. This is particularly important in preseason practice for football, soccer, cross-country, and field hockey.
   —Require players to warm up and stretch thoroughly before participating in rigorous activity.
   —Make substitutions without hesitation when players show signs of disability, injury, or fatigue.
2. *Careful Coaching.* Athletes who are well coached are more skilled, which reduces the chance of injury. Coaches and other athletic department personnel should:
   —Stress safety in performance techniques and elements of play.
   —Analyze injuries to determine their cause and suggest ways to prevent them.
   —Discourage the use of tactics and techniques that increase hazards on the field of play.
   —Plan practice sessions carefully and see that they are neither too long nor too short.
3. *Good Officiating.* Qualified officials who know exactly what they are doing promote enjoyment of the game and protection for players. In this respect:
   —Players and coaches should be thoroughly schooled in the rules of the game.
   —Rules and regulations should be strictly enforced in practice sessions as well as in games. If they are not, the risk of injury will increase in practice and players will get into bad habits which will carry over into games.
   —Officials should be qualified both emotionally and technically for their responsibilities on the field or court.
   —Players and coaches should respect the decisions and ruling of officials. If they don't, tempers will flare and the game may get out of control.
4. *Proper Equipment and Facilities.* Student athletes should not be expected to participate in athletic programs unless they are protected by safe equipment and play on safe fields and courts. Specifically, schools should see that:
   —The best protective equipment is provided for contract sports.
   —Careful attention is given to the proper fitting and adjustment of equipment.
   —Equipment is properly maintained; worn and outmoded items should be discarded. The temptation to try to make equipment last one more year should be resisted when the safely of student athletes is at stake.
   —Proper and safe areas of play should be provided and these areas should be carefully and continuously maintained.
5. *Adequate Medical Care.* (Figures 16-4 and 16-5). Proper medical care is a necessity in the prevention and control of injuries. Athletic educators and school administrators should:
   —See that a thorough preseason medical examination is provided for each athlete and that a detailed health history is taken.
   —Arrange to have a physician present at games, and see that a doctor is available during practice sessions.
   —Adopt a policy to the effect that the physician will make all decisions as to when an athlete should resume participation following an injury. This applies to both competition and practice.
   —Adopt policies on exactly how much medical attention a trainer can perform without a doctor present.

ATHLETIC EMERGENCY INFORMATION FORM

To be completed by Parent or Guardian
(please print)

Name of Student _____

NAME _____ / _____
(parent or guardian)   Signature   Date

ADDRESS _____   PHONE (home) _____

_____   (Business) _____

FAMILY DOCTOR (1) _____ Phone _____

(2) _____ Phone _____

CLOSE RELATIVE (1) _____ Phone _____

(2) _____ Phone _____

In the event parent, family doctor, or relative cannot be reached, indicate your hospital preference:

(1) _____   (2) _____

IF CONTACT CANNOT BE MADE WITH ANY OF THE ABOVE, THE COACH WILL USE HIS BEST JUDGMENT TO PROTECT AND ASSIST THE INJURED ATHLETE IN ACCORDANCE WITH SCHOOL POLICY.

Figure 16-4. Form for placing on record at the school information useful in case of emergency.

SUGGESTED HEALTH EXAMINATION FORM

(Cooperatively prepared by the National Federation of State High School Athletic Associations and the Committee on Medical Aspects of Sports of the American Medical Association.) Health examination for athletes should be rendered after August 1 preceding school year concerned.

(Please Print)	Name of Student	City and School

Grade _____ Age _____ Height _____ Weight _____ Blood Pressure _____

Significant Past Illness or Injury _____

Eyes _____ R 20/ ; L 20/ ; Ears _____ Hearing R /15; L /15

Respiratory _____

Cardiovascular _____

Liver _____ Spleen _____ Hernia _____

Musculoskeletal _____ Skin _____

Neurological _____ Genitalia _____

Laboratory: Urinalysis _____ Other: _____

Comments _____

Completed Immunizations: Polio _____ Tetanus _____
                              Date   Date

Instructions for use of card   Other _____

"I certify that I have on this date examined this student and that, on the basis of the examination requested by the school authorities and the student's medical history as furnished to me, I have found no reason which would make it medically inadvisable for this student to compete in supervised athletic activities, EXCEPT THOSE CROSSED OUT BELOW."

BASEBALL	FOOTBALL	ROWING	SOFTBALL	TRACK
BASKETBALL	HOCKEY	SKATING	SPEEDBALL	VOLLEYBALL
CROSS COUNTRY	GOLF	SKIING	SWIMMING	*WRESTLING
FIELD HOCKEY	GYMNASTICS	SOCCER	TENNIS	OTHERS _____

* Estimated desirable weight level: _____ pounds.

Date of Examination: _____   Signed: _____
                                                    Examining Physician

Physician's Address _____ Telephone _____

Figure 16-5. Health examination form for athletic participation. (Printed by permission of the National Federation of State High School Athletic Associations and the American Medical Association.)

Procedures in the Absence of a Physician

When an athlete is injured and no physician is present, the following procedures should be carried out by the trainer or the coach if a trainer is not available. All athletic employees should be familiar with these important procedures.

1. Make an immediate preliminary examination of the injury.
2. Send for a physician and/or ambulance immediately if the injury is beyond the realm of your ability.

3. Give first aid as needed.
4. Notify the parents, or if they are not available, a designated relative or friend, and inform them of the athlete's condition, what treatment you have administered, or what action you suggest.
5. Determine whether the condition is such that the athlete should be removed from the area. First, ascertain whether such removal would be sanctioned by a physician. Unconscious players or players who are unable to move comfortably should be moved only if necessary and then only with adequate assistance and by proper stretcher techniques.
6. Have an ambulance available for all games involving contact sports. Keep it out of view of both spectators and players. Have the attendants inconspicuously seated but readily available.
7. Use a standard accident report form to record all important information. This form can be used for future reference, especially when the details of certain injuries become hazy memories. Copies should be kept on file in the coach's office, trainer's office, and school nurse's office for reference and for possible use in a legal action.

Duties of the Athletic Trainer

The three basic categories into which the trainers' duties fall are prevention of injury, treatment of injuries, and rehabilitation after injury. Within these basic categories, the trainer has numerous specific duties; the more prominent ones are included in the following list:

1. Require a periodic medical examination for each athlete, and help the physician with the arrangements and record keeping.
2. Work cooperatively with the coaches in setting up and carrying out a program of conditioning for athletes, especially those aspects that help in the prevention of injury.
3. Administer appropriate emergency treatment to injured athletes on the field, in the gymnasium, or in the training room.
4. Apply protective or injury-preventive devices, such as strapping, bandaging, or bracing.
5. Work cooperatively with and under the direction of the physician in respect to
    a. Reconditioning procedures following injury.
    b. Use of therapeutic devices and equipment.
    c. Fitting of special braces, guards, and other protective devices.
    d. Referrals to the physician, health service, or hospital.
6. Work cooperatively with the coaches and the physician in selecting athletic safety equipment and checking it.
7. Supervise the training room, which includes requisitioning and storage of supplies and equipment, keeping records, maintaining an accurate inventory, and managing the training budget.
8. Supervise and, when necessary, instruct assistant trainers.
9. Counsel and advise athletes and coaches on matters pertaining to conditioning and training, such as diet, rest, and reconditioning.
10. Conduct oneself at all times as a responsible professional.
11. Keep accurate and detailed record of athletic injuries and treatments.

INSURANCE FOR ATHLETES

Student insurance for team members is extremely important. An athletic insurance rider can usually be added at a nominal cost to the basic student insurance policy offered through the school. Athletic insurance costs might be paid by the parents, the school, or the booster club, but the athletes must be covered by insurance.

Student insurance with athletic riders usually includes (1) payment of all hospital costs and some physician's fees, or (2) payment of medical expenses after a standard deductible amount is paid by the insured (this kind is less expensive). Insurance for student athletes should contain a major medical clause whereby a high percentage of expenses would be paid for extensive medical care.

STUDENT MANAGERS

Defining the role of a student manager is difficult because it can vary considerably among different sports and with the preference of the coaches. Probably the most accurate definition is that a student manager is an assistant to the coach who carries certain responsibilities in accordance with the agreement between the coach and the manager.

Many responsibilities of the student manager could be correctly labeled as errands, but certain responsibilities involve much more. For example, the manager's duties often include caring for athletic equipment, keeping inventory, compiling, analyzing, and reporting game statistics and preparing equipment and supplies for team practices and games.

A coach should add a reasonable amount of dignity to the team manager's position by including some significant duties and treating the manager with respect. In this way, being a student manager can be a rewarding experience, and the manager can make a useful contribution.

METRICS IN SPORTS

The United States Congress passed the Metric Conversion Act in 1975, which—while voluntary—means the metric system will eventually be put into full-scale use in this country. It is already being taught in many school systems, and science and industry are adopting it. As international athletic competition has increased in scope, the need for a common set of standards has also increased.

In college athletics, the metric system is now in full use. The NCAA rule books for the various sports include metric conversions for the traditional imperial measurements. Progress toward the use of metric measurements has been made in other levels of athletic competition not regulated by the NCAA: namely, high school, junior college, NAIA, and open competition.

Until the metric system becomes universally used in American life, conversions will be necessary. Most are simple, but some can be a bit confusing. For example, a high jump bar set at 7 feet would be at 2.13 meters. However, the metric system is the simpler of the two, once people become accustomed to it and conversions become unnecessary, because metrics are established on the "base ten," whereas the imperial system lacks this element of consistency. To give a working knowledge of the process of converting imperial measurements to metric measurements, the following conversion table is included:

If you know	Multiply by	To get
inches	× 25.4	= millimeters
feet	× 0.3048	= meters
yards	× 0.9144	= meters
miles	× 0.60934	= kilometers
ounces	× 28.3495	= grams
pounds	× 0.453592	= kilograms

Equivalents

1 millimeter	= 0.394 inch
1 centimeter	= 0.3937 inch
1 meter	= 39.3708 inches
1 kilometer	= 1093.63 yards
1 inch	= 25.4 millimeters
1 foot	= 0.3048 meter
1 yard	= 0.9144 meter
1 mile	= 1.6093 kilometers

REFERENCES AND RECOMMENDED READINGS

1. Hardy, R.: Checklist for better crowd control. JOPERD, 52:70, 1981.
2. Horine, L.: Administration of Physical Education and Sport Programs. Philadelphia, PA, Saunders College Publishing, 1985, pp. 270–300.
3. Keller, I.A., and Forsythe, C.E.: Administration of High School Athletics, 7th Ed. Englewood Cliffs, NJ, Prentice-Hall Inc., 1984, pp. 54–193.
4. Kinder, T.M.: Organizational Management Administration for Athletic Programs, 2nd Ed. Dubuque, IA, Eddie Bowers Publishing, 1990, chapter 6.
5. Olson, J., Hirsch, E., Breitenbach, O., and Saunders, K.: Administration of High School and Collegiate Athletic Programs. Philadelphia, PA, Saunders College Publishing, 1987, pp. 228–242.

Chapter *17*

INTRAMURALS AND RELATED ACTIVITIES

The purpose of intramurals is to provide a variety of recreational activities, selected on the basis of their contribution to the development of the individual. Intramurals should be designed to serve the recreational needs of the majority of the student body and not just the athletic elite.

Intramurals are one of the oldest forms of organized sports in American education. The early programs were the result of students wanting to participate in leisure-time athletic activities of their own choosing. These programs were student led, student financed, and student administered and were present on campuses before required physical education and intercollegiate programs appeared.

Traditionally, intramurals meant all sports activities conducted within the walls of a school. The term intramural is derived from two Latin words: *intra* (within) and *murus* (walls). Originally the two words were separate (intra murals), then hyphenated, and finally evolved into one word.

The present concept of intramurals is a program of recreational activities conducted within the institution. Institutions differ with respect to the functions of their intramural programs. Some programs provide a wide range of team sports, individual and dual activities, and recreational pursuits, whereas other programs include only a few competitive sports. The scope of intramurals is often related to the size of the institution, with the large schools usually having more comprehensive programs.

Activities that might be involved in an intramural division are included in the following list. The first two are typically associated with the intramural division, whereas the other two are seen less frequently.

1. Organized sports leagues for both women and men.
2. Special events such as tournaments and meets.
3. Sports clubs, which may include both competitive and noncompetitive events.
4. Extramurals or club sports, which involve competition with teams from outside the school. (Usually this is a separate division from intramurals.)

The selection of programs and the establishment of participation units should be in keeping with sound educational objectives and the interests of the particular student body. Following are 11 guidelines to help ensure this circumstance. (1) The program should be based on the local needs of the students at their own level and on a sound philosophy of education and sports participation. (2) Activities should be available that offer opportunities for each person, regardless of gender, physical ability, race, economic status, or handicaps. (3) Appropriate representatives of the school population, both students and staff, should be involved in planning and administering the program. (4) Equipment and facilities should be shared by physical education and intramurals, whenever possible, to avoid duplication of costs. (5) Awards should be relatively numerous and inexpensive. (6) The program should be free to participants, financed from school funds. (7) The program should not serve as a substitute for physical education instruction or interschool athletics. (8) Activities should be modified to suit the needs and abilities of the participants. (9) Participation should be not only an end in itself, but also the means to teach rules, sportsmanship, and values. (10) The decision-making process in the program should be student-centered with guidance from the directors. (11) Students should be offered both leader and follower roles, and they should learn how to both win and lose properly.

INTRAMURALS AT VARIOUS SCHOOL LEVELS

There is a place for intramurals in school programs at all levels, from elementary school through college; however, the purposes, approaches, and program content are different at each stage of the educational program.

Elementary School

The need of elementary school students to be active, their desire to play, their willingness to accept challenges, and their desire to belong to a group create justification for a certain kind of intramural program at the elementary school level.

Some objectives of intramurals in the elementary school are (1) to develop movement and basic sports skills; (2) to provide moderate competition in a game setting; (3) to provide opportunities for cooperative play; (4) to foster fun; (5) to provide involvement in democratic processes, and (6) to introduce students to play opportunities in a variety of activities.

Simple skills, low organization games, lead-up activities, and modified games should be included. To sponsor a particular activity in the school, the club approach may be used, as well as interest groups or a special theme. Likewise, special events, field days, and mass activities for students are vital parts of the program.

Junior High or Middle School

Excellent opportunities exist for intramural programs at this level, due to the unique needs and interests of this age group. Following are some important objectives of junior high school intramural programs.

1. Provide team activities for the enhancement of esprit de corps and group closeness.

2. Present a wide range of activities to satisfy the various levels of ability and the broad range of interests.
3. Provide co-recreational opportunities to aid in socialization.
4. Offer vigorous activities to dissipate nervous energy and contribute to fitness.
5. Give opportunities for individual achievement and recognition.
6. Offer some interesting special events so that students can have fun, meet new friends, and enjoy both competition and cooperation.

Ideally, intramural personnel or other faculty members should serve as officials, and student helpers should secure the equipment and prepare for the contests. Supervision by adults is important at this level.

Usually, the activities are conducted after school, but some successful programs also utilize hours before school, during lunch, and on weekends. To some degree, transportation problems can be reduced through careful analysis of this problem.

Units of competition may be based on homerooms, neighborhood units, physical education classes, clubs, or pickup teams. A few schools may use a classification index or skill test results for assignment to intramural teams; but normally, administrative limitations of time and personnel prohibit this approach. Students in junior high school ought to have an opportunity to participate at least once each week.

In regard to eligibility, all students except varsity players of the particular sport should be eligible to play in intramural activities. Students should play for only one team at a time, so as not to reduce participation opportunities for other students. But this does not mean that varsity players (if there are varsity sports at the junior high level) could not serve as timers, scorers, and even officials.

Senior High School

The general objective of intramurals at the senior high level is to provide a wide variety of activities, in order to encourage regular participation in team and individual sports and special events. Skill development, a positive self-image, fun, friendly competition, and the development of interest in life-time sports are all valid reasons for a high school program.

Through intramural sports, students can be reached who are inclined to drop out of school or who may be turned off by other school activities. The improvement of self-esteem and the breaking down of social barriers can occur through sports participation.

At the high school level, intramural activities can be conducted before school, at noontime, during activity periods, after school, or in the evening. The ideal time is after school, except that conflicts with varsity sports often arise. To some extent, facility problems can be overcome by playing the sports out of season and through cooperative use of community facilities.

Colleges and Universities

The reasons for and the benefits of intramurals are the same in college as in high school, and the kinds of activities included in the program are generally the same. There are some distinct differences, however, that need to be carefully considered. (1) College and university programs are usually much larger than public school programs. (2) The facilities are more extensive and more available. (3) A large portion of the student body may live in residence halls or apartments, in close proximity to the campus, thus reducing the transportation problem that often exists with public school students. (4) College students have more flexible schedules. (5) A greater variety of circumstances must be considered in light of the eligibility question. (6) Many students at a university live away from home, creating an increased need for involvement in intramurals and other school activities. (7) College intramural programs are relatively large, affording the opportunity for a greater variety of program offerings.

ORGANIZATIONAL PATTERNS

An intramural program can be organized in several ways. Three different patterns are shown in Figures 17-1, 17-2, and 17-3. The educational level, size of the program, and administrative philosophy are all influencing factors. Usually, the intramural program is associated with physical education. However, in some colleges and universities, it is attached to the Dean of Students office, the Student Union, the Interschool Athletic Department, or the Department of Recreation Management.

ADMINISTRATIVE GUIDELINES

The danger always exists of intramurals becoming caught up in the administrative process and becoming more process oriented than people oriented.

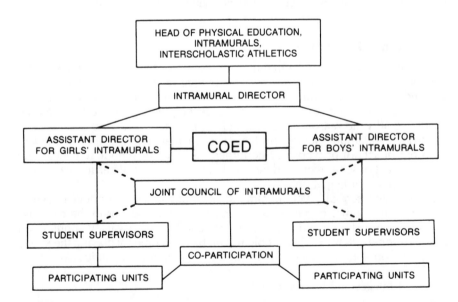

Figure 17-1. Example of a desirable intramural organizational pattern for a secondary school. (Courtesy of Bruce Holley.)

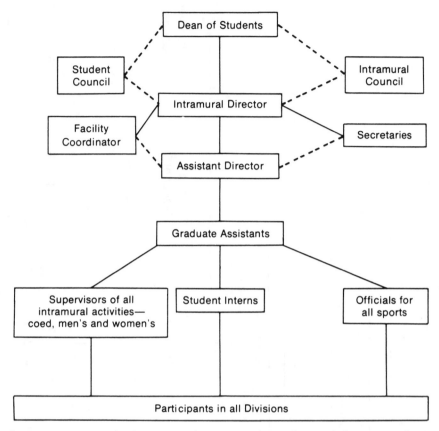

Figure 17-2. An example of an intramural organization for a college, with the program administered under student government.

Intramural administration exists to provide, an effective program for participants, utilizing the resources of the school to meet their needs. The following administrative practices can enhance the intramural program:

1. Student leadership and its development should be a major responsibility of those in charge. This can be accomplished through students participating on the intramural council, serving as assistant directors or supervisors, and qualifying and serving as game officials.
2. The policies and procedures applied should serve the needs and interests of the students.
3. The intramural program should be available to students, faculty, and staff, but the major emphasis should be on the students.
4. The program should foster fair play and sportsmanship.
5. The health and safety of the participants is of vital importance; therefore, adequate precautionary measures are necessary.

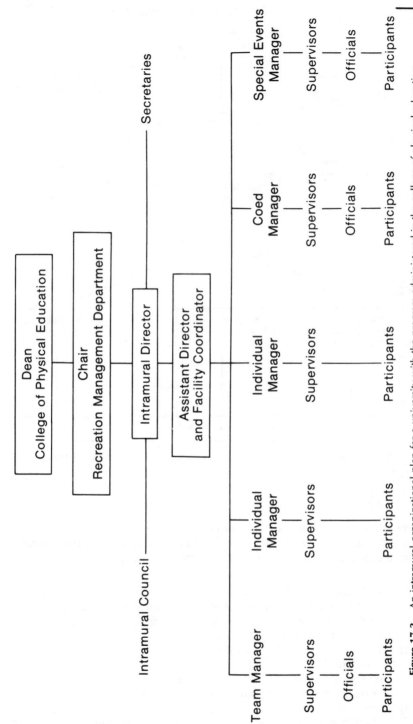

Figure 17-3. An intramural organizational plan for a university with the program administered in the college of physical education.

6. Competition should be equalized as much as possible so that all participants may enjoy rewarding experiences.
7. The program should involve sufficient variety.
8. Novelty and special events may be used for enhancement, but the heart of the program should be sports, both team and individual, that are well planned and conducted.
9. Qualified officials should be provided, because poor officiating is both unfair and troublesome.

Effective *units of competition* are essential to a successful intramural program regardless of the scholastic level involved. The competitive units form the basis for effective organization and administration.

Individual, team, league, and *all-campus* are the units usually found within intramural programs. In *individual* sports competition, the individual is considered a unit because other players are not needed to form a team. *Teams* are developed by groups of interested players, and a team constitutes a unit. A *league* is composed of a logical grouping of teams, such as those representing residence halls. *All-campus* is a tournament that is open to all who would qualify under the definition of the particular event.

Following are suggested events that could be offered during the year. Included are individual, dual, and team activities. Certain of the activities would be conducted separately for men and women, and others would be coed.

Fall	*Winter*	*Spring*
Individual fitness	Individual fitness	Softball
Football (flag)	Basketball	Racquetball
Tennis	Racquetball	Basketball
Horseshoes	Water polo	Volleyball
Bicycle race	Badminton	Golf
Soccer	Arm wrestling	Tennis
Volleyball	Volleyball	5K Road race
Racquetball	Bowling	
Basketball	Wrestling	*Summer*
Handball	Water Basketball	Softball
Table tennis	Tennis	Tennis
Badminton	Road rally	Basketball
Swim meet	5K Road race	Racquetball
		Golf
		Triathlon

TOURNAMENTS

A tournament is organized competition in an activity, usually for a relatively short period of time, which finally results in determining a champion.

The purposes of tournament play include the following:

1. To stimulate interest and develop excellence in the particular activity.
2. To provide challenging competition in wholesome activities.
3. To prepare players for higher-level competition.
4. To determine a champion.

Tournament Terminology

Bracket: The lines used in a tournament chart to show opposing players or teams.

Bye: When a player or team advances to the next bracket without opposition.

Challenge: An invitation to engage in a match or contest.

Default: Failure of one of the contenders to begin or complete a scheduled match.

Division: Normally, a large component of a program, containing one or more leagues grouped under a logical classification, i.e., fraternity, residence hall, graduate, or independent.

Handicap: An advantage given a contender as a means of equalizing competition.

League: The grouping of teams (or organizations) of like characteristics into units for competition.

Match: A contest to declare a winner between two or more opponents.

Qualifying Round: A contest that allows the winners to advance.

Round: The first round in the tournament is completed when all teams have played one match or had a bye.

Seeding: The placement of teams or individuals in different brackets so that those with superior records do not meet in the early rounds of a tournament.

Tie Breaker (overtime or sudden death): A means of declaring a champion after the regular event has ended in a tie, based on points, a period of time, distance, or numbers, depending on the activity. This process ensures an immediate champion.

Types of Tournaments

The particular tournaments described in this section are the round robin, Lombard, challenge tournaments (ladder, pyramid, and funnel), and elimination tournaments (single, consolation, and double). These are the more frequently used tournaments in intramural programs.

Several other kinds of tournaments, which are used infrequently, sometimes fit a situation better than the tournaments mentioned. Among them are the following: Ringer tournament (improvement tournament), Olympic meet tournament, Bagnall-Wild elimination tournament (a modification of the single elimination), combination elimination and round robin, and tombstone tournament. Descriptions of these tournaments can be found in textbooks on intramurals.

Tournaments that are selected for use in intramural programs ought to (1) provide a near equal amount of involvement for all participants (avoid early elimination); (2) provide well-matched competition; (3) be neither too short nor too long; and (4) select a champion with a few other subsequent places also determined.

The five basic criteria for selecting the best kind of tournament are the number of participants, available facilities and equipment, participants' interest, availability of qualified officials, and the nature of the sport.

Round Robin. If sufficient time and adequate facilities exist, the round robin tournament is a good choice. It is superior to other tournaments because it

Rd 1	Rd 2	Rd 3	Rd 4	Rd 5	Rd 6	Rd 7	Check
A vs H	A vs G	A vs F	A vs E	A vs D	A vs C	A vs B	A - H
B vs G	H vs F	G vs E	F vs D	E vs C	D vs B	C vs H	B - G
C vs F	B vs E	H vs D	G vs C	F vs B	E vs H	D vs G	C - F
D vs E	C vs D	B vs C	H vs B	G vs H	F vs G	E vs F	D - E

Figure 17-4. Round robin tournament involving eight teams.

produces a true winner, ranks other contestants, and allows all contestants to play until the end. Each entry plays all other entries at least once; in a double round robin, each contestant plays all others twice. The winner is the contestant who wins the most games.

In scheduling a round robin tournament, the entries are arranged in two columns, as shown in Figure 17-4 under "Rd 1." This provides the pairings for the first round of play. If the number of entries is uneven, a bye is added. (Bye indicates that the entry paired with the bye does not play during that round.) The entry in the top left column remains stationary and the other contestants rotate one position each round. If a bye is necessary, it may be placed in the stationary position. Entries rotate either clockwise or counterclockwise. Counterclockwise rotation is used in the example below. The check round is not scheduled for play. It is the same as round one, and its purpose is to provide a check to make sure that all rounds have been completed correctly.

It is usually best to schedule rounds of play at the same time on the same day each week. This makes the schedule easy to remember. The total number of tournament games required is given by this formula: Total games = $\dfrac{N(N-1)}{2}$, where N represents the number of entries. (N must be an even number. If not, add a bye to the list of participants.)

> *Example:*
>
> 7 teams + Bye = 8 teams $\dfrac{8(8-1)}{2} = \dfrac{8 \times 7}{2} = 28$
>
> 28 games for a single
> round robin tournament.

When the schedule is printed, it should include the date, time, and place for each game, as shown in the following example.

	January 15—Round 1			January 22—Round 2	
	Bye vs. Hotshots			Bye vs. Snappers	
8:00	Snappers vs. Topnotch	Court I	8:00	Bombers vs. Hotshots	Court I
8:00	Bombers vs. Sliders	Court II	8:00	Panthers vs. Topnotch	Court II
9:00	Panthers vs. Flash	Court I	9:00	Flash vs. Sliders	Court I

A win-loss chart such as shown in Figure 17-5 may be posted to report the scores and keep the team records.

If time permits, a *double round robin* provides an interesting modification. It

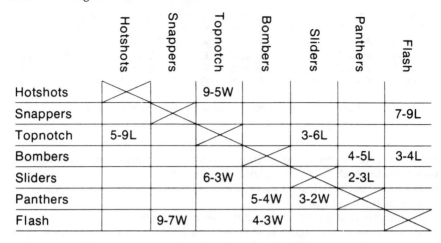

	Hotshots	Snappers	Topnotch	Bombers	Sliders	Panthers	Flash
Hotshots			9-5W				
Snappers							7-9L
Topnotch	5-9L				3-6L		
Bombers						4-5L	3-4L
Sliders			6-3W			2-3L	
Panthers				5-4W	3-2W		
Flash		9-7W		4-3W			

Figure 17-5. A win-loss chart for a round robin tournament.

is even more valid than the single round robin because each entry plays each other entry twice.

Lombard. The Lombard tournament is a round robin played in one day of competition. The number of games to be played is divided into the available time to give the length of each game. As in the regular round robin, each entry plays all other entries. Winners may be determined by adding total points scored by a team and subtracting points scored against it. The entry with the most points left is the winner. More simply, win-loss records may also be used to declare the winner.

Example: Six teams want to play a basketball tournament in which each team plays every other team. They have two courts for 3 hours (6 hours total playing time) to play 15 games. Dividing 15 games into 6 hours (360 minutes) gives 24 minutes per game. Each game could be 20 minutes, with 4 minutes between games.

Challenge. A challenge tournament is one in which the several contestants are placed in a particular order, and then each entry has the opportunity of improving its position (or standing) by challenging and defeating one of the entries above it. The general procedures are as follows:

1. Describe the rules and the starting date of the tournament.
2. Make a signup sheet available.
3. Place contestants on the schedule as they sign up, by drawing or reverse seeding.
4. Challenges begin. If the challenger wins, that person exchanges places with the defeated entry. Otherwise, no change in placement is made.

Once a challenge is placed, the challenged entry must agree to play within a specified period of time or forfeit. This keeps the tournament moving. Usually, a player or team is required to play a contestant from below if a challenge has been made before challenging another player or team above. In this type of tournament, each contestant's objective should be to get to the top by challenging and defeating the contestants above.

There are three kinds of challenge tournaments—ladder, pyramid, and funnel (upside down funnel). These are illustrated in Figure 17-6. In the *ladder* tournament, the entries are arranged in vertical sequence like the rungs on a ladder, then the challenges begin. As a general rule, contestants are limited to challenging only one or two places above. This restriction should be decided before competition starts.

The *pyramid* tournament offers a greater possible number of games because a contestant may challenge not only any player on the same line but also either of the players on the immediate left or right in the line above. For example, in the diagram in Figure 17-6, Player 9 may challenge Players 7 or 8 on the same line or 5 or 6 on the line above.

In the case of an unusually large number of entries, the *funnel* tournament may be a good choice. It combines certain features of the ladder and pyramid tournaments. In the lower portion of the funnel, play is governed by the rules for the pyramid tournament, while in the upper portion play is governed by the rules for the ladder tournament.

Elimination. In elimination tournaments, all competitors except the winner become eliminated. Each entry is eliminated after either one or two losses, depending on whether the tournament is single or double elimination. The bracketing for an elimination tournament is done as follows:

1. Brackets are set up to provide positions for the teams entered if the number of teams is 2, 4, 8, 16, 32, or any other power of 2.
2. If the number of teams is *not* equal to a power of 2, the brackets are set up to the next larger power of 2.
3. Byes are awarded to teams without opponents, making the schedule even. (Example: Use a 16-player bracket for 12 players. Award four byes, two in the upper bracket and two in the lower bracket).
4. To determine the number of byes, subtract the number of teams or players from the next larger power of 2.
5. Place byes as far apart as possible so they are eliminated in the first round of play.

The seeding process places the strongest teams in separate brackets so they will not meet in early tournament rounds. Sometimes there is no seeding, but often between one fourth and one half of the entries are seeded. Any necessary byes should be awarded to seeded teams.

In the *single elimination* tournament, the losing contestants are dropped from the tournament and play continues until only one entry remains. The advantages and disadvantages of this kind of tournament are:

1. The tournament is short and expedient, since one half of the entries are eliminated in the first round and half of those remaining are eliminated in each succeeding round.
2. Even though the winner is determined quickly, the best entry may not win, due to the fact that injuries or an "off game" may cause upsets.
3. Each team is assured of playing only once.

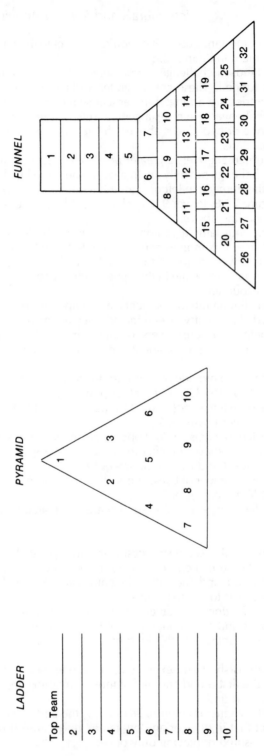

Figure 17-6. Three kinds of challenge tournaments: ladder, pyramid, and funnel.

The formula for determining the number of games in a single elimination tournament is N − 1 (N is the number of entries). For example, 25 entries will require 24 games (25 − 1 = 24). Figure 17-7 shows examples of elimination tournaments for 6 entries and 13 entries. Six entries require a tournament with 8 positions, thus having 2 byes. Thirteen entries require a tournament with 16 positions, thus having 3 byes. The seeded teams are placed to prevent them from meeting each other in the early rounds.

In a *consolation elimination* tournament, the teams are arranged in brackets in the same fashion as in the single elimination tournament. The championship side (first round winners) is a single elimination tournament moving to the right, with a consolation tournament (first round losers), which moves to the left. The winner on the right side is the tournament champion, while the runner-up on the winner's side finishes in second place. Figure 17-8 shows three consolation tournaments involving 4 teams, 8 teams, and 16 teams. Seeding can be done in the same way as in the single elimination tournament.

In the *double elimination* tournament, each entry is assured of playing at least two contests; however, after losing twice a contestant is eliminated. The brackets are established in the same manner as in the single elimination tournament and seeding is also done in the same way. In the double elimination tournament, the formula for determining the number of contests is 2N − 1 (with N meaning the number of entries). Example: with 12 entries, the formula would be 2 × 12 = 24 − 1 = 23 games.

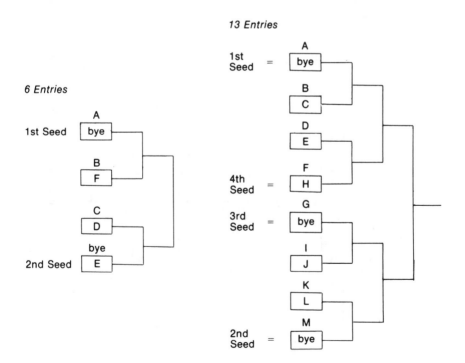

Figure 17-7. Example of two single-elimination tournaments, involving 6 and 13 entries.

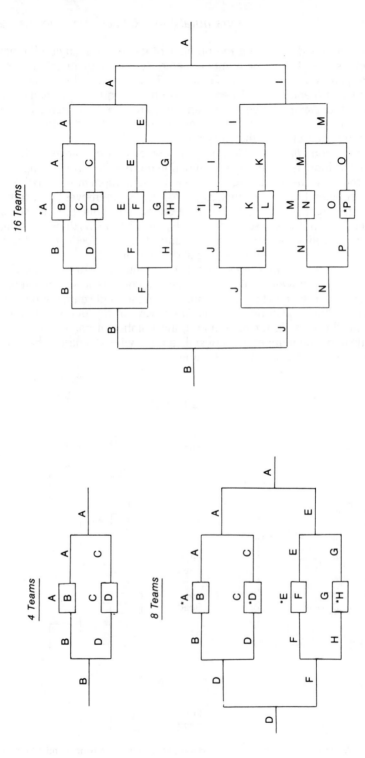

Figure 17-8. Consolation tournaments involving 4, 8, and 16 entries (*indicates seeded entries).

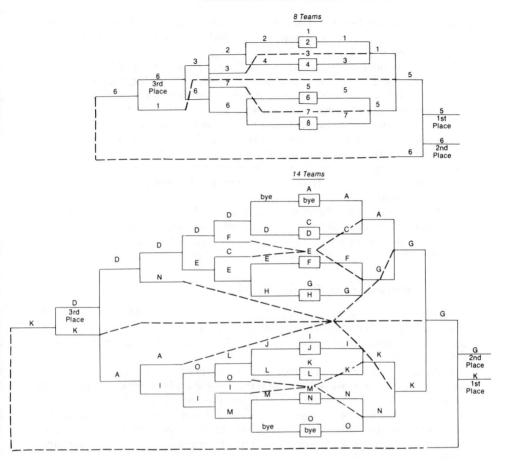

Figure 17-9. Examples of double-elimination tournaments, involving 8 and 14 teams. (Note: Dotted lines may cross each other to different brackets to reduce chances of playing the same team twice.)

The contestants who lose in the first round move to the left, while the winners move to the right. Subsequently, as a team on the left loses again, it is eliminated because it has two losses, while a team on the right that loses moves over to the loser's side (left). If that entry loses again, it is eliminated. Because an entry is not eliminated until it loses twice, the winner of the loser's bracket plays the winner of the winner's bracket for the championship. Refer to the 8-team tournament in Figure 17-9 and follow these instructions:

1. During the first round, the winners move to the right and the losers to the left.
2. Subsequently, when an entry on the winner's side loses, it moves over to the loser's side.

3. Team 1 plays Team 2, Team 3 plays Team 4, Team 5 plays Team 6, and Team 7 plays Team 8. Teams 1, 3, 5, and 7 are winners, while Teams 2, 4, 6, and 8 are losers.

4. On the winner's side, 1 plays 3 and 5 plays 7. Teams 1 and 5 are winners, Teams 3 and 7 are losers, and therefore, they move to the unattached lines on the left side of the tournament (follow the dotted lines). Team 2 plays 4 and 6 plays 8. Teams 2 and 6 are winners, Teams 4 and 8 are losers and are therefore eliminated because they have each lost twice.

5. Team 2 plays 3 and 7 plays 6. Teams 3 and 6 are winners. Teams 2 and 7 are eliminated because they have each lost twice.

6. Team 3 plays 6, Team 6 wins, therefore, Team 3 is eliminated.

7. Team 1 plays 5, and Team 5 is the winner. The loser, Team 1, moves to the left side.

8. Team 1 plays 6 and Team 6 wins; therefore, Team 1 is eliminated because it has lost twice, but it wins third place in the tournament.

9. Two teams remain—5 and 6. They play each other and Team 5 wins; therefore, it wins the championship, and Team 6 places second.

Tournament Classification System

Sometimes in intramural programs, equalization pretournament rounds are played. Assume that four divisions are desired, in which case participants end up in one of four classifications: AAAA, AAA, AA, A. The best entries are in the division AAAA.

Participants first play two or more classification games. If an entry wins both games, it will be in class AAAA. If it wins the first and loses the second, it will be in class AAA. If it loses the first and wins the second, it will be in class AA. If it loses both, it will be in class A. If you can tell that an entry is "sandbagging" or not playing to its full ability, you have the option of placing the entry according to your judgment. Participants then enter tournament play in their respective classes.

With this classification system, the events in the A class can be just as exciting as those in the AAAA group. Many of the participants in the lower class have been relatively unsuccessful in open or unclassified competition. This system gives all entries a chance to compete against others with a similar skill level; therefore, everyone has a reasonable chance to experience success and enjoy the benefits of equalized competition. Figure 17-10 shows how the pretournament rounds are arranged to determine the participants in the four classes.

Seeding

The ultimate objective of seeding is to have the best two contestants meet for the final match. Seeding is important to contestants for tactical and morale purposes. The main problem with seeding is the prospect of human error in evaluating the contestants based on available information.

A general principle of seeding is to place the first and fourth seeds in the upper half of the draw, the second and third seeds in the bottom half, then continue this pattern throughout. This distributes the best ranked contestants in a uniform manner (see Figure 17-7).

QUALIFYING OR CLASSIFICATION TOURNAMENT

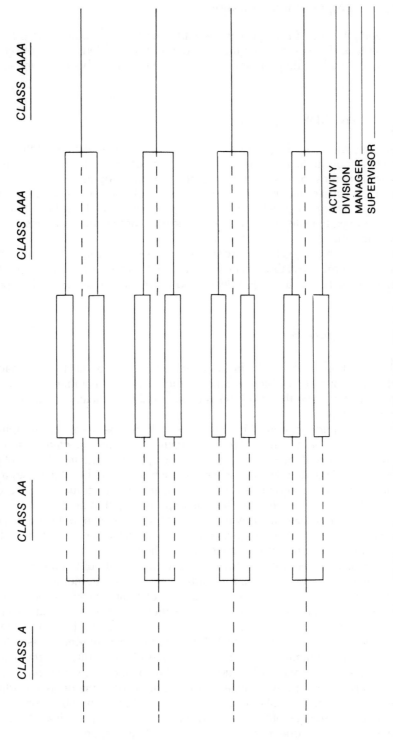

Figure 17-10. Pretournament for arranging the participants into four classes for league or tournament play.

Seeding for 4 and 8 teams can be readily understood, but seedings for 16- and 32-team tournaments are more complex. The detailed aspects of seeding are covered adequately in other sources, particularly in books on intramural programs.

AWARDS

Awards are used to generate student interest, increase participation, and recognize outstanding accomplishments or service. Some leaders consider the awarding of pins, plaques, medals, certificates, and trophies undesirable, saying that it causes students to seek the award and not the true value received from the experience itself. Awards are sometimes called "bribes" that lead students to participate more for the extrinsic rewards than for the intrinsic values of participation.

A carefully managed and conservative awards system can be an asset to most intramural programs. Consistency is important, because an awards program creates expectations among students, and inconsistency results in disappointments.

ELIGIBILITY

The question of who is eligible to participate is one that must be approached with precision and consistency. Since participation is encouraged, the general guideline should be that a person is eligible unless sufficient reason exists to deny eligibility.

Restricted participation in intramurals should not be used as a disciplinary measure for students who fail to meet requirements or expectations in other school programs. If the student performs poorly in mathematics, he is not prohibited from attending English or school lunch or assemblies. Likewise, a student should not be prohibited from participating in intramurals due to poor performance in other areas. In fact, the opposite ought to be encouraged, because intramurals have their own potential for development of the participants and can be an integrating and socializing force, which can help certain students remain interested and want to continue in school.

The main questions that pertain to eligibility are: (1) Should a current member of a varsity team be permitted to participate on an intramural team in that particular sport? (2) Should a former member of a varsity team be permitted to participate on an intramural team in that particular sport? (3) Should an athlete who is trying out for a varsity team but has not yet made it be permitted to participate on an intramural team? (4) Should members of junior varsity teams be eligible for intramurals? (5) Should members of the faculty and staff participate in the same league with students, and if so, should they be on separate teams or play on teams with students? (6) Should part-time students and adjunct teachers participate? (7) Should any limit be placed on the number of intramural activities a person can enter in a given year? (8) Should a participant be able to play on more than one team at a time in a particular sport?

All of the above questions are of concern in determining who can and cannot participate. Other questions would pertain to eligibility, depending on the particular situation.

FINANCES

The financial considerations of any program involve two broad aspects: obtaining a constant and adequate amount of funding and administering the funds wisely toward meeting the objectives of the program. Although an ample intramural budget is important, many effective programs are sponsored with limited funds, especially in the public schools. Shortage of funds should not be used as an excuse for not having a program. The ideal is a secure source of income that is granted on the basis of actual need. Intramural programs are funded in a variety of ways: appropriated funds, student fees, entry fees, equipment or locker rentals, forfeit fees, gifts, and fund-raising projects. Appropriated funds would have to be considered the best source.

RULES AND REGULATIONS

Rules and regulations are used in intramural programs to equalize competition, provide safe playing conditions, and establish standards of conduct. The following guidelines apply here.

1. State the rules and regulations in a positive manner, carrying out suggestions from the intramural council and the players.
2. Establish only those rules and regulations that are reasonable, beneficial, and enforceable.
3. State the rules in simple language.
4. Standardize the administrative procedures for handling violations.
5. Review and update the rules on a timely basis.

PRECAUTIONARY MEASURES

The same precautionary measures must be taken with intramurals as with participation in other aspects of the physical education program. These considerations are discussed elsewhere and they include (1) adequate safety measures for protection of the participants, (2) evidence of fitness to participate, (3) adequate opportunity for student insurance coverage, (4) measures to guard against potential law suits, and (5) providing the best qualified officials available.

A POSITION STATEMENT

Chapters 13 and 15 contained statements of beliefs from the Society of State Directors of Health, Physical Education and Recreation, with which the author concurs and with which all physical education teachers, coaches, and administrators ought to be familiar. The following are statements of belief from the Society about intramurals and other extra-class programs. These beliefs help to give clarity to this aspect of the school program. They are printed with the permission of the Society.

EXTRA-CLASS ACTIVITIES

(Intramurals, Extramurals, Sports Clubs and Recreation Activities)

Every school should provide ample opportunity for participation in intramural, extramural and recreational activities for all students. These programs not only supplement physical education instruction but also afford opportunities for social exchange, enrichment of individual personal resources, and wholesome competition below the varsity level of excellence. Extra-class activities should be consistent with the content and philosophy of the physical education program of instruction. Such activities, if handled properly, can be particularly helpful in promoting good human relationships and community involvement, and in minimizing problems of racial integration, student unrest, and the like.

ABOUT ADMINISTRATION

Extra-class activities should be provided for and financed by boards of education.

School administrators should ensure ample opportunity for all students to participate in individual, dual and team sports, and other suitable physical activities. School transportation should be provided when needed.

Extra-class activities should be administered by school officials, but community facilities and resource persons should be utilized whenever the program can be improved through such use.

Extra-class competition should be equalized, in terms of the age, skill, size and strength of participants.

Policies should be established to protect pupils from injury or over-participation.

—Health examinations should be a prerequisite for participation in vigorous activity.
—Protective, well-fitting equipment for participants, good facilities and equipment, and capable personnel are essential to participants in intramurals and other extra-class activities.
—Boxing should not be included at any grade level.
—Sponsoring of body contact sports below the ninth grade places the school on tenuous grounds, unless the school accepts full responsibility for providing excellent leadership, facilities, equipment, and policies for promoting and protecting the health and welfare of participants.

Awards for extra-class activities are unnecessary. If given at all, they should be simple and of little monetary value, providing only token recognition of an activity satisfactorily completed. Students should be motivated to participate through school-wide emphasis on the values and opportunities inherent in such participation and through the joy afforded by well-planned and well-administered programs.

ABOUT PROGRAM

Education and development of the individual through satisfying and enjoyable participation in selected activities should be the program.

Opportunity to participate in a wide variety of extra-class activities should be provided for both boys and girls of all grades. Activities should be based on the interests, needs, capacities, and level of maturity of the pupils. The program should be broad enough to help meet the needs of pupils who are mentally or physically handicapped or who have social or emotional problems.

Leadership opportunities should be made available to pupils regardless of their sex and skill level.

ABOUT PERSONNEL

Since extra-class program participation is voluntary, the program should be staffed with enthusiastic teachers who possess high-level leadership skills and organizational competencies.

REFERENCES AND RECOMMENDED READINGS

1. Bonanno, D., Ed.: Intramurals and recreational sports. JOPERD, *58*(2):49–63, 1987.
2. Bonnano, D.: Intramurals and Club Sports. Waldorf, MD, AAHPERD Publications, 1986.
3. Bucher, C.A.: Administration of Physical Education and Athletic Programs, 9th Ed. St. Louis, C.V. Mosby, 1987, pp. 90–116.
4. Butts, F., and Kingery, B.: Sports without officials—why not? JOPERD, *3*(3):63, 1982.

5. Davidson, S.A.: Extending the intramural concept. JOPERD, 53(3):68, 1982.
6. Frost, R.B., Lockhart, B.D., and Marshall, S.J.: Administration of Physical Education and Athletics, 3rd Ed. Dubuque, Iowa, William C. Brown, 1988, p. 121–150.
7. Garrett, H.L., and Stanek, F.: Administrative control of intramural sports. Current status. JOPERD, 58(7):94, 1987.
8. Harden, J.P.: Intramural/recreation. JOPERD, 56(8):40, 1985.
9. Little, S.L., and Guse, D.: Campus recreation services. An enterprise in higher education. JOPERD, 59(8):62, 1988.
10. MacTaggart, B.E.: An effective round robin schedule. JOPERD, 55(4):74, 1984.

Chapter *18*

EVALUATION METHODS
AND PROCEDURES

This chapter deals with three important areas of evaluation: *students, personnel,* and *programs.* In addition to these major aspects of education, evaluation is also necessary in connection with such items as educational goals, adequacy of facilities, efficiency of procedures, allocation of resources, discipline, and other control factors. Evaluation of the various aspects of the total operation is the process by which weaknesses are identified; however, evaluation for the purpose of detecting weaknesses serves little purpose unless the information is utilized to cause results. The ultimate reason for evaluation is improvement. Without the intent to improve, why evaluate?

The term *evaluation* is inclusive of exact measurements, subjective measurements, and considered judgments. It involves assessment against defined standards, criteria, or goals. The result is the determination of the relative status or worth of that which is being evaluated. *Tests, measurements,* and *evaluations* are commonly used terms which have certain similarities and certain differences.

A *test* requires a performance by the individual being tested. The performer receives a score representing how well he or she performed. The quality or quantity of an individual's strength, speed, jumping ability, knowledge, and so on are determined by the use of tests.

The term *measurement* includes all tests, but is not confined to them. Some measurements do not require a performance by the person. For instance, measurements of body height, weight, and percent of body fat are not tests.

Evaluation is broader and more inclusive than either of the other terms. It is a process of determining the status of something and of relating that status to some standard in order to make a value judgment. For example, evaluations are made of teaching methods, program content, teacher effectiveness, and student performance and progress. Evaluation is often based on test results in addition to information secured from observations, interviews, questionnaires, and other measures.

286

WHY EVALUATE?

Evaluation should be approached with a constructive and positive attitude and with a sincere desire to accurately appraise and constructively change. The end product of evaluation should be improvement. Without the honest intent to accurately appraise and improve, evaluation has little purpose and, therefore, little justification.

The three steps in evaluation are collection of useful information about the present status; objective comparison of the information against the desired status or condition; and an effective plan to close the gap between the present status and that which is desired.

The two basic forms of evaluation are known as formative and summative. *Formative* evaluation is the kind that is done along the way to identify weaknesses and problems in order that the best solutions can be determined and implemented. *Summative* evaluation is for the purpose of making a final decision as to whether the person or program being evaluated will be permitted to continue. Formative evaluation carries with it no risk because its end is simply to bring about positive change. Summative evaluation, on the other hand, carries with it the risk of elimination. Its final objective is to answer the question of whether to accept or continue with the person, program, or situation that is under consideration.

EVALUATION OF STUDENTS

One aspect of evaluation transcends all others. This is the evaluation of student achievement. Because student achievement is the final result of the total educational effort, educators are vitally concerned with the kind and amount of student development resulting from participation in school programs. They are specifically concerned with the development of knowledge, concepts, and judgments; interests, attitudes, and ideals; strength and skill; and the development of the organic system.

If teachers are to design a high-quality instructional program and teach students effectively, they must obtain considerable information about the students. The more information a teacher has about students' interests, abilities, and needs, the better an effective program can be designed and conducted. Much of the necessary information can be gathered with the use of tests and measurements.

Four ways that measurement is used to evaluate are the following.[9]

Diagnostic. Measurement is necessary to diagnose the differences in abilities, interests, and needs of students in order to plan and conduct effective programs. Objective knowledge about specific student deficiencies is essential to provide both remedial and accelerated programs.

Classification. Sometimes it is an advantage to classify students into homogeneous or heterogeneous groups, whichever is desired for a particular type of instruction, competition, or experience. Such classification is often based on the results of appropriate measurements.

Achievement. Objective measures and accurate records of student achievement and progress form the basis for the selection of program content, for the assignment of grades or marks, and for the advancement of students.

Improve Methods. Objective information obtained from measurements serves as a basis for determining the best methods of instruction and for guiding students into appropriate experiences. Accurate measurements help to determine the success of students and to learn whether students are ready to progress to the next higher level.

Selection of Measurements

Measurements range from highly *subjective* to highly *objective*. Objective measures are based largely on facts, while subjective measures are primarily a result of judgment. Subjective measurement, such as a teacher's evaluation of a student's character, includes some degree of objectivity, but also involves a large amount of subjective judgment. Objective measurement is based on more precise information. A measure is objective to the extent that it will produce the same results when conducted by different people under similar conditions; in other words, when the subjectivity of the test administrator is eliminated. Teachers should strive for a high degree of objectivity in measurement, but still realize that not all important traits can be measured objectively.

In order for a measurement to be highly objective it must have a high degree of validity and reliability. *Validity* is the extent to which the test actually measures what it is claimed to measure.

Reliability is the degree to which all persons using the procedure will achieve comparable results consistently.

It is difficult to say how much time and money should be devoted to the administration of any measurement; but in every case, the value of the results should be weighed in comparison with the expenditure of money, time, and effort. This is *administrative economy*.

Educational application is the degree to which the testing experience in itself is educational or motivational. Measurements should be harmonious with and supplemental to course content.

Many *kinds of measurements* are applicable in physical education programs. They fall into the following categories.

Fitness

Muscular strength and endurance tests
Tests of circulorespiratory endurance
Measures of flexibility
Fitness test batteries

Motor Performance

Measures of power
Agility
Reaction time and speed
Balance and kinesthetic perception
Neuromuscular skill (sports skills)

Nonphysical Performance

Measures of the body structure and body mechanisms
Measures of personality traits such as interest, attitudes, behavior, and character
Tests of knowledge about sports rules, strategies, and techniques

Administration of Measurements

Careful attention should be given to the *administration of tests*. Poorly administered tests can produce results that are misleading and useless to both the teacher and the students. The following are some guides for administering tests.[9]

1. Select and administer a test for a specific purpose; and be certain that it is administered in such a way as to accomplish that purpose.
2. Become familiar with the test and the procedures involved before attempting to administer it.
3. Make proper arrangements for all necessary facilities and equipment and be sure the equipment is in usable condition.
4. Determine the layout of testing stations and have needed equipment in place at the required time.
5. Be sure those being tested appear in appropriate clothing, especially in appropriate footwear.
6. Make early arrangements for necessary assistant leaders to help administer the test. In some cases, a short period of training for the assistants may be desirable.
7. Conduct the test in exact accordance with correct procedures.
8. Have the necessary score sheets, pencils, and scoring scales available.

The test results should be interpreted and used to the advantage of the students and the program. Teachers should constantly be aware that the exactness and correctness with which they administer a test influences its reliability. Test results that might have been valuable become useless when they are improperly administered and incorrectly interpreted.

Application of Results

Among the uses of measurement results are (1) the motivation of students toward achievement; (2) evaluation of the effectiveness of the educational program; and (3) evaluation of student progress. In turn, the results are useful in establishing student marks (grades).

Students generally want to be more knowledgeable, more fit, and more skillful. They are motivated by goals and want to demonstrate their achievements and be recognized for them. Furthermore, they want to see evidence that they are progressing, and they become stimulated by such evidence.

Both written and motor performance tests can assess achievement levels. The results of such tests provide students with evidence of progress or lack of progress in attaining these goals. The lack of this kind of information detracts from motivation.

Student progress is the best indication of a successful program. To determine progress, the goals toward which the students ought to strive should be clearly defined, and sound methods for evaluating progress should be employed.

One means a teacher has for determining progress is periodic measurement of student achievement. Measures of achievement in gymnastics, swimming, basketball, tennis, and other sports help to measure the success of these phases of the program. When achievement is low and progress is slow, the teacher should look seriously at the program content and the methods of instruction.

AAHPERD Fitness Tests

The AAHPERD has two fitness tests that are especially useful and that every physical educator and school administrator ought to know about. They are the AAHPERD Youth Fitness Test and the AAHPERD Health Related Fitness Test.

The *Youth Fitness Test* was first developed in 1957. It was revised in 1965 and again in 1976. This six-item test battery is designed to measure the more important elements of physical fitness. It has updated national norms for boys and girls ages 9 through 17 +. The test should be administered in accordance with the instructions included in the AAHPERD Youth Fitness Test Manual. The six items in the test are as follows:

Boys	Girls
Pull-up	Flexed-arm hang
Sit-up	Sit-up
Shuttle run	Shuttle run
Standing long jump	Standing long jump
50-yard dash	50-yard dash
600-yard run or 12-minute run or 1.5-mile run	600-yard run or 12-minute run or 1.5-mile run

Some school districts have *computerized* the Youth Fitness Test and have thereby made it much more convenient and economical to administer periodically to large numbers of students. Computerization has also made it possible to acquire a printout sheet for each student. A copy of the sheet can be furnished to the parents and the students to serve as a basis for discussion with the instructor. The computerized information can be conveniently stored for long-term use for making comparisons, observing trends, and establishing norms. The computer can also be used to list the winners of both the AAHPERD Fitness Award and the Presidential Fitness Award. It can identify and list those who score low in selected items, and remedial activities can be prescribed for those students. The AAHPERD office can furnish information about computer programs for the Youth Fitness Test.

The *AAHPERD Health Related Fitness Test* was first completed in 1980. It consists of four health related fitness test items especially selected to screen for degenerative conditions, such as coronary heart disease, obesity, and musculoskeletal disorders. The test was especially designed for youth ages 6 to 17 +. Of course, it should be administered in accordance with the instructions in the test manual which can be obtained from the AAHPERD. The manual also contains national norms. The four items included in the test are as follows:

Distance run—cardiovascular function
Skinfold test—body composition
Sit-up test—strength
Sit and reach test—flexibility

The Youth Fitness Test and the Health Related Test were not intended to supplant each other. Instead, they should supplement each other whenever there seems to be a need for both kinds of test.

EVALUATION OF PERSONNEL

Personnel accounting is as much a part of administration as financial accounting. School administrators become involved in the evaluation of both teaching and nonteaching personnel. The evaluation of teaching effectiveness deserves the lion's share of attention; therefore, the emphasis in this section is on teachers. In essence, the measure of good teaching is effective learning, and some important aspects of learning are difficult to identify and even more difficult to measure. Because of this, in order to evaluate accurately, several methods or approaches should be applied. Methods to consider are (1) evaluation by students, (2) self-evaluation, (3) evaluation by the supervisor or administrator, (4) evaluation by colleagues, (5) evaluation of student progress, and (6) comments about the teacher's positive and negative aspects.

In the evaluation of teachers, one should apply insight and wisdom relative to the source of information, its reliability, and how well the information applies.

Following are five basic principles that should be applied in the evaluation of teachers: (1) it should enhance the growth and development of the teacher as an individual; (2) its main focus should be on teaching effectiveness; (3) evaluation should include a discussion of goals for the future and how they can be achieved; (4) it should involve the person in penetrating self-analysis; (5) some aspects of evaluation should be formalized with pre- and postconferences scheduled, and these should be carried on in a nonthreatening environment.

By Students

When teachers are evaluated by students, two influencing factors should be kept in mind: (1) subjective evaluations by students might portray teacher popularity as opposed to real effectiveness; and (2) it is easier to receive high student ratings in certain subjects. For example, a subject that is enjoyable has better potential for high ratings. This is also true for elective subjects, because students enter them voluntarily and usually with positive attitudes because they were not coerced or required to enroll.

Evaluation by students is a method used more frequently at the college level than at lower educational levels, because college students are more likely to approach the matter seriously and are better prepared to make accurate and fair judgments. If conducted properly, however, evaluations by students can be useful at the secondary levels as well. Figures 18-1 and 18-2 are sample evaluation forms which allow students to rate their instructors.

Self-Evaluation

Self-analysis is potentially a great tool for helping teachers improve. The administrator's role is to help the teacher structure the right questions and pursue them with objectivity and thoroughness. The administrator can stimulate and encourage and even suggest penetrating questions that will help generate self-analysis, but the teacher must shoulder the main responsibility for making the process effective and for applying the results in a constructive manner. Figure 18-3 is a sample form that can be used in self-evaluation. It can also be used by a colleague or administrator.

One technique that is particularly useful in self-evaluation is instant video replay of the teacher in action. It is especially applicable in the evaluation of appearance, gestures, mannerisms, and the effectiveness of delivery in the teaching process.

By Supervisor or Administrator

The supervisor or administrator should approach the evaluation process as a resource person and a facilitator. This approach will help to reduce the apprehensions and tension of the person being evaluated. Consequently, the teacher will tend to talk freely and seek help and solutions, which the teacher probably will not do if authority is displayed and threatening impressions are conveyed. A communication of the power to do harm if expectations are not met creates a barrier between the evaluator and the one being evaluated. This condition will usually reduce the exchange of information, sometimes distort or conceal the facts, and almost always delete the potential for positive outcome. Figure 18-4 provides an example of a form that can be used or adapted for use by the administrator or supervisor in evaluating a teacher's effectiveness.

By Colleagues

Often, colleagues have a better perspective of how well an individual functions under given circumstances. Colleagues are generally mature and responsible individuals who have a basis for making sound judgments and are generally vitally concerned about the welfare of both the individual teacher and the students. For these reasons, evaluation by colleagues has high potential for productive results; however, this procedure often causes apprehension among both the evaluators and those being evaluated because colleagues usually do not like to evaluate each other. Also, the process has some inherent hazards. For example, the relationship between two colleagues is sometimes too positive or too negative to allow the evaluator to be adequately objective. Sometimes the evaluator, either consciously or unconsciously, desires to do the other person undue good or undue harm. This possibility must be carefully monitored by the administrator who will apply the results of colleague evaluations. When the circumstances are acceptable, however, evaluation by colleagues provides an additional valuable dimension to the total process. Figure 18-4 provides an illustration of a form that can be used or adapted for evaluation by a colleague.

TEACHER'S NAME _____ DATE _____

COURSE NUMBER AND SECTION _____

INSTRUCTOR EVALUATION

		1	2	3	4	5	6	7
1.	Has an excellent knowledge of the subject matter.							
2.	Is enthusiastic about the subject.							
3.	Is well prepared for each class.							
4.	Makes good use of class time.							
5.	Gives clear examples and explanations.							
6.	Makes helpful evaluations of my work (e.g., papers, exams).							
7.	Clearly explains difficult concepts, ideas, or theories.							
8.	Responds respectfully to student questions and viewpoints.							
9.	Is genuinely interested in helping me understand the subject.							
10.	Is available to students during regular and reasonable office hours.							
11.	Motivates me by his/her example to want to learn about the subject.							
12.	Has produced new knowledge, skills, and awareness in me.							
13.	Starts/dismisses classes at scheduled times.							
14.	Seldom misses class.							

15. Overall rating: _____ Poor _____ Fair _____ Good _____ Excellent

Code: (Place an X in the appropriate square)

1 = Strongly disagree	5 = Agree
2 = Disagree	6 = Strongly agree
3 = Somewhat disagree	7 = Very strongly agree
4 = Somewhat agree	

Figure 18-1. A concise but well designed teacher evaluation form to be completed by students. (Courtesy of Brigham Young University.)

TEACHER'S NAME _____ DATE _____

COURSE NUMBER AND SECTION _____

<u>STUDENT EVALUATION OF TEACHER</u>*

Do you feel that the course objectives were clearly stated?   Yes____   No____

Do you feel that the course objectives were within your abilities?   Yes____   No____

Were the tests and evaluations directed toward the course objectives?   Yes____   No____

How well do you feel the instructor demonstrates those skills he teaches?

Very Well					Needs improvement				
1	2	3	4	5	6	7	8	9	10

How well were you able to learn those skills which the instructor taught?

Very well					Needs improvement				
1	2	3	4	5	6	7	8	9	10

How well do you feel the instructor evaluates your skills?

Very well				Needs improvement				
1	2	3	4 5	6	7	8	9	10

Do you have the necessary equipment to do an effective job of learning?

(comment)

Which of the following is expected of you?

____Memorization and recall.

____Making a judgment about something, using given information.

____Understanding the meaning of ideas or concepts.

____Putting information together in an unusual way to solve problems.

____Examining a complexity and breaking it down into parts.

____Using or applying information in a new situation.

Does the instructor show an interest in you?   ____ALWAYS   ____USUALLY   ____SELDOM

Does the instructor encourage you to ask questions and to state your views?

____ALWAYS ____USUALLY ____SELDOM

Which of the following, if any, needs improvement?

____Speech .   ____Sense of humor,

____Planning for class sessions.   ____Tolerance for students' ideas & views.

____Willingness to help students.   ____Ability to inspire students.

____Enthusiasm,   Other:_____

Figure 18-2. An extensive form with which students can evaluate teachers. (Courtesy of Laramie County Community College, Cheyenne, Wyoming.)

STUDENT EVALUATION Continued.

Does the instructor encourage new ideas and concepts? YES____ NO____

How would you rate your instructor's communications skills—questioning, answering, discussing?

____OUTSTANDING   ____VERY GOOD   ____GOOD   ____ADEQUATE   ____POOR

		Exciting						Boring	
Rank the presentations................	1	2	3	4	5	6	7	8	9	10

Rank the instructional planning   Outstanding   Poor

		Outstanding						Poor	
and organization....................	1	2	3	4	5	6	7	8	9	10

		Outstanding						Poor	
Rank the effectiveness of the instructional methods................	1	2	3	4	5	6	7	8	9	10

Does the instructor make appropriate use of instructional materials such as textbook, films, magazines, manuals, etc.?

                                   YES____   NO____
(comment)

Does the instructor possess an adequate knowledge of course content? YES____ NO____
(comment)

Overall, do you feel the course was good?   YES____ NO____
(comment)

What aspects of the course do you feel were of most value to you?

_____

	Super						Rotten	
Rank the instructor.........	1	2	3	4	5	6	7	8	9	10

Is the instructor available to help you? ____ALWAYS ____USUALLY ____SELDOM

What do other students enrolled in this course think of it?

____LIKE   ____DON'T TALK ABOUT IT

____DISLIKE   ____AFRAID TO SAY

____DON'T CARE   ____DON'T CARE EITHER WAY

Figure 18-2. *(Continued)*

Student Progress

There is a sound argument for the idea that student progress is the only meaningful measure of teacher effectiveness. If all forms of student progress could be measured with sufficient accuracy and consistency, perhaps there would be little use for other forms of teacher evaluation. The first portion of this chapter was devoted to information pertaining to measuring and evaluating student

PERSONNEL EVALUATION

Name _____ School _____ Date _____

Years of Teaching Experience _____ Years in Alpine School District _____

Grade or Subject Area _____

Conference Held: Date- _____ Date- _____ Date- _____

This checklist is used for the purpose of improving instruction and/or evaluation for future employment. This basic set of criteria is the official reference for observation and evaluation. Teachers are encouraged to use this form as a self-evaluation and to discuss these criteria with their administrators.

Final evaluation is to be completed by the principal and reviewed by the teacher. Teacher's signature is only an acknowledgment of having reviewed the final report.

I. TEACHING TECHNIQUES	Superior	Satisfactory	Needs Improve.
Is fair and impartial			
Demonstrates creativity in planning, preparation and implementation			
Varies materials and techniques			
Demonstrates a knowledge of subject matter			
Meets the individual needs of students			
Develops critical thinking			
Uses good English oral and written			
Demonstrates skill in motivating students			

III. PERSONAL ATTRIBUTES	Superior	Satisfactory	Needs Improve.
Shows poise, self-control, tact			
Demonstrates a wholesome sense of humor			
Maintains a professional appearance			
Maintains regular attendance, health, and vitality			
Demonstrates positive attitude toward teaching			
Demonstrates leadership			
Has a good self-concept			
Shows dependability			

Figure 18-3. Example of a self-evaluation form to be used by a teacher. The form can also be used by another person, peer, supervisor, or administrator. (Courtesy of Alpine School District.) (Continued on next page.)

Helps students understand and appraise their own work			
II. SCHOOL MANAGEMENT			
Maintains classroom control			
Shows concern for care and appearance of room and equipment			
Completes all school assignments			
Uses and maintains appropriate school records			
Establishes a positive learning environment			
Shows evidence of daily planning and development of long range objectives			
IV. PROFESSIONAL AND SOCIAL ATTITUDES			
Observes professional ethics			
Adheres to school and district regulations			
Accepts suggestions for improvement			
Shows evidence of professional growth			
Demonstrates genuine liking for teaching and students			
Views own assignment in relation to total school program			
Develops positive parental relationships			
V. TOTAL FINAL EVALUATION			

Teacher's Summary Comment: _____

_____

Teacher's Signature _____

Principal's Summary Comment: _____

_____

Principal's Signature _____

Figure 18-3. (Continued)

TEACHER EVALUATION FORM

Please evaluate the teacher by placing an 'X' in the appropriate square for each item. It is hoped that your comments will be frank, realistic and to the point.

Teacher _____ School _____ Date _____

Period of employment from _____ 19___ to _____ 19___

Secondary-Elementary: _____ Subject or Grade _____

Description of Ratings: P-Poor; F-Fair; G-Good; VG-Very Good; O-Outstanding. Example:

	P	F	G	VG	O
Major and Minor					

PERSONAL TRAITS:	P	F	G	VG	O
1. Dependability					
2. Responsiveness to suggestions					
3. Judgment and tact					
4. Industry					
5. Sense of humor					
6. Voice: quality and articulation					
7. Health					
8. Personal appearance					
9. Initiative					
10. Poise					
11. Ethical qualities					
12. Genuine liking for boys and girls					

Analytical Statement:

SCHOLARSHIP:	P	F	G	VG	O
1. Mastery of subject					
2. Knowledge of source materials					
3. General educational background					
4. Correct and fluent English					

Analytical Statement:

CLASS MANAGEMENT:	P	F	G	VG	O
1. Organization of routine details					
2. Control of classroom situation					
3. Maint. of good "emotional climate"					
4. Adaptability					
5. Attention to physical conditions and appearance of classroom					

Analytical Statement:

OUT-OF-CLASSROOM ACTIVITIES:	P	F	G	VG	O
1. Participation in sponsorship of student activities and in the supervision of out-of-classroom situations					
2. Supervision of hallways or playgrounds as required					
3. Prompt and accurate in filing reports					
4. Prompt in arrival at school and classes					

Analytical Statement:

Figure 18-4. Evaluation form for an administrator, supervisor, or colleague to rate a teacher's effectiveness. This form could also be used by a teacher in the self-evaluation process. (Courtesy of the Provo School District.) (Continued on next page.)

TEACHING METHODS:	P	F	G	VG	O
1. General skill in planning					
2. Motivation of student interest					
3. Provision for individual differences					
4. Creativity					
5. Awareness and use of life situations					
6. Stimulation of critical thinking					
7. Use of resources and instruction aids					
8. Evaluation of student progress					
9. Use of pupil personnel information					

Analytical Statement:

PROFESSIONAL ATTITUDE:	P	F	G	VG	O
1. Cooperation with staff					
2. Attitude toward teaching profession					
3. Parent relationships					
4. Membership in professional organizations:					

    Local: Yes □ No □

    State: Yes □ No □

    National: Yes □ No □

Analytical Statement:

Signature _____ Title _____

Figure 18-4. (Continued)

ADMINISTRATOR EVALUATION FORM

Please evaluate the administrator by placing an 'X' in the appropriate square for each item. It is hoped that your comments will be frank, realistic, and to the point.

Description of ratings: P-Poor; F-Fair; G-Good; E-Excellent; O-Outstanding

In terms of support, the administrator

	P	F	G	E	O
1. has been successful in gaining a high level of respect from other members of the organization.					
2. has been successful in securing a reasonable level of budget and other kinds of support for the programs.					
3. is instrumental in maintaining a high level of morale among the faculty and staff.					
4. helps the organization toward a high level of respect within the larger educational system.					

In Personnel Matters, the administrator

	P	F	G	E	O
1. is fair and impartial in dealing with other employees.					
2. communicates effectively with other employees.					
3. is sensitive and responsive to the feelings, needs, and interests of others.					
4. presents a model and expectations of others which stimulates them to higher performance.					
5. demonstrates desirable ethical and professional behavior and encourages others to do the same.					
6. causes employees to feel both comfortable and challenged in their positions.					
7. keeps the faculty and staff free of unnecessary difficulty, stumbling blocks, and disruptions that might detract from their productivity.					
8. adequately controls conflicts, disputes, controversies, and frustrating circumstances from diluting the efforts of the faculty and staff.					
9. relates well to other people and is respected by them.					

Figure 18-5. An example of an administrator evaluation form. (Continued on next page.)

With respect to management, the administrator

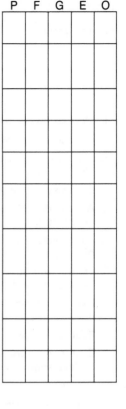

	P	F	G	E	O

1. provides clear direction and adequate insight toward well-established goals.

2. is energetic and productive and utilizes his time and energy in a desirable manner for the benefit of the organization.

3. permits and encourages ample participation by others in decision making.

4. makes decisions that are consistent, timely, and accurate.

5. is efficient and effective in performing his various administrative duties.

6. follows correct administrative procedures in his work with both the staff and higher administrative levels.

7. is a recognized expert in the field of his administration and contributes professionally to the overall good of that discipline.

8. is an effective manager in all aspects of administration, especially in the management of people and financial resources.

9. is consistent, predictable, and forthright in his administrative duties.

10. is both objective and fair in his dealings with other people.

Figure 18-5. (*Continued*)

achievement. Additional information on this subject can be found in Jensen and Hirst: *Measurement and Evaluation in Physical Education and Athletics.*[9]

Unsolicited Information

People who work closely with each other have a good feel for how well the other person is performing. The day-to-day observations and impressions mount up to a large amount of information and clear indications as to a person's effectiveness. The unsolicited comments that are passed on from other people, students, parents, and colleagues provide additional information about the effectiveness of each member of the teaching force. These sources of information can serve a useful purpose when combined with the information obtained through the more structured methods.

Evaluation of the Administrator

Many administrators fail to recognize the importance of evaluating their own leadership. They recognize the need to evaluate everyone else in the organization, yet from the standpoint of overall success there is no one whose performance is more important. Therefore, it is vital that administrative effectiveness

COURSE TITLE _____ DATE _____

PERIOD (TIME) _____ INSTRUCTOR _____

COURSE EVALUATION

	1	2	3	4	5	6	7
1. Course objectives are clear.							
2. Course is well organized.							
3. Student responsibilities are clearly defined.							
4. Course content is relevant and useful.							
5. Assigned workload is appropriate for credit hours.							
6. Assigned homework is *not* just busywork.							
7. Text(s) and other materials have helped me understand the course topics.							
8. Exams concentrate on important points of the course.							
9. Exams are clearly worded.							
10. Exams are good measures of my knowledge, understanding, ability to perform.							
11. Grading procedure is fair and impartial.							
12. Assignments are appropriately distributed throughout the semester.							
13. Course as a whole has produced new knowledge, skills, and awareness in me.							

14. Overall rating: _____ Poor _____ Fair _____ Good _____ Excellent

CODE: (Place an X in the appropriate square)

1 = Strongly disagree	5 = Agree
2 = Disagree	6 = Strongly agree
3 = Somewhat disagree	7 = Very strongly agree
4 = Somewhat agree	

Figure 18-6. Example of a simple but useful course evaluation form to be completed by the students.

be accurately appraised and the results applied toward improvement. Some of the same sources of information as for the evaluation of teachers can be used in evaluating the administrator. In addition, Figure 18-5 illustrates a structured procedure that can be used for self-evaluation and colleague evaluation of those in administrative positions.

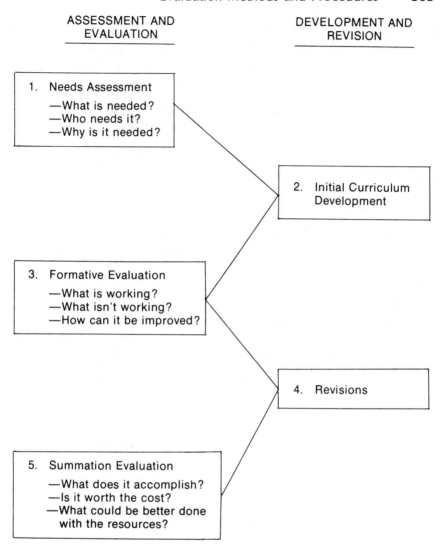

ASSESSMENT AND
EVALUATION

DEVELOPMENT AND
REVISION

1. Needs Assessment
   —What is needed?
   —Who needs it?
   —Why is it needed?

2. Initial Curriculum
   Development

3. Formative Evaluation
   —What is working?
   —What isn't working?
   —How can it be improved?

4. Revisions

5. Summation Evaluation
   —What does it accomplish?
   —Is it worth the cost?
   —What could be better done
   with the resources?

Figure 18-7. A flow chart of the steps involved in curriculum evaluation and development.

EVALUATION OF THE CURRICULUM OR PROGRAM

It is not possible to evaluate curriculum effectiveness totally separate from teaching effectiveness. A school could have a superb curriculum and still not achieve superior results, due to teacher ineffectiveness. Conversely, much can be accomplished through expert teaching even if the curriculum is basically weak. The ideal is a superb curriculum combined with superior teaching.

The purpose of curriculum evaluation is to determine how well the curriculum contributes to the educational goals, and especially how it could be modified to contribute better. The methods of curriculum evaluation can include the following: (1) a determination of the instructional validity—are students learning what is intended as indicated by written tests, skills tests, fitness tests, posture appraisals, information about attitude changes, and character development; (2) student opinions about the curriculum—do they find it interesting, motivating, and appealing; (3) evaluation by teachers and administrators; (4) accreditation committee evaluations (or a committee of outside experts separate from accreditation); and (5) the utilization of a standardized curriculum evaluation scorecard.

Although structured evaluation procedures are important and should be conducted periodically, ongoing curriculum evaluation methods may be even more useful. The ongoing methods include such things as (1) hearing student comments, both positive and negative, about the various aspects of the curriculum; (2) informal discussions among faculty members; (3) feedback from parents and other members of the public; (4) attitudes of board members and administrators toward the curriculum as expressed through encouragement and budgetary support; and (5) the ongoing evaluation of student progress and special achievements.

One of the most useful approaches to evaluation of the curriculum and other aspects of the program is *cost-benefit analysis* in connection with budgeting. This procedure leads to a penetrating study of "what it's worth as compared to what it costs." Chapter 9 includes a section on this useful financial procedure.

One important aspect of curriculum evaluation involves the evaluation of individual courses or units of instruction, especially by the students in the class. Figure 18-6 shows a form that has been prepared for such use.

Figure 18-7 shows a flow chart that illustrates the steps involved in curriculum construction and revision. The flow chart has built into it the impetus to ask penetrating questions about curriculum effectiveness and how the curriculum could be improved.

REFERENCES AND RECOMMENDED READINGS

1. AAHPERD: Motor Fitness Testing Manual for the Moderately Mentally Retarded. Waldorf, MD, AAHPERD Publications, 1986.
2. AAHPERD: Special Fitness Test Manual for Mildly Mentally Retarded Persons. Waldorf, MD, AAHPERD Publications, 1986.
3. AAHPERD: Sports Skills Testing Manuals. Waldorf, MD, AAHPERD Publications, 1986.
4. AAHPERD: Testing for Impaired, Disabled, and Handicapped Individuals. Waldorf, MD, AAHPERD Publications, 1986.
5. AAHPERD: Youth Fitness Test Manual. Waldorf, MD, AAHPERD Publications, 1986.
6. Boyce, B.A.: Grading practices—How do they influence student skill performance? JOPERD, 61(6):46, 1990.
7. Harrison, J.M., and Blakemore, C.: Instructional Strategies for Secondary School Physical Education, 2nd Ed. Dubuque, IA, William C. Brown, 1989.
8. Hensley, L.D., Lambert, L.T., Baumgartner, T.A., and Stillwell, J.L.: Is evaluation worth the effort. JOPERD, 58(6):59, 1987.
9. Jensen, C.R., and Hirst, C.: Measurement and Evaluation in Physical Education and Athletics. New York, Macmillan, 1980.
10. Loughrey, T.J.: Evaluating program effectiveness. JOPERD, 58(6):63, 1987.
11. Petray, C., Blazer, S., Lavay, B., and Leeds, M.: Designing the fitness testing environment. JOPERD, 60(1):35, 1989.
12. Shields, E.: Student ratings of teachers + personnel decision-making = CAUTION!! JOPERD, 55(1):35, 1984.
13. Wood, T.M., Ed.: Measurement and Evaluation—Theory to practice. JOPERD, 61(3):29–44, 1990.

Part V

RELATED ASPECTS

Chapter *19*

FACILITIES AND EQUIPMENT

Winston Churchill is reported to have said that "we shape our buildings, but afterwards they shape us." This statement can serve as a useful guideline for the planning of school facilities: Our schools have a tremendous amount of facilities for physical education and athletics. In fact, more facilities are provided for these programs than for any of the other disciplines in the educational system.

In light of today's spiraling costs, combined with a tightened economic situation, facilities that provide for maximum effective utilization at the lowest cost have to be the rule rather than the exception. It is clear that such facilities cannot just happen; they have to be carefully planned and then managed with this concept in mind.

The administrator has two major concerns about facilities: facility construction and/or renovation, and facility management (priority of usage, scheduling, and maintenance). Let us first discuss some important aspects of facility management.

MANAGING FACILITIES

One of the most important aspects of facility management is a clear definition of the kind of usage for which the facility can be available. The uses should be established into a system of priorities in order that the facility will serve its best purposes and that all concerned will know the relative priorities of its use. Following is a recommended priority system for physical education and athletic facilities.

1. Regular day-time classes and intercollegiate practices and contests.
2. Other activities sponsored and supervised by the department, such as intramurals, rehearsals, evening classes, and free play.
3. Official activities sponsored by other divisions of the school outside of the physical education/athletic department.
4. Activities sponsored by student groups or faculty and staff groups.
5. Approved activities sponsored by groups or agencies not affiliated with the school.

Facilities should be scheduled to get optimum use in accordance with the established priority system and to avoid conflict, misunderstanding, and disappointment due to errors. It ought to be clearly understood that scheduling must be done through the official scheduling office. On occasions when conflict or misunderstanding arises about the use of a facility, the information on the official schedule should apply.

It is recommended that a simple scheduling form be used to record a scheduling commitment and a copy be provided to the one initiating the request (Fig. 19-1). It is also useful to maintain a current master sheet for each teaching station. In the case of a large organization such as a major university, some aspects of facility scheduling are computerized. An example where computerization would be an advantage would be an intramural program that includes a large number of teams in certain sports, such as 400 to 500 teams each in basketball, flag football and softball.

Facility maintenance keeps the facility attractive and protects it from deterioration. Maintenance should be an active consideration in facility planning and construction. If a facility is properly designed and well constructed, the maintenance costs will be minimal. Unfortunately, for many facilities, maintenance receives too little consideration in the planning phase. This results in long-term

FACILITIES REQUEST FORM

Date _____

_____

Area Requested   Rental Fee

_____

Organization

_____

Date(s) Requested   Time

_____

Person in Charge

_____

Mailing Address   Phone

PERSONNEL NEEDED:
   Building Supervisor   _____ cost _____
   Life Guard(s)   _____ cost _____
   Custodian   _____ cost _____
   TOTAL COST (rental fee
      and personnel)   _____

REQUEST APPROVED BY: _____

Figure 19-1. Sample form for the request of facilities.

maintenance problems that can become extensive. On the average, the lifelong maintenance costs of a building amount to about three times the original construction cost, excluding the effects of inflation. With buildings that are poorly constructed or that have poorly selected materials, the maintenance costs run much higher. Highly durable and easily maintained materials on the exposed areas—both inside and outside—are the greatest single factor in the solution to the maintenance problem. Other important considerations include well-trained and conscientious maintenance personnel, adequate maintenance equipment located in strategic places for easy availability and use, and high expectations relative to maintenance among those associated with the use of the facility. Pride in the condition of the facility can make a major difference, and an administrator is in a good position to instill this kind of attitude.

FACILITY PLANNING AND CONSTRUCTION

Careful determination of facility needs for both the near-term and long-term is a responsibility primarily of those in administrative positions. Since the desired program is the basis for facility planning and the projection for facility needs, answers to the following questions are needed. What are the projections of future enrollment? Is the school likely to experience either consolidation or division? How many semesters of instruction in physical education will be required of all students? Is the instructional program to be broad in scope, with opportunities for the development of interests and skills in a large variety of activities? What will be the scope of participation in physical fitness and recreational activities for faculty and staff in addition to the participation by students? Will facilities be available for nonschool use, and if so, what kinds of use and how much? What will be the scope of the interschool athletic programs for men and women? What will be the scope of the intramural program? Will the program include dance activities in addition to sports and athletics? Will the program include aquatics, gymnastics, weight training, or other activities that require specialized facilities? If the facility is for an institution of higher learning, will the program include professional preparation curricula and research? What are the environmental and geographic factors that will affect the content of the program and the need for certain facilities?

Who Should be Involved?

In any locality where the school population is growing or where educational requirements are expanding, careful planning and timely construction of facilities, including the advanced acquisition of land, is an important requirement. This can be accomplished only by involvement of the right people at the various levels within the educational system. It helps for an administrator to have clear insight into who needs to be involved and in what ways.

Following is a list of personnel who are ordinarily involved with planning and construction of facilities. Each situation differs in the amount of involvement of the personnel at each level.

College/University	Public Schools
Board of Trustees or Regents	School Board
Institutional Administrators	School Superintendent and Principal
Campus Planning Committee	State Specialist in Physical Education and
Office of New Construction	Athletics (optional)
Office of Building Maintenance	District Facility Coordinating Committee
Architect	(optional)
Consultant (optional)	Office of Facility Planning and/or Con-
Administrators of the College and Depart-	struction
ment where the facility will be used	Office of Building Maintenance
Program Specialists	Architect
Members of the Planning Committee, some	Consultant (optional)
of whom would come from the above	Administrator and program specialist in
Contractor	physical education and athletics
	Members of the Planning Committee, some
	of whom would come from the above
	Contractor

A *program specialist* is one who is actively engaged as a teacher and/or coach. This person will use the facilities and, consequently, is knowledgeable about the practical questions and problems of use. One or more program specialists should be involved in every aspect of planning from beginning to end. This will help to ensure that the facilities will function as intended.

A *consultant* is a recognized specialist in the area for which the facility is being planned. Such a person is familiar with recently constructed facilities of this same kind and with the latest innovations in design and materials. A consultant can be especially helpful in suggesting to the planning committee the names of architects who are well qualified for the particular project; assisting the committee in analyzing alternatives and determining priorities; advising in connection with the public relations effort; and serving as a coordinator between the program specialists, the architect, and the contractor during the planning and construction stages.

The *architect* is not a draftsman or an engineer or a self-appointed planning specialist. He is one who has completed the required amount of education and apprenticeship and has become licensed by the appropriate state agency to practice architecture in the state. A licensed architect has certain ethical, professional, and legal responsibilities that are not necessarily assumed by lesser planning personnel. School administrators would be well-advised to always work with a fully licensed and reputable architect.

Developing the Idea

The idea of a new or revised facility develops through three important stages: *conception, presentation,* and *selling.*

Conceiving the need for a new or improved facility is the first step toward its accomplishment. The concept usually involves much discussion among those who have a particular interest in the project or who understand the circumstances that would justify it. For example, if it seems that new tennis courts are needed, those directly concerned ought to thoroughly discuss the matter, carefully think about where the need fits in terms of priority and timetable, and what justification exists for the project. They should prepare themselves to defend the idea in terms of cost versus benefit.

After the idea has been conceived and thoroughly discussed by those immediately concerned, a proposal should be prepared for presentation to those in higher authority. Prior to, or in conjunction with the formal proposal, informal approaches can be taken toward generating interest and support among administrative personnel and interested members of the community. Usually some discussion and exchange of information takes place over a period of time. This can provide valuable insight into what the formal proposal should contain once the idea develops to that point. Furthermore, it can pave the way for acceptance of the proposal.

For some projects, such as a group of outdoor tennis courts to be built on school property, little need may exist for public involvement. For certain other projects, however, say an expensive indoor swimming complex to be used by both school and community personnel, extensive public involvement and public support are essential. At this stage, a project steering committee should be organized, with one of its prime responsibilities being the public relations effort. The committee should apply those public relations principles and ideas explained in Chapter 10 that would be useful in the particular situation. This step is crucial because if the public relations effort is not handled effectively, it will result in failure of the idea.

Preparing a Facility Planning Document

A description of program needs should be written well in advance of the initiation of architectural planning to communicate the needs of the school program to the architect. The purpose should be to put into writing the current and anticipated school programs to be offered and to determine the facilities required to house these programs at the optimum level. Here are some guidelines for preparing the facility planning document[9]:

1. The information should be both concise and explicit.
2. It should state the optimal as well as the minimal program needs.
3. It should be realistic in terms of potential financing.
4. It should be both factual and insightful in terms of present and future programming.
5. All aspects of indoor and outdoor facility needs should be considered.
6. A rough draft of the document should be reviewed by selected individuals and their ideas incorporated into the final copy.
7. It should take into account new trends that seem to have an element of permanency, such as (a) additional emphasis on opportunities for the handicapped; (b) application of the community-school concept; (c) equal opportunities for men and women; (d) emphasis on physical fitness and lifetime sports; and (e) the weight training movement.
8. Ample consideration should be given to the use of new products, materials, and equipment, and the application of federal and state legislation that affects programming.

Even the most competent architect should not be expected to know how to adequately plan a building without considerable assistance from the specialists who will utilize the facilities. Thus, one challenge of writing a program is how to transmit a large number of messages from the school staff to the architect, conveying the staff's wishes, needs, and interests in such a way that these items eventually become transformed satisfactorily into wood, concrete, and steel. The better this information is communicated to the architect, the more likely that the building will serve its purposes well and that the owner will be satisfied.

Often, the program is written before the architect is selected. The written program then should not dwell too much on shape or form or other specific aspects, but more on kinds of use, approximate size, special requirements, and particular features that are desired.

Because a written program is so important in transmitting information to the architect, the selected information which follows is taken from an actual written program for a physical education building. To give the reader an overview of what is included in this particular 116-page program, the table of contents is listed.

Introduction
Certification
Space Requirements
Estimated Costs
Location of Building
Air Conditioning and Ventilation
Windows
Acoustical Requirements
Interior Surface Materials
Ceiling Heights
Location of Dressing Rooms
Location of Laundry and Issue Rooms
Elevator
Service Dock
Clocks and Class Bells
Audio, Radio and Television Equipment
Bulletin Boards and Display Cases
Room or Facility Descriptions

Figure 19-2 reproduces a single page in the *Space Requirements* section. Each area within the building is given a facility number. Figure 19-3 is a description of facility 49, taken from page 68 of the plan.

Information Sources

In addition to the ideas that school personnel already have, other information can be obtained by several methods. One example is *field trips*, in which selected individuals travel to locations where similar facilities have recently been constructed. An on-site review of such facilities, combined with direct conversation with those who helped plan the facilities and those who use them, has tremendous potential for helping to sort out strengths and weaknesses. Returning with an adequate amount of useful photographs is fundamental to the success of the trip. Careful pre-trip planning should make sure that the right people are included and that the desired information is clearly identified in the form of a checklist. After completion of the trip, the photographs and the information gathered should be adequately discussed and properly applied.

DRESSING ROOMS	Facility Number	See Page	Total Sq. Feet
Women's Physical Education and Intramural			
Locker and Dressing Room	42	61	10,000
Shower and Toweling Area	43	62	4,000
Lavatory and Toilet Area	44	63	2,000
Hair Drying and Make-up Room Area	45	64	500
Towel and Uniform Issue Room	46	65	600
Women's Faculty Locker, Dressing & Shower Area	47	66	1,500
Women's Swimming Instructor Shower and Locker	48	67	160
Men's Physical Education and Intramural			
Locker and Dressing Area	49	68	5,600
Shower	50	69	1,050
Toweling Area	51	70	1,050
Lavatory and Toilet Area	52	71	240
Towel and Uniform Issue Room	53	72	450
Men's Faculty Locker, Dressing, Shower, and Toweling area	54	73	1,970
Men's Swimming Instructor Shower-Locker Room	55	74	160
Intercollegiate Athletics			
Football Locker, Dressing & Shower Area	56	75	3,500
Other Sports Locker, Dressing-Shower Area	57	76	2,846
Coaches' Locker, Dressing & Shower Area	58	77	456
OTHER ROOMS (36 Total)			
First Aid Room	59	78	150
Swimming Pool Equipment Storage	60	79	576
Dance Property Storage	61	80	840
Costume Construction and Storage	62	81	600
Playfield Cart and Equipment Storage	63	82	250
Canoe and Trailer Storage	64	83	500
Ski Storage	65	84	180
Garage for Driver Training Car and Equipment	66	85	500
Health Department Storage-Room A	67	86	480
Health Department Storage-Room B	68	87	300
Women's Physical Education Department Storage, Room A	69	88	120
Women's Physical Education Department Storage, Room B	70	89	120
Recreation Department Storage	71	90	150
Intramural Equipment Storage Room	72	91	150
Gymnasium Equipment Storage	73	92	2,200
Gymnasium Supervision and Equipment Issue Room	74	93	200
Gallery, Swimming Pool A (40 seats @ 7 sq. ft. ea.)	75	94	280
Gallery, Swimming Pool B (1,000 seats @ 5 sq. ft. ea.)	76	95	5,000
Gallery, Gymnasium A (200 seats @ 6 sq. ft. ea.)	77	96	1,200
Gallery, Gymnasium B (200 seats @ 6 sq. ft. ea.)	78	97	1,200

Figure 19-2. Sample page from the "Space Requirements Section" of a written program for a new facility. (Courtesy of Brigham Young University.)

Facility 49
MEN'S LOCKER AND DRESSING AREA

Floor Area: 5,600 sq. ft.

Ceiling Height: Ten feet

Floor Material: Quarry tile

Wall Material: Ceramic tile

Ceiling Material: Moisture resistant and sound absorbent

General: Located adjacent to F. 50, F. 51, and F. 52;
Lockers arranged on raised pedestal, no legs, solid base, with 106 inches width for the aisle between the lockers;
8 in. benches, 30 in. in front of lockers;
360 dressing lockers, 12 in. by 15 in. by 60 in.; 50 of these to be designated as intercollegiate team lockers, 310 as lockers for physical education and intramurals;
1,800 storage lockers, 12 in. by 15 in. by 12 in.;
Lockers to be arranged on a 5 to 1 basis. All lockers to have louvred doors, perforated backs, and tiers; tops of lockers are to be slanted for cleanliness;
Warm air is to be discharged under storage lockers section, forced upward through each locker (passing through perforations), and carried to the outside through central vents constructed in each locker section;
Mirrors to be arranged on ends of rows of lockers;
Two cuspidors and two drinking fountains, one set near toweling room, one set near entry.

Equipment needed in room:
Benches in front of all dressing lockers;
360 dressing lockers, 12 in. by 15 in. by 60 in., Worley Steel Lockers;
1,800 storage lockers, 12 in. by 15 in. by 12. in., Worley Steel Lockers;
Mirrors;
2 cuspidors;
2 drinking fountains.

Space utilization and importance to curriculum:
Dressing rooms and lockers for all men's activities which will be held in this building.

Figure 19-3. A page from a written plan for a new facility. The information pertains to one area of the total facility. (Courtesy of Brigham Young University.)

Sometimes architectural drawings of a similar facility elsewhere can be reviewed. Borrowing a set of plans enables several people on the local scene to review them without the expense and time needed to take a field trip. Good ideas can be obtained from a review of plans that would not be obtained during an on-site inspection of the facility.

Other useful sources of information are textbooks and articles on facility planning and construction. They include effective procedures to follow, desirable building features, and the advantages and disadvantages of various products. These sources of information are accessible and inexpensive.

Selecting and Utilizing an Architect

Architects have often been criticized for their shortcomings in designing school buildings. Much of the fault, however, lies with school personnel. Often too much responsibility is left with the architect without enough involvement by school administrators and other employees. Even though the architect may be highly competent in architectural design and construction, he cannot be expected to understand all of the functional characteristics that are needed in a physical education or athletic building. Architects have not had first-hand experience with utilization of such facilities and certainly are not experts on the programs that the facilities are expected to accommodate.

Some architects do truly wonderful things in both design and function, but even the best of architects needs all of the useful information available from the program administrators and subject matter experts. The school should get what it needs to accommodate its programs, not only what the architect wants. This places a responsibility on both the architect and the school personnel to do cooperative, intelligent planning and communicate thoroughly with each other throughout the course of the project.

Selecting the right architect is not a simple matter. One must consider knowledge and experience as well as personality and ability to establish rapport. The client should interview prospective architects, view their work, inspect buildings they have designed, and confer with other clients they have served. An architect's ability to provide good service should be investigated from every standpoint.

The planning team for the project has the responsibility of working with the architect on details as the plan develops. Certain decisions must be made expediently in consultation with the architect. The chairman of the planning team should have a degree of leeway in doing this; however, "crisis-type" decisions should be avoided as much as possible.

Planning a Checklist

The checklist presented on the following pages is intended to provide insight into the considerations that deserve attention in the planning process. It also serves as a model for a checklist that could be utilized in an actual planning situation. In order to use the checklist, place the appropriate letter in the space indicated opposite each statement: (A) the plans meet the requirements *completely*; (B) the plans meet the requirements *only partially*; (C) the plans *fail* to meet the requirements.[3] The material for this checklist is from *Planning Facilities*, a publication of the American Alliance for Health, Physical Education, Recreation and Dance, 1900 Association Drive, Reston, VA 22091. It is used by permission of the Alliance and of the Athletic Institute, 200 Castlewood Road, North Palm Beach, FL 33408.

General Considerations

_____ 1. The facility is planned is a part of a well-conceived and well-integrated master plan.

_____ 2. The facility has been planned to meet the total requirements of the program as well as the special needs of those who are to be served, both now and in the foreseeable future.

_____ 3. The plans and specifications have been carefully checked by all agencies and individuals whose approvals are required or desired.

_____ 4. The plans conform to state and local regulations and to acceptable standards and practices.

_____ 5. The plans have been prepared to accommodate possible future additions and expansions in the best manner possible.

_____ 6. Administrative officers, faculty offices, staff offices, conference rooms, workrooms, teaching stations, and service facilities are all properly interrelated and properly located for effectiveness and function.

_____ 7. Facilities for health services, emergencies, and first aid are adequate and suitably located.

_____ 8. The special needs of the handicapped have received adequate consideration.

_____ 9. The building is compatible in design and adequate in control as compared with the other buildings with which it relates.

_____ 10. Adequate attention has been given to making the facilities as durable, maintenance-free, and vandal-proof as possible.

_____ 11. Low-cost maintenance features have received the special consideration that is deserved.

_____ 12. Drinking fountains, restrooms, hair dryers, and other convenience facilities are adequate in number and properly located.

_____ 13. Provision is made for the repair, maintenance, replacement, and off-season storage of equipment and uniforms.

_____ 14. Noncorrosive metals are used in all damp areas such as dressing rooms and laundry areas.

_____ 15. Fire regulations and fire prevention have received adequate consideration. Also, fire alarm systems, both audio and visual, are adequate.

_____ 16. The facility contains adequate and well-placed bulletin boards, trophy cases, and display areas.

_____ 17. Adequate shower, dressing, and locker room facilities are furnished for students, staff members, guests, and game officials.

_____ 18. The proportion of space for different uses and the location relationships have received proper attention in the planning.

_____ 19. Adequate attention has been given to quiet areas for study and concentration.

_____ 20. The plan includes an adequate class signal system (bell or buzzer).

_____ 21. Adequate provision has been made for telephone service, intercommunication, both oral and written, mail service, and stereo.

_____ 22. The lock and key plan is suitable in terms of security and convenience.

_____ 23. The traffic-flow plan is well conceived and adequate, especially at stairways and exits.

Teaching Stations

_____ 1. Teaching stations are of optimum size to accommodate the desired number of students and the particular activities.

_____ 2. Teaching stations are designed with adequate safety zones between separate activity areas, and in connection with walls and fixed objects, smooth surfaces and padding are in locations where needed.

_____ 3. Each gymnasium has at least one smooth unobstructed wall for ball rebounding activities and adequate ceiling height (minimum of 18 feet for elementary schools and 22 feet for secondary schools).

_____ 4. Each teaching station has the desirable accessories, such as scoreboard, seating space, chalk board, bulletin board, floor markings, game standards, power operated partitions (where useful), public address system (if needed), adequate spectator space for the activities planned for the area, and the standard equipment such as nets, mats, and the like.

_____ 5. Adequate storage closets and cabinets properly located and adequately secured.

_____ 6. Special instructional provisions as needed, such as televisions, instant video replay, phonographs and recorders, movie screens, and projection equipment.

_____ 7. Other instructional items are included where needed, such as wall mirrors, exercise bars, floor diagrams, acoustical drapery, and appropriate performance surfaces. (Different surfaces are needed for different kinds of activities such as basketball, tennis, weight training, modern dance, ballet, social dance, or gymnastics.)

Walls

_____ 1. Provisions are made for wall surfaces to be of attractive, durable and maintenance-free materials.

_____ 2. Movable and folding partitions that are power operated and controlled by switches.

_____ 3. Hooks and rings for nets and other attachments are properly placed, highly stable, and recessed for safety reasons.

_____ 4. Where moisture is prevalent such as in a natatorium, shower and dressing rooms, and laundry area, wall coverings are of moisture-proof or resistant materials. Special consideration is given in the case of walls that will be hosed down, such as shower rooms, steam rooms, and possibly, restrooms and dressing rooms.

_____ 5. Walls are free of protrusions and obstacles that interfere with traffic flow or create safety hazards. Corners are rounded and surface irregularities eliminated where desirable.

_____ 6. The wall texture and color of painted surfaces is the best it can be for attractiveness, lighting, and maintenance.

Ceilings

_____ 1. Ceilings in all instructional areas, offices, and meeting rooms are of the material that will provide the optimum acoustical effect.

_____ 2. Adequate consideration has been given to texture and color of ceiling materials.

_____ 3. Moisture-resistant ceiling materials are specified for moisture-prevalent areas.

_____ 4. Consideration has been given to adequate ceiling lighting, both direct and indirect, and both artificial and natural.

_____ 5. Overhead supported apparatus and equipment is secured to beams engineered to withstand stress.

Floors

_____ 1. Floors are made of appropriate materials for the particular activities to be conducted in each location. Performance effectiveness, safety, and maintenance are all considered. Carpeting is placed in areas where appropriate, taking into consideration acoustics, attractiveness, and maintenance.

_____ 2. Floor plates are placed where needed, and they are flush mounted and stable.

_____ 3. Appropriate consideration has been given to flooring material, texture, slope, and drains in shower and locker rooms, swimming pool decks, steam rooms, and other areas that will be hosed.

_____ 4. Nonskid surfaces and strips are placed where needed for safety, especially in wet areas and on stairways and ramps.

_____ 5. Highly durable and easily maintained baseboards are specified.

Electrical

_____ 1. Lighting intensity is in accordance with recommended standards.

_____ 2. Electrical control panels are properly placed and adequately secured.

_____ 3. Where appropriate, lights are controlled by key switches.

_____ 4. Adequate numbers of electrical outlets are properly placed.

_____ 5. Dimmer units are placed in instructional areas and elsewhere, as needed.

_____ 6. Natural light is properly planned in accordance with recommended standards.

_____ 7. Lights are shielded for protection from balls and other game implements.

_____ 8. Waterproof outlets are specified for moisture-prevalent areas and areas that will be hosed.

Temperature Control

_____ 1. Adequate provisions are made in all areas for heating, air conditioning, and ventilation.

_____ 2. Special consideration has been given to ventilation and individual temperature controls in locker rooms, dressing and shower areas, swimming pool, and other moisture-prevalent and odor-prone areas.

_____ 3. Proper ventilation is provided for such places as the wrestling room, equipment storage areas, research animal kennels, and other appropriate areas.

Other Considerations

_____ 1. Throughout the facility, adequate storage spaces are well located and properly designed.

_____ 2. Locker rooms are arranged for ease of supervision.

_____ 3. Provision is made for adequate control of access.

_____ 4. Adequate faculty accommodations are provided: shower and locker room, equipment and supply access, and lounge.

_____ 5. Food dispensary areas have received proper attention.

_____ 6. A well-defined program for laundering and handling of uniforms, towels, and equipment is included in the plan.

_____ 7. Shower heads are placed at appropriate heights for the ages of those being served. In the locker room, adequate attention is given to locker ventilation, placement of benches for convenience and ease of cleaning, height and size of lockers and width of aisle between lockers.

Specialized Areas

In checking the plans, special consideration should be given to such specialized areas as the following:

_____ 1. Athletic training facilities.

_____ 2. Visiting team dressing room.

_____ 3. Dance studio.

_____ 4. Facility for ice activities.

_____ 5. Bowling alley.

_____ 6. Rifle range.

_____ 7. Indoor tennis courts.

_____ 8. A facility to accommodate a large number of spectators.

_____ 9. Research facilities.

Working with the Contractor

Once the plans are complete and the financial and other arrangements have been made to go ahead with the project, it is time to enter into an agreement with a contractor. As a general rule, a project should be put out to bid. All contractors who prepare bids must have access to exactly the same information about the project, so that the bids will be prepared on the same basis and can be logically compared against each other. When a project is put out to bid, the client has a moral obligation to accept the lowest bid unless there are justifiable reasons for doing otherwise. Sometimes, the bidding procedure includes an understanding that the client has the right to approve the subcontractors that the general contractor plans to engage. This assures that the client feels satisfied with all of the contractors who will work on the project.

During the construction phase and beyond, the architect has a continuing responsibility to the client to make sure that the construction is done exactly according to the approved plan. To implement this, the architect works hand-in-hand with the contractor and performs periodic inspections to be sure that the conditions of the contract are met.

In addition, the school should assign an inspector for each major construction project. The inspector should be a school technician whose main responsibilities in connection with the project are to make sure the materials and workmanship are in accordance with the contractual agreement. The inspector also serves as a liaison between the contractor and client, and thereby communicates any clarifications and decisions needed along the way. When the project is nearly completed, the inspector should be involved with the architect and the contractor in semifinal and final inspections. These inspections would result in a list of all of the items that are uncompleted or unacceptable. All of these items would have to be done to satisfaction before the final settlement would be made with the contractor and the architect.

On any large project, a number of changes are made during construction due to additional information that comes to light or the development of unforeseen circumstances. It is an advantage both to the client and the contractor to keep an open door for making such changes when they can be clearly justified. Whenever such a change is agreed upon, a change form should be completed a copy kept by the client, the architect, and the contractor so that there is a written agreement explaining the change. Actually, a change is viewed as a modification of the original contract.

Choosing the Type of Structure

In view of today's exorbitant and accelerating construction costs, the concept of maximum useful space for minimum cost is applicable, also keeping in mind the projected life span of the facility and the cost of maintenance. This requires careful analysis of the basic kinds of structure, the particular design features, and the materials used.

Conventional brick construction of school facilities has been by far the most prevalent and, in the majority of cases, it is still the best kind of construction. The particular features included in a conventional brick structure allow a wide range of choices, in which local needs and individual preferences can be easily accommodated. Practically all of the information presented in this chapter can be applied in conventional brick construction.

In the past few decades, considerable experimentation has been done and some practical use has been made of other forms of construction such as hardshell domes and air-support structures. There is no question that such structures can provide large areas of space at less cost per square foot than conventional brick construction; therefore, these new forms of construction are sometimes worth serious consideration. Let us look, for example, at the advantages and disadvantages of air-support structures, since there has been a mild surge toward the use of these structures during recent years.

Pure air-support structures (Figure 19-4) and cable reinforced air-support structures (Figure 19-5) have certain advantages when compared with each other or with conventional construction. The cable reinforced structures have to have solid walls or some other kind of structure to which the cables can be attached. The advantages of the various kinds of air-support structures as compared with conventional construction are as follows: (1) The cost of air-support structures per square foot is only 25 to 35% that of conventional structures. (2) They are capable of providing a large span of unobstructed space. (3) They are relatively easy and fast to build, and the smaller structures can be

Figure 19-4. A structure at Santa Clara University supported completely by air-fill, with the top placed on a 16-foot concrete retaining wall surrounded by landscaped earth-fill. **A.** Exterior view; **B.** Interior view. (Courtesy of Owens-Corning Fiberglass Corporation.)

put up and taken down during different seasons of the year. (4) The maintenance costs are relatively low. (5) They are easy to light because of the penetration of natural light during the day and their ability to diffuse artificial light at night. (6) They are relatively fire-proof and highly earthquake resistant.

Some of the disadvantages are as follows: (1) The life of the air-support fabric is about 20 years, much less than that of conventional construction. This fact partially offsets the advantage of much lower initial construction costs. (2) In some environments, the architecture of air-support structures is considered unacceptable. (3) Temperature control has been a problem, especially in warm climates. Heat gain is a larger problem than heat loss. For this reason, air-support structures have proven to be more acceptable in colder than in hotter

Figure 19-5. Air-supported structure at the University of Florida at Gainsville, with cable and metal beam reinforcement. Interior concrete walls form important elements of the support system. **A.** Exterior view; **B.** Interior view. (Courtesy of Owens-Corning Fiberglass Corporation.)

climates. (4) In terms of acoustics, air-support structures are less than optimal, but in many cases, the level of acoustics is acceptable. (5) The potential for serious vandalism exists, but the fear of this has not been substantiated in cases where air-support structures have been built.

Additional Ideas

The Park–School. This concept involves cooperative action between school and municipal authorities. It includes joint agreements as to the location, development, and use of the properties for both school and community purposes. In addition to the resulting economy in land ownership and costs of construction, operation, and maintenance, this cooperative approach fosters the desirable multiple use of areas and facilities.

In order to protect the interests of the cooperating authorities and to assure the most effective application of a park–school plan, a formal agreement should be enacted by the parties involved. Their uses of the facilities and their respective responsibilities for the purchase, development, operation, and maintenance should be spelled out.

Although the park–school (or sometimes called the community–school) concept has won wide acceptance in recent years, it still is not applied frequently enough. It should receive thorough consideration in every community and neighborhood.

Storage Space. Often, buildings are constructed with inadequate storage space or with storage space poorly located or poorly designed. Storage is an important element of the total operation, and it should receive adequate attention in planning and construction; however, storage space should be viewed practically. Consider, for example, that a building costs $100 per square foot. The question for administrators, then, is what kind of supplies and equipment and how much of them should occupy storage space at this kind of initial cost, plus interest on the original investment, plus the cost of maintenance. Thus, efficient use of storage space is imperative.

Floor Surfaces. A strong trend has been growing toward the use of carpet in a variety of areas. In some cases, short pile carpet is even used in activity areas. Some administrators view carpet as an expensive luxury; however, it often costs less than other floor coverings. The question of whether to use carpet should be analyzed in terms of relative initial cost, projected replacement and maintenance costs, acoustical advantages, and the positive pyschologic influence it has on those who use the facility.

In large foyers, shower rooms, or other areas where a hard surface is desired, one must decided whether to use concrete, terrazo, or some form of tile. Concrete is the cheapest in terms of initial cost. Terrazo has been found to be highly satisfactory in terms of attractiveness, initial cost, and maintenance. Tile comes in many forms and with a great variation in costs. The merits of any kind of tile should be carefully evaluated in any particular situation.

A decision must be made as to whether to install hardwood floors or some form of synthetic surface in gymnasiums. Hardwood floors have become expensive, and some fairly suitable synthetic surfaces can be installed at less initial cost. It is generally agreed, however, that hardwood floors are still preferable in a gymnasium.

In outdoor areas, the use of *natural or artificial turf* depends on the availability of outdoor space, which in turn, influences the intensity of use. The initial cost for outdoor synthetic surfaces is high; but this kind of surface is necessary if the intensity of use is too great to be withstood by natural turf. In some locations, it is more economical to own a smaller area that is prepared for high intensity use. Additional considerations to be taken into account are the type of surface preferred for the particular activities and the preference of those involved with the program.

Specialized Arrangements. In *locker rooms* and *shower areas*, different arrangements can be considered, with each one having certain advantages. The various arrangements are illustrated in Figures 19-6, 19-7, and 19-8.

Principles of Planning and Construction

1. Each school or school system should have an overall campus plan. People to be involved with this plan should be competent and experienced not only in planning but in working with architects and contractors.
2. The functional capacity of a facility is of prime importance. Practically all other aspects rank below this important consideration.
3. Soundly conceived plans for areas and facilities are not achieved by chance or accident, but rather by thought and action of knowledgeable people who work well together.
4. When a building is ready for use, the true test of the planning occurs. If the building works well, looks good, and wears well, then the planning team has accomplished its purpose.
5. Facilities should be constructed of high-quality materials and workmanship in order to avoid expensive repairs and costly maintenance. Poor quality simply does not hold up under heavy use.
6. All planning and construction should conform to state and local regulations and acceptable facility standards.
7. Facilities should be designed so that they accommodate the needs of men and women equitably.
8. The multiple-use concept should be carefully considered in the case of certain facilities. Application of this concept is basically an economy measure, which can greatly enhance the utility of the facilities.
9. Facilities should be designed so that the different components can be used independently without opening and supervising the entire building or complex.
10. Facilities should permit independent and simultaneous use for more than one activity within the same complex without encroachment or interference.
11. Adequate consideration should be given to possible future expansion of a particular facility, and this might influence design.
12. Relatively small offices designed for one faculty member are much preferred, because having more than one person per office disrupts privacy and efficiency. An oversized office is highly conducive to housing two or more faculty members. The optimum size for one person is approximately 110 square feet.
13. The construction of an undersized teaching station is expensive because it forces the teaching of small classes every term for the lifetime of the teaching station.
14. The special needs of handicapped persons should be taken into consideration in facility planning.
15. Desirable health and safety standards should be adequately considered.
16. Human traffic patterns for spectators and students should provide for movement through corridors and spaces with a minimum of congestion.
17. Initially, the planning should be pointed at the optimal or ideal in view of the particular circumstances. The reality of the restrictions will take over soon enough.

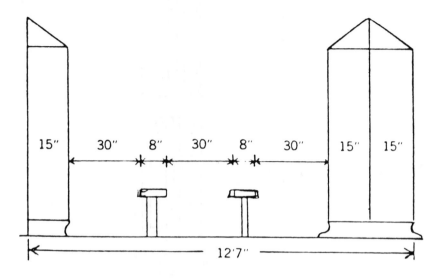

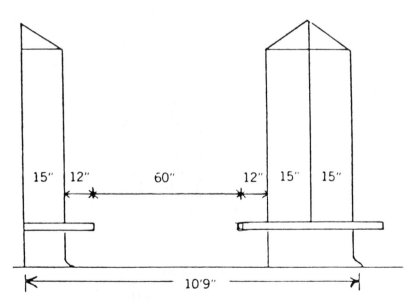

Figure 19-6. Two different arrangements for dressing room benches; isle mount (upper) and pedestal mount (lower). The pedestal mount has distinct advantages in terms of space utilization and traffic flow.

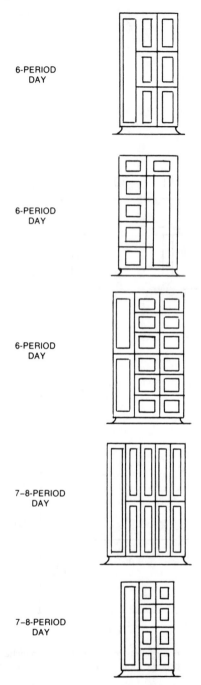

6-PERIOD
DAY

6-PERIOD
DAY

6-PERIOD
DAY

7–8-PERIOD
DAY

7–8-PERIOD
DAY

Figure 19-7. Five different combinations of storage/dressing locker arrangements, with the small lockers for storage of uniforms between classes, and the large lockers for clothes during class.

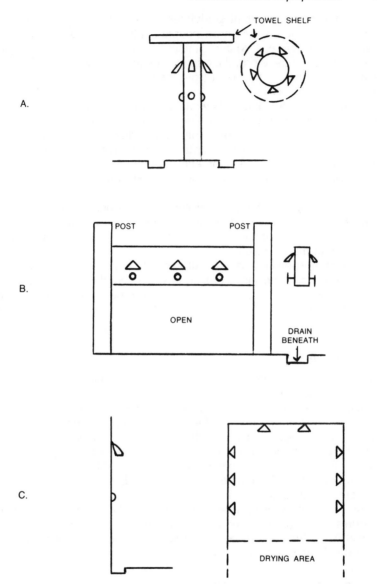

Figure 19-8. Three different shower head arrangements: (A) post style; (B) stainless steel bank; and (C) wall mount.

EQUIPMENT AND SUPPLIES

Although in this chapter much emphasis has been placed on facility planning and construction, administrators are generally more involved on a continuing basis with the purchase and management of equipment and supplies.

One of the most important guidelines in the selection of equipment and supplies is the same concept most people apply in their personal lives, "the best value for the money." Many of the purchases made for the school involve large expenditures; therefore, the one making the purchases must be thorough in searching for the right product from the vendor who will provide the best price and the best service.

Poor-quality equipment usually wears out quickly, is less perfect, and therefore, less desirable to use. Its short life span is uneconomical in terms of the time and money required for ordering, transporting, and handling. In certain instances, it is a good idea to investigate buying used equipment when investing in large and expensive items. Sometimes equipment used for demonstration purposes or that has been repossessed can be purchased at a considerable discount.

When purchasing clothing and protective equipment, proper fit and safety considerations must receive adequate attention. With certain items, such as footwear and the performance implements, their quality and condition can influence performance result.

Equipment must be kept secure. All items should have proper identification labels. Well-defined and sound procedures are needed for checking equipment in and out and monitoring its use. One of the best ways to control loss is to consistently use a check-out form. Figures 19-9 and 19-10 show examples of such forms.

Inventory

Inventory involves keeping an amount of stock that is adequate to avoid frequent shortages and small orders, yet not so large that it occupies an inordinate amount of storage space. Stock, which represents money invested, must be properly secured in order to avoid loss. It should be reasonably protected from fire, dampness, exposure to the elements, or damage by rodents and insects; therefore, it should be stored in areas that are clean, properly ventilated, and protected from extreme temperatures and humidity.

Keeping current and accurate inventory records is an important element in equipment accountability. This requires the use of an appropriate inventory form, of which an example appears in Figure 19-11. Computerized inventory procedures are frequently used by school districts, colleges, and universities. This greatly simplifies recordkeeping, makes the information more readily available, and enhances the purchasing process.

STORAGE AND CARE

Sporting goods suppliers have developed "equipment organizers" that can be transported directly from the issue room to the teaching station. *Nylon mesh bags* are highly useful for carrying balls and similar items to and from teaching stations, and the items can be stored in the same bag in the issue room. Mesh bags can be used for issuing clothing, and the clothing can be laundered while still in the bag, thus eliminating the necessity of sorting and reassembling the issue. *Grocery carts* can be used for storage and transport of light equipment items, and heavy-duty two-wheeled *wire carts* are available for the transport

PHYSICAL EDUCATION ISSUE FORM

Name (print) _____
                          Last   First   Middle

Locker No. _____   Homeroom _____

I hereby accept full responsibility for the following uniforms and/or items of equipment checked out to me:

Uniform Items	No.	Equipment (list items)	No.
Blouse or shirt			
Shorts			
Socks			
Leotard			
Swim Suit			
Towel			
Other			

Address _____Phone _____

Signature _____

* Note: Cross off items when returned.

Figure 19-9.   A sample uniform and equipment checkout form for physical education participants.

and storage of heavier items such as a golf equipment. Inside storage rooms, appropriate hanging devices, storage bins, and shelves are essential.

Proper maintenance of equipment can keep the items in usable condition and extend their life span. Expensive equipment is hard to justify if it is not properly cared for and maintained. Equipment in poor repair results in disruptions and ineffectiveness in the program.

The users of equipment must understand their responsibility for proper use and care and their obligation for payment in the case of nonroutine damage. The time that items are to be returned and the check-in procedures must be clearly communicated.

Most equipment can be effectively cared for by simply using common sense. When equipment requires specialized treatment or care, such instructions usually accompany the equipment at the time of purchase. If additional information or clarifications about care are needed, the distributor is usually the best source. Consistent interest in taking good care of equipment is often more important than special instructions. Following are some guidelines for the care of equipment.

ATHLETIC EQUIPMENT ISSUE FORM

Name _____   Sport _____   School _____
Address _____   Telephone _____   Locker # _____

LIST OF EQUIPMENT

Practice

Belt _____
Cap _____
Guards, knee _____
Headgear _____
Jersey _____
Pads _____
Pads, hip _____
Pads, shoulder _____
Pants _____
Pants, warm-up _____
Shirt, warm-up _____
Shoes _____
Socks _____
Stockings _____
Tights, wrestling _____
Undershirt _____

Game

Coat, sideline _____
Headgear _____
Jersey _____
Pants _____
Pants, warm-up _____
Shirt, warm-up _____
Shoes _____
Socks _____

I am responsible for the articles listed hereon, which are charged to me, and agree that they will not be used for any purpose but the school games or authorized practice while in my possession.

Signature: _____
Date: _____

Figure 19-10. A sample form for the issue of athletic equipment.

INVENTORY FORM

Signature* _____Title _____

Date _____ Room of Location _____

Description	Quantity	New or Used	Condition of Equipment	I.D. # or label

* Signature of person accountable for the items

Figure 19-11. A sample equipment inventory form.

1. The administrative head is the one finally accountable for all equipment and supplies in the organization.
2. Clear procedures should be established and followed relative to loss, theft, damage, or destruction.
3. Equipment should be discarded in accordance with the prescribed procedures and by authorized persons.
4. Accurate inventory and checkout records should be constantly maintained.
5. Procedures should be established to ensure proper use and maintenance.
6. Each individual to whom equipment and supplies are issued should be held accountable. A tight rein must be held on this procedure.

7. Sound procedures must be followed relative to the distribution and collection of equipment.
8. There should be an effective method of marking equipment and supplies to show ownership.

In managing equipment and supplies, an administrator should have positive answers to the following two fundamental questions. Do all of the employees consistently have all the supplies and equipment they need in order to be effective? Do the procedures provide adequate protection against loss, breakage, and misuse, and do they encourage economy and efficiency?

REFERENCES AND RECOMMENDED READINGS

1. AAHPERD: Improvised Physical Education Equipment. Waldorf, MD, AAHPERD Publications, 1990.
2. AAHPERD: Dance Facilities. Waldorf, MD, AAHPERD Publications, 1986.
3. AAHPERD: Planning Facilities for Athletics, Physical Education, and Recreation. Waldorf, MD, AAHPERD Publications, 1986.
4. Bucher, C.A.: Administration of Physical Education and Athletic Programs, 9th Ed. St. Louis, C.V. Mosby, 1987, pp. 387–438.
5. Frost, R.B., Lockhart, B.D., and Marshall, S.J.: Administration of Physical Education and Athletics, 3rd Ed. Dubuque, IA, William C. Brown, 1988, pp. 403–453.
6. Horine, L. Administration of Physical Education and Sport Programs, 2nd Ed. Dubuque, IA, William C. Brown, 1991, pp. 206–243.
7. Horine, L.: Sport facilities. JOPERD, 58:(1):21–42, 1987.
8. Isaacs, L., and Frederick, S.D.: Physical education facilities for the handicapped. JOPER, 51:30, 1980.
9. Jarman, B.: Unpublished Class Notes. Brigham Young University, Provo, UT, 1992.
10. Nalley, C.: A school-park relationship that benefits everyone. Athletic Purchasing and Facilities, 17:24, 1981.

Chapter *20*

PROFESSIONALLY RELATED ORGANIZATIONS

Professional organizations make important contributions to the lifeblood of the particular discipline, so they need to be nurtured and utilized effectively. These organizations help individuals become involved and to know the issues and the trends. They help one to realize that there are few things more interesting than to be on the razor edge of the profession.

Members of a profession must know the organizations that relate to their profession and be at least generally familiar with the purposes, programs, and services of each. Knowledge about these organizations can serve at least two purposes:

1. It helps the administrator better understand how the organization can contribute to the profession as a whole and to the programs of any particular institution or school system.
2. It helps one to better know with which organizations to affiliate and for what reasons.

PROFESSIONAL AND SERVICE ORGANIZATIONS

Numerous professional and service organizations at the national level pertain to physical education and athletics. A brief description of each of these organizations is presented in alphabetic order. Some of the organizations have district and state subdivisions or affiliates. Many organizations pertain to a specific aspect of physical education and athletics. These organizations are listed in the last portion of the chapter.

Amateur Athletic Union (AAU)

The Amateur Athletic Union of the United States, Inc. (AAU) is the largest not-for-profit volunteer organizations in the United States dedicated solely to the development of amateur sports and physical fitness programs. Founded in 1888, the AAU is comprised of 58 AAU Associations that administer and operate AAU programs at the grassroots level.

AAU programs are available to all Americans and are conducted with the

333

philosophy of providing an opportunity for competition without overemphasizing athletic excellence. This ideal of "sports for sports sake" is shared by the more than 4,500 member clubs and hundreds of thousands of volunteers at the grassroots level.

The programs of the AAU are the AAU James E. Sullivan Memorial Award, AAU/USA Junior Olympic Games, AAU/USA Youth Sports Program, AAU/MARS®MILKY WAY® Bar High School All-American Award, AAU/Soviet Boys' Basketball Tour, Chrysler Fund/AAU Physical Fitness Program, Presidential Sports Award, and the President's Challenge Youth Physical Fitness Program.

The AAU publishes brochures and rule books for each of its sports in addition to its bimonthly publication, "*InfoAAU*." The address of AAU House is 3400 West 86th Street, Indianapolis, IN 46268.

AAHPERD

The American Alliance for Health, Physical Education, Recreation and Dance is a voluntary education organization made up of 6 national associations and 6 district associations, with 54 state and territorial affiliates. The membership, which exceeds 35,000, is composed of health and physical educators, coaches, athletic directors, and personnel in safety, recreation and leisure services, and dance. The organization was founded in 1885 by a group of 49 people, mostly educators and physicians interested in promoting "physical training." Today, the membership network reaches into more than 16,000 school districts, over 2,000 colleges and universities, and 10,000 community recreation units.

Following are the national associations that comprise the Alliance:

American Association for Leisure and Recreation (AALR) promotes school, community, and national programs of leisure services and recreation education.

Association for the Advancement of Health Education (AAHE) works for continuing comprehensive programs of health education in schools, the work place, and the community. Position papers are developed on such health topics as certification, drug education, and sex education.

Association for Research, Administration and Professional Councils and Societies (ARAPCS) coordinates the following special interest structures: Aquatics; College/University Administrators; City and County Directors; Outdoor Education; Facilities; Equipment and Supplies; International Relations; Measurement and Evaluation; Physical Fitness; Therapeutics; and Student Members.

National Association for Girls and Women in Sport (NAGWS) is the primary educational organization for professional development of girls and women as sports leaders and advocates for programs of sport and physical activity for all females.

National Association for Sport and Physical Education (NASPE) provides leadership opportunity in physical education and sports development, competition, consultation, publications, conferences, research, and a public information program.

National Dance Association (NDA) promotes the development of sound policies for dance in education through conferences, convention programs, special projects, publications, and cooperation with other dance and art groups.

The AAHPERD holds a national convention each year. In addition, the 6 districts each hold a district convention annually, and the 54 state and territorial affiliates conduct annual conventions. The Alliance and its affiliates sponsor a large number of workshops, conferences, and clinics each year, all of which are aimed at professional development of its members or the solution of particular issues pertaining to the profession.

The Alliance publishes five regular periodicals: *Update, Journal of Physical Education, Recreation and Dance, Journal of Health Education, Research Quarterly for Exercise, Sport,* and *Strategies.* More than a dozen newsletters are prepared and distributed regularly to provide information in specific areas of the associations; and the Alliance publishes 50 to 60 books and films each year. The titles are available in the AAHPERD publications catalog. The home office of the Alliance is located at 1900 Association Drive, Reston, VA 22091.

American College of Sports Medicine

The American College of Sports Medicine is a nonprofit association with an international membership of more than 6,000. Unlike most associations whose memberships are joined together by a single professional specialty, this organization represents over 40 different specialties. Among the objectives of the ACSM are the following: to promote and disseminate medical and other scientific studies dealing with the effects of sports and physical training on people's health; to initiate, promote, and correlate research in these fields; to establish and maintain a sports medicine library. ACSM has five regional chapters, and additional chapters are being developed throughout the United States as the interest of members dictates. Membership is open to any individual interested in sports medicine who holds a graduate degree or who has become specialized in a field related to health, physical education, athletics, or the medical sciences.

The ACSM is a multidisciplinary professional and scientific society dedicated to the generation and dissemination of knowledge concerning the responses, adaptations, and clinical aspects of the human organism engaged in exercise and in recreational and competitive sports. The specific concerns include:

1. The basic physiologic, biochemical, biomechanical, and behavioral mechanisms.
2. The improvement and maintenance of functional capacities for daily living.
3. The prevention and rehabilitation of chronic and degenerative disease.
4. The evaluation and conditioning of athletes.
5. The prevention and treatment of injuries.

The College sponsors an annual national convention, several workshops in various geographic areas, lecture tours by selected sports medicine specialists, and position stands on important sports medicine topics and issues. The publications of the ACSM include the quarterly issue of *Medicine and Science in Sports* and the *Sports Medicine Bulletin*. It has also published the *Encyclopedia of Sports Sciences and Medicine* and a monograph series of sports and medicine. Its address is 401 W. Michigan St., Indianapolis, IN 46202-3233.

American Physical Therapy Association

This association has a membership of more than 30,000 individuals. It has 52 state chapters and 100 district chapters.

The APTA provides a variety of services to its membership and to the profession. These services include the following: sets standards of practice, adopts and enforces ethical principles, and participates in the preparation and revision of the licensure examinations to assure quality physical therapy services for the public; accredits educational programs to assure the preparation of competent practitioners; guides and assists in the development of graduate education opportunities for physical therapists; promotes the exploration of new knowledge in physical therapy; holds an annual conference, conducts continuing education programs, and provides for the production and dissemination of publications to help transmit pertinent information; fosters the recruitment of minorities into the profession; speaks for the physical therapists in legislative and other health policy matters; conducts a public relations program; maintains a placement service; supplies information and advice to members, educational institutions, private and governmental agencies, and other associations.

The American Physical Therapy Association is a member of the National Health Council, the Coalition of Independent Health Professions, and the World Confederation for Physical Therapy. It publishes a monthly periodical entitled *Physical Therapy, The Journal of the American Physical Therapy Association*. It also publishes numerous information pamphlets, which are listed in its brochure of publications available upon request. The Association was founded in 1921. The home office address is 1156 15th Street NW, Washington, D.C. 20005.

Canadian Association for Health, Physical Education and Recreation

This association is the Canadian counterpart of the United States' AAHPERD. The CAHPER is a national, nonprofit voluntary organization which, since its inception in 1933, has been concerned and engaged in providing and extending the benefits of physical activity to the citizens of Canada. Its particular goals are stated as follows:

Act as a strong national advocate on issues pertaining to physically active life-styles.
Create a network of practitioners and researchers.
Exercise leadership and collaborate in the forum of allied organizations that relate to physically active life-styles.
Promote quality programs in educational settings from kindergarten to university.

The CAHPER issues a bimonthly periodical and a newsletter titled *In Touch*. It also publishes numerous pamphlets and booklets on various topics for the profession. The national office is at 1600 James Naismith Drive, Glouchester, Ontario, Canada KIB 5N4.

National Association of Collegiate Directors of Athletics

This organization serves intercollegiate athletics as a forum for its members in their efforts to establish common standards and educational objectives among athletic directors in colleges and universities throughout the United States and Canada. NACDA disseminates information and guidelines pertinent to the immediate problems and issues confronting athletic directors.

NACDA sponsors an annual convention for the major governing bodies in intercollegiate athletics—NJCAA, NAIA, and NCAA institutions. This is the only meeting held regularly with the major governing bodies in one place at one time. This yearly convention serves as a forum for discussing current issues affecting athletics and athletic administration.

NACDA publishes a journal six times annually entitled *Athletic Administration*. NACDA's address is P.O. Box 16428, Cleveland, OH 44116.

National Association of Intercollegiate Athletics (NAIA)

The National Association of Intercollegiate Athletics is an autonomous athletic association made up of the intercollegiate athletic programs of 515 fully accredited 4-year colleges and universities. The fundamental tenet of the NAIA is that intercollegiate athletics is an integral part of the total educational program of the institution. This belief is strongly reflected in the governing documents, activities, and organizational structure of the Association.

Established in 1940 as the National Association of Intercollegiate Basketball, the NAIA (the name was changed in 1952) emerged from a "National Small College Basketball Tournament" inaugurated in 1937 in Kansas City, Missouri. The conversion of the NAIB to the NAIA in 1952 included the expansion of the program to include national championships in golf, outdoor track and field, and tennis. Football (two divisions), cross country, baseball, and swimming were added to the ledger in 1956; wrestling (1958), soccer (1959), bowling (1962-1978), gymnastics (1964), indoor track and field (1966), ice hockey (1968), and volleyball (1969) are the most recent additions. The initial purpose of the NAIA—to provide national championship opportunities to colleges and universities competing below the so-called major level—has indeed been well served.

NAIA organizes and administers all areas of intercollegiate athletics at the national level, including rules and standards, and district and national sports competition. The address is 1221 Baltimore Street, Kansas City, MO 64105.

National Collegiate Athletic Association (NCAA)

The NCAA was formed in 1906. It is the organization through which the colleges and universities of the United States act on matters to do with men's athletics at the national level (recently it has become involved with women's athletics). The association's membership exceeds 980 institutions, conferences, and affiliated organizations. It is devoted to the sound administration of intercollegiate athletics.

The services of the NCAA include the following:

Maintains a central clearing house and counseling agency in the area of college athletic administration.
Enacts legislation to deal with athletic problems.
Conducts research as a means of developing solutions to athletic problems.
Provides financial and other assistance to various groups interested in the advancement of intercollegiate athletics.
Represents the colleges in legislative and regulatory matters.
Administers insurance programs available to member institutions.
Provides a film/television production department.
Promotes and participates in international sports planning and competition by working with numerous national and international organizations.
Sanctions national intercollegiate post-season competition and sponsors national college championship meets.
Compiles and distributes official statistics for intercollegiate sports.
Sponsors a national rules committee for the various NCAA sports.
Provides other services to member institutions as requested.

The particular purposes of the NCAA are stated as follows:

—To uphold the principle of institutional control of, and responsibility for, all intercollegiate athletics in conformity with the Association's constitution and bylaws.
—To serve as an overall national discussion, legislative and administrative body for the universities and colleges of the United States in matters of intercollegiate athletics.
—To recommend policies for the guidance of member institutions in the conduct of their intercollegiate athletic programs.
—To legislate upon any subject of general concern to the membership in the administration of intercollegiate athletics.
—To study all phases of competitive athletics and establish standards therefor, to the end that colleges and universities of the United States may maintain their athletic activities on a high plane.
—To encourage the adoption by its constituent members of eligibility rules in compliance with satisfactory standards of scholarship, amateur standing and good sportsmanship.
—To establish and supervise regional and national collegiate athletic contests under the auspices of the Association and establish rules of eligibility therefor.
—To stimulate and improve programs to promote and develop educational leadership, physical fitness, sports participation as a recreational pursuit, and athletic excellence through competitive intramural and intercollegiate programs.
—To formulate, copyright and publish rules of play for collegiate sports.
—To preserve collegiate athletic records.
—To cooperate with other amateur athletic organizations in the promotion and conduct of national and international athletic contests.
—To otherwise assist member institutions as requested in the furtherance of their intercollegiate athletic programs.

The NCAA home office is located at 6201 College Boulevard, Overland, KS 66221-2422.

National Education Association (NEA)

The National Education Association of the United States was first organized in 1857 as the National Teacher's Association. The basic purpose of this early organization was to elevate the character and advance the interest of the profession of teaching and to promote the cause of popular education in the United States. The name of the association was changed in 1870 to the National Educational Association. In 1907, the National Education Association of the United States was incorporated under a special act of Congress approved in 1906.

Any person who is actively engaged in the profession of teaching or other educational work, or any other person interested in advancing the cause of education, is eligible for membership in the association.

The expressed goals of the NEA are to promote an independent, united teaching profession, professional excellence, and economic security for educators, and to provide leadership in solving educationally related social problems.

The organization has a membership of approximately 2 million. It puts out numerous publications in the form of periodicals, pamphlets, and books. A list can be obtained by requesting the publications brochure. The national office is the NEA building, 1201 16th Street NW, Washington, DC 20036.

National Federation of State High School Associations (NFSHSA)

The National Federation was formed in 1920 and has grown to encompass a membership that today serves 51 state high school associations, 17 affiliate members, 20,000 high schools, 500,000 coaches and sponsors, and 500,000 officials and judges.

The purpose of the National Federation is to coordinate the efforts of its member state associations toward the ultimate objectives of interscholastic activities.

The legislative body of the National Federation is the National Council, made up of one representative from each member state association. The administration is vested in an elected Executive Committee, which consists of 12 representatives of eight geographical sections of the National Federation.

As the national voice of high school activities, the National Federation represents the high school activities of this country. The "Federation family" includes individual national organizations for athletic directors, coaches, contest officials, speech and debate coaches, music adjudicators, and coaches of pep squads.

More than five million publications and materials are printed in the National Federation headquarters in Kansas City, including rule books in 15 sports, a monthly newsletter and a quarterly magazine for athletic administrators.

Through its TARGET program, the National Federation is committed to helping students cope with tobacco, alcohol, and other drug problems. You can contact the National Federation at 11724 N.W. Plaza Circle, P.O. Box 20626, Kansas City, MO 64195.

National Intramural-Recreational Sports Association (NIRSA)

The early growth of intramurals in America was unstructured, but as the intramural movement expanded, there was an increasing effort to share ideas and set standards for improvement. In 1950, William Wasson of Dillard University formed the National Intramural Association (NIA). This was the first national group devoted entirely to intramural sports. It came into being largely as a result of a Carnegie grant to study the intramural programs in black colleges.

In 1975, the NIA changed its name to the National Intramural–Recreational

Sports Association (NIRSA). This name change reflects the expansion of the association to include intramurals, sport clubs, and other forms of recreational sports.

The mission of the NIRSA is to foster the growth of quality recreational sports programs by providing for the continuing growth and development of recreational sports professionals. It offers members the opportunity for professional interaction through state, regional, and national conferences and workshops.

The membership of the NIRSA includes professionals, students, and institutions in the United States and several foreign countries. The majority of the association's membership is represented by individuals involved in programming at the collegiate level. However, a growing number of members are employed in the military, industry, community, and elementary/middle/secondary level school sectors.

Communication within the membership is maintained through periodic publication of the NIRSA *Journal*, Newsletter, conference proceedings, and the annual *Recreational Sports Directory*. Additional services offered to the membership include job placement, sports officials' development, program certification, research grants, media center, numerous publications, and over 40 conferences and workshops each year. The National Office is located at 850 SW 15th Street, OSU, Corvallis, OR 97333-4145.

National Junior College Athletic Association (NJCAA)

The NJCAA was conceived in 1937 in Fresno, California when a small number of junior college representatives met to organize an association that would promote and supervise a national program of junior college sports consistent with the educational objectives of junior colleges. In 1949, the Association was reorganized by dividing the nation into 16 regions, and later it was divided into 24 regions.

The Association was concerned only with men's sports until 1975, when it added a women's division. This division grew rapidly, and now approximately 500 institutions are enrolled in the women's division and 530 enrolled in the men's division. The NJCAA sponsors championships in a large variety of sports for men and women junior college athletes. Its purposes and general functions are essentially the same as those described for the NCAA and AIAW. The NJCAA is the junior college counterpart of those organizations. The national headquarters is located at P.O. Box 7305, Colorado Springs, CO 80933-7305.

National Recreation and Park Association (NRPA)

The NRPA is a nonprofit service, research, and education organization dedicated to the improvement of the quality of life through effective utilization of natural and human resources. NRPA sponsors various publications, workshops, and institutes. It provides direct consultation and technical assistance for the improvement of programs, leadership, and facilities. The Association is also dedicated to the building of public understanding of the recreation and park field.

The NRPA was formed in 1966 by the merger of five pioneer organizations in the park and recreation field: The American Association of Zoological Parks and Aquariums, the American Institute on Park Executives, the American Recreation Society, the National Conference on State Parks, and the National Recreation Association. The NRPA is presently subdivided into the American Park and Recreation Society, Armed Forces Recreation Society, Commissioners-Board Members, National Student Recreation and Park Society, National Therapeutic Recreation Society, and Society of Park and Recreation Educators. The NRPA publishes *Parks and Recreation* (monthly), *Journal of Leisure Research* (quarterly), and several books and pamphlets. The mailing address is 3101 Park Center Drive, Alexandria, VA 22302.

Phi Epsilon Kappa

Phi Epsilon Kappa was founded in 1913 by the students and faculty at the Normal College of the American Gymnastics Union in Indianapolis, Indiana. This professional fraternity for physical educators was initiated to bind members together and to promote a friendly atmosphere among members of the profession.

More than 24,600 members have been initiated into this professional fraternity since its conception in 1913. Among its objectives are "to further the individual welfare of its members and to foster scientific research in the fields of health education, physical education, recreation education and safety education." Publications include the *Physical Educator*, and membership is available through the various collegiate chapters located in colleges and universities throughout the United States.

For further information contact Business Manager, 4000 Meadows Drive, Suite L-24, Indianapolis, IN 46205.

Society of State Directors of Health, Physical Education and Recreation

The Society of State Directors of Health, Physical Education and Recreation was first organized in 1926 in New York City. The Society has five basic purposes, among which are the following: "to promote sound programs of physical education, including appropriate athletics, at preschool, elementary, secondary, and post-secondary school levels; and to study problems affecting the quality of programs and to implement procedures for their solution."

The Society is composed of state directors of health, physical education, and recreation, and their associates. Associate memberships are available for those who have duties in one of these disciplines or who otherwise support the purposes of the society.

Over the years, the Society has issued numerous proclamations, resolutions, and proceedings which have had an impact on school, college, and community programs.

For further information, contact Secretary-Treasurer, The Society of State Directors of Health, Physical Education and Recreation, 9805 Hillridge Drive, Kensington, MD 20895.

U.S. Olympic Organization

Too little is known by sports administrators and the public in general about the purposes, objectives, organization, and procedures of the U.S. Olympic Committee. The following are stated as the Committee's objectives:

Establish national goals for amateur athletic activities and encourage the attainment of those goals.

Coordinate and develop amateur athletic activity in the United States directly relating to international amateur athletic competition, so as to foster productive working relationships among sports related organizations.

Exercise exclusive jurisdiction, either directly or through its constituent members or committees over all matters pertaining to the participation of the United States in the Olympic Games and in the Pan-American Games, including the representation of the United States in such games, and over the organization of the Olympic Games and the Pan-American Games when held in the United States.

Obtain for the United States, either directly or by delegation to the appropriate national governing body, the most competent amateur representation possible in each competition and event of the Olympic Games and the Pan-American Games.

Promote and support amateur athletic activities involving the United States and foreign nations.

Promote and encourage physical fitness and public participation in amateur athletic activities.

Assist organizations and persons concerned with sports in the development of amateur athletic programs for amateur athletes.

Provide for the swift resolution of conflicts and disputes involving amateur athletes, national governing bodies, and amateur sports organizations, and protect the opportunity of any amateur athlete, coach, trainer, manager, administrator, or official to participate in amateur athletic competition.

Foster the development of amateur athletic facilities for use by amateur athletes and assist in making existing amateur athletic facilities available for use by amateur athletes.

Provide and coordinate technical information on physical training, equipment design, coaching, and performance analysis.

Encourage and support research, development, and dissemination of information in the area of sports medicine and sports safety.

Encourage and provide assistance for amateur athletic activities for those who are under-represented such as women, certain minority groups, and the handicapped.

The United States Olympic Committee consists of 31 national sports-governing bodies responsible for the organization and selection of team members for the sports in the programs for the Olympic and Pan-American Games, 11 multisport organizations, and the Armed Forces of the United States, from which directly or indirectly have come substantial numbers of members of the United States Olympic and Pan-American Teams, and representatives from the 50 states and District of Columbia. In addition, individual members include the International Olympic Committee members for the United States and the U.S.A. representative on the Executive Board of the Pan-American Sports Organization.

The United States Olympic Committee has two governing bodies: the House of Delegates, which is the larger body, and the Executive Board, which has the responsibility of conducting the business affairs. The *House of Delegates* consists of representatives from the 31 national sports-governing bodies and the various state Olympic organizations, plus the officers of the United States Olympic Committee and the representatives from the International Olympic Committee and the Pan-American Sports Organization. The House of Delegates meets annually to determine overall policy and to study and amend the constitution.

The *Executive Board* has charge of the ongoing business affairs of the United States Olympic Committee. It interprets and implements the policies and procedures for carrying out the purposes and objectives as set forth in the act of Congress creating the United States Olympic Committee, and in the constitution, bylaws, and general rules of the United States Olympic Committee. Included with the framework of the Executive Board are the United States Olympic Committee officers who form the administrative staff.

The United States Olympic Committee has within its structure numerous important committees which deal with a multitude of responsibilities in the areas of finance, eligibility, game management, and program developments. Two United States Olympic Committee Councils that sports educators ought to know about are The Educational Council and the Sports Medicine Council.

The Education Council has the responsibility for developing and implementing, with the approval of the Executive Board, the various activities under the auspices of the United States Olympic Committee that are designed to promote the spirit of Olympianism and to encourage widespread participation of citizens of the United States in the Olympic movement. This includes sponsoring the annual United States Olympic Academy. In addition, the Council is responsible for selecting the United States delegates for the sessions of the International Olympic Academy in Olympia, Greece.

The *Sports Medicine Council* has the responsibility to promote research and encourage the practical application of information regarding all aspects of sports medicine. This involves the accumulation and evaluation of sports medicine information; the conduct of clinics and workshops for physicians, athletes, coaches, and trainers; the preparation of printed material; and the liaison of the sports medicine function of the United States Olympic Committee with government and nongovernment organizations.

Much additional insight into the overall organization and function of the United States Olympic Committee can be gained by reviewing certain publications of the Committee, particularly the Directory of Personnel. This explains the details of the organization and its constitution and bylaws, which explain all of the established regulations and procedures within which the Committee functions. This and other publications can be obtained from the United States Olympic Committee Headquarters, Olympic House, 1750 Overstreet, Colorado Springs, CO 80909.

SPORTS ORGANIZATIONS

While descriptions have been given of organizations concerned with the broader aspects of physical education and athletics, the organizations with more specialized interests are listed below with their current addresses and the periodicals they publish.

Amateur Basketball Association
of the United States of America

1750 Boulder Street, Colorado Springs, CO 80909.

Amateur Hockey Association of the United States

7901 Cedar Avenue South, Bloomington, MN 55420. Publishes: monthly bulletin, plus an annual publication titled *Hockey/Arena Bix* magazine.

American Bowling Congress

5301 South 76th Street, Greendale, WS 53129. Publishes: *Bowling Magazine* (11 times annually) and *ABC Newsletter* (monthly).

American Camping Association

Bradford Woods, Martinsville, IN 46151. Publishes: *Camping Magazine* (monthly), plus publications catalog, camp standards.

American Water Ski Association

P.O. Box 191, Winter Haven, FL 33882. Publishes: *The Water Skier* (bimonthly).

Athletic Institute

200 Castlewood Drive, North Palm Beach, FL 33408. Publishes: numerous books and pamphlets.

Babe Ruth Baseball and Softball, Inc.

1770 Brunswick Avenue, P.O. Box 5000, Trenton, NJ 08638.

Pony Baseball, Inc.

P.O. Box 225, Washington, PA 15301.

Ice Skating Institute of America

1000 Skokie Boulevard, Wilmette, IL 60091. Publishes: *ISIA Newsletter* (monthly) *Recreational Ice Skating* magazine (quarterly), plus numerous pamphlets and brochures.

International Bicycle Touring Society

2115 Paseo Dorado, LaJolla, CA 92037.

International Softball Congress Inc.

2523 West 14th Street Road, Greeley, CO 80631.

Little League Baseball, Inc.

P.O. Box 1127, Williamsport, PA 17701.

National Amateur Baseball Federation

2201 N. Towline Road, Rose City MI 48654.

National Archery Association of the United States

1750 E. Boulder Street, Colorado Springs, CO 80909.

National Baseball Congress of America, Inc.

338 South Sycamore, Wichita, KS 67201.

National Campers and Hikers Association, Inc.

7172 Transit Road, Buffalo, NY 14221. Publishes: *Camping Today* (monthly).

National Field Archery Association

Route 2, Box 514, Redlands, CA 92373. Publishes: *Archery Magazine* (bi-monthly).

National Jogging Association

Suite 202, 1910 K Street, N.W., Washington, DC 20006. Publishes: *N.J.A. Newsletter* (eight times per year).

President's Council on Fitness and Sport

450 5th Street, N.W., Suite 7103, Washington, DC 20201. Publishes: *Fitness Newsletter* (monthly).

U.S. Badminton Association

501 West Sixth Street, Papillion, NE 68046. Publishes: *Badminton USA* (quarterly).

U.S. Fencing Association

1750 E. Boulder Street, Colorado Springs, CO 80909.

U.S. Field Hockey Association, Inc.

1750 E. Boulder Street, Colorado Springs, CO 80909. Publishes: *The Eagle* (four times per year).

U.S. Golf Association

Golf House, Far Hills, NJ 07931. Publishes: *The Golf Journal* (eight times per year), and the Green Section Record (six times per year), plus numerous pamphlets and booklets.

U.S. Gymnastics Federation

1225 North 10th Avenue, P.O. Box 4699, Tucson, AZ 85703. Publishes: *USA Gymnastics News* (bimonthly), plus several booklets on gymnastics.

U.S. Handball Association

4101 Dempster Street, Skokie, IL 60076. Publishes: *Handball Magazine* (bimonthly) and *National Racquetball Magazine* (bimonthly).

U.S. Ski Association

1726 Champa Street, Suite #300, Denver, CO 80201.

U.S. Soccer Federation

350 Fifth Avenue, Suite 4010, New York, NY 10018.

U.S. Volleyball Association

557 Fourth Street, San Francisco, CA 94107. Publishes: *USA Volleyball Review* (bimonthly).

Young Men's Christian Association of
the United States of America

National Council, 101 N. Wacker Drive, Chicago, IL 60606.

Young Women's Christian Association of
the United States of America

600 Lexington Avenue, New York, NY 10022.

COACHES ASSOCIATIONS

National coaches associations exist for all the well-established sports. These associations are active in updating procedures for conducting sports events, advancement of the sport, and rule modifications. Some of the associations publish monthly or quarterly publications for their membership. For example, the National Football Coaches Association, the U.S. Track and Field Coaches Association, the National Soccer Coaches Association, and corresponding coaches' associations for most of the other sports. These organizations are popular among the coaching specialists, because each organization enhances the advancement of the particular sport and serves a fraternal purpose for the coaches. The addresses of the various coaches' associations can be obtained from the NCAA, 63rd Street and Nall Avenue, P.O. Box 1906, Mission, KS 66201.

SELECTED PROFESSIONAL PERIODICALS

AAHPERD Update

Published nine times a year by AAHPERD, 1900 Association Drive, Reston, VA 22091.

Devoted specifically to Alliance news and features in the broad fields of sport, physical education, recreation, health, dance, and safety. Includes a professional job exchange.

American Journal of Public Health

Published monthly by American Public Health Association, Inc., 1015 15th Street, N.W., Washington, DC 20005.

Promotes personal and environmental health and the development of health policies.

Athletic Administration

Published six times annually. P.O. Box 16428, Cleveland, OH 44116.
Discusses issues and current trends in school athletic administration.

Athletic Journal

Published monthly. 1719 Howard Street, Evanston, IL 60202.
Broad scope of articles on athletic administration, coaching, conditioning, and performance.

Athletic Training

Published quarterly by the National Athletic Training Association, 1001 East 4th Street, Greenville, NC 27834.
Reports on research in athletic training, including the latest in common sports injuries and rehabilitation procedures.

Canadian Journal of History of Sport and Physical Education

Published bi-monthly by the Faculty of Human Kinetics, Univ. of Windsor, Windsor, Ontario N9B 3P4, Canada.
Publishes articles on the history of sport in Canada.

Completed Research in Health, Physical Education, Recreation and Dance

Published annually by the AAHPERD, 1900 Association Drive, Reston, VA 22091.
Annual compilation of research published in over 100 periodicals and abstracts of masters' and doctoral theses in these areas.

Dance Chronicle

Published by Marcel Dekker, Inc., 270 Madison Avenue, New York, NY 10016.
Studies in dance and related arts (critiques of ballet dances, themes, etc.).

Dance Notation Journal

Published semi-annually by Dance Notation Bureau, 505 Eighth Avenue, New York, NY 10018.
Discusses approaches to dance notation instruction and material for teachers.

Dance Research Journal

Published semi-annually by the Congress on Research in Dance, Dance Dept., Educ. 684D, New York University, 35 W. 4th Street, New York, NY 10003.
Encourages research in all aspects of dance, fosters exchange of ideas, resources, and methodology, and promotes accessibility of research material.

Family and Community Health

Published quarterly by Aspen Publishers, 7201 McKinney Circle, Frederick, MD 21701. $64/yr.
Practical information that addresses common goals of health care practices in

teaching essentials of self-care, family and community health care, and health promotion and maintenance.

Health Education

Published semi-monthly by the AAHPERD, 1900 Association Drive, Reston, VA 22091. $35/yr.
Covers such topics as competency, lesson planning, the behavioral aspects of health education, parenting, and legislation. Regular columns provide news, teaching ideas, new resource materials and articles on research, professional preparation, history and philosophy.

Health Education Journal

Published quarterly by the Health Education Council, 78 New Oxford Street, London, England WCIAIAH.
Publishes articles on public health awareness.

International Journal of Sports Psychology

Published quarterly by the International Society of Sports Psychology, Via della Camilluccia, 195-00135, Rome, Italy.
Original papers covering psychophysiological, psychopathological and psychosocial aspects of sport and physical activities.

Journal of Applied Physiology

Published monthly by the American Physiological Society, 9650 Rockville Pike, Bethesda, MD 20814. $270/hr.
Publishes original papers that deal with normal or abnormal function in exercise physiology, respiratory physiology, environmental physiology, temperature regulation, and interdependence of body functions.

Journal of Community Health

Published quarterly by Pascal James Imperato, M.D., Box 43, State University of New York, Health Science Center-Brooklyn, 450 Clarkson Avenue, Brooklyn, NY 11203. Institutions—$89, individuals—$36/yr.
The content relates to all aspects of community health, preventive medicine, and public health.

Journal of Leisure and Recreation

Published quarterly by the National Recreation and Parks Association, Park Center Drive, Alexandria, VA 22302. $20/yr.
Includes topics that contribute knowledge and understanding to the field of leisure studies.

Journal of Sport History

Published three times a year by the North American Society for Sport History, WASSH Sec/Treas, 101 White Building, Penn. State Univ., University Park, PA 16802. Students —$12.50, institutions—$30, individuals—$25/yr.

Publishes scholarly articles pertaining to all aspects of sport history. Additional thrust toward more hypothetic and theoretic sport historiography. Contains literature surveys and book reviews.

Journal of Sport Psychology

Published quarterly by Human Kinetics Publishers, Box 5976, Champaign, IL 61820. $16/yr.

A cross-disciplinary journal that publishes theoretic papers, state-of-the-art and synoptic reviews, position papers, and original reports of basic and applied research in sport psychology. Contains book reviews, research notes, and commentaries.

Medicine and Science in Sport

Published semi-monthly by the American College of Sports Medicine, 401 W. Michigan Street, Indianapolis, IN 46202. $40/yr.

The articles deal with sports medicine and advances in sports sciences.

NAPEHE Proceedings (formerly NCPEAM/NAPECW)

Published annually by the National Association for Physical Education in Higher Education, Human Kinetics Publishers, P.O. Box 5976, Champaign, IL 61820.

Includes papers on biomechanics and exercise, science, motor learning, sports, and professional preparation are published. Reports of general sessions and research abstracts are included.

Public Health

Published semi-monthly by the Society of Community Medicine, Houndmills, Basingstoke, Hampshire, England RG21 2XS. $100/yr.

Includes articles on research and public health.

Research Quarterly

Published quarterly by the AAHPERD, 1900 Association Drive, Reston, VA 22091. Students—$22, institutions—$40/yr.

Publishes original research reports and review articles dealing with human movement, and book reviews.

The Journal of Applied Sport Science Research

Published quarterly by the National Strength and Conditioning Association, P.O. Box 81410, Lincoln, NE 68501.

Provides a peer-reviewed publication for high quality applied sport science research.

The Journal of Physical Education, Recreation and Dance

Published monthly (except July, combined Nov/Dec and May/June) by the AAHPERD, 1900 Association Drive, Reston, VA 22091. Prof. members—$42, students—$22/yr.

Publishes an array of articles, materials, and announcements pertinent to students and professionals within physical education, sport, dance, and leisure studies. Articles range from the theoretic to how-to-do-it. Contains book reviews and special features.

The Physical Educator

Published quarterly by Phi Epsilon Kappa Fraternity, 9030 Log Run Drive North, Indianapolis, IN 46234. $12/yr.

Publishes general manuscripts in the area of physical education, recreation, and safety. Includes sections on comparative physical education, dance, teaching techniques, book reviews and bibliographies.

The Physician and Sports Medicine

Published monthly by McGraw-Hill, 4530 W. 77th Street, Minneapolis, MN 55435. $39/yr.

Contains both research and practical information pertinent to the physician, coach, and trainer of athletic teams.

Chapter *21*

COMPUTERIZATION

To understand where computers are now and where they are headed, compare bicycles with racing cars or, better still, bicycles with jet aircraft. Today's best computers are faster and more powerful than anyone dared to imagine 20 years ago, but they are still bicycles compared to the jet planes they will become.

Computer specialists predict that in a few years a single silicone chip the size of a postage stamp will incorporate the power of a current state-of-the-art mainframe computer with its hundreds of chips. Today's large systems will shrink to the size of a small personal computer. This kind of compression will make it possible to pack an incredible amount of data in a small space, and this will greatly enhance the capacity of computers.

COMPUTER EXPANSION IN EDUCATION

Within the next 10 to 15 years, computers will be in almost every classroom, with computer work stations simple and inexpensive enough to be put in front of almost every student. The student's display screens will be tied into a computer located at the teacher's station. The central unit will have its own large screen, so that work going on at individual stations can be shown to the entire class; the teacher will use the large screen for a demonstration board.

New or complicated technology will not be required. The hardware and techniques already exist and have been in use in classroom-like situations for some time. The need is for scaled-down systems that educational institutions can afford in large numbers. The coming increases in computer capacity will help to accomplish this need, making it possible to pack enormous data processing capacity into small spaces at relatively low cost.

To some degree, this revolutionary change will occur as older teachers and administrators retire and are replaced by younger, computer-oriented professionals. Also, the next generation of parents, many of them already computer literate, will take a more forward view of computer use in education.

Computers can be used for a variety of processes in educational management, including preparing schedules for teachers, students, and facilities; keeping student records; storing personnel data; preparing and monitoring budgets, keeping inventories of and purchasing supplies and equipment; and keeping mailing lists. Computers can also be used to assist teachers in presenting class materials, scoring tests, and printing report cards. Intramural personnel can use computers for scheduling facilities, teams, and officials and for overall record keeping. Some school districts use computers to print reports of fitness tests for each student, including name, age, grade, raw score, and percentile rank on all test items. A computer may enhance any process where information is printed, stored, retrieved from storage, or analyzed.

NEED ASSESSMENT

A crucial responsibility of an administrator is to accurately assess the need for computer application. Some organizations have fallen behind by not addressing this question forthrightly; other organizations simply would not benefit from computerization. In the assessment process, three important questions need to be addressed.

1. Can computerization be *justified* in terms of effectiveness and efficiency?
2. Is appropriate *software* available, or can it be obtained?
3. Which particular *hardware* should be selected to run the software?

Justification

In considering the viability of computerization, the first question is whether a computer system would save time and money and increase effectiveness. Often a specialist within the organization or an outside consultant will need to be engaged to answer this question. In some cases, it would clearly benefit the organization; in other cases, computerization would be more trouble and expense than it is worth. Sometimes the arguments for and against are so close that the decision has to be based on preference.

A case that would favor computerization is a large college intramural program, where computerization could eliminate thousands of human hours each year. For example, a tremendous amount of time can be saved in the scheduling of 400 flag football teams or 500 basketball teams on a weekly basis. Working up the schedule of team against team and applying it to field space and time slots is both tedious and time consuming. Further, computing sportsmanship ratings, power ratings, and officials' ratings can be greatly enhanced through computerization. On the other hand, if there were only 40 flag football teams, computerization would be impractical.

Software

If the assessment demonstrates a viable need for computerization, the next step is to determine the appropriate software. Software is the programming portion or the actual procedures that the computer must perform to accomplish the objectives. Software can be purchased through professional vendors, or it can be developed specifically for a particular application. Packaged programs are the most economical if they fit the need. They are usually well written and can be modified or upgraded. The actual cost of a packaged program is small compared to the overall development cost, because the production cost is spread over many customers.

When a packaged program is not utilized, the alternative is to tailor make the program to fit the circumstance. The more insight the programmer has into the situation, the better the software package will be. Many organizations have their own computer consultants to prepare programs, maintain and upgrade programs, assist with the application, and help improve the computer literacy of other personnel.

Hardware

Once the particular software has been determined, the next step is to decide which hardware to use. Since there is a variety to select from, the following factors should be considered.

1. Will it run your software?
2. Will it be dependable, and will you be able to receive fast and reliable repairs?
3. Are there other similar systems in your organization that could be used when yours is down?
4. Will the hardware require a special environment?
5. Will it still be current in the near future when you need to expand or upgrade?
6. How large a system should you buy?
7. What will be the initial and ongoing costs?
8. Should you wait for next year's improved product?

The question of whether to buy now or wait until later is difficult, because there will always be something better next year. But waiting can become perpetual. Therefore, it is advisable to acquire the most suitable system at the best price and implement the plan on a timely basis.

You can invest as little as $1,500 for a good microsystem, or over a million dollars for a main frame. If you purchase an Apple Macintosh or IBM Personal Computer, the basic system will be $2,000 or less, but additional components, such as hard disk storage and printer capability will increase the price. The key is to purchase the system that will best suit your situation for the present and the projected future.

If you have several microsystems, you should consider connecting them into a Local Area Network referred to as a LAN. Most network software will provide the advantages of larger systems at a fraction of the cost. If a system larger than a micro is being considered, there are a variety of factors to evaluate. The next step higher than a micro is a mini, and then a main frame; the cost soars with these options. Also, these options require the hiring of a specialist to keep the system running and updated. Further, these systems may require a modified environment, such as air conditioning, special power supplies, and a large space. The cost range for a mini or main frame varies from $40,000 to well over $1 million. However, an important consideration is whether a mini or a main frame, along with the necessary expert assistance, already exists in the larger organization. If so, the best approach might be to hook up to the existing system.

ELECTRONIC MAIL

With electronic mail, correspondence is sent electronically rather than by the movement of paper. The telegram was the earliest form of electronic mail. Today's electronic mail is created, edited, stored, and transmitted with computers, and fortunately, the cost of electronic mail is decreasing rapidly.

Each electronic mail message is typed into the computer and edited. The computer then delivers the message to the receiver's "electronic mailbox." Whenever new correspondence arrives, the system flashes a message on the receiver's screen. The receiver examines the correspondence and may answer it or save it. The receiver can make electronic notes on the message just as paper correspondence can be annotated. With satellite communications, electronic mail can be sent around the world almost as conveniently as to the next office.

Facsimile

One popular form of electronic mail is called facsimile transmission. Facsimile (FAX) devices are essentially long-distance copiers. A document is inserted in the sending FAX machine and optically scanned. The information is converted into electrical signals and then transmitted. At the destination, the signals are converted into their original form by another FAX machine. A hard copy of the original is provided, including text, signatures, drawings, and pictures.

FAX devices with built-in microprocessors can run unattended, so correspondence can be sent overnight when phone rates are lower. FAX messages can be sent over high-speed computer networks much faster than over conventional telephone lines, but the costs are greater.

Voice Mail

Voice mail is a form of electronic mail in which messages are sent in the form of human voice rather than written text. Because most people prefer to talk rather than type, voice mail offers an attractive alternative.

Voice messages are digitized and retained in computer storage for future delivery. When the called party comes in, the call is delivered as speech, exactly as the caller spoke it. Also, voice messages may be broadcast to many people simultaneously.

Busy executives are often unreachable by phone, so "telephone tag," occurs when two people call and return calls but cannot seem to connect. Further, time differences make it especially difficult to reach people who are far away. Voice mail diminishes these problems.

Voice mail systems may also be used for dictation. An executive dictates a memo to a secretary; the secretary plays the message as many times as necessary during typing and editing. Voice mail may also be produced during business hours and transmitted during off-hours when phone rates are lower.

Eventually, computers will be able to convert spoken words directly to written text rather than the speech patterns used with today's voice mail systems. At that point, an executive may dictate a memo and have a computerized word processor prepare the finished copy. Stenographers beware!

Electronic Calendar

Each person in an automated office may have an electronic calendar containing confirmed meetings, tentative meetings, and open time slots. Someone wanting to schedule a meeting enters the desired date, time, duration, and a list of the desired participants. An electronic scheduling system can then check the personal calendars of those people to see if all are available. If they are, electronic mail messages are sent informing them of the meeting. If they are not, the system determines a more convenient time for them to get together. Scheduling systems may also be used to reserve rooms and resources such as audio-visual equipment.

Electronic calendar systems also provide convenient electronic diaries of a person's activities. Attorneys and other people who use time billing may use these systems to log the time they spend with each account.

Teleconferencing

With the high cost of travel and the premium placed on the time of busy professionals, more business trips will be replaced by a new kind of meeting—the teleconference. Teleconferencing incorporates audio, video, and computer conferencing techniques. Video teleconferencing (also called video-conferencing) provides much of the atmosphere of personal contact, because it includes visual images of the participants on a screen, along with the audio aspect of the conference.

Teleconferencing requires expensive, specially equipped rooms. But, eventually desk-to-desk teleconferencing may become commonplace, as communications companies increase transmission bandwidths and reduce costs.

EXPERT SYSTEMS

Expert systems is the term given to a computer program that concentrates on knowledge about a particular topic. These systems are spreading into more and more fields and are becoming machine assistants to a range of specialists from surgery to auto repair. In an expert system, the information is arranged in a branching array (If this happens, then what? If that happens, then what?) so that it can discard possibilities one by one until it comes up with a correct answer. In this way, it leads an individual through a step-by-step problem-solving process.

A few expert systems are already on the market. There will be a flood of such systems as computer capacity doubles and redoubles and as software designers are able to develop the packages. Such programs will be powerful tools for a variety of businesses and educational enterprises. They will help run automated factories, provide guidelines for investors to manage portfolios, coach lawyers and judges on precedents in the law, watch bank accounts for abnormal behavior, allow teachers and parents to evaluate a child's development, help teachers and students analyze and improve motor performance, assist athletic coaches with game strategies, help individuals identify health problems and improve health practices, advise people on the kinds of leisure time experiences they need to balance their lives, and a large array of other services and problem-solving tasks.

Voice-activated computers will add a new dimension to the entire scene of expert systems. Instead of having to communicate via a keyboard, individuals will be able to talk with the computer, and it will talk back or carry the message to an intended recipient. The surgeon, for example, will not have to turn away from the operating table. A tiny microphone will aid the surgeon in asking the computer a question, and the computer will provide a calculated response. A similar application might become available in athletic coaching (If the defense does this, what should the offense do? If the offense does that, how should the defense respond? Or, if maximum strength is needed in a given movement pattern, what exercise program should be applied?). There will be one catch to this, and it is not a small one. The computer will have to be carefully taught, and so will the speaker. Voice input-output systems already exist that can recognize only a few hundred words read methodically into the computer's memory, but this primitive system will be greatly improved in the future.

APPLICATION OF THE TECHNOLOGY

Now let us take a "real-life" look at the application of future technology in the lives of a teacher, a coach, and an administrator.

The Teacher

The teacher will be able to conveniently use graphics to illustrate the important points of a lesson. Photographs illustrating good technique in performance will be loaded into a computer with an optical scanner and then reproduced as transparencies or slides. The graphics can be made into a videotaped presentation (stored on cassette) with dubbed-in music for parts of the videotape with no dialogue. This process is called "multimedia."

Computers make it easier and more effective for teachers to keep detailed class records such as student attendance, examination scores, performance scores on physical tests, checklists of skills, and other relevant information. The school will have a central computer for most record keeping and all of the major software programs the administrators and teachers need, including a standard profile of each student. The teacher will have a microcomputer in the office connected to the larger computer, providing all the needed access and storage capacity. In addition, instructional support information, such as equipment inventories and locker assignments and combinations, will be stored on the computer. The teacher may be involved in developing computer-aided instruction (CAI) or computer-aided learning (CAL), such as developing interactive teaching software whereby the student and computer communicate with each other.

Expert systems will be available, some designed for use by the teacher, and others designed for direct use by the students. These systems will help the teacher become more proficient in each area of instruction. The expert systems designed for students will give direct access to the "expert responses" to their questions.

Teachers and students will have access via teleconference to audiovisual instruction by national or international experts. Further, students will have increased access to computerized training machines for the development of strength, endurance, and specific skills.

The Coach

The coach will take advantage of an expert system to plan practice sessions and game strategies. When a question arises, the coach will put the computer on voice mode and then ask questions as if the expert coach were physically present. The expert system will speak in response to the questions. The coach will have access to the best expertise available on almost any question pertinent to the game.

The computer will keep detailed records of the team's training sessions. The coach can type them or give them orally, letting the computer make the proper entries. The records will become available upon request on the screen or in printed form in words, tables, or graphs. The coach will store game and practice films, as well as instructional programs on videodisc. The computer will be able to run the disc, moving quickly to the part the coach wants to see.

On the weekend the coach might attend a national coaching clinic, but will do it in the office. The school's satellite dish will receive the beamed telecommunications signal sent from a central source via satellite. The expert coaches giving the clinic will not leave their schools. A telephone hookup will allow all of the participants to ask questions of any of the experts. Expert coaches will televise live or taped demonstrations using their own athletes in their own gyms.

Much of the coach's correspondence will be conducted by electronic mail sent from the school office at night by the computer—for the college coach, a valuable recruiting tool. The coach will subscribe to databases having information and be able to contact sources for potential recruits across the United States and possibly in foreign countries. The athletic department's computerized mailings will be sent to all prospects as often as the coach wishes.

Indeed, the coach will keep close to the enthusiastic fans with timely messages on a call-in hotline. Also, the coach will be able to produce clinics and visit booster or alumni clubs via satellite or live television hookup.

The Administrator

One responsibility of an administrator is scheduling, which includes (1) scheduling all of the activities included in the program, both classes and extracurricular events, (2) placing each program activity in the appropriate facility, (3) assigning the leader (teacher or coach) to each scheduled activity, and (4) scheduling the participants (students) into the program. All of this will be done largely by computer-assisted procedures. The computer will handle the scheduling from two directions.

1. It will schedule the facilities and leadership for each class and non-class activity, taking into account need and relative convenience of time choices.
2. It will schedule each student on the basis of individual requirements and preferences balanced against the school's requirements.

The computer will be used in scheduling special events by determining the best time or date of an event and arranging the schedule, including the correspondence, contracts, and logistical arrangements. Further, it will be used to record ticket sales, and perhaps even to mail invitations and bills, while keeping accurate account records.

In preparing next year's budget, the administrator will use computer information about past income and expenditures. He will be able to use "what if" projections based on anticipated levels of enrollment and the various sources of income, thus gaining a better idea of the effect of the different variables on the final budget.

Electronic mail will be used for much of the administrator's correspondence. The system will include an electronic bulletin board for general messages, in addition to the memos and other messages sent to individuals during the night. Most of the would-be paperwork will travel over the electronic system.

Further, administrators will have meetings with their peers via a teleconference, both within and outside the organization, thereby saving travel time and money.

REFERENCES AND RECOMMENDED READINGS

1. Haggerty, T.R.: Coping with information overload: A strategy for busy professionals. JOPERD, 61(9):47, 1990.
2. Kelly, L.E.: Computer assisted instruction. Applications for physical education. JOPERD, 58(4):74, 1987.
3. Kelly, L.E.: Computer management of student performance. JOPERD, 58(8):12, 1987.
4. Kelly, L.E.: Telecommunications—electronic mail. JOPERD, 60(7):86, 1989.
5. Mohnsen, B.: Using computers—helping physical education administrators. JOPERD, 62(1):40, 1991.
6. Nicholes, J.: Unpublished class notes. Brigham Young University, 1991.
7. Priest, S.: Teaching microcomputer applications in physical education. JOPERD, 58(6):18, 1987.
8. Stein, J.U., and Rowe, J.N.: Computerized budget monitoring. JOPERD, 60(4):84, 1989.
9. Stein, J.U.: Physical education selective activities. Computerizing choices. JOPERD, 58(1):64, 1987.
10. Taylor, M.S., and Saverance, D.P.: Computers, physical education, and the year 2000. JOPERD, 62(7):38, 1990.

Chapter 22

CURRENT ISSUES

An issue is a problem that has arguments pro and con but is not immediately resolvable. The importance of an issue changes with circumstances and time. Some issues lose significance over time, while others remain unresolved and alive. By understanding current issues, an administrator naturally has a better chance of dealing with them effectively.

Following is a sampling of current issues relating to education, physical education, and athletics, which can provide interesting discussions and debate. Certainly, not all of the current issues are introduced here, but, the chapter does contain a good representative sample.

ISSUES IN EDUCATION

Ethical Dilemmas

Ethical dilemmas in education involve questions for which there are no right or wrong answers. An example of an ethical dilemma pertaining to a broad problem is how to deal with the population boom, because overpopulation can be a serious threat. The natural need is for an effective world policy on birth control, but many individuals oppose such an idea on religious grounds, and some emerging nations see it as a threat to their power—an effort to keep their nations small and weak. However, such nations face the choice of having smaller populations with better living conditions or larger populations that endure severe hardships, often even starvation.

Another ethical problem is education of the masses. Each nation has its philosophy regarding who should be educated and to what extent. The United States has traditionally sought to provide universal education opportunities through the high school level. But is this the best policy in modern times? Should every person be educated to that level? Also, who should have additional education beyond high school, and how should that be determined? Again, there is no "correct answer." Each nation and its political subdivisions must make its own decisions.

Another ethical question is whether handicapped persons should have equal education opportunities in spite of the inconvenience and expense. Some argue that equal opportunities for the seriously handicapped are too expensive and are impractical, while others argue that all humans deserve opportunities for self-actualization, and society is responsible for such provisions.

Moral Education

Religious education has long been important in American schools, though religious education itself has traditionally occurred outside the schools, in keeping with the constitutional requirement of the separation of church and state. However, non-religious moral issues, such as ethical conduct and sex education, are optional topics in the schools. The dilemma is whether such subjects are the proper concern of public education. If moral issues are included in the curriculum, other dilemmas arise regarding the exact content and emphasis. Should certain moral or ethical standards be suggested, recommended, or required? Or, should the students simply be encouraged to develop their own ethics?

Little disagreement exists about whether students need to learn about moral issues and develop standards of conduct. But, there are disagreements as to which standards and who has the responsibility to teach them.

School Violence

Incidents of student violence against other students and against teachers have recently increased, lending an air of fear in some schools. This problem, identified mostly with inner-city schools, is becoming more common throughout the country, regardless of location.

A related problem is the "turned-off" student. Can the student who is not interested in school be reached? The problems of drug and alcohol abuse that we see in students and the larger society are symptomatic of a loss of self-esteem and personal worth. Some educators claim that such feelings result from overcrowded and inadequate conditions, both in the home and in the school. We must cope with the problem, for grave consequences can result from a large number of alienated people. This worry is one of the major reasons for the renewed interest in humanism in education.

Elitism

Another area of controversy is elitism, or education for the superior student contrasted to education for the "average" or typical student. Mostly, the American education system has been directed toward the average student. Hence, it neglects the intellectually gifted and the potential leaders of the future.

The problem of intellectual neglect stems partly from the idea that *elitism* is nondemocratic, because it implies that some people are more deserving than others. The schools should not accept the idea that one person is better than another, but should not ignore that one person may be more talented than another and that all students should have ample opportunity to achieve self-actualization. Some argue that elitist programs should be required; the law requires programs for the average student, and for those well below average. Yet the most talented students are often ignored (except in the area of athletics). True equality demands that all students be given the opportunity to reach their full potential.

Basic Education versus Frills

Currently there seems to be a strong feeling that schools need to give more attention to basic education. Many parents believe schools spend too much on "frills" (nonacademic subjects and extracurricular activities). Supporters of the back-to-basics movement cite the decline in scores on standard examinations such as the SAT and ACT. Several suggested causes include (1) too much television viewing by students, (2) too little homework assigned by teachers, (3) decline in overall discipline of the nation's youth, and (4) deterioration of the work ethic among the youth.

In an effort to improve, some schools have experimented with having the students decide what they should learn based on their views of relevance. However, many students are poor judges of relevance in terms of educational preparation for all aspects of life.

Also, in some programs, the concept of failure has been reduced by going to an "ungraded system." The justification is that students learn more when they are free from the pressures of grades. Further, it is claimed that students will try more difficult subjects when they have less fear of failure. The argument against this approach is that young and inexperienced students are too lacking in self-direction and self-motivation.

Unfortunately, the answers are still unclear as to what kind of education is most worth having and which educational methods are the most effective in producing the desired results.

Teacher Competence

Teacher competence is another area of concern. Some states have become interested in having teacher candidates take competency examinations in the subjects they will teach, because many college graduates do not have adequate knowledge in their specialized subjects. Certainly, such exams could indicate which candidates have the necessary knowledge to be effective teachers. But, in addition to knowledge of subject matter, a good teacher must (1) be interested and dedicated, (2) relate well with the students, (3) be a good communicator, and (4) be able to stimulate and motivate.

Alternative Schools

Alternative schools are educational institutions established to accomplish different goals or a different emphasis than the mainstream public school system. An alternative school might be different, either in curricular content or educational methods. The most prevalent kind of alternative schools are religious-based institutions where religious education is emphasized and is integrated with the other educational content. During the early history of the United States most of the schools were of this kind. In addition to religious-based institutions, other alternative schools include (1) experimental schools, where new or unique educational methods are applied, (2) training schools designed for individuals with special problems, such as discipline, drug abuse, and behavioral deviations, (3) military academies, (4) schools designed for early entry into vocational training, and (5) specialized college preparatory schools. Certainly, some alternative schools are clearly justified and fit well into the needs of society, but there are some alternative schools that advocate extreme or questionable content and methods and that are clearly controversial compared to the mainstream public education system.

Another form of alternative education is the practice of home education, which occurs when the parents do not want their children involved in the public education system or in an alternative school. This practice is certainly undesirable in the minds of most educators.

Discrimination

Three important categories of possible discrimination in education are gender, racial minority, and handicap. In terms of *gender*, the principal question is whether the educational system includes equal opportunities for males and females, and particularly whether any inequalities relate directly to gender. Glaring examples of unequal opportunities related to gender have certainly existed in the past. Fortunately, much progress has been made toward resolving such differences, but there are many situations where gender discrimination still exists. Hence, nonsexism in education remains an important issue that deserves ongoing analysis, monitoring, and improvement.

One of the difficulties relates to interpretation of equality. Some take the position that equal opportunities mean the exact same opportunities. Others emphasize that opportunities should be different (but equal) because the sexes are different. As a result of these different views, the application of the concept of equality remains somewhat confused. A brief description of the current trends of this subject appears in Chapter 23.

Relative to discrimination toward racial *minorities*, affirmative action, both formal (law and regulation) and informal (social conscience), has been steady since the 1960s. Legislation has greatly increased educational and job opportunities for racial minorities and has tackled the school segregation problem. Although a great deal of progress has occurred, the problem is still a long way from being resolved.

Members of the school age population with *handicaps* and special deficiencies are receiving better treatment than ever before, but circumstances are against these individuals, because they have special needs and are in the minority. Therefore, the question of equal opportunities for the handicapped will continue to be one of the important issues.

ISSUES IN PHYSICAL EDUCATION AND ATHLETICS

Place and Function in Education

A continuing issue in America is the place of physical education and sports competition in the educational system. Legitimate questions are asked about what is the function of physical education in the curriculum, whether it is deserving of school credit, and whether it can be justified as a requirement.

Another facet is whether the school is the proper place for sports competition, even though long-standing tradition and public interest appear to accept it. Further, should major emphasis be placed on winning, or more attention given to personal development and lessons to be learned? Also, at what age should students become participants in competitive athletics, and how much emphasis should be on rigorous training for immature youngsters? Those in responsible positions must have good answers to difficult questions such as these.

Curricular Relevance

Leaders of physical education and sports must constantly prove that the programs are worthwhile. Programs must be of high quality, with clear, useful, obtainable goals that contribute to the participants' educational development. The instruction must result in learning new skills, developing the physiological systems, and gaining useful knowledge and attitudes that contribute to social adjustment. The experience must be developmental, and not simply a recreation session or a break from the learning process. There must be educational substance relevant to the students' mental development and their preparation for life. If this fails to occur, there is little if any justification for requiring or even offering physical education for credit.

Cost–Benefit

When the budget crunch hits, do physical education and athletics still have a place in the school program? These activities are unusually expensive in terms of the cost for areas and facilities, as well as other forms of support. In some cases, a choice is made between emphasis on physical education or competitive athletics, with one being partially sacrificed to save the other. Sound arguments can be developed in support of both programs. Those in favor of emphasis on competitive athletics advocate the importance of developing the full potential of those who are naturally endowed (the elitism philosophy), the impact of athletics on school spirit, the entertainment benefit for the student body and public, and the potential for public recognition of the individuals and programs. On the other hand, the advocates of physical education argue the importance of helping all students develop their potential. They argue for the rights of the majority in preference of the few. Often, the best solution is to retain an appropriate balance of emphasis within the financial restrictions.

Another financial issue relates to college athletics. Most colleges and universities expect athletic programs to pay their own way with income from student fees, gate receipts, television revenue, and donations. However, a high percentage of these programs lose money under today's circumstances and have to be supplemented by budgeted funds. Due to constantly rising costs, the financial dilemma is getting worse instead of better. This constant financial pressure contributes to other problems. For example, athletic personnel feel that they must compete successfully in order to survive. As a result, there is (1) too much media promotion in order to attract gate receipts; (2) too much bending of the rules to attract outstanding athletes into the program; (3) too much support for retaining coaches who win, even when some of their behaviors are inappropriate; and (4) too much need for donations to athletics, which otherwise might be available to support academic programs. A strong belief exists that high school and college athletics should be toned down in a number of respects, particularly in the overall cost.

Competence of Teachers and Coaches

Too often, physical education teachers and athletic coaches have the reputation of having few interests beyond the content of the sports page. They are sometimes accused of being disinterested, uninformed, and nonsupportive of academic and cultural programs. Further, athletics is sometimes allowed to drift away from the mainstream of the educational effort, in fact, even become isolated. This undesirable circumstance is far more prevalent at the university level than at any other level. It indicates a lack of competence in terms of perception and understanding of how these activities should blend with the other elements of the educational system.

Other kinds of incompetence are illustrated when physical education teachers follow the practice of simply "rolling out the ball." Such recreation sessions may be wholesome but not deserving of school credit. Further, some coaches are guilty of giving ill-directed leadership involving too much emphasis on winning at any cost or entertaining the public instead of focusing on desirable educational results for the participants.

Violence in Sports

Violence in sports, although less prevalent now, is still an element worthy of concern. Violence results to some extent because of (1) too much emphasis on winning, (2) school rivalries that are out of control, and (3) the prevalence of alcoholic beverages and drug use at athletic events. Actually, it is a wonder there is not more violence in light of all of the precipitating circumstances. Fortunately, the potential for more violence is held under control by the refinement of game rules, authority of game officials, and enforced regulations in stadiums and arenas.

Misdirected Emphasis on Athletics

A basic aspect of misdirection is the diminished emphasis on the positive development of the participants and the corresponding increase in emphasis on the entertainment of the spectators and on recognition for the institution. Booster clubs are putting increased amounts of money into sports programs, facilities are becoming more elaborate, and the rewards given winning coaches continue to increase. These circumstances sometimes get carried to the point that many people think the purpose of the school is to provide a support system for athletic teams, rather than athletic participation being part of the educational process. The issue at hand is one of appropriate perspective and balance. School administrators have a particular responsibility to make sure the elements involved with this issue are held under proper control.

Additional Issues

Following are some additional issues in physical education and athletics that are stated but not discussed. These statements would serve as good discussion topics for class members.

1. Is it desirable for athletic coaches to major in physical education and to teach in the physical education program, or is it better for coaches to teach other subjects?
2. Should the school district and the community consistently strive to cooperate relative to design, construction, and use of sports areas and facilities,

or is it better for each of these agencies to have exclusive use of its own facilities?

3. Should physical education be a required subject in the schools, and if so, at what levels, how much, and for what reasons?

4. Are physical education teachers and coaches usually well prepared to teach the health classes, or should health be taught by health specialists?

5. Should handicapped and injured students be taught separately, or should they be integrated into the regular physical education classes? What are the advantages and disadvantages of each of these approaches?

6. Should restrictions from participation in athletics and physical education be used as a method of discipline in the schools, or should participation in these programs stand on its own merit and not be considered a reward for acceptable behavior?

7. Does participation in competitive athletics inherently contribute toward the positive development of the participants, or is such development dependent on good leadership and favorable circumstances?

8. Does dance logically belong as part of physical education, or as part of the fine arts, or should certain phases of dance be attached to each area?

9. Is it true that more sports skills are learned through recreation programs than physical education programs, and is the teaching of skills a legitimate role of recreation programs?

10. Are posture improvement and weight control important phases of physical education, and is the physical education teacher the one primarily responsible for these aspects of personal development?

11. Should physical education be graded on the same basis as other subjects in the school, such as A, B, C, D, E, or should the pass/fail method or some other system be used?

12. Is it sound to claim that "no person has the right to neglect physical fitness—it is part of one's responsibility as a citizen to keep in good condition"?

13. Should physical education in the elementary schools be taught by the classroom teachers or by a physical education specialist?

14. Should female and male athletic teams be coached by individuals of the same gender, or should the student athletes be coached by the best qualified person regardless of gender?

Chapter 23

A LOOK AT THE FUTURE

What we have done in the past and where we stand now are both less important than the direction we are heading. The past serves as our guide; the present represents our circumstances; and the future holds our hopes and aspirations. Predicting the future with accuracy has become increasingly difficult because the future holds so many options. Yet we must make predictions and estimates, or we have little basis for planning and preparing. What will be our circumstances 5 years, 10 years, and 20 years from now? One reliable prediction is that change in almost all aspects of our lives will be the overriding characteristic. Change will follow change with bewildering rapidity.

SOCIOECONOMIC TRENDS

In the past, most people were able to go through life with a set of attitudes and beliefs appropriate to the age in which they were born. Circumstances relative to science, technology, education, and social values changed little throughout one's lifetime. Even then each generation expressed its frustration with the common phrase, "What is the world coming to?" Today there are many interesting questions about "what the world is coming to" in terms of population, urbanization, work and leisure time, mobility and technology, and the impact of these factors on educational programs.

Population

From the year 1 A.D. until 1930, the estimated world population doubled from 750 million to 1.5 billion. During the next 35 years (1930 to 1965) it redoubled, increasing to 3 billion. The United States Commission on Population states that it will almost redouble again by the year 2000, thus approaching 6 billion people. If the present rate of annual growth had existed since the beginning of the Christian era, we would now have an average of one square yard of earth for each person. That would hardly be enough for mountain climbing, skiing, and long golf drives.

Each minute 225 babies are born, while 140 people die. Each time your heart beats, the world's population increases by one. Human reproduction is self-accelerating. Like compound interest, it spurts upward in geometrical progression.

Most of the world's population is in underdeveloped countries or countries where the natural resources are depleted. These countries also have low literacy rates and weak social structures. Overpopulation and lack of resources contribute to social unrest and political instability and smother efforts to develop better lives for millions of people who are ill-fed, ill-clothed, ill-housed, and poorly educated.

Currently, North America and Western Europe have 17% of the world's population and 64% of the income, as measured in goods produced and services rendered. Asia has 56% of the population and 14% of the income. Ironically, the deprived and underprivileged portion of the population is increasing faster than the affluent portion. The "hunger belt" of Africa and South Asia accounts for four of every five births, while this area produces only one fifth of the world's food.

Recently, certain "Third World" nations have acquired an important status in world politics, because of wealth gained from their petroleum resources. As these nations work toward political maturity, the other nations must help them understand the long-term effects of their actions and work towards international understanding and tolerance.

Americans should recognize that the population problem is not confined to faraway places; our own predicted rate of increase is only slightly less than that of the world. In 1800, the population of the United States was less than 5 million. By 1900, it had reached 85 million, and in the first half of the 20th century, it almost doubled, surpassing 151 million. The United States now has more than 245 million people, and the population continues to grow annually by 2.5 million.

The population increase (excluding immigration) is an expression of the ratio of births and deaths. In 1900, the annual death rate was 17.2 per 1,000 Americans; now it is 9.1 per 1,000. A male child born in 1900 could expect to live 46 years, compared to 73 years today. For females, the gain has been greater, from 48 years in 1900 to 79 years today. What will life expectancy be in the year 2000 and beyond?

In 1940, 7% of the population was age 65 or more, compared to 12% today. The proportion of older members of the population has increased, while the proportion of working age has decreased.

Also of interest is that the average household size is getting smaller. Today it is 2.65 persons, compared to 2.75 in 1980 and 3.14 in 1970; the projection by the year 2000 is 2.35. Reasons for the drop include a decline in birth rate, individual's waiting longer to get married, and an increase in the number of single parent families.

Urbanization

For most Americans the days are gone when open space could be found at the end of the street or around the corner of the block. First came villages and towns, then cities and sprawling metropolitan areas, and finally metropolitan areas joined together to form megalopolis regions. Like inflating balloons, the small communities founded a century or two ago have grown larger, generating problems that the founding fathers never imagined.

The American society was originally agrarian, but because of startling advances in agriculture, the average farm worker today can produce enough food for 70 other persons. At the time of the Revolutionary War, 92% of our population were farmers, compared to about 3% today; some economic experts predict that by the year 2000 fewer than 2% will be farmers. This means each year more people leave the rural areas and go to cities to live and work.

At the time of the first United States census (1790), only 5% of the 4 million population lived in cities of 2,500 or more (small by today's standards). At the Civil War time, we were 20% urban; by 1930, 50% urban; and by 1950, 60% urban. Now we are more than 75% urban, and it is predicted that by the turn of the century 80% will live in urban and suburban areas.

Some major changes within the urban complexes have also occurred. The old districts and central portions of the cities have grown little in recent years, and some have lost population. In contrast, the surrounding suburbs have expanded. As a result, almost everyone in the United States has firsthand experience with some land that was a farm or a forest a decade ago and is now covered with housing, a shopping center, or an industrial complex.

Despite advantages enjoyed by urban dwellers, large cities are often criticized for their congestion, poor sanitation, and lack of order and unity. The central core often suffers from blight and is a breeding place of disaffection and violence. Further, movement into the cities for work and away from them for recreation and other qualities of life contributes to severe transportation and pollution problems.

Work and Leisure Time

The line between leisure and labor has always been tenuous and shifting. Leisure and work are two sides of our shield. The one side, labor, enables us to live, while the other side, leisure, makes living more meaningful. "We labor in order to have leisure," said Aristotle. "Work can ennoble a person, but leisure provides an opportunity to develop perfection and enrichment of character."

In well-established societies throughout history, such as ancient China, Egypt, India, Sumeria, Greece, and Rome leisure and labor became well defined, both having increasing importance. Labor produced material wealth, which was concentrated in the hands of few. Those who controlled the wealth put their leisure to use in a variety of sportive activities, aesthetic and intellectual pursuits. As a result, cultural trends were established and civilizations advanced.

During the past century, tremendous shifts have occurred in the work life of the typical American. The sunup-to-sundown working day has become rare. Most full-time employees in America work 40 hours a week, compared to 60 hours a century ago.

While the work week has become shorter, vacation periods have become longer. At the same time, people are retiring earlier. When we add up the shorter work week, increased vacations, and earlier retirement, we see that Americans spend significantly less time on the job today than they did 50 or

100 years ago. Perhaps our leisure time has increased faster than our ability to use it properly.

A person may possibly buy more of everything, but lack time to do more. For example, to belong to a golf club, a sailing club, and a tennis club requires too much time to participate in each fully. Further, because of the cost of belonging to all of these, one may have to work more and have even less time to enjoy them. Emerson expressed this idea when he said, "If I keep a cow, the cow will milk me."

Even with our increased leisure, we must remain highly selective in order for the time to serve us well. Leisure can be a blessing when used well, but for some it becomes a curse because of boredom, overindulgence, or abuse.

Mobility

The miraculous progress in travel during the past century represents one of the most dramatic changes in man's history. Whether we choose land, air, or sea and whether we travel long or short distances, comfortable and rapid modes of transportation are available.

A century ago, horseback and horse-drawn carriages were the primary modes of travel, although a few rode crudely built trains and steamboats. By the 1920s, many owned automobiles and traveled much by car. Soon, extensive highway systems developed, and the automobile became the king of travel in America.

Today, our most common carrier by far is the automobile, followed by air, train, and boat. In American alone, more than nine million cars are produced each year, and the number of privately owned cars exceeds 100 million. Four out of five American families own cars; in suburban and rural areas, nine out of ten families own cars. Further, a high percentage of all families own two or more cars. To accommodate car travel, the United States now has more than 5 million miles (8 million km) of highways, roads, and streets, including over 50,000 miles (83,000 km) of freeways.

Even though the automobile is the king of travel, other modes have become increasingly important. Airplane passengers in the United States increased from 2.5 million in 1940 to 96 million in 1990. The 600 mile-per-hour (1000 kph) jetliner has put major cities within a few hours of each other. There are more jetliners in the United States than in all other countries combined, and we have nine of the world's ten busiest airports.

Technology

In the *Republic*, Plato described his ideal society as having thousands of slaves to perform the work so that a few at the peak of the social structure could develop their intellectual, physical, and spiritual qualities and thereby improve society. It is believed that at the peak of the Athenian culture there were 15 slaves for each citizen. Automation experts estimate that the average American has the equivalent of 500 human slaves. Our slaves have become available through technology, which is the development and use of mechanical devices and their energy sources. A great variety of mechanical instruments perform an increasing number of functions with unmatched precision and rapidity. Computers, engines, electrical appliances, and other implements perform a phenomenal amount of work, saving human time and energy.

Visualize the amount of slave energy needed to propel an automobile at 60 miles per hour (100 kph). Consider the slave energy required daily to equal the electricity used for running the appliances, lighting, and temperature control in an average American home. Think of the thousands of hours spent making calculations that can be accomplished on a computer in just 30 minutes. Even more impressive is the equivalent energy spent on a four-engine jetliner streaking through space at 600 miles per hour (1000 kph) or a 100-car freight train traveling at 60 miles per hour (100 kph).

Technology experts predict that we shall make far more technological progress in the next 20 years than we have in any equivalent period in the past. The computers of the future will do a decade of work during a lunch hour. There is optimism about electric automobiles, abundant solar energy for heating buildings, and improved household appliances. Further, there will be continuing improvements in almost all kinds of sports and recreation gear. Technologists are truly significant contributors to our lifestyle—both on and off the job.

TRENDS IN EDUCATION

The purpose of education is to prepare individuals to live successfully in society and contribute toward its improvement. Thus, the content of education is influenced by local values and living patterns and by the knowledge, skills, and attitudes that people need in order to earn a living and perpetuate traditions and cultural values. Education is of two general kinds: preparation to *earn* a living and preparation *for* living.

Education has become evermore essential and, as a result, the number of students and the average level of education has increased. For example, in 1900, 60% of school-age children (5 to 18 years) were enrolled; by 1950 78% were enrolled; and now more than 88% are enrolled.

A greater number of students are going on to college. College enrollments increased from 2.5 million in 1950, to 6 million in 1970, and to 11.5 million in 1990. Also, continuing education has greatly increased among adults of all ages.

Relevance

People want education to be both interesting and functional. These concerns influence the accountability of school administrators and teachers. There is mass resistance to the old idea of the school as an ivory tower. Today the outside world is an integrated part of the educational process.

A greater consciousness of work opportunities is a result of career counseling, which shows students the place of work in society, teaches them about work, and introduces them to many career options at an early age. The intent is to counteract the problem of students graduating from school with no idea of what they want to do.

Humanizing

Another trend is toward humanizing the curriculum and the procedures. One complaint has been that education dehumanizes many students or puts them in a lowly position of little respect or human value. Increased emphasis is being placed on "caring for the students." The curriculum is becoming more flexible, and more options are offered to fit the needs of the individual student, rather than bending the student to fit the curriculum. Use of block or modular scheduling, along with a growth in independent study and advanced placement testing, is also increasing.

Teaching Methods

Teaching methodology continues to undergo innovative changes. Specialists are being used more, as are such techniques as team teaching (several teachers instructing portions of a single class). Greater use of mechanized teaching aides and audiovisual equipment is also evident. Teaching laboratories are often equipped with sound cassettes, video cassettes, slide film equipment, and video filming and replay equipment. Further, computers are being utilized more than ever before. The growth of innovative teaching techniques has been rapid and is not likely to slow down in the near future.

Nonsexism

In the field of education, *nonsexism* means equality of educational opportunity regardless of gender. Perhaps the greatest impact toward nonsexism resulted from the passage of Title IX of the Equal Education Act of 1976. The results of Title IX have been felt the most in women's athletics, but it has also had impact in academic areas. Traditionally, women were discouraged from scientific and technical fields of study, because these subjects were "not in keeping with women's interests and talents." Also, women were often discouraged from graduate studies, as they were expected to take up homemaking. During the 1960s and 1970s, numerous discrimination suits became a factor in education. These suits were justified under the 14th Amendment to the Constitution and under Title IX of the Equal Education Act. These actions, along with numerous affirmative action efforts, have helped toward resolution of the sexism problem.

Handicapped

Under Public Law 94-142, public schools are required to give appropriate attention to educating handicapped students. Further, the law encourages mainstreaming (putting students with disabilities into regular classes with non-disabled students).

The handicapped have been shortchanged in education; fortunately, that situation is being amended as new programs for the handicapped are implemented. Several arguments against certain aspects of these new programs have appeared, however. These arguments are not over the rights of the handicapped to an education, but against the high costs. Some individuals question whether the schools can afford expensive new programs for the handicapped at a time when other school activities are being dropped because of money problems. Also, some are concerned that mainstreaming the handicapped may sometimes slow the progress of the whole class. Opponents of mainstreaming see this as a denial of the rights of the majority to accommodate a few.

Also of concern is that some programs for the handicapped are developed only to take advantage of federal grants. In addition, there is concern over whether the handicapped are being used or displayed for sympathy and money-raising purposes. This can be a dehumanizing process.

Adult Education

Adult education is a long-term process, a continuum that extends into old age. Much of the credit for popularizing this concept must go to community-school programs and community colleges. Courses offered in these programs range from exercise to art appreciation to financial planning.

Gerontology, the study of aging, is a growing area of interest. As the youth boom passes into middle age, the average age of the population continues to rise. Also, improvements in health practices and disease control have added significantly to people's longevity. There is growing interest in developing educational programs to help older citizens maintain a high quality of life and continue to be contributing members of society.

TRENDS IN PHYSICAL EDUCATION AND SPORTS

Program Trends

Physical educators are naturally trying to determine the most effective programs for the future, and there are numerous possibilities to consider. Some believe that we seek to meet too many goals, such as physical fitness, motor skills, mental development, and social-emotional adjustment. Perhaps the main goal should be simply to convince and prepare students to incorporate regular physical activities into their lifestyles over the long term. This would be in keeping with the trend toward *lifetime sports*—programs that concentrate on activities appropriate for every stage of life.

The lifetime sports approach goes beyond simply teaching skills; it involves helping people to appreciate and enjoy the activities. If students do not enjoy an activity, they will rarely participate in it either now or later. Leisure activities of adults are, by definition, activities of choice; they are activities the participants find pleasurable. An important achievement of physical education would be to cause a higher percentage of people to voluntarily choose "the active life."

Another program trend is the rising popularity of *outdoor adventure*, including some high risk activities, such as rock-climbing, white-water kayaking, and cross-country skiing. Also, triathlon competitions (swimming, bicycling, and running long distances) and road races, (which boomed during the 1980s), continue to be popular. A continuing problem is that many participants are poorly prepared and careless in their approach to high-risk and strenuous activities.

The *sports for all* (low competition) approach is another growing area in physical education. Especially useful in the elementary school, it introduces young students to organized physical activities in which cooperation is emphasized more than competition. Some children find competition intimidating and frightening. The sports for all approach places more emphasis on mass participation and cooperation to meet a group goal rather than to achieve a personal advantage.

Coeducational activities have become increasingly prevalent in physical education. Some mixing of the sexes occurred in classes in the past, but it was usually limited to such activities as dancing and mixed doubles in tennis and badminton. While coeducation has disadvantages, including some differences in interests and skill levels, mixed instruction is certainly appropriate in many areas of the program.

Another trend is toward fitting *special populations* into the regular physical education program. One example is mainstreaming students with handicaps. Even competitive activities for special populations are on the increase. Special Olympics provides competitive opportunities for people with mental handicaps, while Handicapped Olympics and other competitions have been organized for people with physical handicaps. Also, "master's competitions" (for older people) in many different sports is on the increase. Many people who did not participate in sports in their school years are learning the pleasures of competition in later life.

Sports competition for women has grown rapidly during the last two decades, but the growth rate has leveled off. Also, non-varsity club sports in high schools, colleges, and universities have grown. A parallel trend toward physical education as a purely elective subject is also apparent at the college level. The physical fitness craze continues, and it has spread throughout the different age groups and into many facets of life—schools, businesses, homes, hotels, and resorts. The fitness concept has broadened with the new emphasis being on "wellness," which is inclusive of fitness and overall health.

Improved Technology

New or expanded technology will enable teachers to accumulate, record, and utilize much additional information about the interests, abilities, and capacities of students, thereby enhancing the individualization of instruction.

The benefits of improved technology also apply to athletics with an additional dimension—application of the improved technology to game strategy. For example, the technology will improve the opportunities for coaches to analyze defensive and offensive strategies of their own teams and a large number of other teams. Software packages will become available to cover the best known game strategies.

The improved visual aspects of technology will facilitate the development of the fine points of skill among a larger portion of the population, whereas previously this has been the domain of the expert performers. Visual detailed analyses of the "perfect performance" will become available in a large number of skills, and these will serve as patterns for correct learning.

Leisure Activities

Destination resorts have become more popular, and this trend will continue. Many resorts are placing greater emphasis on lifestyles that enhance health and fitness. The resorts will be facing an older population, and most resorts will try to become year-round attractions adding golf, tennis, racquetball, swimming, weight training, equestrian activities, children's play areas, and summer concerts.

The trend will continue toward "lifetime activities," with continued emphasis on walking and jogging. Golf, tennis, swimming, and cycling will fare well, and cross country skiing will gain faster than downhill skiing.

Manufacturers will do their best to make sports easier and more appealing for novices—young and old. There will be more equipment like oversized tennis racquets, hollowback golf clubs for straighter drives, cayman golf balls for scaled down courses, smaller basketballs for youngsters, more devices to enhance swimming enjoyment, and more versatile bicycles.

How the entertainment dollar will be spent a decade or two from now is up for grabs; there will be a lot of competition for it. College and high school sports will continue to grapple with abuses, and there will be tighter controls in order to maintain acceptance of school sports programs. Professional athletics will continue to be popular entertainment and the leagues will become more international. This will have a popularizing effect of those sports across cultural lines.

In total, the sports and activity craze will continue and even heighten. But, as the population expands and society becomes more complex, pockets of deprived youth and adults will continue to be excluded from opportunities for the active and enriched life.

Health and Fitness

The next 10 to 15 years will bring startling changes in health care—better treatments for a variety of ailments. New technologies in genetic engineering, lasers, optics, and computers will help provide hope and relief to millions of people now hindered by physical and mental disorders. This boost in the human condition will add zest to the lives of a large number of people. Between now and the year 2000, the projected average life span of Americans will continue to increase at least as fast as during the recent past. As usual, the benefits will not be equally distributed. The aggressive and well-to-do will benefit the most.

One factor that will help immensely is the self-help approach to health. Americans are paying more attention to "wellness" through diet and exercise, a trend that will expand as today's youngsters grow to adulthood. More and more employers will build wellness programs into their benefit regimes on the philosophy that staying well is a sound investment for both the employer and the employee. This trend is becoming ever more apparent with the emphasis on smokeless and drugless work environments, pressure to avoid use of alcohol on the job, and provisions for exercise.

Another factor will be the expanding use of computer "expert systems," which will help individuals diagnose and learn the treatments for many kinds of ailments. Such software programs already exist in a limited fashion. The diagnosis is performed by a question and answer route, resulting in the best available expert information about the diagnosed ailment.

Gene engineering will produce a variety of health improvements, including vaccines for certain forms of cancer and other viral diseases and special treatments for some genetically caused conditions. Gene engineering is sure to play a major role in the treatment of brain and nerve damage, which will be especially helpful in treating back injuries resulting from heavy stress or ruptured disks. Also, significant progress is under way toward improved methods of repairing skeletal damage and controlling degenerating conditions, such as arthritis and worn out joints. Some of these processes have strong implications for the treatment and rehabilitation of sports injuries.

Significant strides will be made in the control and treatment of cardiovascular problems. For example, coronary bypass operations will be refined, but at the same time, will be superseded by less traumatic techniques that work as well or better. Lasers will be used more extensively to open clogged arteries, and techniques for preventing and treating acute heart attacks will be improved.

For people with impaired use of limbs, there are two exciting prospects: nerve tissue regeneration and "robot" augmentation. The latter term refers to an automated device to perform programmed functions. A host of other improvements are underway for various physical impairments.

The vast changes that will occur in the health and fitness of the population will result in prolonged life, enrichment, and improved productivity. Longer life, combined with a stable birth rate, will result in a higher proportion of retired people as compared to children and youth.

All of these changes will have implications for various aspects of physical education and athletics. There will be a more uniform need and demand for health, fitness, and recreational pursuits over the total range of the population, as opposed to emphasis on children and youth. Health, fitness, and leisure will be approached more on an individual basis, and to a larger degree, people will become "their own teachers" by using the increased amount of information and the new self-help programs.

INDEX

Page numbers in italics refer to figures. Page numbers followed by "t" refer to tables.